Six Decades of Indo-US-Pak Relations

Six Decades of Indo-US-Pak Relations

By

B.B. Nagaich, Jayant Kumar,
Rajiv Nagaich and Sharda Nagaich

New Century Publications
New Delhi, India

NEW CENTURY PUBLICATIONS
4800/24, Bharat Ram Road,
Ansari Road, Daryaganj,
New Delhi – 110 002 (India)

Tel.: 011-2324 7798, 4358 7398, 6539 6605
Fax: 011-4101 7798
E-mail: indiatax@vsnl.com • info@newcenturypublications.com
www.newcenturypublications.com

Editorial office:
LG–7, Aakarshan Bhawan,
4754-57/23, Ansari Road, Daryaganj,
New Delhi – 110 002

Tel.: 011-4356 0919

First Published: **September 2009**

ISBN: **978-81-7708-216-6**

Published by New Century Publications and printed at Salasar Imaging Systems, New Delhi.

Designs: Patch Creative Unit, New Delhi.

PRINTED IN INDIA

Dedicated to

Our teachers in India as well as in the United States of America and the peace loving people of the globe

Contents

About the Book

This book has been written jointly by a team of four experts, Dr. (Professor) B.B. Nagaich, Col. Jayant Kumar, Attorney Rajiv Nagaich and Ms. Sharda Nagaich, all specializing in different fields. It is different from other books on the subject. The current affairs books generally deal with limited period and limited topics. Normally such books discuss external relations, military and security matters, militancy and terrorism and trade or commerce. Sometimes there is a special article on cultural relations or nuclear issues. The present book, however, is unique as it contains chapters dealing with varying subjects like diversities in India, Pakistan and the United States; cooperation between India and US in economic, agricultural and other sectors; US perspective of India and India's perspective of US; nuclear issues and regional security; Kashmir imbroglio; international terrorism; and strategies of India, Pakistan, US, Russia, and China. The course of events discussed starts from early 1940s and ends with 2009, covering a wide geographical area and a variety of subjects.

Thus, not only the spectrum is very wide but the relations (Indo-US-Pak) cover a long span of time, which could only be done by a team composed of an administrator, a military officer, a financial planner-cum-lawyer and a social worker. The book is useful for a cross-section of readership including statesmen, lawmakers, diplomats, teachers, students, social workers, agricultural specialists, economists, army men and administrators worldwide.

About the Authors

Dr. (Professor) B.B. Nagaich is M.Sc.(Agri.) from Agra University and Ph.D. in Virology from the University of Illinois, Urbana. After his Doctorate, Dr. Nagaich served in Indian Agricultural Research Institute (IARI), a deemed university based in New Delhi and later in CPRI. During service, he rose to the position of Director of CPRI at Shimla and visited all parts of the country and about 2 dozen countries in different continents. He has been going to USA every year to conduct research on current relations. Dr. Nagaich received 2 national awards and the third was Guinness award of the British Science Policy Foundation. He taught as Associate Professor in IARI and as Professor in CPRI and guided several researchers for Ph.D. degrees of various universities. He has published articles on Indo-US Relations.

Colonel Jayant Kumar obtained his Masters degree from H.P. University and joined Indian Military Academy, Dehradun. During service, he received Post-graduate Engineering degree. Later, he obtained M.B.A. degree. He has about 25 years experience in communication network and military matters plus business administration. Colonel Kumar devoted major part of his army service in problematic J&K.

Attorney Rajiv Nagaich is working in USA for several decades. He is an expert on Financial Planning and Law. He owns his own law-firm and has been judged as best teacher by the Washington State Bar Association. He also appears regularly on radio programmes to educate people about elder law etc. During his nearly 3 decades of stay in the US, he has travelled to many countries in Europe and Asia.

Ms. Sharda Nagaich has worked as a member of All India Women's Association (AIWA) from 1960 onwards. Her work resulted in spread of AIWA activities for betterment of women in H.P. In 1982, she moved back to Bundelkhand and began teaching craft-work to girls and ladies in the area and started giving radio-talks for welfare of women in the region.

Preface

Reading and writing the historical, political or cultural accounts provide excellent opportunities to think and look back on the past to enable us to modify misunderstood events or actions, which created disasters. How do you judge a nation which is only 62 years old but at the same time is the product of a civilization that is 5 to 8 thousand years old. This applies to the Indian freedom struggle. The imperial rulers of India depended on their ideologies for developing the colonial rule. The Oxford scholars and administrators turned historians played an important role in British literature on Indian partition. It was noted that the changing contours of external relations were based on interpretations from cherished commonality of objectives. Simultaneously, United States of America was trying to develop business with British India. As early as 1792 official bilateral relations began between India and the USA with the appointment of a Consul General by the President George Washington. During the Presidency of Franklin Roosevelt the mutual understanding improved further.

In fact, President Roosevelt advised the British Prime Minister Winston Churchill to give freedom (Swaraj) to the Indian subcontinent at the earliest opportunity. This suggestion however was not acted upon by Prime Minister Churchill, who wished to delay the freedom as long as possible. To achieve this delay the famous policy of 'divide and rule' was applied by dividing the Indians as a Hindu majority, a Muslim minority, and the so-called Hindu untouchables (termed Harijans or the sons of God by Mahatma Gandhi). They declared the Congress as a Hindu party and Muslim League as a Muslim body, neglecting the nationalist Muslims in the Congress party. Unfortunately, Islamic fundamentalism was growing, and with British encouragement it grew very fast and fattened, leaving nationalist Muslims helpless. Mahatma Gandhi, Jawaharlal Nehru, Sardar Ballabh Bhai Patel, and

Maulana Azad among others, persuaded Baba Ambedkar, the learned leader of the then Harijans, not to pursue separatist policies.

This view was readily accepted by the foresighted leader (Nagaich, 2003). Simultaneously there was a strong support for the freedom (Ghadar) movement of India in the US. Mahatma Gandhi, Rabindranath Tagore and Swami Vivekanand were highly appreciated by many Americans. Bhagvat Gita and Vishnu Purana influenced several American intellectuals. The Wattumal Foundation was set up in the US for awarding scholarships for better understanding between India and the US. In spite of all this, the views of the White House mostly remained indifferent to unfriendly (Dennis Kux, 1993; Ganguly, 1999), contrary to the views of the majority of the US citizens.

Master plan of the Ghadar movement in the US, series of violent activities of the Indian revolutionaries, and the establishment of the Indian National Army (INA) or Azad Hind Fauj discouraged the UK to continue ruling India. Simultaneously, the non-violent or the Ahinsa (Ahimsa) movement by the masses forced the British Parliament to agree to grant freedom to the Indian subcontinent by using a 'divide and quit' policy (Hodson, 1969; Bramha Singh, 1998). Pakistan traces its birth in Lahore Resolution of 1940, whereas India traces its origin in the ancient civilization more than 5,000 years ago (Waslekar, 2005). In the Independence Act for India, the future of 562 micro, mini and large princely states in the subcontinent was left completely with their rulers. They could join India or Pakistan or stay independent. Many analysts feel that the formulation of this provision had a sinister purpose. They think it was hoped that like the Arab world, the Indian subcontinent would also be fragmented into several nations to enable the British to perpetuate their influence in South Asia (Brahmha Singh, 1998).

Sarfaraz Manzoor, a journalist and documentary producer of U.K. visited Mumbai after 26/11 attacks. His parents were born in India and settled in Britain after partition. He came in the end of 2008 and felt that it was a blunder to divide the country and since partition poverty is prevailing in the region (Agencies, December 29, 2008). All the Indian states had merged (Menon, 1985) except Junagarh, Jammu & Kashmir (J&K) and Hyderabad, which faced dilemmas due to the thinking of their rulers. The ruler of Junagarh was a Muslim (Mahabat Khan) but the public was non-Muslim. The state of J&K is a very large state, with three regions, valley, Ladakh and Jammu. Srinagar valley is predominantly Muslim. Ladakh and Jammu both are non-Muslim and the ruler was also a non-Muslim (Hari Singh). Hyderabad ruler was a Muslim (Nizam) whereas the public was non-Muslim. India basically is a multi-religion secular country whereas Pakistan is an Islamic nation.

Fundamentalist Muslims, therefore, became encouraged by the creation of Pakistan and demanded entire Kashmir to be included in Pakistan whereas non-Muslims and nationalist Muslims did not want it. I included terrorism in Kashmir and some other places to show that even different nations are not prepared to accept the views of others because of their own interests. After receiving arms and encouragement from Pakistan, tribesmen launched mass invasion of Kashmir. Pakistan first supplied arms but later sent its regular troops (Chopra, 1990). Pakistani forces invaded J&K as they thought the Hindu ruler might merge his state with India (Akbar, 1985; Khan, 1970). Pakistan itself accepted this fact, which was also recorded by UNCIP in 1948.

When the invaders were nearing Srinagar, the ruler offered to accede to India if the Indian army saved Srinagar from loot, arson and rapes meted out in other parts of Kashmir (Chibber, 1998). Mehar Chand Mahajan, the then Kashmir Prime Minister, flew to Delhi to persuade India to send the army. Nehru was reluctant at first but Sheikh Abdullah interceded. As a result tl1e accession was signed after considerable delay and 300 soldiers of the Indian army were airlifted next day, using civilian Dakota aircraft, to expel the invaders (Mahajan,

1963). This operation found whole-hearted support of Sheikh Abdullah and Muslim workers of the National Conference, who rallied public support to provide the army with civil trucks as well as food. Srinagar and some other areas were saved.

While accepting merger Lord Mountbatten, in his reply dated October 27, 1947 to the Maharaja, stated, "as soon as law and order have been restored and her soil is cleared of invaders the question of accession should be settled by the people". Subsequently, on 1st November Mountbatten made an offer to Jinnah to resolve the Kashmir issue through people's verdict. But Jinnah declined the offer. However, the invader is still occupying the area that is called Pakistan Occupied Kashmir (POK) or Gulam Kashmir by India and Azad (free) Kashmir by Pakistan. Before the entire Kashmir could be liberated Nehru (persuaded by Lord Mountbatten) submitted the case to the United Nations against the wishes of several Indian leaders and also the army officers but later regretted having done so (Lok Sabha debates, 1963). Pakistan admitted in the UN the entry of its troops and other irregulars into J&K. The Security Council in a resolution, dated August 13, 1948, proposed a three-step solution.

1. A cease-fire. This happened on January 1, 1949.
2. Pakistan to pull out of the state completely. It has not happened so far.
3. Future of the state to be decided by the people, after the first 2 steps are taken (Bhattacharya, 1994; Chopra, 1990; Chibber, 1998; Vas, 2000).

Between 1951 and 1958, the Security Council appointed five representatives, three of whom were the US citizens, to study the question of implementation of the UN Resolution leading to a plebiscite. None of these representatives could come to an agreement. They were of the opinion that a plebiscite would create more problems. This fact was accepted by the UN. Since 1958 no representative was appointed by the UN on this issue. Thus it is clear that for the UN, plebiscite was a dead issue in 1958 itself (Lakhera, 2000). Later, the Secretary General of the UN himself expressed almost similar opinion in Islamabad. The Indian Government asked the state Government to convene an elected Constituent Assembly to debate and give its conclusion on accession. Accession was ratified by the state Constituent Assembly of J&K, based on adult franchise, to complete the wishes of the masses (Mahajan, 1963). Pakistan however, still occupies the northern areas (POK) but no developments have taken place there and the public is highly dissatisfied. Indian J&K had several democratically elected governments, which have time and again stated J&K to be the integral part of India. Pakistan has on the other hand, through sponsored terrorists (Nayar, 1998), been threatening the public to stay away from elections. This has not been agreed to by most of the people of J&K. Therefore, what now remains to be done is to hold a plebiscite in POK, after withdrawal of Pakistan troops from that part of Kashmir. The Secretary General of the UN, Kofi Annan, during his visit to Pakistan on March 11, 2001 stated that the UN resolutions could not be applied. He further suggested that for the solution of Kashmir imbroglio Lahore declaration should be made the basis.

The United States, however, did not accept the merger of Kashmir into India as a legal act despite the Maharaja of Kashmir having signed an accord of accession. They suspect that Maharaja did not even sign the accord. This laid a strong foundation for difficulties and a strained relationship between India and the US (Dixit, 1995, 1998). Thus the goodwill, which prevailed until then started being washed down. In the UN the US sided more or less with the Pakistani view whereas Russia considered the merger of Kashmir with India as proper and legal as per the Freedom Act. It is true Anglo-American plans did not succeed in dragging India into a plebiscite net but the real issue of vacation of Pakistan's aggression receded into the background. With this start the US from time to time has opposed the merger of Kashmir, disregarding the declaration signed by the concerned parties. The US considers all of Kashmir as disputed territory and not as an integral part of India, whereas it agrees with merger of other princely states as legal. The US has continued economic cooperation with India and a military partnership with Pakistan (Cohen 1985; Dixit, 1998).

When President Zia was proceeding to Sri Lanka straight from Dhaka, Prime Minister Rajiv Gandhi invited him to stop over at New Delhi. Rajiv asked President Zia to enter into an agreement not to attack each other's nuclear facilities. Zia was taken aback for a moment but quickly recovered and welcomed the proposal. Pakistan openly was expressing that India (perhaps in collusion with Israel) was planning to attack Kahuta installations. Therefore, the proposal was highly important to Pakistan. Three years later the accord was signed in 1988 (Khan and Parthasarthy, 2004).

The nuclear tests carried out by India in May 1998, succeeding Pakistan's receipt of Chinese and Korean help on nuclear arsenals and also the testing of Ghauri missile, ignited fire in the relationship between India and the US. According to the former Ambassador Richard Celeste Indo-US relations at the Asia Society, he spoke passionately of the nearly one million strong Indian-American community and reiterated that it could form the intellectual bridge to resurrect the mutual relationship to its full potential.

According to Indian authorities it was vital for India to declare itself a nuclear weapon-state for security reasons. Despite the fact that Indian Prime Minister, Rajiv Gandhi, as early as 1988 proposed "Action Plan for Ushering in a Nuclear Weapon-Free and Non-Violent World Order, none of the nuclear powers realized the cost of their cynicism to revise their action plan to usher in a nuclear weapon free world (Rajiv Gandhi, 1988). On the contrary, France and China detonated nuclear weapons in spite of strong opposition throughout the world and neither the US nor any other country imposed economic sanctions on them or cut off relations or trade. Also the US itself started "sub-critical" testing of its stockpile of nuclear weapons and missiles to improve their reliability and efficiency. After President G.W. Bush took over nuclear arsenals were tested about half a dozen times. Simultaneously the US and some other nations placed economic sanctions (which were later withdrawn by President Bush) on India and Pakistan for their nuclear tests.

In spite of a series of 14 high-level talks between Jaswant Singh, Emissary of the Prime Minister, and Strobe Talbot, Deputy Secretary of State, the US disagreed with India on its need for the 1998 Pokhran-II tests, although they agreed to fight terrorism on an international level. On one hand the US dislikes military regime in Myanmar but supports the same in Pakistan. India and the NAM nations have not been able to digest these facts and openly state that knowing fully well the role the China-Pakistan team is playing, the US is closing its eyes and is continuously encouraging China by declaring it as the Asian leader.

In fact it has been suggested by some that, with the approval of the US, China continued helping Pakistan with arms, M-11 and Hatf missiles and by providing nuclear technology. At the same time the US desired India and Pakistan to become party to signing CTBT (although the same was not ratified by its own Senate), which India had been declining to do mainly because it viewed the CTBT as discriminatory in nature. Pakistan had been denying it on the ground that India was not doing so. In the light of the foregoing, it is very difficult to comprehend how India and the US would come to common terms unless they leave the paths they have chosen to follow. President Bill Clinton invited Prime Minister Nawaz Sharif to visit the US in December, 1998 to discuss economic issues and to follow up matters that arose in London conversations between the Deputy Secretary of State and Pakistan Foreign Secretary. In these meetings some of the sanctions were withdrawn to help Pakistan but not India. The US has recently given trillions of dollars and weapons to Pakistan, despite North Korea-Pakistan-Iran etc. nexus in proliferation, with this money it is purchasing military equipment.

This partisan attitude angers the government of India and complicates the problems for smooth Indo-US relations. Actions like these and previous concessions/favours to Pakistan created misgivings in the minds of Indians, who already believe the US to have 'pro-Pakistani leaning'. In spite of this, relations have slowly improved in the post cold-war era due to trade-ties and technology transfers. Indo-US relations briefly chilled due to India's nuclear tests but after the visits of President Clinton & Bush and Prime Minister Vajpayee and Singh to the US in later years they improved.

The former US Ambassador to India R.D. Blackwill had said, President George W. Bush had a global approach to Indo-US relations consistent with India's rise as a world power. The US operation 'Enduring Freedom' after the September 11 terror attacks continued and India passed on information on terrorism. It also continued its punitive actions against terrorist infiltrations in J&K under the cover of Pak army fires and elsewhere in its territory. One stand off between Indo-Pak forces came as Secretary Colin Powell reached Islamabad, before flying to New Delhi in 2001. Skirting the issue of terrorist camps in Gulam Kashmir/POK Donald Rumsfeld told George Fernandes, on November 5, 2001, that the current war against terrorism would riot end after Afghanistan. "We will be pursuing terrorists wherever they are. We began with Afghanistan because Al Qaida is there." He also spoke of strengthening military-to-military ties between India and the US, including training and exchange of personals. During President Bush's period there have been considerable improvements in Indo-US relations because of economic treaties, joint military exercises and civil nuclear energy deal.

For Indian Foreign policy Gandhiji had proposed a commitment to freedom based on democracy and a pledge to encourage reason and impulses of peace in international affairs. He was of the opinion that "...Democracy is not a state in which people act like sheep. Under democracy, liberty of opinion and action is jealously guarded. I am not pleading India to practice non-violence because it is weak. I want her to practice non-violence being fully conscious or its power. No training or collection of arms is required for realization or this strength." The presumption was that since India has no expansionist designs against any other nation, it would not race any threats. This was also supported by the fact that since India is not taking sides with any power group and is desirous of cooperation, and friendship with all countries, power group equations should not adversely apply to India. Another presumption was that the establishment of the UN provided both oral and procedural basis for conflict resolution through peaceful means, nations like India need not bother for large army using sophisticated arms.

Many learned authors have written valuable books on the ups and downs of the Indo-US political relations. However, they are available only in the libraries and most of the people are not aware of the history. Therefore, when I came to the US in 1995, the idea to write a book on different aspects of Indo-US-Pak relations was suggested by some experts. The intention is to let the interested people know the facts, with emphasis on recent events, so that people would be better equipped to judge and assess where things have gone wrong. However, whenever the Indo-US relationship is discussed it is hardly possible to leave out Pakistan, Bangladesh, Russia or China (referred to as star nations). One or the other country always figures out in these discussions. As I continued to develop the manuscript, it became apparent that each move has its utility. Accepting the validity of one approach does not necessarily imply rejection of another. It is not a matter of an action being right or wrong. Every approach offers a unique contribution to improving mutual relations and has implications for understanding each other views. There is a clear place for secularism and pluralism, especially in a society/world that is becoming increasingly pluralistic and secular.

The material for this book has been collected from various sources including Parliamentary records, Congressional records, proceedings of conferences, books, magazines, newspapers and journals. It may be mentioned again that the idea is to detail the facts with least comments. At times essential views have been expressed for helping the readers. Opinions expressed by different authorities are only theirs. I do not intend to affect the feelings of any community or country and am indebted to Dr. Steve P. Cohen of the Brookings Institutions, Prof. Salim Rashid of the University of Illinois, Dr. J.P. Singh of Washington University, Dr. Shiv Kumar of the Central Potato Research Institute, Dr. J.P. Mishra of the Indian Council of Agricultural Research, Mrs. Neha Gohil of Yale University and Dr. M. Blaufarb of California, who all helped by sending literature or by giving their valuable suggestions on the subjects of their specialization. I am also indebted to my daughter-in-law Jamie Nagaich, son-in-law Yogesh Mudgal and Saket Sengar for their assistance on the computer. Also the help of USIS, AFP, API and PTI for supplying information and photographs is acknowledged, as is the kindness of the dignitaries, who very kindly gave personal interviews. I hope that not only the scholars but also other people will find this book useful for promoting mutual understanding and cooperation between different nations for peace & welfare of humanity.

B.B. Nagaich

Introduction

By B.B. Nagaich

The unique feature of India is that democracy and economic growth were never mutually exclusive as well as majority kept religion out of politics. After independence the electorate has been growing in size and becoming increasingly demanding for accountability. However the bad part of Indian elections or democracy is that the poor, underprivileged and uneducated vote in greater numbers than the rich and educated people. Consequently more and more unwanted unsocial elements are getting advantage and as a result politics is becoming criminalized and corruption is increasing. Communal strife (town or region specific) studied by Harvard scholars has shown that in a sample surveys for over 20 years, communal violence in India is sporadic and specific to some localities. There are many unfinished tasks for a six decade old nation like eradication of poverty, illiteracy and basic medical care of all citizens particularly in remote rural areas. However the nation never left hope and resilience. Secularism found its place in the constitution in 1976, through 42nd Amendment, although it existed in the society for centuries. Mahatma Gandhi (father of the nation) regarded secularism as "Sarva–Dharma-Sambhava" or equal status of all religions and is being followed by majority of people.

Preparations for Freedom (*Swaraj*)

Mahatma Gandhi did not address any public meetings in Srinagar after arriving there on August 1, 1947. Although it was a vital visit and many politicians wanted Gandhiji to address at least one meeting to counter Mohammad Ali Jinnah, who visited Kashmir earlier and offered the ruler, Maharaja Hari Singh, a blank check for joining Pakistan. Gandhi insisted on neither holding meetings nor suggesting Kashmir to accede to India. He suggested to the leaders, who met him there, that the people themselves and the ruler should jointly decide the future of the state. Mahatma Gandhi's confidence in the communal harmony, for which the Kashmiris are well known, was apparent from his actions. He said his sole hope and prayer was in Kashmir becoming a beacon light in the subcontinent. Sheikh Mohammad Abdullah, the President of Kashmiri National Conference was under preventive detention due to leading a movement.

Gandhi was unable to meet Sheikh but conveyed his views through Mrs. Abdullah, who met Mahatma. Even without public meetings, thousands gathered in Gandhi's prayer groups. People urged him to ask the ruler to release Sheikh Abdullah. Gandhi refused by saying that he had not come for political purposes. He also said that the question of determining the will of people should be worked out between the Maharaja and the Kashmiris to avoid any conflict later.

On his way back via Punjab, Gandhi stopped at the refugee camp at Wah, near Rawalpindi (now in Pakistan), full of aggrieved Hindus and Sikhs. Their main goal was to move away form the land, which was soon to become Pakistan. Despite the strong anti-Muslim sentiments in the Wah camp, Gandhi emphasized religious harmony, which he had found in abundance in Kashmir. He asked refugees to accept the assurances given by Jinnah and his party leaders that the minorities would be quite safe in Pakistan. He left his disciple, Doctor Shushila Nayyar, in the Wah camp to dispel their fears. Gandhi had seen and heard personally how serious the situation was in Punjab. Therefore he told the Congress leaders, who came to see him off at the Lahore railway station that "The real test is soon coming." He asked them to remain calm and quiet as well as to respect the Pakistani flag, if the new nation gives equal rights to all citizens and full protection to all religious minorities, such as Buddhists, Hindus, Sikhs and Christians etc.

Soon after Gandhi's visit the passions and fears aroused by the acceptance of partition started taking a heavy roll of innocent Hindus, Sikhs and other minorities in the state of Punjab. Cyril Radcliffe was still to announce the exact boundary between Pakistan and India (West and East Punjab, respectively). This uncertainty created false hopes, anxiety and tensions. Sikhs desired to get access to their religious shrines like Nankana Sahib. Future of Lahore was still debated and undecided. Although it was generally presumed that Lahore in all probability would go to West Punjab, Hindus and Sikhs hoped for it to go to East Punjab and so they gathered here. Muslim extremists also gathered in Lahore to maintain their hold. Punjab Governor, Evan Jenkins, informed the Viceroy, Louis Mountbatten about continuous deterioration in the state (Chibber, 1998).

Lahore was having a series of stabbings, murders and bomb explosions. Consequently, in Amritsar also a major explosion left about 50 people dead. Communal riots and arson were reported along the proposed border in the Radcliffe award of the Boundary Commission. Jenkins, who opposed partition from the very beginning, was very much concerned with the difficulty of reaching agreement on the division of assets & liabilities between the two Punjabs. There were only two weeks left for the partition, when he wrote, "It would have been difficult enough to partition within six weeks, a country of 300 million people, even if all concerned were friendly and anxious to make progress." To make matters worse people were divided and there was very little Monsoon rain that year, which threatened the Kharif crop. In addition, because of migration much work could not be done in the fields, leading to extreme food shortage.

Punjabi Congress leaders informed Jawaharlal Nehru about manslaughters in Punjab. In turn Nehru wrote to Mountbatten, that the situation in Punjab was deteriorating steadily and more trouble was expected in the coming days. Therefore, he suggested that military pickets be posted in the city side by side with regular police pickets to help them in preventing looting, arson, manslaughters and to reassure terrified citizens. Mountbatten agreed with Nehru and conveyed his suggestion to the Governor of Punjab, who turned it down, informing that there was only one infantry battalion left and they had been posted in the city of Lahore. Intelligence reports mentioned that the Akali Sikh leader Master Tara Singh had plans to blow up special trains carrying Pakistani staff to Karachi. The Viceroy invited M.A. Jinnah, Liaquat Ali, and Sardar Patel for a special meeting on 5th August. Gerald Savage, an officer of the Punjab criminal investigation department (CID) reported that Master Tara Singh was committed to taking revenge on Muslims and was collecting arms.

In view of the Master Tara Singh's hold on the Sikh community, the government was reluctant to arrest him. In his report, Savage himself suggested that Master Tara Singh's arrest could lead to further troubles. Liaquat Ali was interested only in safeguarding Muslims and Pakistani officers going to other areas in special trains and suggested precautions to be taken for these trains. In his opinion Sikhs were likely to rebel on the announcement of the Radcliffe Boundary Commission award. Ultimately, Mountbatten made a bold decision to order the arrest of Master Tara Singh and his aides, by the Punjab Governor. Jinnah kept silent. Patel did not agree with the CID report sent by Gerald Savage. Jinnah later told the Viceroy that he favoured arrest of Tara Singh but did not want to express his views in the presence of Patel. Tension increased day by day as did the stabbings, looting, murders and arson. Therefore, Mountbatten wanted to hurry up all the arrangements. Even if Radcliffe had handed over the award of the Boundary Commission on the expected date of 9th August, there would be very little time left to take necessary precautions before August 15. According to the staff of the Viceroy, Mountbatten was showing signs of fatigue with forgetfulness and flashes of ill temper (Campbell-Johnson, 1951).

The North-West Frontier Province (NWFP) was also

showing apparent signs of tension, though not to the same extent as Punjab. The interim Congress government, under the able leadership of Abdul Gaffar Khan (called Frontier Gandhi), was refusing to hand over the territory to Pakistan (Chibber, 1998). Although the referendum had been lost, Khan's government still claimed majority in the provincial legislature. On persuasion from Mahatma Gandhi and Nehru, Khan Sahib was willing to cooperate with Pakistan, provided the NWFP was given the same autonomy as was given to the princely states of India. As the Viceroy did not want any future conflicts with the Pakistani government, he wrote to NWFP Governor, Lieut. General Lockhart to persuade Khan Sahib the leader of the interim government to resign before the transfer of power. Meanwhile Nehru, after discussing with his colleagues, submitted to the Viceroy the names of the members of the founding cabinet of independent India, who would take office on August 15, 1947. He had been heading the interim government at that time. The list included Sardar Vallabhabhai Patel, Abdul Kalam Azad, Babu Rajendra Prasad, John Mathai, Jagjivan Ram, Baldev Singh, C.G. Bhabha, Rajkumari Amrit Kaur, Rafi Ahmad Kidwai, B.R. Ambedkar, Shyama Prasad Mukherjee, Shanmukham Chetty and N.V. Gadgil, all the important patriots in different parties.

Freedom (*Swaraj*)

Lord Mountbatten was under so much tension that he wrote to his daughter, Patricia, "It may not be realized at home but I am in the act of bringing off a coup second only to the 3rd June plan, and sincerely hope that by August 15 I shall be able to turn over power to only two central Governments for the whole of India." The fact that an estimated 600,000 lives were lost and nearly 14 million people were involved in the largest forced migration in history was explained as the inevitable fall out of the administrative decisions which Louis Mountbatten had to implement without any choice, as British Parliament had already passed India's Freedom Act plan on June 3. The

British Raj ended at midnight on August 14-15, 1947 and India's Tricolour was raised on Delhi's Red Fort in place of the Union Jack (Hodson, 1969). During British rule, the policy of divide and rule was successfully pursued and the communal divide between Hindus and Muslims had been nurtured both overtly and covertly. There had been an increase in rivalry among the communities to seek more favours by way of communal reservations in services and popularly elected bodies.

After the traumatic partition (Bramha Singh, 1998) Prime Minister Jawaharlal Nehru's announcement of independence from British rule was, similar to Abraham Lincoln's Gettysburg Address, a tale of victory and tragedy. About the same number of people died in the US civil war as in India's freedom movement, which led to the India-Pakistan partition. Roosevelt's action to grant freedom to the Philippines in 1946 impressed Indians greatly. Roosevelt gained popularity in India for his domestic reforms and anti-colonial views.

On August 15, 1947 an ancient civilization was re-born declaring the end of foreign dominion. There was one land with two nations—India and Pakistan (which further split later into 2 countries—Pakistan and Bangladesh). Eventually fragmented India defined itself as the biggest democracy in the world with the potential to become one of the worlds leading nations in the century. Ironically there are more Muslims in India than in Islamic Pakistan. Some consider the Kashmir dispute as a Hindu Muslim conflict that began several decades ago. However, our views are different. India had been warding off invasions from the North-West even before the birth of the Prophet Mohammad. The first battle of Panipat was fought in 1556 between two Muslim empires as a power struggle. For Pakistan even now it is a power struggle and not a legal matter. In history books Emperor Akbar is referred to as "Great" because he understood the Indian psyche and accepted the old Indian concept of unity in diversity. Due to his policies the Moghul Empire lasted about 200 years and only when

Aurangzeb adopted staunch views and disturbed traditional pluralism the empire started crumbling.

As expected the Pakistanis extolled Aurangzeb and not Akbar. After the Moghul Empire the East India Company of U.K. organized mercenary forces to safeguard its economic interests by arranging alliances with local rulers. The famous freedom struggle or the Ghadar movement of 1857 (called mutiny by the British) was a joint Hindu-Muslim event to overthrow the autocratic foreign rule. The event did not succeed and the East India Co. was replaced by British rule with their educational system and administration. Hindus adopted themselves quickly to the new environment. Muslims, in general, did not like to change because they thought that the changes were against Islam. Most of them clung to the traditional Madarsa's and avoided modern schools and scientific knowledge, looking to the Arab world for guidance, indirectly denying themselves progress.

Jinnah was a shrewd barrister and initially a member of the Indian National Congress. Realizing that he could not match Mahatma Gandhi and Nehru, Jinnah became a leader in Muslim League. To gain power, he sided with the British "divide and rule" adventure and pressed for an Islamic State. During Indian Civil Disobedience Movement, the British announced "Communal Award" for separate electorate not only to minorities but also to Harijans (Schedule castes). This was seen by Hindus as an attempt to disrupt not only national unity but also the Hindu unity. Ultimately reservation in place of separate electorates was agreed upon.

In his August 11, 1947 address to the Pakistan Constituent Assembly Jinnah said, "In course of time all these angularities of majority and minority communities will vanish. We are starting with the fundamental principle that we are all citizens and equal citizens of one State. But Pakistan's feudal leaders did not have Jinnah's perception and did not maintain his secular views. On his deathbed Jinnah confessed to his doctor that, "the creation of Pakistan has been the greatest blunder of my life." With the partition the Intelligence Bureau of Pakistan was split further. The services formed their own intelligence Directorates (ISI). The ISI was mainly responsible for military and external intelligence. Islamic fanaticism was supported by ISI and Pak army which played significant roles in fomenting and sustaining the Kashmir imbroglio. Pakistani civilian and military rulers sent terrorists across borders and later used them to create terror in J&K that could have been otherwise easily contained.

Despite being religious urban and educated Pakistanis avoid extremism. With Afghan war unlimited funds, arms and ammunition came to ISI through the CIA, with both the US and Saudi Arabia helping. Slowly the ISI took over the policy making in Afghanistan, Kashmir, narcotics & drug deals, terrorism and counterfeiting Indian currency. However, the White House (at that time busy with the master plan for Europe) mostly remained apathetic to the subcontinent where more than one billion people resided. There was a time when the Britain guided the US on India as Washington had yet to make its own strategy. The US therefore drew on London's experience on the subcontinent.

Later, the US structured its own formula, taking into consideration its own strategy and also the cold war that had just started. India's refusal to join in the military pacts against communists made the US woo Islamabad and England became the follower. Britain and the US supported the demand for a plebiscite in Kashmir to please Pakistan. When Washington changed London followed the suit. It was therefore crystal clear that there was something paradoxical about the relationship between India and the United States. Indians like most of the things in America. Life, Time and Newsweek magazines are widely read in India. Indian children adore Superman, Batman and Archie comics. The youth has a clear preference for reading Max Brand, Louis L' Amour, Zane Grey and Sudden novels. They also love wearing jeans, listening to 'pop songs' from Elvis Presley, Madonna and Michael Jackson.

Indian science, medical, engineering and agricultural students scramble to get into American universities and once they come to the US, they normally do not want to return to India. Therefore, it is stated by many that India prepares graduate students for settling in the US. Indians enjoyed watching 'I Love Lucy', Disney movies and Laurel and Hardy Shows on television or videos. There was goodwill and strong support for India's freedom movement in the US. In fact Lala Hardayal, a famous Indian freedom fighter (teaching at Stanford University) founded the Ghadar movement (freedom struggle) in the US. Wealthy California farmers supported this movement and leading American newspapers published articles supporting India's freedom struggle.

Therefore, it was a surprise that the Indians' liking for America was not reflected in Indo-US official relations. Normally, India and the US should have been close friends as both gained independence from Great Britain and both were allies during the world wars. India's population and security burdens were and are still heavy. Although nearly 30 per cent of its people are among the World's poorest and despite hostility from the Pakistan right from the painful partition, India with more than 600 million voters has remained a vibrant democracy and a supporter of democracy (like US) since its independence. This achievement alone was more than enough for the White House to admire India. Americans appreciated Mahatma Gandhi, Tagore and Swami Vivekanand. Books like Bhagvat Gita, Vishnu Purana and Gitanjali etc. made a great impact on American thinkers.

However, surprisingly the views of most of the senior White House officials were often indifferent or unfriendly and sometimes estranged (Dennis Kux, 1993; Dixit, 1998). Therefore, most of the Indian politicians, bureaucrats and Indian intellectuals have become suspicious of moves from Washington, instead of visualizing them from the American point of view. Besides Kashmir, international control of atomic energy, Palestine and Indo-China were some other issues on which the two countries did not agree with each other (Alan James, 1969). India's non-alignment was unenthusiastically accepted by the US (Immerson, 1999). Similarly, Joseph Stalin regarded Nehru as a "bourgeois democrat". Contrary to expectations, free India decided to remain in the commonwealth and aligned with the US and Russia both.

One critical period in the Indo-US relations began when America felt threatened by communism in the mid 1940s. China, the world's most populous country, became communist and joined the USSR block. The White House was afraid that the communist tide would move down to South Asia and engulf India, Pakistan, Afghanistan and Myanmar (then Burma). However, Jawaharlal Nehru did not take communism from Soviet Russia and China so seriously.

In fact, he was oriented towards socialism and, along with A.G. Nasser of Egypt and J.B. Tito of Yugoslavia, he started the non-aligned movement (NAM), a concept that he was articulating even before independence. He propounded the famous Hindi Chini Bhai-Bhai (Indian-Chinese brotherhood) and Panchsheel (Five principles) theories. Such was Nehru's trust of China and Chou, the CIA report mentioned, that he dismissed a letter from the then Burmese Premier (Ba Swe) cautioning him in dealing with Chou. Nehru declared Chou-en Lai to be a very honourable person. "The Chinese diplomatic effort was a five year masterpiece of guile, executed and probably planned in large part by Chou-en Lai," according to CIA report. Some believe that Roger Baldwin (the Founder of the American Civil Liberty Union) too influenced Nehru's foreign policy. Many of Baldwin's remarks on US Foreign Policy have found a place in Nehru's books and statements. In the 2nd World War, the US and Chiang Kai-shek were allies against Japan. As a token of benevolence to Chiang Kai-shek, the US seated Formosa as one of the permanent member of the UNSC.

In reality at that time itself Nehru wanted the US to agree to mainland China's acquiring veto power in the UN and to

Formosa's being an ordinary member, possibly to favour Chiang Kai-shek. Although the proposal to give mainland China veto power was based on its population, unfortunately the Nixon and Dulles team considered it to reflect a communist bias (Immerson, 1999). Much later the White House agreed to mainland China's becoming a permanent member of the Security Council (which was the desire of Pandit Nehru, as informed personally by Late Shankar Dayal Sharma and Pandit Parmanand (former President of India and freedom fighter, respectively). It is also quoted in Keesing's Contemporary Archives 1950-52, p. 10847. The US later also awarded China the most favoured nation status but China is not willing to accept Formosa as a separate country. Therefore, the question of Formosa being a member of the UN does not arise.

Such differences in perception between New Delhi and Washington led to an important cause of friction between India and the US. V.P. Dutt, a leading expert on China, wrote that "The Americans have fully come around to the policies that Nehru pleaded with them for many years and which they spurned so haughtily and for which they described Nehru as the 'lost leader' of Asia. Suddenly they found everything Chinese unique. The Chinese acupuncture the most felicitous system of the treatment, and so on. The refrain in USA today was there are no flies in Beijing (1990).

Anxious to contain China and communism, the US started arming Pakistan despite India's continuous objections. Pakistan joined the US sponsored SEATO military pact in 1954 as well as CENTO. India was furious about the US supplying arms to Pakistan (Cohen, 1985, 1992) and began to look towards the USSR for friendship. India believed that Pakistan would use its new arms against India and it repeatedly asked the US not to increase the arms race in the subcontinent by sending additional armaments to Pakistan. The US, aware of Pakistan being hostile to India since independence over the Kashmir issue kept telling India that Pakistan would not use the arms against (you), although it (US) had proof that Pakistan had indeed always done so (Bhattacharya, 1994; Chibber, 1998; Dixit, 1995; Ganguly, 1993; Lamb, 1967).

Contrary to the assurance given to the US, Pakistan later became a close ally of China and formally retreated from SEATO in 1972. These differences in the perception of the two countries continued further and increased friction-between New Delhi and Washington. Consequently, India developed better relations with Soviet Russia and slowly walked away from the US. Another vital reason for it was that Moscow supported New Delhi on Kashmir imbroglio while Washington supported Islamabad. It may be noted that whenever Great Britain talked about Kashmir, it only mentioned the Muslim majority section of the Srinagar valley. It never referred to the Hindu majority Jammu region and the Buddhist majority Leh-Ladakh region. The US echoed the British statements. Because the Soviet Union supported India on Kashmir, New Delhi reciprocated by keeping quiet on the Russian invasion of Hungary in 1956, while criticizing the Anglo-French invasion of the Suez Canal.

The US showed resentment by backing out from its earlier commitment of financing the Bokaro steel plant. Russia grabbed this opportunity to strengthen its relationship with India and happily financed the steel plant, after the US had backed out. Finally, this convinced the US that India is not non-aligned but with the U.S.S.R. (Immerson, 1999; Prajapati, 1998; Thornton, 1992). In spite of rocky relationship between India and the US there were always important pro-India voices in the US. John Kenneth Galbraith, Chester Bowles, Senator Hubert Humphrey and Dean Rusk wanted the US to finance the Bokaro plant. After receiving a letter from President Eisenhower allaying Indian concerns, Nehru told Ambassador George Allen it was not the "US motives" that disturbed him but the "possible consequences of this action," both internationally and internally on India and Pakistan (Dennis Kux, 1993). In 1959 when President Eisenhower visited India, Nehru told him "India has given you her most valuable thing-a part of her heart." In 1961 Nehru referred to President John F. Kennedy's government as the friendliest government that India had ever encountered.

The other critical period began when China attacked North-eastern India in 1962. Nehru, who had propounded the slogan 'Hindi Chini Bhai-Bhai' (Indo-Chinese brotherhood theory), was himself greatly shocked. According to him, India was like a brother to China and he had been advocating for China's inclusion in the world forums. Since India always wanted to live in peace with its neighbours it was not ready to fight a war with China. The border war was short but ferocious. The Chinese forces had already prepared for a mountain war before crossing the border. The Indian troops were routed because they were insufficient in number and they were using old weapons, as compared to the Chinese (Hoffman, 1990), who had been preparing for a mountain war.

Twenty days after the attack India wanted help but Russia did not come forward. Instead the US the perceived ill-wisher, helped India by airlifting 60 planeloads of automatic weapons and ammunition. America's response to India's time of need was unhesitating. In 1963 Dean Rusk stated that the US would not wait for negotiations or legislation to give India a quick assistance in the event of another Chinese attack. Another critical period commenced apparently in the mid 1990s. In the beginning of 1998 Senator Sherrod Brown, International Relations Committee member, had cautioned that the US-China nuclear agreement would lead to further development of Pakistan's nuclear capability and pose a serious threat to India. He emphasized that China had already transferred nuclear technology and material to Islamabad although it had been promising not to transfer the same.

As an example of the irresponsible and dangerous action of China, the sale of magnetic rings and other technology was quoted (Brown, 1999). To make matter worse Pakistan refused to allow the International Atomic Energy Commission (IAEA) to inspect its atomic plants. Thus, India was faced with a dangerous situation, a nuclear capable Pakistan mostly in the hands of dictators, supported by China. Soon after Senator Brown's statement Ghauri missile trials by Pakistan and deployment on Indian borders prompted India to detonate nuclear bombs. Pakistan's nuclear tests followed, proving Senator Brown's predictions to be true, which were unfortunately not listened to by the White House at that time.

To improve Indo-US relationship Senator Lauch Faircloth wrote to President Clinton stating that the US policy and economic sanctions were having opposite effects and Washington was in fact alienating the world's largest democracy and one of America's long-standing allies. Senator Jesses Helms, Chairman of the Foreign Relations Committee, also supplemented views of senator Faircloth, who urged President Clinton to work closely with Congress to overcome impulse and reclaim the US position as India's leading trade partner.

Referring to the post-nuclear test (Pokhran II) meeting between Clinton and Nawaz Sharif in 1998, December, Prime Minister Vajpayee's principal secretary, Brajesh Mishra said, US move to resume lending to Pakistan while keeping a ban on India shows partisan attitude. He further said the discriminatory attitude creates an unhelpful atmosphere in India. It had been alleged that despite tons of evidence on China's continuous help to Pakistan's nuclear program the US had been keeping silent and maintaining a soft attitude on China. The Monetary Fund & International Institute of California mentioned that both China and the US had not acted impartially on Pakistan 's nuclear and missiles programs.

Till recently, the US had not taken any action against China on supplying M-ll and other missiles to Pakistan, despite many US senators' asking for sanctions against China. The US intelligence agencies had informed the White House that China had given a full design of atomic weapons to Pakistan and had supplied purified uranium enough to prepare at least two nuclear bombs. China also trained Pakistani scientist in purifying uranium and supplied prepared Tritium gas enough for ten nuclear bombs as well as other nuclear products. In August 2001, the Deputy Secretary of State led a delegation to Beijing regarding China Metallurgical Equipment Corporation (working closely with the government) transferring technology for Pakistan's Shaheen 1 and Shaheen 2 missile programs.

These clandestine transfers were in clear violation of the MTCR as also other international agreements. This time, foolproof evidence provided by the CIA through their satellite watch as well as pressure from Senators Joe Biden (now Vice President) and Arlen Specter etc. ultimately succeeded to make slapping of sanction on CMEC and Pakistan's National Development Complex possible by the US administration, despite denials by China (India Abroad, September 14, 2001).

Similarly, Pakistan was desperate to counter India's superior military power, so it turned to North Korea, which tried to replicate Pakistan's success in developing a nuclear bomb based on enriched uranium, found in plenty there (Seattle Times, November 24, 2002). The American reaction to the Pakistan-North Korea missile nexus confirms that the US is not going to cool its supports for its favourite general in Islamabad. KPS Gill, President of Conflict Management Institute and Dr. Ajai Sahni, the Director of the same institute, while discussing at Pentagon opined, "Some of the ISI know bin Laden's whereabouts --- not the hierarchy but some lower level members know." They termed 'China-Pakistan-North Korea is the new axis of evil,' a triangle threatening world peace (India Abroad, November 1, 2002).

During a press Conference on 5th January, 1999 the US Ambassador at New Delhi had asked a very unusual question from India as to how many atom bombs are required for its security and per bomb how many missiles are needed. The answers were to be submitted along with solid information. Retaliating to the statements of Mr. Celeste, India mentioned that its requirement depended on what changes were taking place in the world and particularly in the region. The matter was not so simple as many items of this type of controversy were related to issues that may not have been visible but they were very important.

According to several defence experts, actually the US was not worried about how many nuclear bombs India possessed but in reality it was worried about rapid acquisition of knowledge India was gaining about nuclear technology and that some day it may be as good as some of the P-5 allies. Therefore, it (US) was trying its best to stop development of all nuclear programs and their militarization by India. Now, many suspect that thru some visa curbs and other regulations the US is trying to discourage employment and contacts to Indian IT specialists. The US state department Director of policy planning said not only North Korea but also India, Pakistan and Israel should be stripped of their nuclear weapons. The NPT should be made universal," as if the P-5 nations are not in the universe or they are only countries to which the nuclear programs are useful" (Times of India December 12, 2003).

India's foreign policy is based on peaceful co-existence (panchsheel), self-reliance, non-alignment, de-colonization, disarmament, restructuring international economic order and anti-racialism. Prime Minister Nehru laid down the basic parameters of foreign policy coupled with the concept of non-alignment in the bipolar world. Consistent with our traditional values of democracy Nehru promoted global disarmament, equality, economic cooperation and non-violence. Our basic considerations are a plural democratic secular society and the well being of our people as well as our neighbours.

Therefore, Indian peace-keeping operations formed an important aspect of our international activities and also in relation to our neighbouring nations. Speaking at the 12th summit of SAARC at Islamabad Prime Minister Vajpayee said the region had talent, resources and markets to make it an economic powerhouse, "all it needs is political will." Earlier he had suggested one currency (SAR) for the whole South Asia, which was very much liked by former Prime Minister Jamali (PTI December 13, 2003) and BIMSTECH proposal (free trade between Bangladesh, India, Mayanmar and Thailand). On this occasion, he proposed creation of 'Poverty Alleviation fund', to which India was to have made contribution of US$ 100 million to be used outside India (TNN January 5, 2004).

In this summit terrorism in any form was not acceptable to SAARC nations, which signed a 10-point social charter and suggested that a single visa can boost tourism in the region. A homemade bomb exploded on September 29, 2007 outside a crowded city park in Maldives, for the first time, wounding about 12 foreigners. Muslim majority Maldives islands, in Indian Ocean, are renowned for tourism and the nation is one of the members of the SAARC nations. It is not known whether the bomb was aimed to harm tourism industry or whether it was an act of Islamic Jehad.

India's Neighbours

Bhutan: The King of Bhutan visited India and had discussions with the President and Prime Minister of India. India had been helping in the implementation of Bhutan's Five-Year Plans. Some of the portions of the seventh Five-Year Plan (1992-97) as well as the eighth were being assisted by India. Important projects like the Paro airport terminal building construction, Kurichu hydroelectricity project in eastern Bhutan, agricultural development, the health program, education, road & bridge construction, communication systems, electrification in many areas etc. are the ongoing programs, about to be completed, in which India is playing an important role. In addition, New Delhi is also cooperating with the kingdom of Bhutan in the fields of higher education, technical education (including agriculture), survey & training for renovation of culturally important places and historical monuments.

Thus economic cooperation between India and Bhutan has provided an ideal model (both being SAARC members) for friendly and cooperative relationship for others to follow. Bhutan's operation to flush out India insurgents came in for special praise at 2004 SAARC Summit from Prime Minister Vajpayee. He said "courageous" action was an outstanding example of Bhutan's sensitivity concerns of a neighbour (Times of India, January 4, 2004). Recently, the king of Bhutan visited India and signed an agreement for connection of its five border towns with different Indian cities. He also initiated democratization of Bhutan and is working on elections based on its new constitution. The Bhutanese refugees are being threatened in Nepal and the US has come forward to settle some of them in the US. Inflation has taken Bhutan also in its folds. Price increase has been quite heavy in 2008.

In fourteenth SAARC meetings in Delhi in 2007, Afghanistan for the first time participated as the eighth member and several other countries participated as observers. For country's development President Hamid Karzai, who was shocked by a suicide bombing in Kabul, is prepared to meet & talk to Omar Abdullah and former Prime Minister Hekmatiyar. He reportedly said, "Esteemed Mullah, sir, and esteemed Hekmatyar, sir, why are you destroying the country?" This suicide bombing on September 29, 2007 killed about 30 people and wounded several.

Nepal: Nepal has a special relationship with India because of its long tradition of sharing history, culture and religion as well as population. Several exchanges of high level visits take place often between India and Nepal. Liberalizations of economies in both neighbouring countries led to improvements in economic relations. Mutual discussions resulted in establishment of a framework for treaties of Trade and Transit. Since Nepal is a landlocked country passage and port facilities for transit are a must for its stable trade and economy, both countries trade materials with each other. The new bridge (Sirsiya) at the Raxaul border linking the two nations at a place where heavy traffic was creating problem is a welcome project.

Agreement on the Kali River is also a sign of good neighbourly relations. Recently, Rajbiraj Industrial Estate was handed over to Nepal formally. Proposals were exchanged between India and Nepal for the renewal of a bilateral trade agreement, which expired in December 2001. An agreement on controlling terrorism in the region was also signed between the two neighbours. The treaty of peace and Friendship of 1950 has been renewed. Nepalese and Indian citizens will be given privileges for some economic activities, employment, resident and ownership of property in each other's territory.

In 1954 Nepal became a UN member with India's help. A dose friendship between India and Nepal is clear from the fact that the former King and Queen had attended the 50th independence anniversary reception given by the Indian Ambassador in Kathmandu. They were later killed in a shoot out in the palace (Press, June 3, 2000). To take maximum advantage of this situation the ISI of Pakistan has lately made Nepal its important place because there is no visa or passport requirement between India and Nepal. Finding of explosives from Pakistani diplomat, Mohammad Arshad at Kathmandu is only one example.

Despite a peace and friendships agreement there was a hijacking of an a Indian Airlines plane due to which flights had to be cancelled but later these were resumed, Both the nations are SAARC members. In December 2000 there were anti Indian demonstrations and violence by the fans of an actor Hritick Roshan. They alleged that the actor made anti-Nepal statements, which Roshan denied. It is suspected that anti-Indian communists and ISI agents ignited the fire as they were unhappy because of the release of a film 'Mission Kashmir' by his father, Rakesh Roshan. India is now willing to sell its vehicles after the Supreme Court gives its verdict on the pollution problem (Press, June 14, 2000). A work-plan for 2000-2001 between ICAR and ICIMOD (dealing with Nepalese agriculture) was signed on March 15, 2001 to strengthen cooperation between the two nations for improvement of agriculture. The Prime Minister of Nepal visited India along with his wife in March 2002 to discuss bilateral issues, particularly Maoist attacks in Nepal and mutual economic cooperation. He met Prime Minister Vajpayee and other Ministers.

Nepal deported employees of the Pak embassy, who were caught with Indian counterfeits and US dollars. Indian police handed over several Maoists, who were quietly getting medical treatment in India. On the visit of Nepalese Prince to India, Prime Minister Vajpayee promised help required to end violence in that country. Nepal started moving away from India and closer to China. After king Gyanendra took over the government by dismissing Prime Minister, India feels worried because ISI, understand mafias and Maoists can join hands to create serious problems in the region. Already Mumbai underworld is getting its supply of arms and ammunition from Nepal. The monarchy has deployed its force also to crash the Maoists in western Nepal. According to the Amnesty International violence and human rights abuses have increased because of declaring emergency by the king Gyanendra to control Maoists. Democracy had finally been restored by appointment of G.P. Koirala as Prime Minister, who visited India and the Indian Prime Minister gave him a substantial monetary help for economy improvements.

Lately, Maoists have joined to work peacefully with the government in the interest of the nation. Nation's leading party has announced its support, in 2007 September, for declaring the country a republic. Thus it clearly is moving the government a step closer to ending monarchy or making it very weak. In view of improving education and health programs, India decided to donate 13 crore and seven lakh rupees to Nepal in 2008. Newly elected Prime Minister Pushp Kamal D. Prachand said Maoists would like to renew the old agreement with India signed in 1950. According to him this agreement is discriminatory and needs a change. He also said the King should leave the palace voluntarily. The king of Nepal had therefore, vacated the palace in the end of May, 2008 and moved in the summer house, Nagarjun palace. Price of rice has increased in Nepal and consequently it had to put ban on export of rice in 2008. Acting Parliament of Nepal passed a resolution approving election of Prime Minister or removal by a simple majority. Thus it was indication for Maoists to form the government. However since Maoists did not get majority for forming the Chairman of the constitution committee, they decided not to join the new government. Rambaran Yadav, the leader of Nepali Congress, has been elected as President of Nepal.

After demonstrations against Chinese policies in many countries Nepali & Tibet-Buddhists had started demonstrations in Kathmandu to show unity with Buddhists and also to oppose Olympics in China. More than 700 demonstrators were rounded up by the police, in front of Chinese embassy.

Nepali Prime Minister visited India during the middle of September, 2008 to discuss 1950 agreement, Kosi river flood control and other matters of mutual interest to both countries. In January 2009 two Indian head priests of Pashupatinath temple were asked by the government to resign and replaced them with Nepali priests. As a reaction other priests did not allow Nepali priests to enter the temple and also did not take part in any religious activities. Supreme Court interfered and Prime Minister Prachand restored the position of Indian head priests to replace Nepali priests. After controversy on retirement of the military Chief, Katwal, Prachand resigned and it appears there may again be a new revolution by Maoists (PT May 5, 2009). Senior Communist leader Madhav Kumar was elected as new Prime Minister of Nepal on May 23, 2009.

Bangladesh: During the 1990s interactions between India and Bangladesh (earlier East Bengal turned into East Pakistan) were carried out very frequently and several high level visits were exchanged. Both countries became SAARC members and contributed to its programs. The Indo-Bangladesh joint

Working Group met for the first time in New Delhi to discuss bilateral problems on security related matters, cross-border movements, visa related issues and in the end took stock of the situation on the border between the two countries. Indian Border Security Forces and Bangladesh Rifles also had their meetings in New Delhi and Dhaka to make an attempt for curbing illegal immigration of citizens of Bangladesh to Indian West Bengal, which share culture and language with Bangladesh. Other topics of discussions at these meetings were trans-border crimes and repatriation of about 6,000 Chakma refugees from Tripura on a voluntary basis. Bangladesh assured that it will not give sanctuary to Indian insurgents in that country. India has also agreed for additional transit facilities to Bangladesh for trade with Nepal and Bhutan. The exiled writer Taslima Nasrin desires to settle in Kolkata permanently. She wrote in her book on Lajja how Hindus and women suffer in Bangladesh and for this she was punished.

A big eye-sore in cordial relations was the Ganges water sharing and Farakka dam, which was resolved by both countries during Vajpayee government and Sheikh Hasina's regime. The Bangladesh Festival of Arts was inaugurated jointly in New Delhi. The second meeting of Indo-Bangladesh Joint Business Council was held in Dhaka. The Bangladesh railway signed an agreement with India to purchase diesel locomotives. In December 2008, there was tension between India and Bangladesh on drilling of hydrocarbon in the sea near Bangladesh border and two warrior ships were posted by Bangladesh. First India became unhappy but luckily they withdrew from the spot to remove tension.

After an interval of about 25 years India-Bangladesh train called 'Sonar Bangla Special' was started in January 2001 from Petrapol of Indian West Bengal (Agencies, January 21, 2001). Bus travels originating from Calcutta (now Kolkata) and Tripura to Dhaka began to facilitate travel between the two friendly neighbours (Agencies, July 12, 2001). In April 2001 Bangladesh Rifles captured an Indian post and killed 16 Indian

(B.S.F.) soldiers after torturing them on Assam border (Agencies, April 20, 2001). After this incidence Indian-Bangladesh border situation became tense, particularly because Bangladesh rifles again tried to recapture the vacated Indian post (Agencies, April 24, 2001). The Indian government lodged strong protests over the events and Bangladesh government assured that the incidences will be enquired into and the guilty officials will be suitably punished. The Prime Minister of Bangladesh had stated that due to this border problem the ties between the two nations will not be affected (Agencies London, May 13, 2001).

However after Ms. Khalida Zia took over as the Prime Minister in October 2001, Hindus and other minorities have been subjected to harassments. A Hindu Principal of a school was killed by two Muslims in November 2001. Minorities Parishad therefore, organized a rally and its President V.P. Datta warned that if harassment of minorities continues they would have no alternative but to use rifles. According to the Indian State Minister of Home Affairs there are more than 1,000 Madarsas on the Bangladesh border, being helped by ISI for encouraging anti- Indian activities. Despite these events India has been liberal to allow 40 Bangladesh products to be imported into India without any tax or duty, as decided in a meeting at Dhaka in 2002. After the term of Ms. Zia is over it was agreed that for holding the elections in the country an interim government shall be formed which will arrange for free elections.

In 1990s, President Musharraf of Pakistan had exiled the former Prime Ministers Bhutto and Nawaz Sharif. Same way former Prime Ministers Sheikh Hasina and Khalida Zia were exiled from Bangladesh. Earlier both of them were given one week-time to submit the details of their property. Sheikh Hasina and Khalida Zia have now been imprisoned on the charges of corruption. The interim government did not want both former Prime Ministers to remain in politics. Dictatorship had launched a crackdown since assuming power in January,

2007. About 160 former ministers and political leaders had been convicted. Eight terrorists of Jamt-ul-Mujahideen Bangladesh (JMB) were arrested before proposed elections. They also recovered large amounts of grenades, blast materials and Jehadi literature from them. Main political parties of Bangladesh had to threaten to demonstrate against the past dictator government unless their leaders were freed to take part in the elections due towards the end of 2008. If this was not done they would start a countrywide agitation. Ultimately in the elections held in December, 2008 after seven years, former Prime Minister Sheikh Hasina won with an absolute majority. After her victory she announced that the country would be working with neighbours in eradicating terrorism. This way it became clear Bangladesh, which was earlier following Pakistan policies of imposing dictatorship in the country, democratic forces succeeded once again.

On November 16, 2007, cyclone Sidr struck Barisal area near Dhaka. About 5,500 people were reportedly killed. There was huge loss of property and 3 million people had to leave their houses to become homeless. This was not as severe as the one in 1991. Indian President Pratibha Patil offered help. UN, USA, Saudi Arabia and UK were the major donors of aid but the aid was slow. Taslima, Nasreen residing in Kolkata was flown by the government out of Kolkata to Jaipur and to Delhi after violent protests by Muslims. Afterwards she went to Sweden to get medical treatment. Think Tank Observer Research Foundation organized a conference and there former Foreign Secretary of Bangladesh said it is necessary for Bangladesh to have friendly relations with India. Islamic experts have suggested the government that in the new policy they should give up the idea of equal rights to women. Instead they should be given only the rights which are absolutely necessary. A mutiny in the Bangladesh Rifles (BDR) was quelled on 25th February, 2009 after Prime Minister granted general amnesty to rebel soldiers, not involved in killings. A senior officer of BDR was the ring leader. About 75 military officers died. One of the banned organization in Myanmar has been giving training to Bangladeshi Islamic terrorists since 1980, as per news of Daily Star from Bangladesh.

Myanmar: India shares about 1,400 kms with Burma. India's relations with Myanmar (separated from India in 1935 and made independent in 1948) have always been friendly. They improved further in 1994-95 with several exchanges of visits of delegations between India and Myanmar. A delegation visited India to survey and discuss operational details relating to boundary demarcation between the two countries. In January 1995 senior officers of both nations held talks for operating the Border Trade Agreement. A large number of Myanmar trainees came to India in mid nineties for different courses on agriculture and farm machinery, computers, journalism & mass media operations, land surveys, banking services, railway operations and telecommunications. Indians have sympathy for restoration of democracy in the neighbouring country and continued attempts to set up democratic government without any outside interference. China's military supplies to Myanmar are therefore, being watched very carefully in India. A few years ago there had been an agreement between the two nations for closer cooperation and trade during a week-long visit of General Maung Aye.

A 4-member delegation led by Chan Nyin, Deputy Minister of Science & Technology visited New Delhi on December 2001 for finalization of work-plan between the two nations. Lately, it has been reported that soldiers are harassing by burning villages of minorities on eastern border with Thailand, where they are taking refuge. China has made agreement with Myanmar to purchase their gas. Recently military government, which took over in 1988, increased the duration of house arrest by one year of the famous leader of the country, Aung San Su Kyi, who is supporting democracy in the nation. She has been under arrest for a very long time since she returned. Su Kyi's father founded Burmese

Nationalist Movement and Burmese Communist Party. Her mother was Burma's Ambassador to India in 1960. Su Kyi continued her education in New Delhi at Lady Shriram College. After her marriage she started the struggle for democracy in Myanmar. Recently, hundreds of demonstrating Buddhist monks marched past barricades to the residence of Su Kyi, pressurizing the government with the icon of long struggle for democracy (AP, September 22, 2007).

The struggle is continuing for about a month and crackdown is more severe than ever before in the 44 years of military rule. Security forces clubbed or tear-gassed protesters and fired shots in the air. Hundreds of Buddhist monks and demonstrators were arrested. About fifteen people were killed. Refugees are coming in India and desire India to intervene. This happened during the period when an Indian Minister had gone to Yangon for agreement between India and Burma for exploration of natural gas etc. Foreign Minister Mukherjee said in New York that India had already told Myanmar government to release Su Kyi and to abstain from violence, because it could make the situation much worse and out of control. Further, India desires the situation to be resolved peacefully through dialogues expeditiously. Myanmar should also consider a probe into violent incidents in the country. Important nations are keeping a close watch on the situation in Myanmar. United Nation's representative had gone for discussions with the government but nothing concrete came out (Seattle Times September 30, 2007).

In 1988, last peaceful uprising was crushed by military, killing about 3,000 people. Since then military rule has been maintained, arresting Buddhist monks, students/ dissidents for quashing opposition by force. China had since been the chief patron of Myanmar rulers and also the beneficiary. After global outrage military government started releasing the arrested monks and dissidents. The government has also asked Aung Kyi, a moderate minister, to develop relations with Su Kyi to deflect criticism because of its crackdown on mass protests and for appeasing the UN. Both Su Kyi and the military government have agreed to meet with and cooperate. In addition to India, the US, European countries and many South East Asian nations demanded release of Su Kyi to show that the country is now a responsible nation of the globe.

In the beginning of May, 2008 the country faced a heavy cyclone 'Nargis' leading to death of thousands of people. There has been heavy destruction of property and about 10 thousands of people are missing. This also destroyed rice crop in Myanmar, which was very good this year. The country had planned to export 6 lakh (0.6 million) tons of rice. However, failure of the crop led to heavy price rise. India, the US and many other countries have begun to send relief materials.

Naval vessels from Myanmar and Bangladesh are facing each other after former nation began exploring in the area for oil and gas. Bangladesh is planning to send its diplomats to Yangoon to resolve the territorial dispute.

Sri Lanka: Earlier referred to as Ceylon always had good relations with India, with mutual understanding and good neighbourliness. On the request of Sri Lanka, India had sent an Indian Peace Keeping Force (IPKF) to fight terrorism for a short period. Sri Lanka is also a SAARC member. India had expressed its great shock on the unfortunate assassination of UNP candidate for the post of President and offered all help for forensic and ballistic assistance in investigation of the tragic murder. At the same time it conveyed its happiness on the election of Chandrika Bandarnaike Kumartunga as the Head of the State in 1994 and envisaged keen interest in further improving bilateral relations.

A few months after elections, the Foreign Minister of Sri Lanka visited India and held discussions with Indian Government on mutual ties, reforms in constitution, economic policies of new government, the peace process and keenness for more cordial relations. The Government of India in turn fully reciprocated the same. The same year second meeting of Indo-Sri Lanka joint Commission was held in New Delhi, which resulted in several measures like restoration of preferential tariff margins on agricultural produce from Sri Lanka, reduction in tariffs on items of export interest to Sri Lanka, extension of a new line of dollar-dominated credit, permission to open a branch of bank of Ceylon in Chennai. Same year another important meeting was held on civil aviation to enhance Sri Lankan flights. About 8,000 Sri Lankan Tamil refugees returned to their home country voluntarily in 1994.

It may be noted a very large number of Tamils came back to India after the Sri Lankan army took stern action against LTTE and attacked Tamil areas. The fight between government forces and LTTE is continuing and India has agreed to give all the humanitarian help to Sri Lanka to fight terrorism but did not agree to give arms and army. It also expressed its happiness over the mediation Sri Lanka is getting from Sweden to solve this problem. After becoming Prime Minister Ranil Vikram Singhe visited India in December 2001 and met several Indian leaders and expressed hope to solve terrorism in his country. It asked for India's help. For increasing bilateral trade, Sri Lanka also asked helicopters for transport (Amar Ujala December 28, 2003). Chief telecom Officer of Sri Lanka visited India for resuming telecom service between the two nations. Recently elected Prime Minister Mahinda Rajapaksa also desired help from India for peace process in that country (Times of India April 7, 2004).

Despite India being affected with Tsunami tragedy at the end of 2004, India sent 1,500 soldiers to help Tsunami victims in Sri Lanka. India also gave 23 million US Dollars and this was highly appreciated by Sri Lanka. At the Hindustan Times Leadership Summit in New Delhi on October 13, 2007 Sri Lankan President Mahinda Rajapaksa stated, "While my government remains determined to fight terrorism, we are equally committed to seeking a negotiated and sustainable solution to conflict in Sri Lanka." He also spoke of the 'home grown solution' based on Indian model of federalism. Fighting between troops and rebels, who want autonomy in the north and east, had worsened during end of the year. Two senior officers of Sri Lankan army stated that LTTE has good cooperative relations with Al-Qaida and some other terrorist organizations.

During army attacks on LTTE dominated areas citizens of other nations have also been seen and it appears the rebellion may not last for long, although LTTE had carried out two unsuccessful aerial attacks. Ultimately President Rajpaksa declared death of LTTE Chief and his cooperating leaders. This brought end to about 25 years of LTTE militancy. Now there is anxiety for settlement of Tamil refugees and Indian Security Adviser has gone to Sri Lanka, followed by the Secretary General of the UN Chief for talks on settlement of Tamil refugees. During his visit, the Secretary General confirmed use of heavy arms, which was against the promise made by the army. This caused heady losses to the life of civilians and their property.

Pakistan: Since the very birth of Pakistan as an Islamic state, Indo-Pak relations have been estranged or indifferent. Before partition Hindus in the land to be Pakistan were massacred resulting in retaliatory Hindu-Muslim riots in secular India. At that time West Pakistan was the granary of India and East Pakistan was the major producer of jute and rice. Thus very foundation of Pakistan was based on hatred; it started the Kashmir imbroglio, mentioned earlier. The hatred ideology resulted in the splitting of Pakistan and the creation of Bangladesh in 1971. The relations between India and Pakistan sometimes showed short-lived improvements. Apart from religion, the authoritarian and dictatorial attitude of the Civil and Military rulers of Pakistan have been the main causes of differences between the two neighbours, both of which are SAARC members. Due to the negative attitude of Islamabad 'Free Trade Agreement' had to be postponed in Kathmandu meetings of SAARC (Vikas Dwivedi, New Delhi, December 23, 2002). Throughout the existence of Pakistan the strategy has been to raise a slogan of religious and military threat from India to divert public attention from internal problems. During this period four wars were fought and each time after the captured territory and the prisoners of war were handed over, the attitude of the rulers changed, setting aside the agreements signed already.

It may be mentioned that an important politician and a former Air Marshal Asgar Khan stated, in an interview to a leading newspaper that in 1965 Pakistan sent its army to Kutch and started war. Similarly, in 1971 it created such a situation in East Pakistan that India had to retaliate. India did not start fights and was never a danger to Pakistan, he said (Press Islamabad, May 5, 2001). Addressing a gathering in Islamabad on the occasion of 54th Independence Day, President Musharraf said despite freezing the defence budget, Pakistan was secure from external aggression. "Unfortunately, however, our threat emanates from within. Our economic malaise coupled with intolerance and extremist attitude in certain quarters are the termites eating us from within," he declared. At times there were short spells of cooperation and understanding leading to agreements, treaties on sharing of water from rivers originating in India. Under agricultural and cultural pacts several agricultural scientists were trained in Indian institutions and visits of leading artists were exchanged. India gave Pakistan the Most Favoured Nation (MFN) status for better trade but the latter has not reciprocated the same to India so far. India has unilaterally liberalized visa policies for visitors and allowed the free flow of books.

Since the beginning Pakistan's ISI has been supporting terrorism in various parts of India and simultaneously Pak authorities have been denying the same. It is only now that ISI had accepted that Islamabad was helping cross-border terrorism in J&K (Agencies, March 29, 2002). The attack on Srinagar Assembly Building, the murder of Daniel Pearl, the attack on the Indian Parliament & American Centre all are considered heinous crimes aided by ISI. ISI's Kashmir and

Afghanistan cells will not be closed as stated on T.V. by former Head of ISI and Communication Minister Javed Ashraf Kazi (Agencies March 19, 2002).

Even the hijacking of the Indian Airlines plane on Kathmandu-Delhi flight by five Pak nationals was a part of 'Operation Ramadan' of ISI. Such actions in the past forced Kashmiri Pandits to leave the Kashmir valley. Similarly the minority population of Pakistan was reduced from about 22 percent at the time of freedom to about 2.5 percent at present because of forced conversions and treatment meted out to them. Murder of Hindus, Sikhs and Christians by militants or non-participation by Pak Air Force/Navy/Army Chiefs in the functions organized to welcome the Indian Prime Minister at Wagah border did not affect the Lahore declarations between India and Pakistan. Both nations renewed their statements on Kashmir and other issues as well as discussed mutual cooperation. But Pak sponsored insurgents were being simultaneously pushed into the Kargil sector, under army cover. Therefore, can there be any peace with Pakistan where Pak army or ISI are not participants? Will it work for the Indian Defence Forces to hold consultations with the Pak army on cross border terrorism? The answer is No; it does not seem to be possible.

On coming to power Sharif had outlawed presidential powers to dismiss an elected government, installed his nominee as Chief Justice of Supreme Court and forced army general Jahangir Karamat to resign. Later Musharraf took over as the Chief Executive of Pakistan in a coup after arresting Sharif and many others political figures in the country and ultimately managed to become the President with powers to dismiss even elected government through the National Security Council. The referendum for Gen. Musharraf to remain President was declared illegal by a learned judge Tarik Mahmood. He had to resign and is now afraid for his life (Agencies April 17, 2002). Similarly a member of the Election Commission, who considered judging a referendum beyond the scope of E.C. also resigned. Pak media too was against a referendum. The editor of a leading paper "The News" had to resign due to pressure from the government as he did not take action against the reporters disclosing the death of journalist Daniel Pearl.

When Indian and Pakistani military delegations met they realized that they were fighting a difficult battle in Siachin. Such exchanges were very limited. Later, Indian Army Chief, General Roderigues sent an invitation to General Arif Nawaz to visit India, but he was not allowed to do so. Afterwards, General Karamat favoured army-to-army contacts, but nothing happened. Generally, it is the Pak army that has shown more reluctance to discuss, although both armies realize talking is better than fighting. Such a dialogue is likely to remove the wrong perception of the Pak army in the presence of 'Indian threat'. Former military attaches from Pakistan stated that Balluch, Mohajir and Pathan generals usually show more understanding to Indian views on Kashmir than the Punjabi generals. Politicians also pressure the Pak army to become rigid.

In the first round of the Siachin glacier negotiations, both sides agreed on their respective pull back places but the Pak politicians did not let their army sign the agreement. In May 1998, General Karamat, after consulting his corps-commanders, advised Prime Minister Sharif not to detonate nuclear devices in Chagai hills. Sharif made presumptions to declare Karamat's cowardice at cabinet meetings, perhaps not knowing the opinion of corps-commanders.

Shortly afterwards, Karamat had to resign. Thereafter, Pakistani generals became afraid and they had to adopt a more hard-line stance than they would have otherwise liked to take. It is impossible to expect open discussions between the two armies under such an atmosphere where the Pak generals remain prisoners of their politicians just as the politicians have been in the hands of army generals many a times. Organization of Islamic countries had agreed to give membership to India in

June, 2002 due to its large Muslim population. But due to threats from Musharraf to leave OIC, they withdrew their decision as per information from 'The News' (Amar Ujala May 27, 2003). After several years of cease-fire on the LOC Pakistan has been carrying out firings on the border in 2008. Indian army had been complaining of the same. For the first time Military Adviser Brigadier Mohammad Iqbal agreed with the statement of Chief of the India army, Deepak Kapur, and said whenever Indian forces open fire to repel entry of terrorists from Pakistani side, it is misunderstood by Pak forces (Agency August 8, 2008).

For controlling cross-border terrorism India did not agree to the Pak proposal of international observers watching the border but suggested joint patrol of the border by an Indo-Pak army team, while addressing journalists at Almati 'Asian Security Meetings' (Agencies June 5, 2002). Later the Kyoto News Agency mentioned that Pakistan had disagreed with the Joint Vigil proposal of India (Tokyo July 8, 2002). After removing Rafiq Tarar from the post of President and declaring himself President, Musharraf visited India in July 2001 for the Agra summit meetings with the Prime Minister. But mainly due to treating cross border terrorism as freedom struggle by Musharraf these meetings could not achieve much.

However Musharraff said that Pakistan would neither reduce its 11 percent increase of the defence budget nor involve itself in an arms race with India. In his opinion, in view of India's aggressive posture Pakistan is compelled to allocate the maximum share of its resources to defence. Despite US etc. desiring to hand over twenty terrorists/ culprits, residing in Pakistan, to India he did not do it. ISI is reportedly working hard to establish its foothold in Uttranchal for sinister purposes. However in spite of tension between the two nations mutual trade increased. In the first half of 2001-02 exports from Pakistan went up by about 7.4 percent and import by nearly 17.8 percent. With Safta Pakistan will benefit in many ways. It will have choice of products at lower costs.

As a part of confidence building measures it was agreed between India and Pakistan to begin trading on the LOC in Kashmir and on October 21, 2008 trading started on Kashmir-LOC raising hopes for reducing tension and illegal trade. Musharraf appointed Zafarullah Khan Jamali to lead government as Interim Prime Minister, who was later replaced by Sahaukat Aziz. Musharraf was elected for the post of President in 2007 elections and had resigned from the post of Army Chief. Pakistani advocates were agitating against Musharraf's election. Yusuf Raza Gilani became the 24th Prime Minister of Pakistan on March 25, 2008. Taliban arrested Pakistani Ambassador to Afghanistan and about 30 security and other personals. They demanded US$ 500 million and release of 10 extremists for release of Ambassador Tariq Azizuddin and warned that if movement against Taliban was not stopped they would start killing arrested personals (Hindustan, July 21, 2008). Defence Secretary Robert Gates said all major terrorist net-works have a safe haven in Pakistan. Al-Qaida, Taliban, Haqqani network, Gulbuddin Hekmatyar are separate groups but work together creating a big problem to the US and NATO in the terror war (PTI March 3, 2009).

Indo-Pak Chamber of Commerce submitted its recommendations to the Indian Prime Minister after concluding its meetings. They showed desire to increase trade and regularize unauthorized deals to get more revenue and suggested different ways to improve trade between the two countries. According to them the trade should not be held in ransom to unsolved problems (Amar Ujala July 9, 2003). Later Shaukat Aziz became P.M. of Pakistan and said his country did not want to start arms race with India. In October 2005 J&K, POK & northern areas suffered worst tremors and lost over 85,000 lives. India, US and many other nations provided help to Pakistan. Despite J&K being affected, India sent plane loads (25 tons) of relief materials and offered to provide helicopters.

However, Musharraf declined to accept pilots lest they may see training camps for terrorism and illegal bunkers. Therefore, helicopters were not sent but India opened 5 points on LOC for relief/medical treatment and also to talk to relations on phone free of cost. Extremists in Pakistan, who were opposing British award of 'knighthood' on Salman Rushdi have retaliated by honouring and giving award to Osama Bin Laden. According to Bruce Riedel, the Ex Director for South Asia on the National Security Council, "if you were to look around the world from where Al-Qaida is going to find its bomb, it's right in their backyard." Three more extremist organizations, namely Army of Prophet Mohammad (Sipah-e-Sahib), Tahriq-e-Jafariah, Tanjim-e-Nifaj came to limelight recently. President Musharraf handed over the post of the military chief to the former ISI head, Asfaq Kiyani, after relinquishing the post. If he is confirmed as the elected President by the Supreme Court, this would bring the civil rule a step closer to democracy.

On November 4, 2007 President Musharraf declared 'Emergency or Martial Law' suspending Constitution, removing Chief Justice and arresting many leaders, as Supreme Court was expected to rule out legality of Musharraf's re-election as President in November itself. More than 25,000 people (mostly lawyers, politicians and media personnel) were arrested including Benazir Bhutto and the former Chief Justice of Supreme Court. After Bhutto's murder in December, elections were held in February, 2008. Pakistan has again been suspended from Commonwealth pending restoration of democracy and the rule of law. Finally Nawaz Sharif returned to Pakistan after several years of exile. Gilani became its Prime Minister. Like other countries Pakistan also faced heavy inflation and food shortage in 2008. American security forces have disclosed to New York Times that they have clear evidence that ISI Officers are busy working against American fight against terrorism. Further they have tapes of the talks between ISI and terrorists regarding July, 2008

Fidayeen attacks on Indian Embassy in Kabul. According to them Pakistan is directly encouraging violence in Afghanistan including attacks on NATO forces (Agencies).

After 26/11 Mumbai attack Pak Prime Minister and President had to accept that terrorism has deep roots in Pakistan and whole world is defaming Islamabad. According to the Dawn, terrorism is the enemy of Pakistan and must be destroyed completely. Because of poverty and unemployment youth is in the grip of Jehadi organizations. Almost similar are the views of the News, which agrees that entire globe defames Pakistan and western nations should come to the rescue of Islamabad so that the nation can overcome the worst situation. After the statement of the Indian Prime Minister that there is no chance of a war between the two neighbours, there is a great relief in Pakistan. Swat valley Taliban received $6 million, through a back channel, from Zardari government for agreeing to a cease-fire, as per Italian news agency AKI report. In the first week of March, 2009 Taliban blasted Rehman Baba mosque in Peshawar. This Sufi religious mosque was very popular among ladies for its religious activities. Despite terrorist's earlier warning the government did not take proper security measures and is quiet on this bomb blast, although it took destruction of Ram's birthplace mosque destruction in India very seriously.

Landmarks in the History of Modern India

- 1857-58: Ghadar movement (mutiny), the first freedom movement, leading to British government assuming administration of India. Unofficial Indo-US relations commenced.
- 1921: Mohandas K. Gandhi begins Ahinsa Satyagraha (peaceful non-cooperation movement) as a start for freedom movement.
- 1930: Mahatma Gandhi calls for peaceful civil disobedience by Dandi march; Indian national Congress issues grievances declaration.

- 1940: Muslim League demands Pakistan for Muslim majority regions of India.
- 1945-46: Freedom movement gains momentum in India and abroad; Constituent Assembly elections held.
- 1947: India and Pakistan (East and West) gain freedom from British rule and Princely States get choice to merge with India or Pakistan.
- 1948: Mahatma Gandhi assassinated; Pakistan invades Kashmir, leading to two Kashmir; Nehru takes Kashmir issue to the UN.
- 1950s: The US, in the interest of containing Communism, supplies arms to Pakistan despite India's protests.
- 1958: First end of Democracy in Pakistan as generals seize power.
- 1959: President Eisenhower visits India and receives a warm welcome
- 1961: Prime Minister Nehru visits Washington and holds talks with President Kennedy.
- 1962: China launches attack on North-eastern India by crossing international boundary; US helped India.
- 1971: East Pakistan becomes independent Bangladesh; US 7th Fleet deployed to Indian Ocean; Taiwan expelled from UN and replaced by Beijing government.
- 1981-82: Prime Minister Indira Gandhi visited Mexico and US and held talks with President Reagan.
- 1984: Rajiv Gandhi became Prime Minister after death of his mother.
- 1980s: American investment in India increased.
- 1996: No Indian party obtained absolute majority in elections; BJP emerged as the largest single party; several coalitions gained and then lost power.
- 1998: Indian (Pokhran II) nuclear tests, after Pakistani Ghauri missile tests; followed by Pakistan's nuclear tests. The US imposed economic sanctions on India and Pakistan.

- 1999: India developed medium range Agni-2 missile. Kargil conflict and the US asking Pakistan to honour LOC. Military coup in Pakistan. US fifth on the list of Foreign Direct Investors in India. BJP coalition again in power in India.
- 2000: President Clinton visited India and Prime Minister Vajpayee paid a return visit to US to herald a new era. Russian President Vladimir Putin visited India.
- 2001: President George Bush desired to establish friendlier ties with India, leading to waving off economic sanctions. The US started international movement against terrorism, in which India participated. US Secretaries visited India.
- 2002: US Secretaries paid visits to India. Indian Prime Minister and some Senior Cabinet Ministers visited the US to discuss bilateral issues and joint military exercises.
- 2003: Deputy Prime Minister, L.K. Advani and Prime Minister Vajpayee visited the US and had discussions with President Bush and other senior officials
- 2004: Prime Minister Manmohan Singh visited the US to participate in UN meeting and discussed with the US President.
- 2005: Prime Minister, Defence Minister and Foreign Minister visited the US to sign agreements on Defence, joint military exercises, nuclear energy.
- 2006: President G.W. Bush visited India and signed civil nuclear energy cooperation agreement with India.
- 2008: Prime Minister Singh visited Washington when Indo-US civil nuke deal was at the finish line. Condoleezza Rice visited New Delhi for completing formality of nuke deal and made it a legally-binding, after Bush made it a law.
- 2009: William Burns, Deputy Secretary and Hillary Clinton, Foreign Secretary visited India and had talks with Prime Minister and other Ministers on mutual relations.

"India chose her places of pilgrimages on the top of hills and mountains, by the side of holy rivers, in the heart of forests and by the shores of the ocean, which along with sky, is our nearest visible symbol of the vast, the boundless, the India" (Rabindranath Tagore).

1

India, Pakistan, and the US: Socio-Politico-Economic Diversities

B.B. Nagaich and Sharda Nagaich

Pandit Jawaharlal Nehru regarded secularism as freedom of religion and conscience subject to their not interfering with each other in the basic concept of governance. Dr. S. Radhakrishnan considered secularism as equality and religious tolerance. Concept of democracy is similar in all nations. However in India the unique feature is progressive empowerment of those suppressed for centuries and who are now aspiring to win through ballot boxes. What Indians perceive as tolerance, originating from universal humanism, may be considered by many as lack of will. This perception influences security policies too. In 1947 when India (Bharat/Hindustan) declared itself a secular and democratic state, it also had to agree to painful partition on the basis of religion.

India and its Diversities

To some it may mean practical compromise to avoid bloodshed whereas to others it may be an indication of weakness of will. At the time of independence many scholars predicted division of India, beyond Pakistan and Hindustan. The most enduring division in India is between the north and the south. The foresighted Indian sages thoroughly devised ritual of pilgrimages to reinforce unifying ideology. Survival of India as a single entity baffles many. They fail to understand why India remains a single entity, when unification of Europe could not materialize even though diversity in India is far greater than in European nations. Pakistan, though much smaller, however, did split into Pakistan and Bangladesh, both Islamic nations.

The overwhelming majority of Indians still live in rural areas i.e. in villages and small towns, which were in terms of Mahatma Gandhi the Real India (Nagaich, 2004). Rural India is mired with poverty with abundance of illiterate people. Only about one fourth of the entire population (which is over a billion at present) lives in metropolitan areas. Old Delhi was once the capital of the Hindu rulers followed by Muslim Empires. New Delhi, the present capital, is very largely North Indian and Hindi/Punjabi speaking.

Although New Delhi's residents all understand Hindi, the national language, some prefer to speak Punjabi or Urdu or a regional language in their homes. A significant portion of the population of New Delhi and other metropolitan cities speak English at work and their mother tongue at home. Unlike other Indian cities except Chandigarh, New Delhi was carefully planned during British rule in early 1930s. After independence it remained the seat of centralized power in this nation of several nations, with Tricolour (having Ashok Chakra) as its national flag. Its streets are witness to what has transpired in the nation. The effect of population explosion is crystal clear in the combined Delhi and New Delhi.

At the time of independence there were only about 25,000 automobiles in Old and New Delhi combined and the streets were not as crowded as now. However, after independence there were influx of workers and businessmen. With the passage of time several research institutions and human welfare organizations came into being and in the areas surrounding the city industrial townships or residential colonies developed. Therefore, the streets are full of people, cycles, cars, buses, motorbikes, scooters and the three-wheelers etc. From the high Himalayan region in the North the majority of the Indian subcontinent rivers-Ganges, Bramhputra, Sindhu (Indus), Yamuna, Satluj, Ravi and Vyas etc. flow down nourishing crops in the fertile plains called

Doab of the Indo-Gangetic belt, starting from Amritsar to Kolkata and beyond. It is in this region where the 'Sanatni' or 'Vedic' civilization sustained for more than 4,500 years. Various invaders including Harappans, Aryans, Greeks, Hunes, Muslims, Portuguese, French and British came and were absorbed and shaped the nation of nations or the subcontinent.

In terms of modernity the British (the worst exploiters) had the greatest impact. Some of the Muslim invaders brought many customs from their areas and have changed very little. However, most of the other migrants became part of the Hinduism or what is termed Sanatani or the Vedic Hindu culture.

In the middle of the eighteenth century a large section of the society started the first freedom struggle, which was termed mutiny by the British. However, the movement did not have unity and the premature clashes led to its downfall. The movement also had supporters in the US. In the second quarter of the nineteenth century the second freedom movement gained momentum and Mohandas Karamchand Gandhi (later called as Mahatma Gandhi) converted it into a mass movement through his "Ahinsa" Ahimsa or "Satyagraha" (non-violence) struggle. Under his leadership Indian National Congress (earlier guided by Bal Gangadhar Tilak and Gopal Krishna Gokhale) became the single largest party of Hindus, Muslims, Sikhs and Christians for driving the British away.

At the same time there were other freedom fighters like Bhagat Singh, Chandra Shekhar Azad, Udham Singh, Veer Savarkar, Pandit Parmanand, Subhash Chandra Bose and Bhai Parmanand etc., who believed in 'tit for tat' and supplemented Ahinsa with Hinsa (violence) to light the freedom fire. Unfortunately, excepting Savarkar and Pandit Parmanand none of them survived to live in independent India and consequently did not get the fame they deserved. Some ambitious Muslims did not want to tolerate a Hindu majority Indian government because they considered Muslims to be successor of Moghuls

(Mughals), the last Muslim rulers, who were in conflict with British (Young India, June 5, 1924).

These separatists considered India as the property of Mohammad, as reflected in a prayer song of Muslims- 'Bharat Mohammad ki Jagir hai'. Therefore, they wanted a separate Islamic country be carved out, comprising the areas with Muslim majority irrespective of the fact whether these areas were contiguous or not. The British government grabbed the opportunity and happily agreed to partition India against the wishes of the Congress (Ganguly, 1999; Garry Hess, 1992). Most of the Indians desired a population movement before independence to prevent killing of innocent people because of religious fundamentalism. But this was not to be and on August 14-15, 1947 Pakistan (in Eastern and Western India) and the present India respectively became free amidst a lot of bloodshed, particularly in western Punjab. Pakistan's treasuries were empty and Mahatma Gandhi asked the Indian government to supplement them. This and his patronizing Muslims annoyed extremist Hindus and one of them shot and killed him a few months after independence. Pandit Jawaharlal Nehru, a close associate of Gandhi became the first Prime Minister of India with Sardar Ballabh Bhai Patel as the Home Minister. In Pakistan Jinnah, the undisputed leader of the Muslim-League, became the President with Liaqat Ali as the Prime Minister. In India Lord Mountbatten, the last Viceroy, became the Governor General. Sardar Patel (Home Minister) successfully united the princely states, including Junagarh, Hyderabad and J&K into the Indian Union. To get something one has to lose something. About 15 million people were uprooted and displaced as a consequence of Pakistan's birth. India obtained freedom but only after a lot of bloodshed instigated by the ambitious group of people from Pakistan, who got paid back later in the same coin when in 1971 disgruntled population of eastern part of their country (East Pakistan) was separated as an independent nation called Bangladesh.

The British did leave the legacy of English education, and a network of civil service, which was created by them to rule India. The railway, telegraph & postal service were the other legacies given by the British. However, there was no industry worth the name and there was a serious food shortage for 350 million people. Illiteracy was predominant and society was divided by cast and class systems, which were encouraged by previous rulers. In the Western and Eastern provinces there was great tension between Muslims and non-Muslims. Over ambitious politicians fanned the fires. Immediately before Kashmir merged with the Indian Union with the consent of its ruler, Maharaja Hari Singh, Pakistan's army and Mujahideens, intent on annexing it, attacked the state, Indian army pushed the illegal occupants away from most of Indian J&K.

However, Pandit Nehru, acting much against the wishes of the Indian army and several leaders took the case to the U.N. A cease-fire was declared, and Pakistan continuously occupied a third of Kashmir (POK) or Gulam Kashmir (GK), which could not be liberated and merged with the rest of Kashmir. Since then the cease-fire line has been viewed as the international boundary between India and Pakistan. However the POK/GK population has never been given the Pakistani legal rights and there has been no development in the region. As a result the people of POK have been resenting it and there have been several demonstrations within the state and abroad. On the other hand, Indian J&K had several elected governments, which carried out developmental activities.

With an increase in population from 350 million to a billion plus India's situation became more urgent. Family planning is therefore crucial for India's progress. Population in India currently growing at the rate of about two percent per annum, is about half the pre-independence growth rate. This decline has taken place despite a tremendous reduction in child mortality. However, at the present rate of growth, India's population increase is equivalent of Canada's population every two years. Therefore, it is clear that further decrease in the population growth rate is necessary. The population pressure on its land is about 12 times that of the US. Forests have been cut down very much and the pastures are things of the past. Land holdings have been divided several times, with the result that the holdings are so small that in many areas these can no longer support a family.

Large-scale hunger or famine was predicted for India in the future (Malthus, 1978). There are no industries particularly in rural areas worth naming. About 70 to 80 percent of the population directly or indirectly is relying on weather dependent agriculture. Urbanization is taking place as villagers move to cities seeking employment and better opportunities. As a result slums are increasing in metropolitan cities. Like other cities, Delhi and Bombay (now Mumbai) have attracted people from all over the country. However, Bihar, Uttar Pradesh, Madya Pradesh, Rajasthan, Haryana and Punjab have contributed the most to Delhi's increase in population followed by separate colonies of people from Bengal and the southern states. People from neighbouring countries such as Nepal, Bhutan, Bangladesh, Burma, Tibet, and Afghanistan have also taken refuge in Delhi as well as in other areas in the country, further increasing the diversity in the nation.

Although the overwhelming majority of India's population is Hindu, other religions are well represented. "India has two million gods and worships them all. In religion all other countries are paupers; India is the only millionaire" (Mark Twain). Hindus worship land, rivers, mountains, certain animals, some birds, trees, wind, sun and moon. In other words all different components of nature are treated with respect. There are more Muslims (over 124 million) in India than in any country including Pakistan, with the exception of Indonesia. The main reason for the population explosion in India, according to census, is the reluctance of Muslims to follow 'family planning'. This has affected their economy adversely. The Christian (20 million) population is larger than that of many European countries.

There are also Buddhists (8 million), Jains (4 million) and other faiths such as Sikhs and Jews. India is having large diversity, and this is reflected in the differences in languages, food, dress, festivities and worship places from area to area. In the villages of India where Muslim population is less, Hindus, Muslims, Sikhs and Buddhists live happily in peace. On March 21, 2008, Hindu festival 'Holi', Muslim festival 'Baravafat', and Christian festival 'Good Friday' were celebrated on the same day happily in the country without any problem. However, in cities with high Muslim populations, politicians and extremist religious leaders exploit religious sentiments and do not hesitate to create communal disturbances, if they stand to gain.

It is easy to blame majority community or the government for educational backwardness of minorities. Minority should however themselves give priority to modern education for their economic growth and must not restrict themselves to religious education only. This is luckily changing slowly. Secondly, minorities were requested not to resort to allured or forced conversions and whenever conversions are carried out there has always been retaliations of various kinds in different parts of the country. Orissa and Karnataka are known for such acts. Some of the States have therefore brought out laws for not converting from one religion to another but others have not bothered about the same. In the middle of 2008, hate fire was sparked in Orissa by killing of a Hindu Swami, who was leading opposition to conversion of Hindus and wanted conversion back to Hinduism. This angered non-Christian tribal communities, which were already angered by conversions. On the top police arrested a large number of these tribal people flaring the fire. Similar troubles started in Karnataka when Hindus started agitations for alleged conversion activities by some Christian groups, particularly a sect called the New Life Fellowship.

The unique longevity and size of Indian history have made Indian society the world's most complex human tapestry. The

Varna system deformed to caste system had contributed significantly to Hinduism durability by organizing generally accepted rules for peaceful coexistence of even incompatible groups of population. Job oriented caste-system has thus proved to be one of India's important assets and one of the liabilities as well, undermining the structure it is supposed to hold together. To retain and protect their traditional beliefs, they resolved not to marry outside the limits of their groups. With education, inter-caste/religion marriages are becoming quite common. Most castes were associated with unique jobs. Nowadays one can find upper caste people working side by side with lower caste or schedule caste people (Harijans or untouchables) in factories, fields or offices. Traditionally, Brahmins were supposed to preach, teach and preside over many Hindu rituals. Kshatriyas (warrior class) were expected to fight the invaders. Later Sikhs also took the same job in North western areas. Vaish were supposed to carry out trade. Since freedom, all citizens have been promised social justice and equality. The untouchability was abolished by law. Harijans (legally termed Schedule caste) have been given preference for education and government jobs for bringing about social justice and equality. The powerful law of Karma or duty offers ultimate rationalization by believing in what we deserve, based on sum total or the balance of all that we have done in the past. Political empowerment was translated into economic muscle for the nation's disadvantaged sections and over half of the countries business establishments, i.e. 51 percent, are owned by OBCs, SCs and STs (TNN September 8, 2008). Hindus are often called the most tolerant people for whom the ideal goal is Moksha, which helps in dampening effect on jealousy and personal aspirations. Thus, many feel that by virtue of their faith in reincarnation, the Varna system, the goal of Moksha as well as the law of Karma (duty), Hindus have become passive or more tolerant to hardships, social injustice, sufferings and easy satisfaction or less aspiring.

The most recent examples to prove this point are the

agitations for shrine lands going on in J&K valley, Jammu region and many states in India. In many cities in different states there are government Hajj houses for the convenience of Muslims going for Hajj pilgrimages and they also get government subsidy on travel for this purpose. However, as per agitations in the Kashmir valley, for Hindu Amarnath Yatra no land should be allotted temporarily on rent near Amarnath for erecting tents for Hindu pilgrims. To counter this demand Hindus in Jammu region demanded that forest land must be allotted temporarily on rent for erecting tents during Amarnath Yatra but the ownership will remain with the government. After several days agitations in Jammu and other cities in India Central government agreed to rent out forest land temporarily for Amarnath Yatra and Jammu agitations were stopped when security forces could not control the agitations but separatists in Srinagar valley threatened parliamentarians and state legislators to resign or face the consequences and they approached the office of the UN in J&K. The extremists/protesters even fired the security forces at several places showing that the agitations are not limited to locals. This strengthens the suspicion that Pakistan-backed separatists have been stocking passion in the valley for separatism on some suitable occasion.

The most famous heterodox thinker who emerged in ancient time was a Hindu prince, Siddhartha Gautam, better known as Gautam Buddha (Enlightened one). He won tens of thousands of devout disciples to his Sangha (Buddhism). Buddhism has spread from India to Southeast Asia, Sri Lanka, China, Korea, Japan and other parts of the world. Like Hindus, Buddha also viewed life as full of pain and sorrow. To reduce suffering, he preached the middle path of restraint, non-possession and non-violence (Ahinsa). His Sangha was free of caste but like Hindus treated cows as sacred animals not to be harmed as they are by Muslims. Similar to Buddhism, Jainism (another heterodox school of faith) also believed in Ahinsa, which has remained mostly a potent theme in Indian history.

Hinduism absorbed Buddhism, Jainism and Sikhism, which have become a Hindu alternate way of life. It is paradoxical to think that the great Mauryan dynasty (Chandragupta and Ashok), which ruled some parts of South Asia for almost one and a half centuries, while defending India's frontiers had emperors who had faith in non-violence and exalted the Rule of Love. These emperors united Afghanistan's areas east to the Khyber Pass and the Hindu Kush mountains with North India.

Islam was born with the flight of Prophet Mohammad from Mecca to Medina. Islam spread with ferocity towards the West and to the East. Both Islam and Hinduism are more than mere religions. The sacred Quran guides, inspires, dictates, and controls every path of action, behaviour, aspiration and goal of Muslims. A true Muslim believes, there is only one God, Allah and Mohammad is his Prophet. The insistence upon the all-pervasive monotheistic power of God gave Islamic nations its cohesiveness and strength. Murder of the fourth Khalifa Ali (Mohammad's son-in-law) lured a large Muslim population to become Shia, the rest of them remained Orthodox Sunnis. Thus in the Indian subcontinent Islam has an external origin, its roots in Western oil rich sands. Therefore, orthodox Muslims are expected to travel to Mecca for pilgrimage (Hajj) at least once in lifetime, if not more. To establish Islam on Indian soil about 50,000 Arab troops came to conquer the plains of lower Indus in the eighth century. To them Hindus or non-Muslims were Kafirs (infidels), who had the option to either become Muslim or to die. Thus, Sindh became the first predominantly Muslim province. The Mughal power at its peak was maintained by a big military administration and resorted to forceful large-scale conversion. To increase their population further, they do not resort to modern family planning measures on the pretext of this being an anti-Islamic practice. They are getting all the facilities for their religious travel for Hajj including travel subsidy but if Hindus expect similar facilities for Amarnath Yatra in Kashmir, even on payment, Muslims object. Although those Muslims living on the Yatra route get a good business, giving land on rent for tents is not relished by separatist Muslims, as shown by agitations in Kashmir during middle of 2008 for which Ghulam Nabi Azad, the Chief Minister, withdrew the land ordered to be given for Yatra tents and resigned.

Thus it is clear that India has a very heavy burden of population, and internal as well as external security. Its diversity, reliance on weather for agriculture, small & marginal holdings of land, scarcity of industries particularly in rural areas and illiteracy all lead to slowing down the growth of country's economy. Family planning and attainment of self-sufficiency are very important for the progress of the country, which plunged into the world market by liberalization and industrialization. Luckily after boom in economy, the percentage of people living below poverty line is down to less than 26 from 55 in 1972-73. In 1958 the average annual income was Rs. 300 but now it is Rs. 20,900 approx. After the US and China, India has the largest air force with about 1130 fighter planes. In 1947 the country was producing only 1,400 megawatt electricity whereas in 2005 India produced about 1,20,000 megawatt electricity. In 1951 literacy was 18.33 percent but in 2001 it was about 65 percent.

Therefore, it is clear that the country still has shortage of energy as well as literacy. Its security is always at risk as it is surrounded by failed or failing countries like Nepal, Pakistan, Bangladesh, and Myanmar. For several decades Muslim fanatics from across-border have been creating problems to India as well as to their own countries.

Post-Independence Period: "Long years ago, we made a tryst with destiny and now the time comes when we shall redeem our pledge…At the stroke of the midnight hour, when the world sleeps, India will awake to life and freedom"(Jawaharlal Nehru). Priorities of Pandit Nehru were to eradicate poverty, illiteracy, increase food production, clothing and housing. During his 17-year tenure the growth of social and political consciousness overtook the growth of economy and millions still remained below the poverty line. Nehru desired to live in peace with Pakistan and in 1960 he made a treaty with President Ayub Khan to share Indus water, with the support of Eugene Black of the World Bank. However, his policies for peaceful coexistence suffered a reversal in 1962 when China invaded India. He could have built a powerful army to defend the border but he believed in brotherly relations with China and other neighbours and did not think of improving/ modernizing and strengthening the army. Shocked as he was, he succumbed in 1964. Lal Bahadur Shastri took over as Prime Minister and resolved the problem of Ceylonese (now Sri Lankan) Tamils by entering into an agreement with Colombo.

However, Ayub Khan thought that he could annex the entire Kashmir from India with the Help of superior arms and Patton tanks supplied by the US (Ganguly, 1999; Grower, 1995; Chibber, 1998; Chopra, 1990; Jha, 1983). Shastri made the Indian army march into Pakistan up to Ichogil canal, next to Lahore. They also captured Haji Pir pass and Tithwal but were stopped for Tashkent Agreement. Shastri and Ayub Khan met in 1965, with the Russian Premier Kosygin as mediator and signed an agreement to settle the dispute amicably and India returned the captured territory to Pakistan. Shastri died in Tashkent itself and Indira Gandhi took over. She remained at the helm of affairs for nearly 20 years. She accelerated poverty alleviation by abolishing privy purses of princes and by nationalizing banks. She also helped the liberation of Bangladesh from Pakistan, which was highly appreciated by the majority of Indians and Bangladeshis, although the US disapproved and sent its nuclear powered warship the Enterprise of the 7th Fleet in the Indian Ocean. Indira Gandhi believed in self-sufficiency of food and arms. During her administration the country had its "Green Revolution" to eliminate food shortage. She also opted for a close alliance with the Soviet Republic due to continued economic and military support of Pakistan by the US, which was resented not only by Indians but also by many Americans. In 1984 Indira Gandhi succumbed when her Sikh Security guards shot her due to their anger over the Blue Star Operation of the Indian army to evacuate Bhinderanwale terrorists form the 'Golden' Temple.

Her son, Rajiv Gandhi, become the next Prime Minister. Rajiv Gandhi enjoyed immense popularity. He dreamt of modernizing the country before the 21st century and he did begin to work towards that goal. In 1988 he desired an "Action Plan of Ushering in a Nuclear-Weapon-Free and Non-Violent world Order". Unfortunately, he dissipated his popularity. In 1991 he was assassinated by a Sri Lankan LTTE terrorist. Prime Minister Narsimha Rao, who succeeded him, introduced a liberalization program crafted by his finance minister Manmohan Singh (at present Prime Minister). The US became the largest foreign investor in India. Later other governments who followed continued the liberalization policy and the US remained as the large foreign investor in the country.

The last government to come was Bhartiya Janata Party (BJP) alliance with Atal Bihari Vajpayee as the Prime Minister. This government believed in taking India into the next century as a nuclear power for national security but simultaneously declared No First Use (NFU) policy. It also believed in having peace with the neighbours. Therefore, the Indian Prime Minister took a bus ride to Lahore 1st February 1999 and signed an agreement with the Pakistan's Prime Minister Nawaz Sharif, called the Lahore Declaration. Unfortunately, Pakistan did not respond properly and in fact sent its military infiltrators and Mujahideens (holy war fighters) across the J&K border to capture nearly 25 Kms. deep and about 150 Kms. long Kargil sector territory with a view to cut off Siachin region and eventually annex this area also (Nanda, 1999; Mohan, 2000; Behl, 2000). However, Indian forces cleared the invasion after 74 days undeclared war.

Fortunately, the US asked Pakistan to vacate illegally

occupied Indian territory and after they were pushed out during Operation 'Vijay' from the majority of the area, Pakistan did oblige by vacating the remaining area. After the US imposed economic sanctions on India, S. Korea has become the largest investor (FDI), pushing back the US to fifth position, which is now improving slowly. In 2004 election Congress party again came back in power and in 2009 it won more seats for 15th Lok Sabha. The National Intelligence Council of America wrote that by 2020 India will become world power along with the US and China. However, at present India is far behind the US and many other countries in education, working atmosphere, law and order problem, transport & communication, basic facilities like electricity or other energy resources. There are plenty of possibilities but long term vision is lacking. According to the Brookings Institution for poverty alleviation India will need about 3-4 times more energy in 2030. At present India is on 5th place as far as energy consumption is concerned. We are not only behind developed countries but also behind a developing country like Brazil. For such a large energy requirement India needs a comprehensive energy production program. We have several energy ministries like coal, petroleum, natural gas, non-conventional and renewable energy besides electricity and atomic energy but there is lack of proper coordination between these energy ministries. It is well known that we import about 2/3rd of our petroleum products by spending huge amount of valuable foreign exchange. By saving spending on import of petroleum products we will be able to spend on schemes for employment generation and poverty alleviation. Simultaneously we will not have to remain dependent on the nations supplying power oil to us.

Problems in Rural India: Rural India still seethes with many struggles, unemployment/underemployment and malnutrition are very important problems as no industries have been set up in these areas. Consequently, a very large proportion of the poor people live in rural areas. The tragic news of farmers committing suicide, moving to cities and begging on city sidewalks accompanied developments. Therefore, to the bulk of the poor land, water and forests make up the vital resources and it is around these that the current problems are likely to intensify. This forces the rural youth to move to cities to get employment leads to slum developments (Nagaich, 2004 & Tharoor, 2007).

In 1991, 36 percent of India's population lived on less than one dollar a day, which after a decade reduced to 26 percent due to economic reforms. We should not forget that India is still a nation of rural poverty, slums, pollution, corruption, clean water scarcity, unemployment, under employment, malnutrition, lack of good education and inadequate health-care (Tharoor, 2007). The last decade saw job seekers increasing to a level of about 40 million. If these job seekers stand in a row, the queue will be about 20,000 kilometres long, more than three times India's coastline. One of every three persons in the world lacking good drinking water is in India. The nation has entered the 21st century with about 46 percent of its population illiterate. No nation has more blind people than India. Million of Indians suffer from malnutrition. The poorest are mainly rural Indians.

Around 40 percent of the poor Indians are landless labourers, 45 percent are the under employed marginal farmers. Of the remaining, about 7 percent are the unskilled artisans in rural areas. Others like old and disabled etc. make up the rest. Despite the economic advances India made recently, malnourishment among the children is very high. Chemical addiction is also on the increase. During 2008-09 there was a record reduction in exports and also import showing effect of global recession on the Indian economy.

Indian on Nuclear Disarmament: India has suggested that the NAM take the lead on nuclear disarmament by organizing a Global Conference for arriving at an agreement for a time bound plan for the elimination of nuclear arsenals. It is well known that the momentum for nuclear abolition has become stronger now that ever before. In February 1998, over 100 political leaders, including several heads of States, signed a statement for eliminating nuclear weaponry. Former President Jimmy Carter, former Chancellor Helmut Schmidt and former Prime Minister of Canada, Pierre Trudeau were some of those signatories.

A number of other developments have bolstered the disarmament movement. The most important opinion was offered in July 1996 by the International Court of Justice at Hague on the use of nuclear weapons. The court declared that under all conceivable circumstances the use of nuclear weapons would violate the principles of International law. It was also declared that the nuclear powers were obliged to conduct negotiations leading to complete abolition of nuclear arsenals. About a year later 61 senior army officers from 17 countries declared that long-term international policy must aim at complete elimination of nuclear weapons. The former Chief of the US Strategic Command, General George Lee Butler, was the most important signatory to this declaration. Similarly in August 1966, the Australian government convened a commission on elimination of nuclear weapons and prepare plans for their elimination, which has been the Indian view since 1988. Despite several movements for complete abolition of nuclear arsenals from the face of the earth, more than 31,000 nuclear weapons remain in the stocks, although the Cold War ended more than 15 years ago. The expansion of the US led NATO has created further insecurity in the minds of Russians and their allies. Therefore, the Russian Parliament 'DUMA' did not like to ratify the Strategic Arms No-First-Use-Agreement and declared that nuclear weapons could be used against even a conventional invasion of its soil. On the other side, the US has already started sub-critical testing of its nuclear stockpile to improve efficiency and reliability. Even more serious is the announcement by President Bush on the potential use of nuclear weapons in retaliation to chemical and biological attacks. In view of the above refusal of the US

Senate to ratify CTBT it is unlikely that NPT would succeed. Many non-nuclear States, which were party to NPT, are now thinking of revising their commitment if there is no progress on disarmament as per clause VI of the treaty. North Korea has already withdrawn and conducted nuclear or missile tests. Iran is also following the suit. Israel is already a non-declared nuclear power. Japan is having a second thought after North Korea's nuclear plans. In the US itself protesters marched on the Oak Ridge nuclear weapon plant and outside Lawrence Livermore National Laboratory on August 2003 to protest against atomic bombings in 1945 and development of new nuclear weapons. Hence, India must take 3 steps. First, it should declare that it is willing to put its nuclear weapons on the negotiating table to force the nuclear powers to eliminate their arsenals. This had already been declared by Vajpayee. Second, it must offer to host a global conference itself (not NAM) to plan for a nuclear weapons free world. Third, it must present an updated version of the 'Action Plan for Ushering in a Nuclear-Weapon-Free and Non-Violent World Order', proposed by late Rajiv Gandhi in 1988.

Pakistan and its Diversities

Pakistan was carved out of the colonial India on 14th August, 1947 as an Islamic State on the demand of Muslim League, led by M.A. Jinnah. The first President was Jinnah, who not only appointed Liaquat Ali as Prime Minister but also appointed other Cabinet Ministers. After death of Jinnah, Khwaja Nizamuddin was made President. On murder of Liaquat Ali situation became unstable and overambitious service personal Gulam Mohammad managed to become Prime Minister and since then the question is continuously asked whether position of President is higher or that of Prime Minister is higher.

Afterwards there were about a dozen Prime Ministers and about ten Presidents, heading the government during six decades. Geographically, the present Pakistan is on the North-western side of India separated from Afghanistan by the Durand Line, traversed by the Khyber and Bolan Passes, the two historical invasion routes from Mid-east in the subcontinent. At the time of traumatic birth, it was on both sides of India, called as East and West Pakistan. After continuous neglect the East Pakistan was liberated as independent Bangladesh. The present Pakistan comprises of about 803,940 square kilometres. It is surrounded by four countries, i.e. Afghanistan, on North and Northwest, China in the Northeast, India on the Southeast and Iran on the West. In the South, it has a coastline of about 1046 kilometres on the Indian Ocean part commonly referred to as Arab Sea.

M.L. Khanna, Dr. K.C. Nirula, Dr. B.L. Dutt and L.C. Sikka (who had moved from Pakistan) informed the authors about the sad events they and minorities had faced during painful partition of the Indian subcontinent. These four specialists, on reaching India, were absorbed in the Central Potato Research Institute, Shimla where they were working with B.B. Nagaich.

Pakistan has a wide range of weather conditions, varying from mild hot and dry conditions in the west and southern parts of the country to very cold and snowy weather in the north and northwest. Generally Pakistan's climate can be called as mild arid subtropical, with majority of the country receiving an average of less than 250 millimetres of annual rainfall. The desert areas such as Chagai and Sibi receive much less rainfall, whereas northern areas get abundant rains measuring more than 2,000 millimetres. Most of the country receives rain as a result of southwest Monsoon, like India in the period between June and September. During summers, majority of the country becomes hot with temperatures ranging between 35 to 40 degrees centigrade, much less than most of India. Winters in the hills (Himalayan, Karakorum, Hindu Kush and K 2) remain below zero degree centigrade for several months. The eastern plains are part of the Indus (Sindh) river plains. The other important rivers are Satluj,

Vyas and Ravi etc. in the region. The plains also have a vast network of canals for irrigation and famous for agricultural production. In fact, before partition, this region used to be called granary of India.

Officially referred to as 'Islamic Republic of Pakistan' or the land of the pure, Pakistan is administratively organized as a republic with Islamabad as a newly built capital city of the nation. This country owes India its share of debts that India paid for it in 1948-49. At that time it was agreed that Islamabad will pay 3 percent interest on the same but till today nothing has been paid. The republic has four provinces (States)-Baluchistan, North West Frontier Province (NWFP), Punjab and Sindh. In addition there is one region, federally administered Tribal Areas, and one capital territory, i.e. Islamabad. Besides the above areas, there are Pakistan occupied parts of disputed territory called Azad Kashmir/POK or Gulam Kashmir (GK) and the Northern areas of Gilgit & Balistan. Pakistan's constitution was framed in 1956 but it was abrogated only two years later.

In 1973 its present constitution was adopted subsequent to an extended military dictatorship. The constitution was again modified several times to suit the needs of the governing group. Lastly, it was modified on coup by Musharraf in the year 2001. After the coup Nawaz Sharif, the biggest rival of Musharraf, had to flee the country about 7 years ago by trading prison for exile. Basically, like India, the country has three main branches of administration, namely, legislative, judiciary and executive to run the country. Similar to India, Pakistan also has the Prime Minister and the President, following Parliamentary system. Immediate past President is General P. Musharraf and the present President is Asif Ali Zardari. Although after independence the nation has mostly been administered by the military dictators, during democratic set up, the President dominates the decision making process particularly in security and defence matters, with Prime Minister and Defence Ministers playing subordinate roles.

There were about a dozen Prime ministers in the period when democratic governments were functioning; during rest of the period Dictators were working as Presidents or Heads of the government.

Demography: In Pakistan diversity is much less as compared that in India or in USA. In 1947 the population of both regions (East & West) of Pakistan was about one-third of Indian population. In July 2003, it became at 150,694,740, with about 2 percent annual growth in the present Pakistan. There are four important ethnic groups recognized the Islamic Republic, Baloch, Pastun or Pathan, Punjabi and Sindhi. People migrating from India at the time of partition were termed as Mohajirs and the rest as Haquiqis. Urdu, the language spoken by about 8 per cent people is the official language of the nation along with English. Majority of the people (nearly 58 percent) speak Punjabi and about 12 percent speak Sindhi. About 46 per cent Janata is literate (Sathasivam, 2005). At the time of birth, minority population mainly Hindus used to be around 12 percent but now it has decreased to about 2 to 3 percent due to killing, forced conversions, or running away to foreign lands to protect themselves. Consequently about 97 percent Pakistanis are Muslims, with Sunni majority (seventy seven per cent). Shias are in minority in most of the republic, excepting in POK. Ahmadias, Bahavis and some other sects have been outcaste from Islam. Very small numbers of Christians, Hindus, Sikhs and other religious groups make up the remainder of the Pakistani population, resulting into virtually very little diversity. Although Pakistan is an Islamic State, it calls itself secular, constitutionally. Its legal system is based commonly on English laws, from time to time it has increasingly included Sheriat Islamic laws to give it a pure Islamic identity. Transparency International carried out 'Global Corruption Barometer 2007' survey and found that in 2006 about 15 percent population was greasing palms to get their works done but in 2007 about 30 percent population is greasing palms to get their works done. Police is the most corrupt department. Corruption however decreased in media and judiciary.

Economy: Like India, Pakistan is also a developing nation with lots of socio-economic difficulties. Religious orthodoxy and dictatorship hampered its development, which India did not have. Fortunately, foreign aid inflows from different countries along with movement of people to foreign nations did help republic's economy to some extent temporarily. In 2002, CIA estimated Pakistan's GDP to be about US$ 295.4 billion, which amounts to US$ 2,000 per capita GDP. Like many developing nations Pakistan is also heavily burdened with public debts, which is around US$ 32.35 billion. About 35 to 36 percent people are living below the poverty line. Unemployment rate is about 8 percent, with a very high figure of under employment. Industrial growth was estimated to be around 2.5 percent only with heavy expenditure on defence.

All these factors lead to poverty. Similar to India, Pakistan is also dependent on services sector, which accounts for about 51 percent of the GDP. Industry accounts for about 25 percent of the GDP and agriculture to about 24 percent. Most of the people in labour force from Pakistan serve in the Middle-East nations in the service oriented works and as drivers in the western countries. The remittances sent home by these persons contribute significantly to republic's GDP. Pakistan is also lucky to be a member of the American Security system in South Asia and gets sophisticated military hardware and dollars for different operations as well as wave offs of debts. According to the CRS report for 2006, Pakistan is the number one purchaser of the military hardware from the US, amounting to about 4.6 percent of its GDP. Pakistan's important industrial products include textiles, processed foods, beverages, construction materials, paper products and fertilizers.

The country produces sufficient natural gas and electricity but does import fuel oils. Like many other countries, Pakistan also faced heavy price increase and shortage of Food in the

2008. The same year in the month of July the inflation had reached to the level of 21.53 percent. New leaders are scrambling for foreign cash to ward off economic meltdown at a time when the country is facing soaring violence by Islamic fundamentalists. President Asif A. Zardari returned from all-weather friend China in October with a promise of assistance but no public commitment other than two more nuclear-power plants. Since 2001, the US has given Islamabad more than US$ 10 billion in aid (monetary and military). The donors in the West are distracted by the global financial crisis and recession in their own countries. Despite slowdown of economy Pakistan has announced a 15.5 percent increase in defence budget because it is getting dollar rains from the US to fight terror war.

After 1971 war, Pakistan did see a temporary weakening of Islamic unity at the national level, thereby resulting in social instability and wide spread civil unrest and violence (Sathasivam, 2005). Baloch people and Northern area residents always feel threatened by the immigration of non-Baloch in Baluchistan and Sunnis in Northern areas & POK/GK. The threat to the national unity posed by Sindhi nationalist movements and the conviction that India is encouraging in these internal conflicts are the events worth mentioning. A big domestic threat to Pakistan is the rise of Islamic radicalism in the north and north-western areas. Several militant groups remain active within Pakistan and carry out sectarian violence and sabotage almost every week. Some of these extremist groups also attempted assassinating Pakistan's top political and military leader.

The sectarian violence between Sunnis and Shias has been encouraged by the rise of radicalism in the neighbouring Afghanistan. The Afghan militant groups that fought Russian occupation forces operated mainly from Pakistan, with the help from USA. Many of these groups amalgamated to form Taliban and govern Afghanistan. They invited Al-Qaida in the region and hosted them. Following the defeat of Taliban regime in 2001, the remnants of Taliban and Al-Qaida (who were formerly equipped by CIA) are resting in Pakistani tribal areas and operate from there, where the US cannot penetrate. After September 11, 2001 attacks in the US, Musharraf had promised to prevent extremism and rein in Jehadis. But even after more than 10 years these promises remained unfulfilled. Nor have the US and the West realized that enormous investments on their ally on terror have failed. Taliban and Jehadi trainings are continuing on Pakistani soil to embark on missions in Afghanistan and Kashmir and finances are not a limitation.

The Economist (July 2006) pointed out these issues and called Musharraf as destroyer of democracy and never serious for preventing terrorism. Other economists have predicted that long term sustainability of Islamabad's economic growth is uncertain and heavily dependent on the US or international economic institutions. Through IMF the US has promised help to Islamabad for easing the economic hardship. IMF has given Islamabad US$ 7500 million loan aid in the end of November 2008 to overcome the hardship. President Zardari went to Saudi Arabia in November to seek assistance to overcome cash strapped economy. The country needs funds urgently to tide over its trade and budget deficits. Earth quake of the magnitude of 6.4 hit the Baluchistan area in October 2008 and is supposed to have killed about 300 people. Despite international help promise, Jamaat-ud-Dawa, a designated terrorist group pledged to build 1,000 temporary homes for survivors in the affected area to expand group's influence in the backward region. The group was designated a terrorist organization in 2006 by the US for cooperating in spreading terrorism in J&K. Troops and foreign relief agencies were helping communities in remote valleys.

Pakistan is one of remorseless tug and pull between civilian and army leaders or between moderate and radicals. Therefore it neither became a permanent democracy nor a permanent military dictatorship. The main casualties are therefore, the rule of law and national integration. Pakistan has long seen Jehadi movements like creation of Taliban as a counter to Indian and Russian influence in the neighbouring Afghanistan, the Western diplomats and analysts, in Kabul, said. At Jamia Islamiya, a Quetta religious school, Taliban sympathies are on flagrant display and students have gone with their teachers' blessings for suicide bombings in Afghanistan, residents said. One former Taliban Commander informed Pakistan Intelligence officials had jailed him because he did not go to Afghanistan to fight.

The religious parties have recruited for Jehad in Kashmir and Afghanistan since 1980s, when Pakistani ISI ran the resistance by Mujahideen and funnelled money to them from USA and Saudi Arabia said Hussein Haqqani, the author of a book on relations between the Islamists and the Pak security forces. In return for help in Kashmir and Afghanistan the intelligence services would rig votes for the religious parties and allow them freedom to operate said Haqqani as per New York Times information. India has since long been saying this. Pakistan however, had been rejecting the allegation. But Diplomats in South Asia and interviews with residents on the border have confirmed that POK and Quetta are the important bases for terrorists and Taliban, respectively (Seattle Times January 21, 2007).

In the centre of Islamabad there is a red mosque, where extremist Islamic education is given to thousands of students. They all live here and Prime Ministers, Army heads, as well as Presidents patronized it. ISI has its head quarters near this mosque and has been financing it for Jihad. The Officers of ISI have been visiting here for Namaz. Two years ago, the extremists, under the leadership of Abdul Aziz and Abdul Rashid Gazi, have been pressurizing the government for applying Islamic rules and Sheriat in the country. It is considered that they had close relations with terrorists including Al-Qaida. They made this mosque as the main place for planning and carrying out agitations because the government was not willing to start military operations in the mosque for the fear of harm to the students. Ultimately the government had to take military action for clearing the mosque from undesirable extremist elements. After a few months Red Mosque has again started playing the old game. Girl students of school Jamia Hafza demonstrated in front of the house of Co-President of PPP (the ruling party) for release of Maulana Abdul Aziz, who was arrested in July, 2007. The Imam has been released in 2009 and started playing old game. In 1994, Pakistani authorities, with the help of ISI, created Taliban to protect their interests in Kashmir likely to increase problems of Af-Pak region. Now the Talibans are threatening its creator. The newly elected government will have a hard time in correcting the mistake committed by the military and ISI for the last more than three decades. Taliban has demanded $500 million and release of 10 extremists in exchange for its Ambassador to Afghanistan. Taliban have occupied Darra Adam town in North-West Frontier Province of Pakistan (Agencies Islamabad May 2, 2008).

Terrorists have also occupied a national highway. Administration had talks with Taliban through tribal leaders but no concrete results came out of these talks. In May 2008, the US became unhappy to know that Pakistan government had to liberate two hardcore terrorists, Mulla Obedullah Akhund and Mulla Mansoor Dadullah to get released Tariq Ajizuddin, Pakistani Ambassador in Afghanistan. Same year, in front of the Denmark embassy in Islamabad bomb was blasted. Before this 18 people died in Mardan city bomb blast in May and in March more than 40 persons died in Sia-Sunni violence of extremists. Taliban actually desires to weaken the Karzai government. Afghan government officers have stated that foreign workers, particularly more and more Indians have been attacked because they were trying to construct roads in remote areas. Bomb blast in front of Indian embassy is additional proof for hatred against Indians, who are helping the reconstruction program in Afghanistan. Without naming any country it has been suspected that ISI is encouraging such activities.

In fact President Karzai had to threaten that if such actions are not stopped Afghani army will have to attack shelter areas in Pakistan after crossing the border. In fact Af-Pak region-Taliban announced cooperation with each other and this is likely to increase the problems of the allied forces. Therefore it is crystal clear that terrorism giant, which was encouraged by this very nation, has become a danger for Islamabad itself. In 2006 about 1,100 persons died and in 2007 about 1,250 persons lost their lives. Asif Ali Zardari, the Co-chairman of the ruling party (PPP) while speaking in Socialist International Congress in Greece did accept that terrorism is spreading from Pakistan but according to him international politics is responsible for such an action. In the 1st week of July about 100 Taliban attacked a police station and arrested 14 security persons including officers in a tribal area in North western Frontier province (PT July 11, 2008).

Later in Swat valley attacked a security force post and arrested about 30 police personals and killed three officers (Agencies). For the first time the US has agreed that Pakistan government and some of their organizations have close relations with terrorists. This was stated by Condoleezza Rice in an interview to "The Politics" and "Yahoo News" (Hindustan, August 9, 2008). Adm. Mike Mullen, Chairman of the US Joint Chiefs, visited Prime Minister Gilani on 18th and told that there would be no compromise on strikes by the US in Pakistani northwest (AP September 19, 2008). The US helicopters flew into Pakistan's militant-infested tribal border and returned to Afghanistan as tribesmen opened fire.

To condemn the US, Shiite Muslims burnt the US and Israeli flags on 23rd September and 5th October, 2008. Militants from tribal areas are reportedly running away to settle mostly in Karachi. Just after Islamabad accepted involvement of Pakistanis in Mumbai blasts President Zardari said the Taliban was trying to control the nation after enhancing its power in a large part of the country in tribal areas. Barely 2 days after this statement the same President gave in to the ultra Islamic extremist organization by signing an agreement to make Sharia a law for the country (TNN February 17, 2009). Islamabad paid US$ 6 million to Swat valley Taliban for cease-fire as per Italian news AKI report. This agreement was however broken down within a few months after Taliban started occupying areas like Buner to become nearer to Islamabad to which the Pak military retaliated by killing Taliban militants. On March 3, 2009 15 terrorists attacked Sri Lanka cricket team in Lahore in a crowded Liberty Chowk. They fired bullets on the bus for about 20 minutes, injuring 6 members/officials of the team and killed the same number of policemen.

As usual some of the Pak politicians have started blaming Indian intelligence for the same. Similarly, attack in Lahore police training institute is presumed to be organized by Betullah Mehsud, who is stating that the attack is part of the revenge for killings in tribal areas and if this does not stop the US would have to pay for the same (Hindustan April 1, 2009). Taliban which had demolished about 40 mosques has lately been using the mosques as admission centres for recruiting youth for training for Jehad. Lately there had been a move for recruiting ladies for terrorism training. There is in general an atmosphere of disbelief in terror fighting Pakistan. Army does not have faith in the present laws. Public has lost faith in their leaders. In a situation like this administrative officers are recommending implementation of strong anti-terror laws, which is also the liking of army. According to 'The News' army does not want that the arrested terrorists should get undue benefit from the weakness in rules and escape from punishment. Therefore, military Chief and the public are pleading for stronger punishment. This happened during Musharraf's rule but the same Musharraf used these strong regulations against Nawaz Sharif. Although in the operation after April 26, 2009 more than 1200 terrorists were killed but surprisingly none of their leaders is included in the list

(Agencies June 7, 2009).

With popularity falling and options narrowing, President Musharraf was meeting former Prime Minister Benazir Bhutto for a possible US-inspired power sharing arrangement as he thought his days were numbered. He gave up his role as army Chief for retaining the post of President. He could not retain both after elections, which were due in October- November but were held in February, 2008. Supreme Court was threatening to knock him out of the office entirely. On 10th September Sharif returned home from London, where he was residing. Since he was likely to set up a power struggle between three aspirants and could jeopardize Musharraf's deal to share power with Benazir Bhutto, a former prime minister also in exile. He was likely to rally support among the opposition to contest Musharraf's re-election for another five years presidential term. Therefore he was arrested at Islamabad airport and deported within 5 hours. After about 10 weeks Sharif again returned to Pakistan and the government turned blind eyes to let him to come to Lahore. Extremists and Al-Qaida militants saw development of power sharing as a serious challenge to their survival and together with Taliban started terrorism in Rawalpindi etc and captured Pak security forces in Waziristan to "nip the evil in the bud". Police allegedly swept Islamabad to arrest the opposition leaders, vowing to obstruct Musharraf's re-election. According to Aijauddin (2006) a question that is lurking unanswered as yet in Pakistan is that to what degree will President Musharraf be willing to transfer power, how much and to whom?

Pakistani advocates and many political parties were agitating against Musharraf's election as President in 2007 elections. The US strongly criticized crackdown on political opposition before Supreme Court rulings on the re-election of Musharraf. As President, he made his loyalist, Asfaq Kayani (former ISI head) to ultimately succeed him as army chief. Former Prime minister Bhutto returned from self-imposed exile and escaped narrowly suicide bombings that killed 139 people and injured about 450 during her motorcade journey to her house in Karachi on 19th October, 2007. She had been pleading to fight extremism and for restoration of democracy. She thought it was an act of fanatic Zia supporters. She was later killed on 27th December, before elections.

Consequently there were riots in the entire country and the elections were postponed for 18th February, 2008. Richard Hass, president of Council of Foreign Relations, said the attack reveals "one of the fundamental realities of Pakistan today is that the government is not in total control of the country." According to Bruce Riedel, the former Director for South Asia of the National Security Council, if the terrorists have to look for the bomb it is right there in the backyard of their safe haven. According to many US analysts Pakistan has every thing Bin Laden or Mullah Omar would require for their activities, i.e. political instability, a net-work of extremist Muslims, abundance of anti-US youth & public, secluded training camps, electronic technology, direct access to the West and reluctant security services. On the top this country has abundant supply of arms and money from the US.

On November 4, Musharraf declared a state of emergency (Martial Law in the eyes of many) suspending country's constitution and firing the Chief justice of Supreme Court. Police arrested the leaders and lawyers protesting the move. Supreme Court was expected to rule within days on the legality of Musharraf's re-election as President. Western nations advised Musharraf to hold elections according to schedule. Defying the US, Musharraf continued crackdown and arrests, which have exceeded 25,000, Including Ms Bhutto, Chief Justice Chaudhri and Bhagwan Dass, lawyers, media personals and politicians.

On being sworn in as civilian President, Musharraf promised that emergency will end on December 16 and elections would be held on January 8, 2008. Musharraf had dissolved parliament on November 16 after it completed its 5-year term and appointed Mohammedmian Soomro as interim prime minister to guide the elections in emergency-ruled nation. Agitations were continuing for one reason or other. Therefore once again Pakistan has been suspended on November 23 from Commonwealth pending restoration of democracy and the rule of law. After elections, Yusuf Raza Gilani became the 24th Prime Minister, on March 25, 2008, of the 13th National Assembly of Pakistan and it was expected that Indo-Pak cooperation will continue to grow. Gilani announced to keep a watch on 15 thousand Madarsas being run in Pakistan but PML-Q party supporting the government has shown disagreement with this watch on Madarsas, which are giving Islamic education to youth. The new government also announced that it is having talks with terrorists and reached cease-fire with them.

According to the new deal Security forces will not search terrorists in Swat valley. The most dangerous terrorist of Waziristan, Betullah Mehsud, the leader of Taliban, and his close Maulvi Omar told 'The Nation' that their talks with the new government seem to be successful. Mehsud has also direct link with Al-Qaida and is suspected for killing Benazir Bhutto. While giving interview to Daily Times the Governor of the Northwest border state, Ovas Ahmad Gani said Taliban Commander Mehsud spent three Arab dollars every year for purchasing arms and these funds come not from donations only but mainly from Narcotics trade. He also said he had informed US and UK about poppy cultivation in the region but enough attention was not paid. Taliban had captured one district, Rashidan and arrested several government servants and policemen. Taliban had also launched an agitation in tribal areas for total implementation of Sheriat laws. According to Taliban commander Maulvi Fakir Mohammad all the males should stop shaving beard and made it compulsory for them to raise beard soon (Press Trust, May 5, 2008). Influence of Taliban has been increasing in Pakistan (particularly in southern Waziristan) and Afghanistan. Fed up with such activities Pakistan had imposed ban on 3 more terrorist organizations in Khyber Pass region and even started some military action against them. Well known 26/11 terrorism in Mumbai (particularly in Taj Palace hotel), conceived in Pakistan, was condemned throughout the world and India demanded extradition of 20 terrorists from Pakistan. Pakistan did not do the same despite initial promises and also denied involvement of Pak citizens in these terrorist acts. Instead the politicians and also army officers threatened action against India in the event of war.

Pakistani forces on Indian border were alerted and reinforced to get ready to fight with India. Even Taliban promised to fight with Pakistani army against India. On the other hand India suggested Pakistan to remain away from hysteric war cry and arrest the culprits and try them properly in Pakistani courts, if Islamabad is not happy to surrender them to India, despite 1987 SAARC agreement on the same. Today the entire world is looking at South Asia, particularly Afghanistan, Pakistan and Hindustan or India because of 26/11 Mumbai attacks. Everybody is worried how to control the terrorists, sheltering in Pakistan. Even the UN demanded that terrorist organizations must be wiped out. Pakistan on the other hand blamed India for terrorism in Lahore to distract attention from Islamabad and not only blamed India for the attacks but also arrested 4 Indians. However the Taliban organization, Ansar Mohajir, accepted the responsibility of Lahore terrorism, which Pakistan had been throwing on the shoulders of India. Tufan Vazir claimed to be the commander of the same organization and informed the Pak daily newspaper 'The News' that his organization had carried out the attack to revenge US attacks in Waziristan (Agencies, December 29, 2008).

According to Wall Street Journal Lashkar Commander, Zarar Shah, arrested in POK, has agreed that he had trained terrorists involved in 26/11. The commander Zaki-ur-Rehman was also arrested in POK with him. However no one in right mind would expect Zardari to hand over the culprits to India despite its repeated demands to do so because military will never allow it (Hindustan Times December 11, 2008). President Zardari said to NY Times reporter, in December, 2008, that the Mumbai attacks were directed not only at India but also at Pakistan's new democratic government and the peace process with India that Islamabad has initiated. Federal Bureau of Investigations (USA) and Indian government gave strong proof independently to Pakistan and are waiting to see what Islamabad is doing in this connection (Agencies January 5 and 6, 2009).

First Islamabad said that India has given information but not proof. Later it accepted that Kasab is a Pakistani citizen but according to news from Dawn the terrorists themselves had planned the attacks and no other organization was involved. General Ahmad Shuja Pasha, the head of ISI, said he himself would like to go to India for helping in the investigations. Meanwhile the longest fight between the terrorists and Indian security forces termed 'Mini Operation Sarpvinash' continued on the 7th day on LOC to eliminate the terrorists hiding in thick forests in the bunkers in Poonch area (Hindustan January 8, 2009). 79 days after 26/11 Pak Interior Minister Rehman Malik said that Mumbai attacks were planned partly in Pakistan and so far six men were arrested for heinous crimes. VoIP calls made by terrorists to their handlers repeatedly were traced to a serving colonel and also included the name of a 'major general sahib.' Taliban's growing power is clear, but question can be raised about Zardari's blunt acceptance and its timing. It coincided with Islamabad's demand that it needs concessions on J&K in order to help the US in Afghanistan.

Although Zardari is right that the Taliban wants to take over Pakistan—those who play with fire will be hurt by fire. By encouraging Taliban, Pakistan set in motion the political reconfiguration of Af-Pak region—the political border between the two nations has practically ceased to exist. Pakistan again gave evidence of double talk by releasing Hafiz Sayeed, the founder of LET and the Chief of Jamat-ud-Dawa, who masterminded the 26/11 Mumbai attacks. Just after his release Sayeed said he will continue to work against India on Kashmir (PT June 4, 2009). Former President Musharraf accepted that ISI has good relations with terrorists. Mastermind of the blasting of Indian embassy in Kabul, Sirajuddin Haqqani is also having friendly relations with ISI. ISI had taken help from Haqqani in getting the kidnapped Pak Ambassador released (PT London June 9, 2009).

President Musharraf resigned before impeachment proposal by the new government and decided to stay in Pakistan despite willingness of the US and Saudi Arabia to allow him to settle in those countries. Mian Sumro the President of the upper house became the acting president. On September 6, 2008 Asif Ali Zardari was elected President by a good margin. He has a tacit approval of the US. He has promised a tough fight against Al-Oaida and Taliban extremists. His election coincides with a stepped up effort of the US to fight against the extremists in the tribal areas. Two days after resignation of Musharraf two fidayeen attacks occurred in Takshila in which about 80 people were reported killed and more than 100 injured. It is expected by the analysts that situation in Pakistan is likely to deteriorate and Taliban is supposed to become more active in that country (Agencies & PT August 19, 2008).

Pakistan's government had to face rising anger for ground attacks by the US in Waziristan, a haven for Taliban, killing US forces in Afghanistan. But after September 3, 2008 incidence army Chief General Kayani vowed to defend Pak territory "at all cost." US commanders complained Pakistan did very little to control Taliban and militants from recruiting, training and sending them in tribal areas. On September 20 about a thousand kg of explosives were used to blast Marriott hotel in Islamabad killing at least 53 people and injuring 260 others. It is suspected Al-Qaida is behind this attack although little known Fidayeen-e-Islam took the responsibility several days later. Pak religious & political leaders as well as Taliban are furious about US strikes in October 2008 in tribal areas on the pretext of deaths of civilians. The US had intensified cross-border strikes targeting Al-Qaida and Taliban militants or hideouts in N.W. areas bordering Afghanistan. Political leaders condemned these attacks as violation of the sovereignty of the nation.

The UN declared Islamabad unsafe for families of its international staff unsafe and ordered children to be out putting Pakistan at par with Afghanistan, Iraq and Somalia. Pakistan is already under pressure to combat terrorists responsible for attacks at home in neighbouring Afghanistan. Its lack of serious action met with a blur of suicide bombings that killed about 1200 people since July, 2007 (Seattle Times October 3, 2008). Taliban had issued a new 'Farman' in NWFP asking people to marry their daughters to terrorists and also asked them not to send girls in schools. According to a news in Dawn, announcements are being made from mosques that public should list their daughters with them so that girls can be married to mujahideens. Those who oppose this proposal their daughters would be married forcefully to terrorists (Hindustan, January 3, 2009).

After long denial of existence of terrorist training camps and sanctuaries in Pakistan and POK, Musharraf admitted, "There are sanctuaries of Al-Qaida, which combined with the remote mountainous terrain makes the task difficult of finding the militants" (TNN January 25, 2009). Few days after President Zardari also accepted this fact but caved in to the pressure of Taliban and made Sharia a law for the nation. To this Richard Holbrooke (special US envoy) said that Swat was a reminder that, "US, Pakistan and India face an enemy that poses direct threat to our leadership, our capitals and our people."

Former Prime Minister Nawaz Sharif and his younger brother Shahbaz Sharif (Chief Minister of Punjab) were debarred from polls by the Supreme Court. This widened the rift between PPP and PML (N) or between Zardari and Sharif, whose supporters agitated and clashed with policemen in Lahore and other places (PTI February 26, 2009). Some analysts believe that Kayani may ultimately gain from this rift between Zardari and Sharif. Ultimately government had to release Iftikhar Mohammad Chaudhuri, who took over as Chief Justice on 21 March. Defence Secretary, Robert Gates, said all major terrorist net-works namely Al-Qaida, Taliban, Haqqani group, Gulbuddin Hekmatyar network and other affiliated groups have a safe haven in Pakistan. They are all separate organizations but work together to create problem for war against terror. In May 2009 Taliban started crimes on minorities in some areas and consequently a large number of Sikh and Hindu families had to leave their homes to find shelter somewhere else.

Military: Nation's armed forces are divided into three branches like that in India and many other countries, the army, the navy and the air force. Each branch is controlled by one Chief of Staff of that branch. The three Chiefs have a joint committee (JCSC) for coordination and integration the operations of the three branches. JCSC is headed by a military officer, getting highest pay in the military, other than the three service Chiefs. JCSC Chief is the military adviser to the President of the nation. A proposal for a new National Security Council is in the offing, which will be headed by the President, comprising of politicians and military chiefs. The country has been having a sizable military force including several paramilitary organizations to match with the forces of the arch rival- India.

The army consists of the nine area commands. Major operational formations are divided into 22 divisions, 38 separate Brigades, 3 light anti-tank regiments, 4 air defence commands and 1 strategic force command. There are about 2,500 battle tanks, about 1,250 armoured soldier carriers and around 1,700 artillery units (Humayun Khan & Parthasarthy, 2004; Sathasivam, 2005). Looking at the size of the country, the army is proportionately very large costing a high proportion of the GDP.

However, the country has been getting lot of financial help and military equipment from other nations in the name of different projects. It has been reported by NY Times that the US has spent about 100 million dollars on secretly guarding Pakistani nuclear arms for the past 6 years. Some however, state that the US is actually controlling the nuclear stocks, after 9/11. According to Press Trust news Pakistan is going to build two more atomic plants with Chinese help. Each of them will have the capacity of 350 megawatt. The government however has not given detailed information to the National Economic Council and has released the information to various agencies. Because of Pakistani nuclear ambitions not only India but many responsible European nations are worried. It is well known that economic situation of Pakistan is not very sound yet it has announced that it will increase defence expenditure by 15.5% during 2009.

United States of America: The Great Melting Pot

The US is the most powerful democratic nation on the globe and gives emphasis on human rights. Its economic power has an impact on the process of globalization. It is a country with 5 percent of world population, utilizing 25 percent of world resources and creating 25 percent of world pollution. It is not reasonable to expect that any nation can have a rigid foreign policy uniformly. The US National Security Council document 'National Security Strategy for a New Century' avoids coupling of the ideals of democracy and human rights with West Asia-and many other Islamic countries. The US is concerned about control of Pakistan's nuclear weapon program and its terrorism (Hindustan July 19, 2008). The omission of the words "democracy and human rights" in the US goals for West Asia and Pakistan is in sharp contrast to other areas like Africa and South East Asia, where promotion of democracy is the central focus of the US policy. Some call it double standard.

The US is however the undisputed leader in the fields of science and technology, education as well as army, agriculture and medicine etc (National Academy of Sciences Report, 2005). However, the situation is now changing. In 2004 China has trained about 6 million graduate engineers, India has trained about 3.5 million and the US has trained nearly 7 million. According to many the days are not far off when Chinese and Indian engineers will surpass the number of American engineers, although they may or may not be better than the US trained engineers.

Never before has any nation dominated the world in power and in so many diverse fields but it avoids any coupling of the ideals of democracy and human rights with West Asia. The National Security Council document of the US emphasizes only peace and stability in that region (National Security Strategy for a New Century, May, 1977). Public is becoming more and more aware to denounce weapons of mass destruction, even their own. On August 10, about 1,000 people rallied outside the Lawrence Livermore National Laboratory to protest against the administration's move to develop new nuclear weapons. There was a similar march in Oak Ridge on the same day to symbolize the victims of Hiroshima and Nagasaki atomic bombings of 1945.

The US is about four times the size of India, with Canada to the north and Mexico to the south. Unlike the Himalayas, bordering India from East to West in the north; the US Rocky Mountains run from north to south, resulting in free flow of the icy winds from Northern areas to South. Consequently the entire continent remains cool, even in summers as against hot the climate of India. Not going into details about the climatic diversity, particularly in the overseas states, it may be mentioned that only a small population of about 3 to 5 percent is dependent on agriculture in the US, unlike that in India where about 70 to 80 percent of the population is dependent on agriculture directly or indirectly. Still the US has been feeding its own population as well as that of many other countries.

The Mississippi, Missouri, Colorado, Platte, Hudson, Ohio and Colombia are some of the important rivers in the country. However their water generally flows unobstructed and is not used for irrigation, like the canal system in India. In the US rains and snow are the major sources of irrigation coupled with tube well water. Economic prosperity of the US depends mainly on industries, agricultural and natural resources. Population of the country is almost one-third of that in India, originating from different parts of the globe, resulting in great diversity of culture, dress, food and religious festivities etc. Luckily the year 2007 has a record of birth of 4.315 million babies. Majority of Americans are Christians, either Protestants or the Catholics. Muslims, Jews, Buddhists and Hindus are also living happily without many problems, despite occasional disturbances created by certain fanatic groups or organizations.

The Native Americans are the American Indians or the Red Indians (as referred to by Indians from India). They now live on their reservations and even now apply their own rules in their respective territories. Christopher Columbus, who had a plan to go to India, reached the American continent in 1492 and considered the same to be India. Therefore, he called the residents as Indians. This is why the Native Americans are still called Indians. Till today this day is celebrated national day throughout the US and turkey meat is eaten on October 25. Following the tradition of settlers, 'Thanksgiving' day is celebrated as it was done on the first harvest of the puritans in the Plymouth Colony in November 1621.

The US was also ruled by the British originally and became independent much earlier than India but it is not a part of the Commonwealth, although it is one of the strongest allies of Britain. The official language of the US is English (simplified English). However a substantial amount of the population particularly in southern states speaks Spanish. Some speak French, Italian, German, Greek, Chinese, Arabic, Japanese, Hindi, Punjabi, Korean etc. in their homes, depending on the country of their origin. Education to a certain level is compulsory and free in the US. Most of the people are educated with strong national feelings. To sum up, most of the nations are represented here and they follow a wide variety of customs and traditions.

According to many the US colleges are the nation's alcohol-drenched institutions. About 12 million undergraduates drink 4 billion cans of beer in a year, each spending nearly US$ 446 on alcoholic drinks, much more than they spend on soft drinks and text books together. Experts suggest working with larger community so that students do not abuse hard drinks in private houses and liquor bars rather than confining programs on campuses, fraternities and sororities only. The other serious problem which came in light was sexual exploitation of females during 1999-2004 in the *top* military academies. More than 50 percent females informed that they have been sexually abused. For sometime gun culture has become prevalent in schools, colleges and the residential colonies. This forced the US Supreme Court to begin hearing, after 70 years, on this aspect in March, 2008 to decide whether the residents should be given freedom to own the arms or not. In Texas teachers in district schools have been allowed to keep a gun for their safety, while teaching. Parents of the children have not objected to the same.

The country has adopted a Presidential type of democracy since independence, based on two strong parties and not the Parliamentary system. The important Presidents of the US were George Washington, Thomas Jefferson, Abraham Lincoln, Theodore Roosevelt, Franklin Roosevelt, Harry Truman, Dwight D. Eisenhower, John F. Kennedy, L.B. Johnson, R. Nixon, Gerald Ford, Jimmy Carter, G.W. H. Bush, Ronald Reagan. Bill Clinton was the 42nd President in the millennium and G.W. Bush was the 43rd President. In November 2002 mid term elections GOP gained control over Senate, Congress and the While House. Senator Barack Husain Obama became the 44th President of the US. He assumed the charge of President on 20th January, 2009 and is the 1st African American to become a President. Although women have equality with men in all walks of life in the US, so far no woman has been lucky enough to be the President or vice-President of this great nation. This country has attracted intellectuals and scientists from all over the world because of much better living standards, environment, political freedom and better facilities. The maximum Nobel Laureates have been from the US.

According to a survey conducted in 2000, 49 US girls out of 1,000 became mothers in the age group between 15 and 19 years, which is earlier than in many western countries like Sweden, France and U.K. Boys and girls mostly chose their life partners and marriages are performed in a simple manner in the US as compared to those in India. The divorce rate is higher in the US in relation to that of India and many other parts of the world but less as compared to some of the European countries. Population increase is very well controlled in the US as people voluntarily follow family planning strictly irrespective of their religious affiliations. On an average the US citizens work harder than the Indians or Pakistanis in their own countries. This automatically helps in attaining prosperity of the nation and its residents.

Although, a large number of Indians have settled since the 1960s, immigrants poured into the country between 2000 and 2005, arriving at a greater rate then any other group. Almost every third person in Edison is of Asian Indian ancestry. Many are new immigrants who came to work as physicians, engineers and high-tech experts. About 2.3 million people of Indian origin including America-born, now live in the US, as per 2005 census. High-tech companies, especially Microsoft have hired large number of Indians in Seattle region. According to Census by 2002, Asian-Indians out-numbered American-Indians.

Asian-Indians also have large communities in New Jersey, New York, California and Texas etc. Their average annual income is more than US$ 60,000, higher than the national average. Like huge diversity in India there are dozens of languages and regional differences in culture, politics and cuisines. From 2006 to 2007, many states showed a decline in foreign born immigrants. The wave of immigrants entering the US slowed down during last two years as the economy faltered. Surprisingly India is one of the most pro-American country in the globe and Pakistan is one of the most anti-American nation. The Pew Global Attitudes Survey report of January 2005 mentions that out of 16 nations, about 17 percent Indian said they liked US. Only Americans (83 percent) had a more favourable view.

The nation is by and large one of the most prosperous democracies and by far the strongest in the world. It produces large amount of arms and ammunition and is the biggest supplier of the same followed by Soviet Russia. The nation believes in the free trade with necessary controls to safeguard its own interests as well as those of its allies. The US strongly discourages communism from the very beginning and had organized various regional pacts to contain communism in the world and to keep away prevalence of communist influence in their own country. Slowly and slowly these regional pacts gave way to development of the bipolar world. These alignments resulted in the fights between the US and its allies on one side and the USSR and the communist nations on the other side. Of these the North Atlantic Treaty Organization (NATO) is the most important.

After the break up of the USSR, NATO has expanded tremendously, including many of the old WARSAW pact East European countries. Any country which did not side with the US was usually considered probably aligned with the communist group. In this tussle a third world of non-aligned nations (including India) emerged. The non-aligned countries were considered unfriendly and received very little aid as compared to its allies or the cooperating nations, like Pakistan and Turkey etc. Therefore, both intellectually and economically too, the US has maximum say in the world affairs, including the control over the UN and the World bank, international aid giving agencies, particularly those located in the US. The US has taken part in all the world wars and also the regional wars as a leading partner.

The country has enormous military strength, including the nuclear arsenals, one of the greatest intelligence-organizations and spying-agency and also the ICBM system. Its nuclear stockpiles are the largest in the world and it has not agreed to the Russian proposal of cutting down the nuclear arms for the reason that to maintain the effective strength the US requires at least two thousand to two thousand and five hundred nuclear weapons. James Robin, the spokesperson of the Foreign Affairs Department stated that the US cannot come below the 2500 weapons whereas the Russians wanted to cut them down to 500 level in all the countries. The proposal was to immediately bring them down to 1,000 to 1,500 level and later limit them to 500 only. Robert Maning, the Director of the Asian Studies Council suggested to the US that the opportunity, which came after the end of cold war, should not be lost and the Soviet proposal must be reconsidered. However, it was not acted upon and the opportunity of enacting the nuclear non-proliferation treaty has been lost for the present and the near future. Recently Russian President Medvedev said on October 8, 2008 that his country will respond to US missile shield plans in Central Europe and that Russia will not resort to hysterics over the issue.

Just before the last millennium, the US economy as well as that of many other nations started declining. "Over the past couple of decades, the American economy has become increasingly resilient to shocks," the Federal Reserve Chairman Alan Greenspan, told the Senate Banking Committee in the middle of September 2001. Flexible labour, deregulated markets and technological advances "have enhanced our ability to absorb disruptions and recover," he said. Boeing kept Washington out of the last recession in the

1990s but the US may not be lucky this time. In 1990, when the last recession began Boeing employment was at highest. The company did not start cutting jobs until 1992. It eliminated about 33,000 jobs over the next four years, but as the national economy swung into an early phase of the technology boom there were enough jobs. At present Boeing has already started cutting the jobs and similar is the situation with most of the airlines as also many corporations.

Even if the air travel picks up and airlines start recovery with the Federal aid being given, Boeing is likely to remain as it is. Economists say the job cuts by Boeing alone are sufficient to tip the US into recession like situation. By one estimate, Washington State loses 1.7 jobs for each Boeing job lost. Consumer purchases were affected adversely because of Boeing and airlines etc. lay off as these had negative effects consumer confidence. After his retirement Greenspan wrote a memoir in which he criticized Bush and Republican-controlled Congress on spending and deficits (The News Tribune. Com). He said that Bush Administration abandoned its principles and paid little attention to fiscal discipline.

The other important reasons for the economic downturn were the recent terrorist activities followed by US involvements for retaliation. Operations Enduring freedom, Anaconda and others in Afghanistan and afterwards war in Iraq by the US government and later nation building activities in these countries are also affecting US economy. Nasdaq, heavy with tech shares, fell by about 15 percent in early years of the new century and more or less similar was the fate of Dow Jones. The prime rate, on which generally the loans are based, fell by about 5 percent. The rate cuts sharply reduced mortgage rates and kept the housing market from collapsing. "Lower mortgage rates and lower lending rates are an advantage now compared to last recession," said Dong Pederson, Conway Pederson economics.

Despite higher consumer spending in 2003 end and some other signs of improvement of economy in most of the states the gas prices went beyond US$ 2 per gallon in 2003 and afterwards. Luckily they have started coming down in October 2006 and later in November 2008. Many libraries are behind the locked doors. Staff protested third closure in 2 years because of shortfall in city revenues. According to the non-partisan Congressional Budget Office sources the Federal government posted a record deficit and accumulated a record over one trillion in new debt. Senator Kent Conrad of North Dakota, a budget committee member, had stated that President Bush needs to come up with a long range plan to get the economy back on the track (Seattle Times News Services, August 27, 2003).

Therefore active involvement in wars, unnecessary economic aids and tax cuts, should be avoided as much as possible. Luckily many shares have begun moving up. With citizens flush with money from tax cut and record mortgage refinancing, the US economy has started going high after many years. The GDP was at more than 7 in 2003 and in later years. Oil prices, which were very high in 2004, 05 and in 06 have begun coming down but rose again in March, 2008 to US$ 110, in May crossed US$ 135 mark and in June it rose further by another 11 dollars. In July it touched US$ 146.95. Many expected the prices to go up to US$ 150 despite request from the World community not to increase prices further. Fortunately, due to less demand and strong dollar the oil prices came down to below US$ 114 in August 2008 and much lower (below US$ 55) in November. But the US is again facing recession in 2008. Famous investment banking firm Lehman Brothers had to be liquidated. Insurance conglomerate AIG and some others had to be bailed out.

The US House and Senate leaders had to agree on a US$ 789 billion economic stimulus. Consumers are trying to cut spending. Sale of three car companies is down to minimum. Star Bucks has decided to close its 600 outlets. Boeing was having mechanics strike for several weeks. There were substantial job losses which resulted in unemployment number increases greatly in the past 10 months. For most of the last decade the US was a nation of borrowers and spenders, not savers. The personal saving rate dropped from 5 percent in 1990s to 0.6 percent from 2006 and 2007 and household debt grew much faster than personal income.

Till recently the Americans thought they were becoming richer due to the statements that there houses as well as stock portfolios were appreciating much faster than their debts. But the facts were otherwise (NYTNS February 16, 2009). According to network readiness index rating the US had become fifth from first ranking in the use of info-tech. The first place had been taken by Singapore. Luckily the situation began to improve and the interest rates have been cut down by half a percent in 2007. With oil prices rising in 2007 and 2008 people started facing a prolonged recession. Economy was at its worst in October, 2008. Mortgage system crumbled while regulators jousted. Unemployment rose to 6.5 percent and may hit 8 percent by the end of 2009. Some economists predict that GDP would shrink at a 5 percent pace or even lower in 2009 as a result of squelching of credit by banks and a plunge in consumer spending.

Al-Qaida (the Base), which plotted 9/11 events, is not a fixed point any longer. It has migrated from the Afghanistan to the heart of killer, be it in New York, Madrid, London, Mumbai or Delhi. Al-Qaida is an inspiration with its twin towers of Bin Laden and Ayman al- Jowahiri, possibly hiding somewhere near Quetta (Pakistan). They are the promoters of the brand Jehadi. Not the West alone, Israel, India and Indonesia are their battlegrounds. Although Pakistan is the origin country, the US is unwilling, for its own reasons, to call Islamabad's bluff. President Bush and his team knew it very well that its ally in terror-war is the safe haven for Jehadis. Therefore, they were pouring dollars to wean it away but it did not work. President Obama is also using the same old spectacles and raining dollars in Islamabad. Let us see what happens. Pakistan is the most anti-American country in the

World, as shown in the PEW Global Attitudes Survey Report.

According to Bush doctrine the US national security strategy will be based on 'American Internationalism' that reflects the union of values and national interests. With UN agreeing to disarm Iraq, the US sent its army in preparation, to attack Iraq. The UN team of inspectors reached Iraq and started their work but could not find weapons of mass destruction, as alleged by the US. A classified report of the Senate Select Committee on Intelligence (2006) revealed that US intelligence analyses were disputing the alleged links between Iraq and Al-Qaida, while administration officials were asserting the links to justify invading. Iraq was attacked mainly by the US and Britain to throw out Saddam Hussein. In a way war was won after killing several army generals and soldiers as also capturing entire Iraq. Later Saddam Hussein was also captured and his trial started. He was awarded death sentence in 2006. Guerrilla fight has been going on after the end of major war.

Reconstruction work began and oil production restored. An interim government had been installed, with Allawi as the head. The US was asking for soldiers from other countries, besides those of 6 participating nations. India did not agree to send its soldiers because UN was not involved actively. The overall situation in Iraq is not encouraging, because insurgency is widespread. Although elections were held in January 2005 and Nouri al-Maliki was elected the Prime Minister, sectarian violence is becoming more common. First an important Shiite religious leader was killed and later a Sunni leader, helping the US, was killed in 2007 in Anbar province. More than 6,200 Iraqi civilians died. The war in Iraq has surpassed the length of World War 2, by now lasting for about 5 years. Casualties of the US and allied soldiers are also rising. More than 4,550 US soldiers/citizens have died since the waging of military operations.

The death sentence on Saddam Hussein was executed on December 30, 2006. Grounded in 2003 Iraq's air force returned to the skies in 2008 and took complete control of airspace from the US. By the end of 2008 President Bush realized the truth that the US and many other countries had wrong information about WMD in Iraq and Saddam Hussein was attacked despite opposition from several nations and he expressed sorrow for the same (Agencies & Hindustan December 3, 2008). To give himself a cover for withdrawal from Iraq and diplomatic push with Iran, President Obama is teaming himself with people like Hillary Clinton, Robert Gates and Jones, who would not be lampooned.

After November, 2006 elections, things became different for President Bush and also for the US to some extent. Democrats seized control of the House of Representatives and defeated 3 Republican Senators, riding a wave of voter discontent. The era of Republican rule in Washington ended, putting a proudly unyielding President on notice that the voters wanted a change, especially on the war in Iraq. Peace in Iraq is still far from sight despite surge in the army. About 2.32 million people are reported driven from their homes in Iraq. The US has some evidence to show that Iran is helping insurgents in Iraq and Afghanistan. As per information of Washington Post a shipment destined for Taliban was intercepted by on September 6, 2007.

According to one estimate, about 27 Democratic victorious House candidates campaigned against free trade. Therefore, a Democratic Congress is likely to increase farm subsidies, making it difficult to win market opening concessions from Europe that are needed to revive the stagnant Doha round of talks about world trade negotiations. Bush needed to devote a substantial portion of his State of the Union address to motivate pro-trade forces in the country to educate the public. The fact is that export of goods and services accounted for about 10 percent of the US domestic product in 2005 and 20 percent of GDP growth for the year. Manufacturing exports have increased about 82 per cent over the previous decade to provide nearly 5.2 million jobs, one sixth of all manufacturing jobs in the US. About one–third of all agricultural area in the US is planted only for export.

Moreover, imports do control prices in the country. If the US markets are closed to foreign-products, other countries also may close their markets to the US products, which would cost jobs and economic growth both in the US and elsewhere in the globe. The economy, particularly of the developing countries will be affected adversely. Bush administration officials state that they are doing their best to combat unfair trade practices by China and other countries. However, they will have to be more open and confrontational, if necessary, to win public support for free trade. According to the treasury Secretary (August, 2006), productivity gains are benefiting upper-income and well educated Americans but not average workers. Wage growth was stagnant for the first five years of the Bush administration. For the past year however, wage growth was about 2.8 percent but it came late in the recovery, when the economy is already softening.

It was estimated in Cornell and Massachusetts Universities that the US may lose nearly 40,000 jobs in China, India, Mexico and other nations also if MNCs restructure operations and shift production overseas to cut costs (US-China & Economic and Security Review Commission Report, 2004). Notwithstanding its cooperation with the US in anti- terror war, Pakistan is probably the most "anti-American Country" in the world right now, according to the report of Congressional Research Service (CRS) and the PEW Global Attitudes Survey Report. According to many US experts, today no other country on earth is more dangerous than Pakistan and not Iraq. It has all the things Bin Laden could desire.

During the middle of the year 2002, the US possessed unprecedented and unequalled strength and influence in the world. The US President decided to translate strength and influence into decades of peace, prosperity and liberty and he submitted to the Congress "National Security Strategy of the US". In several areas the Bush doctrine differed from the policy laid out by President Clinton, particularly in the assertion that the US will act pre-emptively either through the UN or alone against terrorists and 'rogue nations' if necessary.

Bush Administration asked the Congress for US$ 42 billion more next year for the war in Iraq and Afghanistan. This would make spending on the wars to US$ 189 billion in 2008, amounting to a total of more than US$ 600 billion for Iraq alone since the US-led invasion. In August 2008, nation's unemployment rate rose to 6.1 percent from 5.7 percent in July. Unemployment bolted for the first time in 5 years and is expected to rise further in the coming months. Already about 40 to 50 lakh jobs have been lost by January 2009. Economists consider it a strong recession. The funds established to in insure bank deposits is feeling the pinch and could be forced to tap the tax dollars. The Federal Deposit Insurance Corporation's insurance could be forced to tap tax dollars through a treasury department loan if lending corporations fail. General Motors also declared itself bankrupt. Treasury came to rescue several corporate victims of housing and credit crunches. Additional failures of large banks or savings and loans companies seem likely according to many economists. According to some specialists, US is heading towards deflation. After the Fed's rate cut, interest rates at a quarter of one percent are close to zero. So your US$ 100 in a US bank one year later will be worth about US$ 96 one year later. Federal Reserve Chairman Ben S Barnanke predicted a sober assessment of the economy and prospect of recovery. According to him recession will end in 2009 and the year 2010 will be a year of recovery (NYT NS February 24, 2009).

2

Indo-US Economic Cooperation

B.B. Nagaich and Rajiv Nagaich

In more than six decades of Indo-US trade relations political and security aspects attracted more attention than economic aspects, although controversies over economic and trade relations deeply influenced political and security matters. The planned socialistic pattern adopted in independent India was useful to lay the foundation for modernization and development of industries, which the private sector was unable to understand at the time of freedom. Only the government had the needed resources for the massive investments. The socialistic pattern meant that India would rely upon pervasive government ownership and a strong-handed public direction of key industrial, financial, communications and transport sectors (Ayoob, 1977).

According to Professor John Adams of the North Eastern University (USA) such a doctrine was inevitable because only the State could mobilize the capital essential to commence development across many fronts and allocate investments for the required projects for maximizing social improvements and reforms. According to him, because of the emphasis on indigenous self-reliance, India worked on import substitution rather than export orientation and promotion. The expectation was that aids flow faster than the earnings through exports and that would cover the shortfalls in domestic resource mobilization programs (John Adams, 1966).

Consequently, Indo-US trade growth was very slow. In 1970-71 out of India's total export, 13.7 percent was to USSR, 13.5 percent to USA, 13.3 percent to Japan and 11.3 percent to UK. India's import from USA was 27.7 percent, from UK 7.8

percent and that from Japan was 5.1 percent. In 1978 India's export was up to about 22 percent to the US. India's share in the US imports in 1977 and 1978 were down to only 0.53 and 0.57 percent, respectively. Interestingly, India's import from USA increased by over 47 times in 2002-03.

Hurdles in India's Development Efforts

The private sector had to face several disadvantageous regulations. Manufacturing has been hobbled for decades by job destroying labour laws, a decrepit infrastructure that could not provide reliable electric power or other sources of energy. Similarly rails and roads were also sometimes lacking which inhibited movement of finished products between plants and markets. Owing to costly labour laws did not allow manufacturing to be globally competitive (Alan Greenspan, 2007). The government required industrial firms to obtain government licenses for setting up production units, adding more equipment or converting a plant to produce products even slightly different, for any reason. This so called the 'License Raj' hindered India's development in the 1970s and 1980s (National Trade Estimate Report, 1987).

In addition special restrictions were designed by some politicians to favour their friends or favourites or relations. Big industries were required to obtain clearances from antimonopoly authorities. For getting industrial license and monopoly clearance the documentation and procedural formalities took about 2-3 years. This tended to discourage large industrial houses and the sole beneficiaries were the bureaucrats. Government domination of industries was by rules and regulations, which ensured that foreigners could not bring any unnecessary products or divert needed resources.

Imports were curtailed as much as possible. After sometime the burden of strong bureaucratic controls on the economy started stifling economic development. Mismanagement and consequently inefficiency increased much more than expected and the need for alterations in economic policy became extremely necessary. India's socialism did very little to improve the lot of the poor it was supposed to help. Income disparity increased particularly in rural areas and in the industrial areas during the first thirty years of independence. The nationalization of the banks in the early 1970s contributed to marshalling resources from the rural areas and the "green revolution" in the agriculture sector revived agricultural productivity and increased food production in the nation.

Industrialization and changes in the trade policies helped in the rapid development in Indian exports in the late 1970s and in the 1980s. Exports further increased with new economic reforms in 1990s. The devaluation of the rupee in 1966, on the suggestion of the USA, made India's exports competitive and also attractive. By 1971, pursuit of import substitution policy started building a suitable base for the exports, which later multiplied with the growth of industries, coupled with the modified industrial policies of the governments.

In the beginning of the 1980s it became very clear that the economic development was only slightly ahead of the population increase and that too was much behind that of the Asian "tigers". According to Professor Adams, the basic trend of India's economic development was set in the early 1980s with a growth of about 5 percent and gaining speed to reach 6 percent with the continuation in the reforms after 1991. Unprecedented growth in the economy was likely to continue but the reforms in democratic India would have to be cautious and gradual with regard to the importance of the international aid, external trade and foreign investments in assisting economic development. In retrospect, with the exception of agriculture in the late 1960s, it is hard to see much impact of aid, which was always tiny on a per capita basis." According to him, external corporate engrossment is crucial. Indian firms in general are as far behind the modern technology in the 1990s as they possibly were in the 1970s and cannot hope to catch up except by borrowing technology. Their access to markets or brand names and the reputation for quality is not near to what is required. According to Professor Adams, the chief American role will be through its corporate involvement rather than trade alone.

Due to tension with Pakistan China and consequently the deployment of significant resources to the nuclear programs, missiles and other security requirements and their effect on the economic development is not very heavy. Ranging in the area of 3 percent of the gross domestic product (GDP), India's defence spending is probably where it ought to be. It is much less than the top twelve military power States. In the budget of 1999-2000 the allocation for India's defence was 2.3 percent of the GDP, less than 4.04 percent in 1986-87 despite the fact that inflation during this period was double digit for most of the time and cost of weapons and equipment has been going up between 5 to 15 percent. Petrol and diesel prices more than tripled during this period. Movement cost of personals and freight increased three to five times. The pay and allowances of the defence personals have increased more than three times.

Thus, the current levels of the budget allocation do not leave extra funds for capital expenditure. Regretfully, over the years, decision-making process in the defence affairs has been taken over by the bureaucracy and unless defence services are involved in strategic thinking of government there cannot be any improvement, The US Central Intelligence Agency had also mentioned in its recent report that Indian defence expenditure is only about 2.7 per cent of the GDP. This expenditure is much less although it has plenty of people available for recruitment in army. Somewhat lowered tariff barriers freed entrepreneurs to participate in international competitive markets. Both export and import of goods rose sharply in relation to GDP. Net software exports went up from US$ 5.8 billion in 2001 to US$ 22.3 billion in 2006 (Alan Greenspan, 2007).

Any burden is more than offset by the regional and domestic security benefits, including quashing the regional separatism, envisage the political and economic consequences vis-à-vis expenditure. If India had lost one of its wars with Pakistan or if Punjab or Assam had became free what would have been the results. Professor Adams said, "India's army is well behaved, so cheap at the price." In the emerging security environment, a minimum deterrence is a strategic imperative.

However, India should not get consumed in a nuclear arms race as the concept of power shift from military muscle to economic power is the new reality. India's long-range policy should be to improve economic performance. Its economy should be integrated in the new International Economic order, because it is the economic development and its friendly image, which will give India a lasting deterrent and a better peace dividend. According to the Congressional Research Service report, India was second on defence spending even after Pakistan (which is one-sixth in size as compared to India). Pakistan spent about US$ 5.1 billion in 2006 as against US$ 3.5 billion spent by India. Thus the defence spending of Pakistan works out to be 4.5 percent of the GDP and that of India works out to be 2.5 percent of the GDP, a trend witnessed since 1991-92, although Defence authorities have been requesting Indian government to increase it to a level of about 3 percent of the GDP.

Despite the ups and downs that the economy faced the national income of the country increased from Rs. 87,000 millions in 1948-49 to Rs. 1,33,000 millions in 1960-61 and to Rs. 6,01,000 millions in 1974-75, This achievement was also reflected in the growth of per capita income. At constant prices, with 1960-61 as the base, per capita income rose gradually from Rs. 305 in 1960-61 to Rs. 341 in 1974-75. The virtual trebling of the Indian population in the last 50 years has created strains on the economy. This is why top priority has been given to family planning and welfare programs to overcome the present neutralization of the economic gains by population multiplication.

The Twin Problems of Poverty and Unemployment

Removal of poverty and attainment of self-reliance are India's two most important objectives. The consumption standards of those below the poverty line are to be increased from Rupees 30 a day to a minimum standard of Rupees 60 a day. A major thrust is on providing opportunities for employment. Development plans are already on their way for tribal, difficult and backward areas. Plans have been implemented for accelerated agricultural and industrial outputs and for non-inflationary financing of the developments. After two years of poor growth, stock markets in 1999 scaled new peaks and the manufacturing sector was firmly on a growth path but slid down in 2000.

Surveys have shown that apart from impressive growth of information technology and software companies, sectors like cement and steel have registered rapid growth during the year 1999. Out of 86 sectors surveyed, growth in 46 exceeded 10 per cent and in 16 sectors growth exceeded 20 percent. The companies surveyed account for 65 percent of the total production. While colour TVs, refrigerators, clocks and other consumer durables had an impressive growth even during the slow down of 1997-99 period, cars and auto components showed signs of recovery in 1999 sliding down in 2000. Growth in steel and cement production is significant as these sectors have a substantial impact on the rest of economy. Steel had grown 11.5 percent and cement by 18 percent, indicating revival of construction activity in 1999 but showed slum in 2000. Car production has gone up by 44 percent indicating move in economy in 1999, which could not be maintained in 2000. Sugar and Vanaspati (hydrogenated fats) productions have also gone up compared to their low performance last year. In export, paper, malted food, processed fruits and vegetables have slowed down. In 2000 there was extremely high-rise in price of petroleum products. Agriculture was badly affected by worst Monsoon in last 11 years. Consequently, agriculture production came down by 19 percent and this trend continued in the Rabi crop of 2000-2001.

During 1st half of 2004-2005 India's exports grew by 24 percent. The index of industrial production (IIP) went up to about 8 percent as compared to nearly 6 percent in 2003-04. This was supported by a big growth of 14 percent in capital goods. In the oil sector, the crude has increased by 8.8 percent compared to 5.1 percent in the previous year. Electricity generation increased by 8.3 percent during April-August, 2004 compared to 2.2 percent growth during previous year. Basic chemical production increased growth by 19.2 percent. The textile industry, TV, refrigerators and working machinery showed vigorous growth in production. Consumption of electricity, oil, textile, durables increased sharply in 2004. Since then oil import has been increasing every year. Industry grew at fast speed and service sector maintained its growth, whereas agricultural growth slowed down. Investment and consumer demand accompanied by low rate of interest increased economic growth.

Foreign exchange reserves rose to US$ 141.5 billion by the end of March 2005, leading to an expansion of monetary base. Average inflation for the year was at 6.4 percent. The year also saw a very high rate of bank credit. The biggest boom resulted from high demand from manufacturing firms. Thus growth prospects for Indian economy are bright and inflows of foreign investments are making India among the fast growing economies of the globe. Global economy grew only by 4.8 percent, whereas India maintained its rapid growth for the third year. In 2005-06 GDP in India was about 8.1 percent. Trade, hotels, transport and communications rose by double digit rates. Despite problems agriculture also rose to 2.3 percent. Robust activity in the manufacturing sector was encouraging. Indian companies raised about US$ 40 billion, of which nearly 25 billion was from overseas.

Foreign exchange reserves increased by US$ 10.1 billion and stood at 151.6 billion on March 31, 2006. The inflation rate in the period ending in the first quarter of 2007 went up to

6.49 percent, highest in two years. In May, 2008 inflation again went up to 8.1 percent level, highest in 45 months. In the end of July inflation reached to the extent of 12.01 percent, the highest level in 13 years. Foreign exchange reserve also fell down slightly during this period. In 2006-07 the economy witnessed robust growth of about 9.2 percent. The only exception is the agriculture. During 2006-07, the manufacturing sector grew by 12.3 percent. The service sector now accounts for nearly three-fifth of GDP. Within service sector, trade, hotels, transport and communications and financial services recorded double-digit growth. Another positive feature is the sharp rise in savings and investments. Inflation did remain a major concern during 2006-07-08, with inflation remaining around 6.0 percent and rising up to 11.89 in July 2008, due to cotton, iron ore, fuel and manufactured products. Government had to impose ban on export of certain food grains to contain the price rise. Exports showed a good growth, rising by 20.9 percent, pushing India's share in world merchandise exports to 1 percent.

During the same period, imports grew by 26.4 percent, mainly due to increase in oil prices. There was a reduction in silver and pearl imports. Capital flows remained high and India's foreign exchange reserves rose by US$ 47.6 billion to US$ 199.2 billion on March 30, 2007 but came down to about 300 arab in August 2008. GDP growth at 8.7 percent in 2007-2008 is the same as average of the past five year period. Agriculture, despite poor monsoon in many areas, grew at 2.6 percent as was the average growth during 2000-01 to 2007-08. Food grains production touched a record high in 2007-08, with a total production placed at 227.3 million tons. Industrial growth at 8.6 percent is less than 10.6 percent in 2006-07. The services sector maintained its double-digit growth at 10.6 percent in 2007-08, higher than the previous five-year average of 8.9 percent. Trade and hotels reached a higher growth of 12.1 percent as against 11.8 percent in 2006-07. Another important feature is sharp rise in savings and investments.

Foreign reserves with the IMF were US$ 520.70 million in June 2008 as against 450.80 million in 2007 but came down in August 2008.

Some of the constraints, which hampered the process of growth, have been removed to a great extent. It was hoped that recent increase in price levels will be contained by 2008 September. However there was no effect till November despite international crude oil prices tumbling down. There is a large buffer stock of food grains and the Indian economy has been better than that of the so-called Asian "tigers" etc. It is now 3rd in the world behind US and China (Ashok Kapur, 2006; Tharoor, 2008). Despite Rupee appreciation, exports showed a good growth, rising by 23 percent in terms of USD in 2007-08. Export growth was due to petroleum and crude products, gems & jewellery, iron ore, non-basmati rice, cotton, transport equipment etc.

While India's exports to its largest trading partner, USA, showed a decline, exports to UAE and China remained good. 2007-08 imports increased by 27 percent, mainly due to higher oil imports (both fuel and edible), capital goods, chemicals, gold, silver, precious stones and pearls. Due to higher growth in imports the trade deficit widened by 35.5 percent (SBI Report, 2007-08). However the efforts made so far to minimize the inflationary tendencies in March 2008 were not very successful. It reached the level of 12.44, the highest in several years, but came down in single digits in the 2nd week of November. This year because of maximum reduction of industrial growth by about 3 percent level there is possibility of a recession or even deflation in India. October was marked by seven 500+ point drops. It is the worst performance in terms of percentage losses. Foreign Institutional Investments (FIIs) have contributed significantly, while domestic mutual funds tried to slow down Sensex fall, worst in 29 years.

Banks have gone bust and jobs are being cut. High price rises and recession adversely hit festive spirit. Experts predict that India is likely to hit deflation. Diesel prices sky rocketed on the pretext of international prices of crude oil going up. However crude oil prices came tumbling down in November and afterwards but the government is still to act seriously on price reduction for consumers on the pretext of losses to the oil companies indicating extra high charges in government expenditures. It has been announcing price reduction but reduced the price by only 25 percent of the increase it had made earlier. Inflation came down in March, 2009 to less than 0.5 percent level and below zero in June, showing the possibility of deflation. Reserve Bank however took measures to prevent deflation. During 2008-09 exports and imports reduced to a great extent.

Indo-US Trade and Economic Cooperation

As India adopted import substitution policy, its exports did not grow rapidly. In 1977 India's export to the US was only US$ 776 million. Next year it was up by about 22 percent. India's share in the US imports in 1977 and 1978 were only 0.53 and 0.57 percent, respectively. In these two years, India imported US goods worth US$ 76 and US$ 948 millions, respectively, having a small favourable balance. The main items exported by India were pearls, precious stones and clothes. The important items exported by the US were the machinery, transport equipment, fertilizers, chemicals, edible oils, wheat and cotton (The US Embassy, 1979, New Delhi). In 1950 the US aid commenced when the first Technical Cooperation Agreement was signed. From 1951 to 1967, the US provided 54.3 percent of the total foreign aid received by India and was the largest donor followed by European Economic Community (Singh, 1973). In the years 1951- 1971 the US provided assistance worth US$ 9,801 million approximately, out of which about US$ 5,324 million was in the form of food aid (Palmer, 1984).

During seventies in spite of foreign policy differences, Robert McNamara, the World Bank President allowed India to become a major beneficiary of its development funds of which the US was the principal contributor. The US did not object to India receiving aid to the extent of 40 percent of the IDA funding. In the 3rd 5-year plans the World Bank's share of the total external assistance was 11.3 percent, rising to 53.5 in the sixth plan (1980-81 to 1985-86). In 1981 when India applied for a huge amount of IMF loan of US$ 5.8 million, the US opposed initially but later abstained and the loan was sanctioned.

The scope for the Indo-US commerce is almost limitless. At present, we are far from reaching its potential. India's new economic policies and more open approaches, despite strained relations due to 1998 nuclear tests, have fostered momentum. Between 1991 and 1996 Indo-US trade increased by 83 percent. In the first eight months of 1997 it increased further by another 18 percent. This trade at the end of 1997 exceeded US$ 10 billion level. Encouraged by these facts the influential minority leader Senator Richard Gepphard suggested that America should give MFN (most favoured nation) status to India too. He was surprised by the United States conferring MFN status to China where its own citizens are not respected.

Richard Celeste, the US Ambassador, on January 9, 1999 stated at Jaipur that the next century would be mutually beneficial based on Indo-US cooperation and that in the near future the US will increase its direct investment, 5 times in India. FDI in India over the past eight years grew to US$ 4.7 billion from US$ 2.8 billion in 1996, whereas in China it grew to US$ 80 billion in the same period. The annual investments from the US have fallen 44 percent in the past 5 years from US$ 737 million to US$ 414 million in 2003. However, overall trade figures with Indo-US two-way trade are up from US$ 10 billion in 1990s to US$ 17 billion in 2003 (India Abroad, September 24, 2004). While inaugurating a meeting of High Technology Co-operation Group, US Secretary of Trade Secretary (K.D. Gupta) and India's Foreign Secretary (Shyam Saran) both stated that the two countries need to increase cooperation in the fields of Defence Technology, Data

Privacy and export licensing etc. (Agencies 20th November, 2005).

In the IT sector India is contributing a lot for the US economy but four of the states, namely, New Jersey, Connecticut, Washington and Maryland have enacted regulations which prevent foreign organizations from taking contracts for data processing. According to the data issued by Electronic and Computer Software Cooperation, Indian IT firms had exported items worth Rs. 283,780 million in 2002-03. In the previous year it was to the tune of Rs.234280 million. Thus, there was an increase of about 21 percent. About 61 percent was exported to the US markets. Therefore, the US is the biggest market for Indian IT sector and any attempt to prevent Indian IT experts from working in the US is a thing of great worry to the country.

Some critics argue that outsourcing to India and China is the root cause of job shortage in the US. During 33rd meetings of the Indo-US Business Council Commerce Minister of India, Kamalnath, gave an interview to the PBS TV and stated that during the last two years India has invested heavily in the US. This way India has opened several new jobs in the US. According to him whatever outsourcing has been done to India by the US that is much less than the jobs created by India in the US. He considered trade and investments as the two lane highway leading to job creation (Agencies, June 15, 2008). President Obama and Foreign Secretary Clinton had been arguing against outsourcing during their Presidential campaigns. Therefore, President Obama's proposal to reduce the concessions to the outsourcing American multinationals is no surprise to Indians. Obama desires to cut tax concessions up to 2011. This way, expenditures of outsourcing companies will increase by 35 percent. But if 70-75 percent savings due to Indian services is compared the companies will gain even after paying the additional taxes, due to removal of tax concessions.

Japan is India's second largest trade partner, accounting for 5.3 percent of India's foreign trade. The US is the largest partner and accounts for 14.5 percent trade (Ram, 2000). Sino-Indian trade has also been galloping- it has crossed US$ 25 billion mark and the US$ 40 billion target for 2010 is likely to be achieved in 2009 itself.

World Trade and Intellectual Property Rights

World Trade Organization (WTO) became effective from 1955. India is one of the founder members of the WTO and a signatory to Uruguay round of General Agreement on Tariffs and Trade (GATT). Obligations and disciplines incorporated in the agreement on agriculture relate to agreement on market access, domestic support, export competition/subsidy, sanitary and phyto-sanitary measures, and trade related intellectual property rights (TRIPS). India has to phase out all quantitative restrictions (QRs) by April 2001. Removal of QRs does not mean free trade. Nations are free to regulate imports through tariffs. However, the imports of various commodities would depend on the price difference and production cost. In the case of domestic support, if the aggregate measure of support (AMS) does not exceed 10 per cent of the total value of agricultural production in a developing nation, the product specific or non-product specific support may not be reduced (Gehlot, 2002).

Thus, India is exempt from reducing subsidies. While addressing the meeting of academic representatives and investors in London, Indian Finance Minister Chidambaram said that heavy subsidy given to farmers in developed nations in Europe and America is against he interests of the farmers in developing nations. The developing nations are finding it difficult to export their agricultural produce on competitive rates (Agencies 5th February, 2005). With import duties slated for ultimate elimination later, the developed countries have come up with novel ways of blocking their markets and there is need for immediate for discussions to combat non-tariff impediments to free the trade in the interest of developing nations, where 80 percent of the world population reside.

Unfortunately these countries have little or no say in the global institutions. Global governance is highly centralized and there is hardly any possibility of breaking the monopoly of developed nations. The developed countries are adamant about their agricultural subsidies. In that case how can the developing countries export their agricultural produce? The Seattle lesson is now loud and clear, the rich nations have not understood how to give more and take less from poor nations. Rich and poor countries have clashed repeatedly in the seven-year WTO talks. The EU said that it would slash farm tariffs by 60 percent as a part of a new global trade pact. The US exchanged harsh words with China and India, trading blame for stuttering steps toward a world trade pact. The US began by pointing its finger at India and China. China retorted sharply. India rebutted the charge, "who's holding up this round I think are the large developed countries...that are looking for commercial interests and enhancing prosperity rather than looking for content which reduces poverty."

The US offered to cut official aid to its farmers to below US$ 15 billion a year, from previous offer of US$ 17 billion, but found no support from Brazil, another strong exporter of agricultural produce. Indian Commerce Minister cited domestic subsidies as one of the main areas of dispute and insisted that around 100 nations backed India's position on proposals for special import tariff measures called special safeguard mechanism (SSM) (AP July 22, 2008). Next day he poured cold water on attempts by the US and EU to jolt stalled talks forward by stating that developed nations must propose "real" cuts.

As regards climate change and the environmental issue, Kyoto became the symbol of all that is wrong and the problem figures high as a global issue. Developed nations are resisting change while India, Brazil and many other developing nations are demanding their rights. Developing countries are asking for putting caps on global warming and assuring that Indian emissions levels will not exceed those of developed countries.

Whatever level the developed countries agree to, India will maintain its emissions below it. According to Indian view it cannot be blamed for global warming. It is the result of policies of developed nations and they have to agree to their share for the wrong.

One of the important issues in the international trade is protection of Intellectual Property Rights (IPR) and patents. A few such cases are the problems between India and America as the West had already a free lunch on our bio-diversity (Mishra, 1999). The World Trade Organization and many other nations including the US believe that all the nations should have the IPR laws of international standards to benefit all the countries of the globe disregarding the sovereignty over bio-diversity. Till then the nations having such laws must see that they do not infringe the rights of those who do not have them, otherwise the same would lead to serious differences as has happened between India and the US on Basmati rice, Neem (Margo) and Haldi (Turmeric) etc. Lately 'Yoga' was also patented in the US. Yoga is an important part of the Indian culture since ages and foreigners were coming to India to learn it. Now we will have to take permission to teach Yoga and pay royalty for the same. India did not have very good IPR regulators till now.

Even now some people advance arguments against IPR. For instance, the IPR guarantee leading to higher prices works for the disadvantage of consumers. Undoubtedly the patented medicines and other materials are more expensive than the non-patented ones. However the non-patented articles lead to competition that tends to keep the prices of the patented material from going very high. The patented materials on the other hand have a guarantee of the quality as against non-patented inferior or the spurious materials, which can many times lead to the health hazards. Therefore, in the long run, the guarantee of the patented material through its quality benefits the individual consumers and eventually the society or the nation. In this manner, the effective implementation of the IPR laws-is likely to improve the usage of the manufacturer or the supplier of quality materials. In view of the above it is necessary that for balancing the price there should be non-patented materials too. Another argument, which is sometimes advanced against the patent-right is that the IPR guarantee inhibits technology transfer to the developing and underdeveloped countries. This is not necessarily true.

In fact the IPR implementation in most cases encourages technology transfer as it is presumed that the rights holders must have patented and taken copy rights of the trade-marked products in their home countries and abroad and unless technology is transferred properly, it may create legal problems (Debroy, 1998). Most important benefit of IPR laws is promotion of creativity, discoveries, inventions and innovations by making conditions and environment highly suited to the ambitious inventors/scientists, artists/artisans and writers by giving them guarantee that they will get their recognition and due material benefits arising out of their patented materials.

If any country or a society does not ensure it, creative people and inventors are likely to get discouraged and move to other places where the environment is more suitable towards guaranteeing money and fame, leading to 'brain drain'. It may not be out of place to mention that an Indian American, Ananda Chakrabarti, one of the first scientists to receive a patent for genetically engineered micro-organism, after a lot of controversy and also a court case, got what he had been aspiring for. As regards copyrights, effective regulations on IPR and copyrights can protect the interests of creative people; in the absence of effective and proper copyrights cheap copies of material may lead to flooding of markets, which adversely affect the local creative individuals. Under these circumstances not only the markets for local products are affected adversely but gradually piracy is also encouraged. On account of improper IPR regulations, piracy has been encouraged against Indian products. It is a well-known fact that the pirated videocassettes of the Indian motion pictures are available openly in markets in India and abroad, leading to huge losses of revenue both to the producer as well as to the government.

Since India is emerging as a major producer and exporter of the computer software etc., it is essential for the Indian manufacturers to have better and effective rules and regulations on IPR to protect its own interest abroad where its computer software etc. is currently being pirated. Similarly, India must protect its valuable age-old knowledge and the natural wealth from being pirated by Western nations. The well known examples are patenting of Neem (margo) in the US, salt-sugar solutions (with or without starch), Haldi (turmeric) and Pricolive in the US and France as well as Basmati rice under different names by the Rice Tec Company of Texas for which court cases were on way and demonstrations were held and are still in going in some cases. Alphonso & Dussehri mangoes, Darjeeling tea, Kolhapuri chappals and Chanderi and Kanjipuram saris are at risk. Indian government has recently worked out some effective IPR regulations and has taken up steps lately to prevent patenting of Adrakh (ginger), Zira (cumin), Dhania (coriander), Ilaichi (cardamom) or other herbs and medicinal plant material etc. without its knowledge, in future.

The new law which came into force in 2005 recognized IPR. This act involved modifying third Indian Patent Act of 1970, in a phased manner. India became a member of Paris Convention and the Patents Coop-Treaty in 1998. Since then two amendments in 1999 and 2002 were made. The third amendment is the final amendment for the new act enacted in 2005. It may also be stated that margo, turmeric, Raulfia, castor, ginger etc. and now pepper, Karela (bitter gourd), brinjal (eggplant) and lately Yoga too have been patented. It may not be out of place to recall that Europe saw the strong opposition to a patent on margo but this challenge was however first turned down by European Patent Office. The US did not even admit Indian opposition to patenting of margo products (azadurachtin etc.) in its territory, which had been patented by the US company, WR Grace.

In the beginning of 2005 the EPO had to agree with India and abolish the patent of WR GRACE. Anti-bio-piracy activities should take encouragement from granting IPR to the Kani tribe of Kerala (India) in recognition to their use of Jeevani, which is non-steroid stimulant for combating stress and fatigue comparable to, Ginseng's (Chau Chee Khoon, 1999). Therefore, Indians are now seriously working on how to prevent robbery of their age-old knowledge and practices, which were intended for human welfare, free of cost. Indian Food Policy specialist Professor Devendra Sharma informed that at least six US and French firms have patented the salt-sugar solution (with or without starch) in different names. These solutions have been in use in rural India for generations to prevent dehydration from dysentery and diarrhoea etc. and have been described in ancient religious books and no body should have right to deprive Indians from manufacturing them or get its patent without giving royalty or without consulting India. These patents were given as early as in 1992 secretly and the same came to the notice of Indians only recently.

In what has become an oft-repeated problem, another composition from traditional medicines has been patented by a US pharmaceutical firm. The medicine is an herbal-mixture of bitter gourd (karela), eggplant (brinjal) and derivatives of jambolina (jamun), with several other herbs added to make it an edible composition. The US Company has taken jamun and eggplant derivative mixture for the US patent. The Indian pharmaceutical industry is already alarmed that traditional medicine patenting in the West, which have growing market for alternative systems of medicines, will ring the death knell for business of the Indian enterprises exporting herbal medicines. The recent controversies of patents for cotton seed, turmeric, margo, basmati rice and for the edible items like Dosa, Pullao and even Curry has brought out "the basic inadequacies, inherent limitations and the very serious consequences of the existing patent system," dealing with IPR. Basmati rice has been found in several archaeological excavations too.

Therefore, the patent taken by the *Rice* Tec Company amounts to a robbery and it deserves to be cancelled without much delay. After the taking of patent, protests were also held by Thai farmers in front of the US embassy in Bangkok (Chau Chee Khoon, 1999). *Rice* Tec had claimed its Basmati rice to be better than Indian Basmati. However the US Patent and Trademark Office (USPTO) said on September 11, 2000, that *Rice* Tec has filed statement cancelling its earlier claim 4 and 15-17, after Indian agency, the Agricultural and Processed Food products Export Development Authority (APEDA) filed re-examination request. In March 2001 USPTO struck down a few more claims. In August 2001 USPTO has upheld *Rice* Tec patent on a "superior strain" of Basmati rice. According to the ruling the brand name Basmati has to be dropped by the US Co. but it can sell Texmati, Jasmati or Calimati by writing on packages that its rice *is* "superior to Basmati". Rice Tec Co. was granted the right for Rice lines Bas 867, RT1117 and RT 1121 (India Abroad, August 31, 2001). On one hand, India has to block others from claiming exclusive rights to the word Basmati. On the other hand, it has to claim that right for itself. India has won the first, one Indian official said. "We now need to fight and win the second". In reality this ruling has opened a legal minefield.

The Indian authorities can now file a fresh appeal with the USPTO or move civil courts in the US, which is very expensive. They were however negotiating under the aegis of WTO for including Basmati in the 'geographical indication' category, with the case of Scotch whisky as a precedent. The TRIPS unfortunately excludes the patenting of plants and animals but it does provide protection for plant varieties. This again ignores the question of nation's sovereign rights over its bio-diversity and historical innovations. It is against this backdrop that the relevance of the Convention on Biological

Diversity (CBD) becomes a must for the developing nations (Mishra, 1999).

Visualizing its after effects on the economy in future the proposing country (USA) has later refused to ratify it. However with an unusual display of skill, the Ambassador Ting Wen Lian of Malaysia succeeded in negotiating CBD, which recognizes the sovereignty of nations over their biological resources. It mentions that the access to the bio-diversity for a foreign entity shall be based on mutually agreed terms and subject to prior informed consent of the donor country. It introduces a strong concept of country of origin of species. Therefore, instead of chasing unyielding western patent laws, action must be initiated within the framework of CBD. The CBD parties could bring the recalcitrant nations.

Another conflict between Indian and the US was on anti-dumping charge of the US on Cold Rolled Steel products of 5 nations. The US International Trade Board has however, given judgment against anti-dumping charges. On the other hand, Clinton administration criticized the Indian IPR rules and patent guarantees alleging that these were adversely affecting the US firms, which were losing about US$ 500 million annually as they were manufactured in India without any royalty to the US. Therefore, many of the US firms were removing their recent most medicines from India. Further, cinema, home videos, and TV trades were also violating agreements. American industry, according to them, had lost US$ 60 million in 1997 alone. To this India counteracted by stating that India and some other nations which do not presently recognize product patents in the field of drugs, food products and chemicals have been allowed a transition period of 10 years for patenting such products. The US has put India and another eight countries on its priority list of close watch. According to them these countries have failed to safeguard the US patents and copyrights. Therefore, the US has suffered a loss of about 91.4 crore of Dollars during 2007. These areas include Software, Music, Entertainment and Books. They have therefore, advised India to take strong steps on patents, copyrights, trademark safeguards, particularly in pharmaceuticals.

Market Demography

Statistics have also led to the myth of the Indian market. Apparently, there are about seven hundred and eighty million consumers of cooking oil, seven hundred and six million consumers of tea. Four hundred and fifty million buyers of casual footwear, forty million television set owners, two and a quarter million automobile owners have been estimated. Thus the list of India's consumption potential is very tempting. Simultaneously there has been a propaganda drive launched in different parts of the globe by governments over the past several decades offering a magical 250 million middle class consumer base. In fact the task before the multinationals in India is a far more formidable one. Some indicators are to be found in a pioneering nation wide survey carried out by Delhi based National Council of Applied Economic Research (NCAER).

Although this survey has found a consuming population ranging between 168 to 180 million for the durable items and 504 million for consumable items, the actual number of consuming households for the durable items like the refrigerators, motorcycles and scooters and the cosmetics such as nail polish and lipsticks are not more than 70 million. It is not only the unique profile of the Indian consumer that has posed so many hurdles for the MNCs. It is mainly the mosaic of markets in this country, which is almost full of the local brands. These have competed for every inch of the ground with the multinationals, which despite their tremendously superior financial resources and professional skills have found it very difficult to compete in prices and the reach offered by the consumers.

There are some of the interesting lessons to be learnt from a few multinational brands, which have successfully competed with local brands and made a good headway with the Indian consumers. The cell phone boom in very recent years is one lucky example, which did not have to compete with local brands. Brands like Motorola, Nokia, Ericsson etc. have made big inroads because of the advantage of the not so good telephone network across the country. Similarly, soft drink giants like Coca Cola and Pepsi are gradually acquiring a monopoly over drinking habits of the consumers by keeping prices competitive and trying to reach out beyond the metropolitan cities. These are some of the rare success stories underlining the preference of the markets if they desire to tap even a small percentage of the available potentials. So far, much time and money have been wasted by the international corporations in attracting the Indian consumers and make them change their ways to suit the multinational brands rather than vice versa. This is easier said than done, especially if it involves substantially lowering the prices of products of standard qualities sold across the whole world. However, it is only by going native that the multinationals can eventually hope to win over the Indian consumers through competitive prices.

Opening Up of the Economy

The trend of the progress that, first swept European countries and later some of the Asian nations, has begun to commence in India lately. It is very difficult to comprehend why many Asian nations, which opened their markets at the same time as India, today enjoy a level of prosperity, which could not be attained in India. Not only Japan and South Korea, but also Taiwan, Singapore, Indonesia, Malaysia and Thailand have leaped ahead, although very lately some of these countries like Japan and Indonesia etc. have got into economic troubles. India could plead its size, diversity of problems and huge population for lagging behind. However, what is surprising is the fact that more populous country like China has also transformed itself into a major economic power with a higher standard of living than that prevailing in India. Some of the experts assign America's help in this regard as an important factor besides other reasons. India's per capita GNP of US$ 1,400 is much lower than that of all aforementioned Asian countries. For example China's GNP is US$ 2,920; Indonesia US$ 3,800; Thailand US$ 7,540 and Malaysia's US$ 9,020. As in the developed European and American continents, most of the people in Southeast Asia are well fed and well dressed. However in India, only the upper class and the middle class have begun to enjoy the decencies of the West. The most depressing fact is that a little less than 30 percent of the population still living below the poverty line. What has really gone wrong and how can one correct it are the questions in the mind of the majority of the people dealing with the subject. The general thinking is that India ended up adopting the wrong policies of closed-door economy and the so-called Socialism.

Despite facing the disadvantages of being a responsible democracy from the very beginning, fortunately it has now discovered appropriate policies & programs and these models are likely to deliver the goods sooner or later. The dominant features of the socialistic patterns were the principal role of the public sector with very limited role of the private sector. There were restrictions on multinationals, high tariffs and strict controls on foreign exchanges, all leading to literally no competition and very little introduction of the newer technology. The new policy is expected to reverse the process leading to an open market economy with enough competition and newer technology introduction. The experience with liberalization suggests that public investment is very crucial to efficiency and proper development and should not be taken for granted under all situations. An ideal system conducive for efficiency does not exist even today and is very much called for. This may take sometime before the benefits of the liberalization start flowing into rural areas.

For an average Indian, economic reforms mean that the brand products not available readily are now available with local merchants. The complacent executive who drifted with the tide are being pushed aside by those determined that their firms may not miss the big wave. There are four broad areas where the license Raj left corporate India groping in the dark. The first is how to focus and make strategies. The second is taking a long-term view on employees and products. The third is giving some thought to the consumer. Fourth is the need to separate the roles of promoters and managers. To seek the guidance, Western, particularly the US management practices are being used. Under five-year plans, industrial Licensing and Monopolies and Restrictive Trade Practices Act, the Indian firms were left with no room to move, and prone to financial sickness.

The main skill required of an executive was an ability to burrow through the office records of the bureaucracy. The executive was supposed to know how to economize on advertising, worker training and also product development. After 1991, competitions became tough. Soon the red tape officers were replaced with go leaders. The new environment demands a visionary Chief Executive Officer, who is a go leader. Indian business attitude was suffering on two counts. One was not to bother for investments on employees. The second was not to bother for investing in the products. Tapping the growth potential of every worker is the new philosophy. Leading the groups are knowledge-based persons adopting modern methods of handling workers. The Bangalore based Info-sys gives stock options to its workers and has a personnel turnover rate a fifth of the software industry norm. About 70 percent of the Indian companies now have a human resource development strategy and 12 percent more are ready to practice it soon. Products got short drift because there was very little competition.

A good example is the Ambassador car, which is typical representative of the Indian product non-development. In a world of practically no consumer choices there was no necessity for it to develop. In 1947 the concept of quality improvement was non-existent. Today, the terms like quality management and benchmarking are normally heard over cocktail parties. What however bothers is that this should have happened in 1965, if not in 1955. Quality has many sources in the international philosophy. The main source for India however, is in the numerous joint ventures being set up by the US companies. Today the rejection rate on the automobile subsidiary is one-twentieth of international levels in Hewlett-Packard India, and it has not missed a delivery in two years.

Similarly in sectors like software, consumer products and telecom where 40 percent of foreign direct investment has come from the US, Western quality standards are commonplace. If a firm takes to corporate strategy and product development it will do so because it needs to search and retain customers. Nowadays the companies have to compete with each other to try catching the client. The importance given to buyers constitutes a major break through for Indian Industry and it finds its reflections in the post 1991 marketing and advertising. In this nation about 98 per cent of the businesses are run by a family. Even of the 500 largest, 80 per cent are run on family ties. Therefore, it will take long time for professionalism to work its way out. There have already been some institutional responses. Indian company-boards have been breaking up into specialized committees like in developed nations.

It is proper time that the Indian industries should accommodate the interests of the stockholders, partners, customers, workers and the public on priority over those of the promoters. The changes have recently started. For example, Reliance Industry and some others have lately been listed on the New York Stock Exchange. This means that their accounts must meet the US accounting standards. Many Indian companies have started exploring overseas markets too. Globalization means facing stiff competition, i.e. producing good quality materials and rendering good quality after sale-service. One thing is however clear, if the Indian Managing

Director looks anywhere, his first choice is the US for success. After 1991 the market for books on business management has doubled in India. Nearly 90 per cent of the books on management sold in India have been written by American authors.

Agriculture, which accounted for more than 50 percent of the economy of India at the time of independence from Britain, even now continues to constitute far more than one third of the economy of the country. Fortunately agriculture has been in the hands of the people and not on the pattern of the Russian model, it flourished with the help of the government run R&D programs and more importantly because of the private initiatives. Although government was not the owner of the farms, there was plenty of the government support by way of the research and technology transfers, leading to productive materials and scientific methodologies. Land reforms, giving appropriate rights to the actual tillers, adequate subsidies on critical inputs, credits and supervision by government field workers gave a good jump to the agricultural development. Thanks are due to the US Aid, Ford and Rockefeller Foundations, etc. who initially supported agricultural researches, which were followed up vigorously by the Indian government agricultural research institutes and the agricultural universities work mostly managed by the scientists trained in the US or in India.

As a result, from being an importer of food grains, the country became an exporter and a model for other developing nations in Asia, Africa and some of the Latin American countries. Famines in India are now a history; food grain production has kept ahead of the population growth; agricultural produce export is the backbone of the country's export. As against the predictions of the FAO and other experts, the "Green Revolution" in the country increased the yields of India's food crops like wheat, rice and potatoes etc. This became possible because of a number of factors like improved seeds, fertilizers; irrigation, credit, plant protection and lastly but more importantly the will of the farmers. After nationalization of the banking, financial agencies were given instructions to expand their network and also to issue agricultural loans even if these lead to losses.

Thus, government intervention in several ways helped agricultural growth. Expansion of irrigation projects also helped in the insulation of the agricultural economy to some extent from the vagaries of rainfall. The introduction of support price also helped in the boosting of production. This way, the joint efforts of the governments and the private sector resulted into a tremendous boost to agriculture. The governments constructive interventions at all levels and the supplementary efforts of the individual farmers created a situation which led to the agricultural development in the country and not being on the pattern of cooperative farming of the USSR which provided inspiration for India's socialist model. Therefore, it is clear that the hypothesis that food production increase supports the socialism is no more true. The efforts of public and private sectors in the field of agriculture responded very favourably to Indian conditions. In other words, an indigenous growth model coupled with borrowed growth model provided the success.

Therefore, it could also be argued that the socialistic pattern retarded the industrial and economic development of the country. As mentioned earlier; the domination role of public sector and very strict controls over private initiatives were some of the key problems. After arriving at these conclusions the government began to relax its controls in the 1980s. Public sector domination in industry had substantial justification at the time of independence in the year 1947 as massive investments were required for oil, power, coal, steel etc. The private sector at that time and also two to three decades thereafter was not adequately developed to cope up with the above mentioned requirements. Even at present with regard to the domestic industrial houses, there are only a very few (about half a dozen), who can manage massive requirements essential for big projects.

Domestic industry therefore, on its own, cannot promote growth. Licensing and import controls and high tariffs at one time were necessary to protect Indian industry from excessive external competition. Not only Japan, but also other Asian industrial nations have given adequate protection in one form or the other. Even the United States considered it essential to resort to voluntary restrictions from Japanese automobile industry to give protection to its own automobile companies.

Although lately government of India considerably liberalized import policy, restrictions on import of consumer goods were continued for the protection of domestic industrial houses. External investment has been kept out of core sectors generally but permitted in other sectors with the provision that the foreign stakes should not be more than 40 percent of the project. It can be stated that investment by the multinationals (MNCs) could have boosted industrial development during the past two or three decades. Many however argue that this statement does not have much evidence, if our experience after liberalization is carefully analyzed. India has been given a very low rating on sovereign risk by most of the important rating agencies, even though our economic fundamentals and with all the liberalization programs, direct foreign investments are to the tune of about US$ 2 billion.

In the key infrastructure areas, foreigners find it a risky business to invest in the country without any guarantee. In other areas, the domestic markets at the present income levels are not large enough to sustain as the volumes required for viability are rather very high. Therefore, the Indian pattern of industrial growth seems to revolve around the public sector as the growth engine. Import controls, play a limited role for multinationals and licensing appears to be the present day pattern and it is hard to argue against these except that the present form of licensing can perhaps be modified to make it more practical. Thus, the unfortunate task of taking the load of building the industrial infra-structure naturally fell on the government because only governments could bear the heavy load of massive investments with comparatively low returns. In other words, public sector investment is generally made for the inefficient use of capital. However, it did help to build a base for the private sector and also for some public sector industries, which resulted in the growth of high profit domestic enterprises. Along with the strengthening of the private sector, it did encourage the growth of capital markets for very big financing.

It is a different matter that compared to a 5.5 percent growth rate in the preceding decade. Export growth was 10 percent in the period during 1991-1996 as compared to 8 percent in the previous decade, only slightly higher in the post-liberalization period. The infrastructure public sectors are slowing down. However, the cutbacks in public sectors' investments have not been replaced or supplemented by any major investments by the private entrepreneurs. As an example, the annual addition to the power production of about 3,000 megawatts in 1990s is considerably less than 5,000 megawatts annual increase in the preceding five years.

Therefore, it is evident that the private sector alone cannot sustain growth on its own. The inability of private investment to speed up the slackness in public sector investment is one of the most important problems. Those who consider the inefficiency in public sector alone as the cause for India's ills must also recall that several companies, even those belonging to the leading industrial houses, have often become sick in due course of time. A series of scandals in private sector have shown that the in-built safety of the corporate world in the advanced nations and the strict management accountability to the share-holders are mostly lacking the private sector in our country. Therefore, public sector surpasses the private sector in credibility in accounting procedures because its dealings are subject to strict audits, precedents and mechanisms. Delays and inefficiencies are certainly there but the potentials for the large-scale frauds have been reduced greatly.

In view of these, leading foreign institutional investors expressed their preference for some of the pioneer public sector companies and not the corporate companies because he law enforcement or regulating agencies do not take seriously the misappropriations of funds in private companies. More than sixty years after independence, the country still does not have strict protection of the rights of the share-holders and mechanism of take over to improve efficiency and honesty. The competition after reforms has set restructuring in motion for both industrial and financing sectors to increase the efficiency and to avoid scandals or scams. Therefore, it means that the present slow growth rate is likely to improve. This thinking has however been clouded by the May 1998 nuclear blasts in the country for which economic sanctions had been imposed by several nations. The world economy appeared to be set firmly on a path of growth. It is estimated to have grown at 3 per cent in 1997, making it the third year to reach such a level. Inflation has fallen in most countries. The output is surging and heavy fiscal deficits are broadly down.

The US has been leading the way with booming conditions for the last several years in succession. Europe too has been growing at a rapid speed. Globalization and the technologies are the keys for this growth. Asia's tigers were however in trouble for some time. The world economy is having structural changes due to its slowing down to 2.5 percent in 1998 with a little recovery in 1999. Thanks to globalization, facilitated by the increasing importance of information technology, a new economy system has been prevailing throughout the world. India has been a leading partner in this. Since the beginning of the second half of 1997, South East Asian countries have been facing big crisis in economic situation. This crisis, which had adversely affected the region, continued to widen and deepen the onslaught in most of Asia.

The Indian economy with strong fundamentals virtually remained untroubled. India's export growth was, however, somewhat down on account of steep depreciation of the currencies of South East Asian nations, which competed with India in the price of commodities like readymade garments in world trade. Banking and financial system remained impervious to this 'bubble' effect because of avoiding erratic investments and maintaining quality of its assets. The growth rate of the domestic Indian output in.1997-98 came down to 5 percent from more than 7 percent per annum in the previous three' successive years. The uneven distribution of rainfall in the year 1997 during monsoon and later unusual rains in winter both had their toll on the agricultural output, lowering its growth rate by about 2 percent. Similar has been the situation in 2004 to 2006 period also. Less domestic and foreign demands brought down the industrial output to 5.7 percent during the year 2000 as against 6.4 percent growth recorded in the previous year.

The industrial and services sectors provided the impetus to overall growth, while there was a slow down in agriculture sector due to inadequate and erratic rainfall in several states. The industrial sector attained a growth of 7.8 percent in 1999 April to March 2000 as against 4 percent in April-March of previous year. In 1999-2000 three industrial sub-sectors, namely, manufacturing, construction and mining, registered higher growth rates than last year. The services sector attained a growth rate of 8.6 percent this year than that of 8.3 last year. The growth rate of the financial services rose from 6.1 percent to 10.6 percent in 1999-2000. During 1999-2000 exports achieved a growth rate of 13.1 percent as against a fall of 5.1 percent in 1998-1999. Due to increase in international oil prices the imports rose by 8.9 percent as against 2.2 percent increase last year.

The major factor responsible for slow growth of non-oil imports was decline in imports of capital goods, gold and silver. Strong foreign exchange reserves and Reserve Bank's timely actions in foreign exchange markets ensured stability of domestic currency (SBI Annual Report). In the year 2001-02 trends in GDP growth was largely driven by good agricultural performance. Low inflation, strong growth in foreign exchange reserves and huge stocks of food grains increased nation's economy. A decade of economic reforms began to show improvement in Indian economy and further reforms are expected to put the economy on better footing.

The inflation rate dropped to international levels of about 3 percent for the first time in the decade. The year 1999-2000 ended with an annual inflation rate of 3.7 percent as against 4.8 percent in the previous year. The revised estimates for the fiscal deficit for the year 1999-2000 at 5.6 percent of GDP exceeded the budget estimates of about 4 percent mainly due to the Kargil conflict and the havoc caused by the super cyclone in Orissa. In 2001, India moved to 115th place from 128th place in 2000, on the Human Development Index. The Human Development Report of the UNDP classified India among the medium human development countries. India ranks high on HD Report's technology achievement index. It ranks No.7 globally in science and technology talent highlights government support, turning out thousands of graduates.

Overall, the HD Report ranks India at 63rd place in terms of technology development index. At this stage the US companies could however, provide a range of techniques that could contribute to India's infrastructure development and industrial modernization. Power generation is an important key sector where Indo-US cooperation could help greatly. Luckily India and the US have signed an agreement for co-operation in civil nuclear energy program, which is likely to begin soon. This agreement is likely to boost energy production with no green house emissions .India's needs are expected to double in the next decade and the greenhouse emissions must be reduced for preventing an adverse impact on the climate. The US firms can help in these aspects and also in the telecommunication products and services that are required in India to expand and modernize its network in rural areas. But the US investors get discouraged with heavy paperwork required by Indian bureaucrats. Therefore, with all the liberalization the investments from the US are not to the level expected.

Speaking at Jaipur in 1999 the US Ambassador Celeste stated that the US was planning to encourage its direct investment in India nearly five times. However, as per recent figures the US is no longer at the top of list of the countries investing in India. Foreign Direct Investment (FDI) from the US dipped sharply in 1998 and shrunk further to the fifth position, around US$ 219 million flowing between January and May 1999. South Korea led the table with its FDI amounting to US$ 727 million approximately, followed by Mauritius. British and Japanese investments amounted to about US$ 236 million each. The US Treasury Secretary Lawrence Summers, said on January 17, 2000, during his visit to India, "My hope is that apart from building a mature and strong relationship between India and the US, there will be a separation of tracks on which different issues play up." After delivering a letter from President Clinton to Prime Minister Vajpayee, he also met the Finance Minister, Yashwant Sinha, who asked for the revival of the Indo-US joint Commission, which had met last time in 1996. Sinha also informed Summers that the Indian government was planning to hold "India Road Shows" to project the country as an investment destination in various sectors.

India and the US have formally entered into an agreement to create a forum to promote economic cooperation between the two nations. Yashwant Sinha, who was in the US for the World Bank and International Monetary Fund-meetings, signed the pact along with Summers on April 17, 2000. The forum is part of the broader economic and commercial dialogue between the two nations as envisaged in the "Vision Statement" issued jointly by President Clinton and Prime Minister Vajpayee during President's visit to India in the month of March 2000 (India Abroad, April, 21, 2000). The first meeting of the dialogue was held in San Francisco in June. Norman Y. Mineta, delivered an address in the meeting. He said, "the more we expand commercial cooperation and technical assistance, the more we improve economic security and quality of life for people at home and abroad."

According to a senior official, these projects could have a potential value of more than US$ 6 billion. Elaborating on President George Bush's vision of Indo-US relations, Ambassador to India Robert D. Blackwill said Washington is set to collaborate on the entire range of issues that confront the globe. The Ambassador told the select audience in Mumbai "Rather, President Bush has a global approach to US-India relations, consistent with the rise of India as a world power." He added that the US is India's biggest trade partner, with two-way trade in 2001 expected to exceed US$ 14 billion. However foreign direct investments flowing into India is only a tenth of the amount that goes to China. Important reasons could be the trouble that Enron has had in Maharashtra and bureaucratic delays. During the visit to Moscow, Indian Foreign Minister, Yashwant Sinha agreed with the Russian Prime Minister to form a Task Force to investigate the possibility of furthering cooperation in trade and investment in joint projects from Indian Rupee Funds (Amar Ujala, March 14, 2003).

The economic development in 2003 has so far been very good as compared to that in 2002, when widespread drought in several states brought down growth rates. In 2003 majority of areas received abundant rains by August and the Reserve Bank of India has upgraded the GDP rates. It has escalated the growth rate to about six percent this year and about 10 percent in the coming years whereas the Confederation of Indian industries has projected a growth rate of about seven percent for the current fiscal years. The foreign exchange reserves are heading for a record of over US$ 100 billion mark from the current $85 billion mark (Times News, December 21, 2003). Value of rupee has also risen.

The expanding foreign reserve has also rung alarm-bell as the Indian products would become more expensive. The central and state governments are spending lavishly. The rising petrol and diesel prices however, are a thing to be watched. Remarkable progress is being made on the telecommunications front but the speed of port-and airport development is slow. With good rains, farm sector is expected to grow by about six percent whereas industrial and services sectors are expected to expand nearly 6.5 percent and 7.5 percent, respectively. Therefore, all the signs indicate a credible turn around in the Indian economy and the government will have to speed up the pace of economic reforms and cut down deficits. Prospects of development in 2004 were not as good as in 2003 due to 25-40 percent less rains in many areas. Inflation is already back. With India's economy improving there were visits of several world leaders from France, Australia, US, Ireland, Russia and Great Britain and agreements were signed in the energy sector, defence, science and technology and trade etc. all within a few months in 2006.

Survival of the Fittest

Ten years after India liberalized its closed economy and threw most of its sectors open for foreign firms, some of them are still finding it difficult to compete and crack the market. The year 2002 saw a few MNCs quit India to go native as they could not compete with other units. BMW motorcycles, Blue Bunny ice cream, Power Gen, Indonesia paper giant Sinar Mas and Australian Broadcasting Co. Nine Gold have raised their hands or sold out to local companies. Reasons for their failure were: miscalculations about the size of market, wrong strategies, flawed joint ventures and a hostile environment as cited by these companies. MNCs are finding that obsolete technologies do not work and the products have to be modified to suit the needs of Indians. Most of these ventures made the wrong choices or used wrong strategy mentioned Gautam Mahajan, the managing director of Inter-Link India that helps foreign companies transition into the Indian and Asian markets. Earlier, Inter-Link had helped Alcoa, GE, Rock-well and Xerox. Sometimes high pricing also makes take off rare in

India (India Abroad, November 8, 2002).

For long time the US considered South Asia a low priority areas. The Bush administration however, took a major policy decision to enhance the US-South Asia relations. It has therefore created a new position for Assistant USTR for South Asia, almost parallel to SAARC. The USTR is generally the lead government agency for inter-agency coordination of economic policies. USTR head Robert Zoellick mentioned that the creation of the office of South Asian affairs reflects "the increasing importance of the region to US economy and national security". The new office will cover Afghanistan, Bangladesh, Bhutan, India, Nepal, Pakistan and Sri Lanka.

Indian Investments Abroad

Indian corporations are bullish on investing in the US with the regulatory authorities approving US$ 225 million in April, 2005 to January, 2006 period. Majority of the Indian investments abroad are in the US and about US$ 2159 million have been invested in the last decade. Next to US, is Russia with investments to the tune of US$ 1763 million, Mauritius US$ 1038 million and Sudan $964 million according to a survey by FICCI and Ernst and Young. Indian companies are going in sectors like IT, healthcare, Telecom, textiles, automotive and financial services etc. In 2004-2006 period, software and BPO accounted for maximum investments, nearly 58 percent followed by healthcare, about 17 percent.

Because of Indian economy improving, Indian industries are investing in foreign countries and foreigners are investing in India. In 2006-2008 period also some of the leading Indian companies have acquired several foreign firms. Thus, business and tourist traffic has increased tremendously, resulting into a great shortage of accommodation for the increased number of people, who visit Indian metropolitan cities like Delhi, Mumbai, Bangalore and Chennai. Recently, an Industry leader has estimated that India needs another 100,000 rooms immediately- more than double the current amount. The government has approved 300 hotel projects. Most of them are likely to be completed within a 3-year period and that should increase capacity by about 75,000 rooms. Till then high rents and low availability are expected to continue in the near future. The worst situation may arise during key events, such as the Commonwealth games in 2010 and the cricket World cup in 2011, unless the approved projects get completed before these events.

With an estimated US$ 8 billion spent on overseas mergers, acquisitions and expansion, 2006-07 turned out to be a year of global consolidation for Indian multinationals. India, which itself is seeking massive foreign investments, is for the first time witnessing its companies invest more capital abroad this year than the inward flow of overseas investments, which was a little more than 5 billion only. The build up of the foreign reserves of about US$ 140 billion helped. Luckily the FDI has lately broken US$ 10 billion barrier and has the strong possibility of the trend holding or even increasing.

Foreign Institutional Investors (FII) pumped investments during 2007. The market crossed 11 billion in September itself, surpassing US$ 10.8 billion recorded in the whole of 2005. It is expected to cross US$ 12 billion. As India's economy boomed in recent years, it diverted its new found wealth (raised from high-tech sector) into political and defence fields to stake a claim as another world power. It is expected that the 2-year 'Chandrayan mission', which was blasted off from Sriharikota on October 21 will enhance its nuclear power status. Chadrayan's mapping instruments are a joint project with NASA.

What started simply as the US Bank-investments problems the situation slowly engulfed the entire financial sector across the globe, including India. There is a consensus that the global problem in heading towards a prolonged recession. India is no longer a closed economy and is thus not insulated from global bad economy. Our economic figures are certainly better than those of other countries already suffering. But the government seems to be under illusion that our economy is not going to be seriously affected like other parts of the world. It is considered that our agriculture sector, supposedly sound banking system and consumers are great assets. A fiscal stimulus with wide spread reduction in excise duties and service taxes etc. would be proper combination for good economy cum good politics. Despite record low international price of crude oil (below US$ 50 a barrel), UPA government has refused to cut down the sale price of oil to the level it was before international price went up. Farmers are suffering because of high diesel price and so are the transporters, who ultimately charge it form the consumers. However what is a clear indication of industrial crisis beginning also in India, revenues from federal excise in October-November 2008 are 8-9 percent lower than those in 2007. Despite economic slow down American magazine Forbes has listed 47 Indian companies as important globally.

Hawala Deals and Terrorism

Financial Intelligence Unit (FIU) of India reported in 2008 a number of suspicious transactions through different banking channels. According to the report these transactions doubled in a year. It found more than 130 suspicious cases related to terrorism financing. In about 300 cases, the FIU discovered that the banks and other financing institutions were not even aware of the identity of the client or their background information. These accounts were initiated by fictitious persons based on forged documentation. Luckily government having passed the Prevention of Money Laundering (PML) Bill, India is prepared to become a regular member of the FATF, which has headquarters in Paris and the regional Asia Pacific Group in Australia. FATF members are obliged to share information relating to an accused so that the accused can be arrested anywhere across the national boundaries.

3

Indo-US Agricultural Cooperation

B.B. Nagaich

Look at the globe, India and the US cannot be seen together. Perhaps no two countries are physically farther apart. However, after Indian independence both nations worked in close co-operation in the field of agriculture (particularly in the initial planning phase) till India achieved its "Green revolution" about 40 years ago, despite predictions of famines by authorities (Malthus, 1798). The potential of Indian agriculture largely remained untapped as the nation was unfortunately under 800 years of rule by parasitical regimes. The main objective of these regimes up to 1947 was revenue appropriation. There were hardly any improvements in varieties, irrigation and floods. Farmers were given no incentives to produce more. India is the second most populous and the seventh largest country in the world. It has an area of 3.29 million sq. kms only. Pressure on land is therefore, higher than the world average. Increasing population has been the cause of concern throughout the globe in general and in India in particular. More than seventy percent of its population is agricultural-based and lives in 600,000 villages. Its total cultivable area is 184 million hectares, which is divided into fifteen agro-climatic zones that cater to incredibly diverse habits. Settled cultivation in this country probably began over 7,000 years ago in the Indo-Gangetic plains.

However, being rich in fauna and flora, India became one of the early centres of domestication of several important crops including rice, barley and sugarcane. A large number of food and fibre crops are grown in the country from the distant past. Even then weather dependent agriculture has never been solely a means of profit. For a very large proportion of population it is not a very profitable economic proposition. It has been and still is a livelihood and a way of life. The concept of farm as a factory is alien to majority farmers. Traditions and small size make Indian agriculture heavily dependent on cattle. Animal wealth of the country is quite rich consisting of 760 million livestock and has achieved number one position in milk production in the world. Cattle are used here for milk production and also for draft purposes to a great extent.

The Indian tropical and subtropical region, which is indeed a vast area, permitting harvesting of fishes all the year round. The Famine Commission, Irrigation Commission and the 1915 Committee on cooperation made a number of recommendations for the agriculture based rural population. The Royal Commission on Agriculture was appointed in 1926 to examine the report on the development of agricultural and rural economy. However, it is the responsibility of agricultural scientists to ensure that the growth in agricultural production surpasses the growth in population and to see that mankind does not suffer from hunger and malnutrition. It is highly satisfying to note that in India the rate of growth of food production has been above the population multiplication during the last many decades, through combined efforts of farmers and scientists.

It is the result of the recommendations of various commissions that a Research Institute and Agriculture College was established in the eastern part of the Indo-Gangetic belt in Pusa, Bihar with the generous donation of Mr. Henry Phipps, an American Philanthropist. As gratitude an important unit in Delhi's Indian Agricultural Research Institute was named after him. The Imperial Council of Agricultural Research (ICAR) was formally started on July 16, 1929 to promote, guide and coordinate agricultural activities in the country (Randhawa, 1986).

After 1947, the Imperial Council of Agricultural Research was renamed as the Indian Council of Agricultural Research and was rejuvenated to help finance and oversee research and development work in the fields of agriculture and allied subjects, including animal husbandry, fisheries, transfer of technology and agricultural education etc. After independence, due to food shortage a high priority was given, by the government of India, to agriculture. Several committees were set up to explore the possibilities for higher food production in the country and for import of cereals. The US helped from time to time by supplying wheat and maize to India through its PL-480 program and through Rockefeller/Ford Foundation experts deputed to India (Randhawa, 1986). Thanks to them.

University Education Commission

In 1948-49, the University Education Commission, under the chairmanship of Dr. Sarvapalli Radhakrishnan, recommended that a system of rural universities be established to supply skilled persons for meeting the need of the nation. The Commission observed, "A new beginning is desirable, with freedom to create a distinctive tradition as to purposes, spirit and methods". According to the commission a rural university should include a ring of small resident colleges for undergraduates, with the university facilities at the centre. Each rural university should be autonomous to work out its own program, syllabus, curricula and examinations.

Through its concept of rural universities, the University Education Commission introduced the Land-grant College philosophy of the US in India. The earliest advocate of the agricultural university idea was Pandit GB Pant, former Chief Minister of U.P. and later Home Minister of the government of India. In 1950, Major H.S. Sandhu and A.N. Jha, Chief Secretary of U.P. visited the US. On return they reported that if such a university were established in Tarai region at the foot hills of Himalayas in U.P. it would give an impetus to agriculture not only in Tarai but also in the other areas of the state. Pant accepted their recommendation. This ultimately resulted in establishment of the first agricultural university at

Pantnagar and later a series of agricultural universities in the country.

From 1947 to 1950 the Indian government was confronted with the problems of partition, particularly the rehabilitation of refugees from eastern and western parts of India, *i.e.* Punjab and Bengal, now in Pakistan and Bangladesh (earlier East Pakistan). In 1952 the Government of India handled the problem of food shortage energetically and an Indo-American team was established for this purpose. Dr. FW Parker of the US AID was made adviser to the Ministry of Food and Agriculture from 1953 to 1959. He took interest in the use of chemical fertilizers and in the scheme of agricultural universities on the pattern of land grant colleges. Parker influenced the Rockefeller Foundation to take interest in the agricultural development schemes in India.

Consequently in 1956 an agreement was reached between the government of India and Rockefeller Foundation. The agreement had two main objectives: (I) Foundation was to assist in the post-graduate school of the Indian Agricultural Research Institute, and (II) the Foundation was to assist in the development of national research programs on the improvement of Maize (Corn), Sorghum and Millets initially. Thus the passionate concern of Dr. Parker and the Rockefeller Foundation assistance in the improvement of certain cereals will always be mentioned with happiness and gratitude.

In 1963 the Agricultural research Review team, headed by Dr. M.W Parker of the USDA, was appointed by the Government of India to suggest suitable changes in agricultural research and development. The other members of the team were Dr. R.L. Lovorn, Dr. O.S. Ross, Dr. E.E. Cheema, Dr. L. Sahai, Dr. K. Ramiah, Professor P. Maheshwari and Dr. S.K. Mukerjee (as Liaison Offlcer). As a result the I.C.A.R. was made a fully autonomous organization, bringing all agricultural research institutions under *its* control and reconstituting the governing body of the Council, making it a body of the eminent scientists or those with a profound knowledge of agriculture and related subjects (Randhawa, 1986).

In 1957, Dr. Ralph W. Cummins arrived in India to direct the Rockefeller Foundation's field programme till 1966. India honoured Dr. Cummins by naming the Cereal Research Laboratory of the Indian Agricultural Research Institute after him. Dr. Albert Moseman, who had been a member of the first Indo-American team and who was the then Director of Agriculture programs for the Rockefeller Foundation in New York, also-gave support to the projects in India. The second joint Indo-American team, set up on September 12, 1959, by Dr. M.S. Randhawa as Vice President of the ICAR, had three representatives of the land grant Universities in the US. They were, Dean Arthur D. Weber, Dean A.E. Darlow and Dean Arthur L. Deering. Dr, M.G. Weiss represented the USDA. The Indian members of the team were Dr. B.N. Uppal, Dr. L. Sahai, S.B. Lal Singh, P.D. Nair, Dr. M.D. Patel, Dr. K.C. Naik (Secretary), Dr. J.S. Patel, and Ibne Ali.

The team submitted its full report in July 1960, mentioning that there was widespread demand from many states for establishment of the agricultural universities. The team recommended that assistance in establishing an agricultural university should only be granted if it meets the following conditions.

1. Autonomy.
2. Agriculture, Veterinary, Animal Husbandry Home Science, Technology and Science colleges are established on the same campus.
3. The integration of teaching to provide a composite course.
4. The integration of research, education, and extension is a must.

All India Coordinated Research Projects

The All India coordinated research projects are land marks in the history of agricultural research and development. The field work in India is based on the concept of Multidisciplinary

Team-Work developed in US under conditions somewhat similar to those in India. The I.C.A.R. was interested in improving maize production using hybrid vigour in the crop, which has led to spectacular results in the US and later in many other countries. On the invitation of the I.C.A.R., the Rockefeller Foundation, which had been carrying out fruitful research on crop improvement in Mexico, Central America and the Caribbean region, deputed two specialists on corn to visit India. These scientists were supposed to study the present position regarding the cultivation of the crop so as to make recommendations for stepping up production.

Therefore, Dr. S.J. Wellhausen and Dr. U.J. Grant, corn experts of the Rockefeller Foundation program in Mexico and Columbia came to India to study the position of maize crop research and production in progress in this country. For the first time a new approach to research on the improvement of crops was formulated. Instead of financing research on boundaries of states the financing was on the basis of the major agro-climatic zones for research planning and funding. States and the Central experts all are involved in planning and action. States administer the work, provide the land and laboratory. The Centre (ICAR) would provide the leadership and financial assistance. Rockefeller Foundation agreed to make available the world collections of germ-plasm. The project was so successful that within 4 to 5 years high yielding hybrids became available. After reorganization of the ICAR in 1955-56 the then Director General, Dr. B.P. Pal applied this-concept for improvement of all major crops and animal sciences in the country with equally good success. Thanks to the US and the Rockefeller Foundation as well as the Indian Farmers and scientists who all joined hands to achieve this breakthrough.

Agricultural Universities

The first agricultural university to be established on the Land-grant College pattern was the G.B. Pant University of

Agriculture and Technology founded in 1960 at Pantnagar. This university has an excellent record of achievements to its credit in the field of education, research and extension education with the collaboration of the University of Illinois. The university started programs of practical training for agriculture and veterinary graduates. This university is serving as a model to other agricultural universities, which were established later, Like Punjab Agricultural University at Ludhiana (Punjab) with collaboration from Ohio University and Jawaharlal Nehru Krishi Vishwa Vidyalay at Jabalpore (M.P.) with collaboration with the University of Illinois. The role of coordinated projects was expanded in the State Agricultural Universities also. Consequently, all the agricultural organizations, Central Agricultural Institutes (38 in all), the National Research Centres, the Agricultural Universities (21 in all) and the commodity Coordinated Research Projects (52) along with the State departments worked together on the production of food crops. This way, India not only wiped out its food shortages but achieved the so called "Green Revolution" to become surplus in grains, potato and other food articles and provided a model for other developing nations of the third world to follow.

PL-480 and Intensive Agricultural Development Programmes

In the late 1950s due to succession of droughts the production of food grains dipped alarmingly. In 1958-59, the production of food grains was only 66 million tons, much less as compared to the production in previous year. As a result the country had to import large quantities of wheat under the PL-480 arrangements with US as well as purchases from other countries. It was estimated that unless a concerted effort was made to overcome the food crisis, there would be a shortfall of about 28-30 million tons by 1966. In view of the serious food situation inherited from British rule, Government of India formed an Agriculture Production team, in collaboration with the Ford Foundation, in 1959 to study the food production. The team was composed of 13 US scientists as its members and the Chairman was S.E. Johnson, an expert in the field of Farm Management.

There were 11 Indian scientists and officials as members of the same team. The team recommended that in each State having irrigation or assured rainfall and a good yield potential should be selected for intensive agriculture. The efforts should be concentrated on the most promising areas for wheat and rice production. For rice, there were 25 important growing districts. For wheat, there were 18 selected districts in Punjab, U.P., M.P. and Bihar. These areas were expected to increase India's food production more rapidly than others, if fertilizers, plant protection measures, high yielding variety seeds, irrigation water, improved practices and proper supervisors were allocated. Attention to other areas should also continue.

The idea was based on the US experience where the key to the increased production and productivity or the agriculture revolution was the adopting of what is called a 'package' of practices. This package usually included mechanization, greater use of fertilizers, widespread use of cover crops and other soil conservation practices, irrigation, use of improved varieties, a better balanced feeding of live stocks, effective control of pests and diseases, as well as the use of weed killers and growth regulators. The package idea is actually a system approach to the problem of increasing agricultural productivity and production. The other unimportant factor is the stabilization of farm prices, the role of cooperatives for the credit supplies and marketing. All these measures resulted in higher and higher production.

In 1951, President Truman initiated the first of many of the shipments of the US food aid to India. This enabled India to avoid famine. However, due to extended haggling in the Congress and anti-India statements the public appreciation was lacking. On the other hand USSR received good comments for a much smaller food shipment that arrived before the US shipment of wheat. After Chester Bowles took over as the US Ambassador, his enthusiasm and goodwill had a positive impact to offset the frictions in the Indo-US estranged relations. Ironically, India was first to procure not only food but also arms from the US, before the outbreak of fighting in Kashmir.

A year after the US Congress voted US$ 190 million of food aid and at a time when India was seeking substantial development aid, it was asked how India could justify spending large sums for arms. In the end India succeeded to seek and got far cheaper 54 C-119 transport planes. By that time the "Green Revolution" in India had taken its deep roots, for which the US scientists and organizations assisted considerably and deserve compliments because opposite was predicted by authorities (Malthus, 1798). Simultaneously mainly due to the untiring efforts of Ambassador D. Moynihan, the US administration agreed to utilize its accumulated PL-480 funds for further research and development work in India and were finally written off. Consequently the Indo-US ties improved tremendously during that period.

US-India Agricultural Knowledge Initiative Board

This AKI board was created to continue Indo-US cooperation in Agriculture and allied fields. The fifth meeting of this board was held in Washington DC on June 14-15, 2007. The board discussed agenda items, including progress in the four areas and also announced a number of planned activities as given below: HRD institutional capacity building, Agro-processing and marketing, Water management, Biotechnology, General and other related activities. The AKI Board was apprised of other activities undertaken in related areas by other US agencies, viz. USDA, USAID, USTDA, US State Department etc. About a month earlier Indo-US AKI Workshop on Indian Libraries and Information System under the US-India bilateral program was organized by the IARI,

New Delhi on May 16-17. The Library partnership between the National Agricultural Library (India) and the National Agricultural Library (USA) is under human resources development component of the AKI program. The Group discussed modernization of National Agricultural Library and the Networking of NARS Libraries and NAL, USA.

Intensive Agricultural District Programme

Intensive agriculture district program (IADP) was started on a 'pilot' basis in 1961 in seven selected districts to increase all round agricultural production. Subsequently it was extended to nine more districts. In all these districts attempts were made to place all the available resources, such as production supplies, credits, and technical staff at the service of the farmers. The facilities provided in these districts were as follows:

1. Adequate and timely supplies of production requisites like improved seeds, fertilizers, pesticides herbicides and implements.
2. Timely supplies of the required credits through cooperatives.
3. Arrangements for marketing to enable the farmers to obtain reasonable price for their marketed produce.
4. Adequate storage facilities for storing farm produce, if required.
5. Intensive educational efforts through demonstrations and on the job training courses through extension specialists.
6. Strengthening of transport arrangements to ensure movement of supplies and staff.
7. Village planning for increased production, including the live stock improvement programs.
8. Strengthening of village organizations such as cooperatives and the 'Panchayats'.
9. Establishing workshop for making and repairing agricultural implements and starting of seed and soil testing laboratories.

Arrangements were also made for evaluating the program from year to year and constant gradual development was reported. Such a package of practices was evolved for all the important crops and for each agro-climatic zone. Specific recommendations were made regarding the variety to be sown, the seed rate to be used, the time of sowing to be adopted, etc. In many package areas, the seed of the recommended improved variety treated with Agrosan GN was supplied in sealed bags. Recommendations were made regarding the quantity of fertilizers, and also the doses and time when these would be applied by the farmers. This strategy was an important development in Indian Agriculture in the sense that for the first time the available findings of agricultural research were selected for adoption in the field. The Directors of Agriculture in the States were asked to review the package of practices for-crops annually so that the gaps were brought to the notice of researchers and the package of recommendations were improved further from time to time.

Agricultural Research and Development

The reorganization of the ICAR was an important achievement and it played the key role in the agricultural development in the nation. The rejuvenated ICAR is responsible for the advancement of the agricultural education, research and transfer of technology, which are vital for the transformation of traditional agriculture into a highly productive agriculture. The infrastructure developed after the formation of the new ICAR, paved ways for the breakthroughs in agriculture through the coordinated approaches. On the basis of trials conducted by Indian scientists with Mexican wheat, the Government of India took a bold decision of importing 18,000 tons of Lerma Rojo-64-A and Sonora-64 varieties of wheat from Mexico for distribution among farmers. For farmers, "seeing is believing" and the national demonstrations laid in the fields of several farmers served as windows into a new world of plenty and prosperity awaiting our farm community.

This along with triggered researches for varietal improvements, plant protection practices and agro-techniques led to the "Green Revolution". The introduction of improved varieties of wheat, for which Indians owe thanks to the Nobel laureate Dr. Norman Borlaug, the US help and the passionate work of the ICAR scientists in the field as well as in the laboratory all contributed to the nation's agricultural development. Above all is the acceptance of the new varieties by the farmers whose efforts helped India to march forward to achieve self-sufficiency in food grains, potato and also in sugar production during the eighties.

In 1965 (part of 1st phase of agriculture development), India was dependent on other countries for food grains and at one stage it was declared by world authorities that India would face a great famine in a decade. However, in 1995 (part of 3rd phase), there were surplus food grains, potatoes, sugar and onions, etc. in the country, which could be supplied to others (Table 3.1). Perhaps, Indo-US agricultural cooperation is the best example of close relationship between the two estranged democracies. By the advent of the second phase, India and the US had several ups and downs in bilateral relations.

Therefore, India started becoming independent of the US cooperation in the food front and high value crops. Even then there is no international seminar, symposium or a conference either in India or in the US in which active participation of scientists from the other country is not there. This shows Indo-US cooperation in the field of agricultural science and development is even now quite significant. An Indo-US joint Workshop on 'Curriculum Development under the Agricultural Knowledge Initiative (AKI)' was organized in New Delhi from January 22-23, 2007. The US-India AKI Board met on June 14-15, 2007 in Washington DC. The board discussed agenda items, including progress in the four areas and announced a number of planned activities. In addition it was agreed to set the dates of the next meeting for 2nd half of

February 2008.

Table 3.1: Production of Agricultural Commodities

(million tons/million bales)

Year	Population (crore)	Food grains	Oil seeds	Potato	Sugar cane	Cotton
1951	361	50.82	5.16	1.66	57.05	3.04
1961	439	80.02	6.98	2.72	110.0	5.60
1971	548	108.42	9.63	4.81	126.37	4.76
1981	685	129.59	9.37	9.67	154.25	7.01
1991	846	176.39	18.61	15.21	241.05	9.84
1995	900	191.09	21.42	17.94	271.23	12.11
2000	101	205.91	21.16	24.15	309.31	14.50
2005	101	208.6	27.10	23.91	281.17	18.50

In 1996-97 the agriculture sector reached a peak growth rate of 7.9 percent. Uneven distribution of rainfall in 1997-98 and untimely rains in the winters had their toll on the agricultural output, lowering its growth rate to an estimated negative of about 2 per cent. In 1998-99 the growth rate stepped up to reach foodgrain production to 203.60 million tons and potato production to 22.50 million tons. Agriculture sector was once again affected by the worst monsoon in 11 years in Kharif 2000, when production went down by 2 percent in 1999-200 and the Rabi crop was not as good as last year. The year 2001 roved to worse than 2000.

The Production System Research has been designed for applied research. It prioritizes research needs taking care of all the subsystems like crops, livestock, natural resources, socio-economic and their inter linkages. The need for 2nd "green revolution" is being felt now because per capita annual food production between 1991 & 1995 was 192 kg but now it is about 174 kg only. Similarly, per capita pulses-production was 15 kg and in 2007 it is only 12 kg. In 1970s, the population was between 550-600 million but now it is estimated to be beyond 1100 million.

Thus population explosion has exceeded food, pulses and

oilseed production. Secondly farm-land is being diverted for other uses, putting additional pressure for 2nd green revolution. The second green revolution should not based only on commodity approach but mainly population control & on the system approach involving pulses, oilseeds, fruits, vegetables, animal husbandry products, soils and Sea-foods. Special Spokesperson of the UN has stated that wrong policies of the US and Europe are mainly responsible for price increase of the food articles throughout the world. According to him both of them are using a substantial amount of food for production of bio-diesel because of which food has become in short supply causing heavy increase in prices. Therefore, UN has prepared a plan for solving the food problems by the end of June, 2008. The Deputy General Secretary John Holmes said he will arrange a meeting in the beginning of June in Rome to solve high price problem.

Uruguay Round Agreement

After several years of negotiations the Uruguay round of multilateral trade agreement was finalized on 15th December 1993. This is a landmark in the trade negotiations under GATT as it deals not only with traditional goods but also extends to new areas, like IPR, agriculture etc. The root cause of distortion of international trade in agriculture is the massive domestic subsidies given by industrialized countries to their agriculture sector for several decades. This led to excessive production and import restrictions to keep foreign agricultural products and their dumping in international markets.

To minimize such dumping exports and for keeping markets open for efficient agricultural products producing nations, the beginning has to be in the reduction of massive production subsidies in the industrial countries as well as reduction of export subsidies and minimum market access commitment for foreign agricultural producers coupled with food stock holding and food aid operations. The US and European officials maintain that subsidies protect farmers from the vagaries of weather and price fluctuations. The 2002 farm Security and Rural Investment Act approved by the US Congress and signed by President Bush boosted support to farmers, which was further increased by the majority Democratic party in 2007. President Bush had sought to place a ceiling of US$ 200,00 on payments to farmers per year, but the Democratic party set it up at US$ 1 million (US$ 2 million for a couple).

Under pressure from developing countries at the WTO, however, they pledged to cut subsidies. Their plans are sketchy, but trade officials from Brazil to India were hoping for additional progress at the Cancun conference in September (Seattle Times, September 6, 2003). However, these hopes ended in a dead-lock even in other meetings held later. In the case of developing countries, it is obligatory to reduce domestic subsidies only if the total aggregate value of subsidies given to farmers is in excess of 10 percent of the value of total agricultural production of the country. The subsidies given to small and marginal farmers are exempt from any reduction commitment (Mishra, 1999).

On the other hand, the US through its Commodity Credit Corporation (CCC) will help farmers economically for large scale production of several commodities, making it impossible for Indian farmers to compete in international markets. The issue that has created an impasse in the Doha round of talks in WTO is the US government's refusal to reduce subsidies paid to its farmers. The rest of the world, including staunch allies of the US in Europe, is one in calling USA's position as unreasonable. After negotiations broke down in Geneva, in 2006, Indian Commerce Minister and European Trade Commissioner observed that the US was asking too much from others in exchange for doing too little itself. The US described these allegations as false and misleading.

During 2007, WTO talks of the G-4 in Germany did not succeed. Intentions of the European nations and USA were quite clear. They wanted to pour their cheap food grains in developing countries and were emphasizing that developing countries must open their markets but were not agreeing to reduce subsidy to their farmers. They even attempted to put a wedge in the unity of developing nations. After their attempts failed, USA put taxes on jewellery and some other Indian products. Presently, an American family pays on an average US$ 320 a year in farm subsidies, through higher taxes and higher food prices, as per a recent study by the Heritage Foundation. These subsidies, particularly for cotton, increase poverty in Africa by reducing the cost of American cotton, which results in depression of prices of African cotton produced by small farmers. Similarly on emission of greenhouse gases, increasing global warming, the developed countries which have been emitting these gases are trying to impose cut on carbon emission by the developing countries.

However, if we look at the per capita carbon emission data, the US emits carbon 20 tons, EU 10-15 tons and India only one ton. Despite this the developed countries do not want spend on reduction of their carbon emissions. In 2008 WTO meetings India and other developing nations were again disappointed. Developed nations are not prepared to sacrifice even a bit. They want that countries like India, China, Brazil and South Africa should bear entire load. According to many if these proposals are accepted developing nations will not be able to safeguard their economy. UN is eyeing globally on ecological disasters. There is likelihood of loss of Aral Sea to Soviet-era irrigation and the melting of Himalayan glaciers (feeding rivers for quenching the thirst of 500 million people). China is planning to dam upper Mekong, reducing water flow to about 65 million South-eastern Asians. As long as globalization increases industrialization, climate change will continue. If climate change has been caused by West it is their responsibility to help correct it, otherwise climate change will be taken as an act of aggression by rich against the poor.

Subsidies

Domestic subsidies in India fall in two categories, namely

(i) non-product specific subsidies given for fertilizers, water, electricity, seeds and credit, and (ii) product specific subsidies given for specific crops, in the form of support price given for about 20 agricultural commodities. According to the calculation of the Ministry of Commerce, the total aggregate value of our product and non-specific subsidies (total AMS) the average of three years (1986-87 to 1988-89) was minus. About 76 percent of agricultural holdings in our country consist of less than two hectares and they account for 29 per cent of the area. None of the seven export subsidies listed in the Uruguay Agreement is being provided to farmers/exporters in India.

With increase in production and export subsidies as well as volume of dumping exports, international prices of agricultural commodities will rise and this will help our country to make exports more competitive in world markets. We have potential to increase, agricultural exports of a wide variety of products particularly rice, wheat, cotton, jute, potatoes, sugar, fish, meat, fruits and vegetables etc. The terms of trade will shift in favour of agricultural products and create additional purchasing power in rural areas in the next few years. A part of additional purchasing power will be ploughed back as investment in agriculture, which will further accelerate agricultural production.

An eight-member delegation of the USDA called on the Minister of State for Agriculture on May 14th, 1998 to discuss the ongoing bilateral cooperation in agricultural research, plant protection, etc. Both sides agreed to have further deliberations on various issues between the officials from the US Agriculture Research Agency and the Government of India Directorate of Plant Protection and Quarantine. According to the Prime Minister of India, the country has achieved food security. The I.C.A.R. has played a pivotal role in these accomplishments.

He also said that the challenge before us is how we can double our food production to become a major exporter of food in next ten years. Our GDP growth target of 7-8 percent cannot be accomplished unless we achieve 4-5 percent growth in agriculture. Higher investments in agricultural research and education will be made for better utilization of financial and human resources. According to him a policy on optimum use of land, water and genetic resources will soon be launched in a sustainable manner. It will include consolidation of land, use of 80 million hectares of marginal and wastelands, agro-forestry and improvement of rural marketing infrastructure. The policy is to boost up agro-processing industries and agribusiness in rural areas to increase farm income, and help resolve rural employment problem.

Indian Medicinal Plants

India is an emporium of spices, medicinal and aromatic plants. Nearly 80 percent of the drugs mentioned in pharmaceuticals are available in natural form in this country. This nation embraces tropical, subtropical and temperate zones in plains, valleys and hills. There are humid, arid, semiarid and dry regions, with or without irrigation. The traditional medicine in this country functions mainly with oral communications in rural areas. Thousands of birth attendants or Dayees, bone setters, skilled acupressure technicians, eye surgeons or Satias, snake bite specialists and herbal physicians (Vaidyas) form an autonomous community supporting public health system. A second system is the classical society of scientific practitioners. Traditional system consists of those with organized medicinal foundation explained in ancient classical literature like Charak Samhita, Sushruta Samhita and other manuscripts covering treaties on different branches of medicines, like Ayurveda, Siddha, Unani and Tibetan. The major resource base of traditional treatments is mainly plants, supplemented by animal products and minerals.

Gardens for conservation of plants are about 30 large and medium size botanical gardens and about 125 small units of some private parties or botany department of universities. The

ICAR is operating an All India Coordinated Research Project on Medicinal and Aromatic plants. The Central Council of Research in *Ayurveda* and *Siddha* (CCRAS) has four farms for maintaining about 300 plant species for planting by growers for pharmaceutical or research purposes. The Council of Scientific and Industrial Research (CSIR) has three institutions for research in cultivation of more than 25 species of medicinal plants being used in modern medicine. In addition to the above there are two state funded research institutes, which maintain more than 100 medicinal plant varieties, including endangered species and wild plants, in addition to several private companies.

There is little updating in available information, at the world level on changing demand of phyto-chemicals and their analogues to plan production for export. Stray report in Trade journals suggest that market for tropane alkaloids is estimated to be about US$ 100 million per annum and the price of hyocyamine or scopolamine varies between US$ 350-1400 per Kg. Digitoxin costs about US$ 1100 per Kg. and digoxin sells at an even higher price. These items can be produced in India. However, since there is very little local demand and since large manufacturers import basic chemicals to formulate the end products there is little commercial cultivation. As far as Periwinkle cultivation or manufacture of its VLB alkaloids are concerned, 500 Kg. leaves produce 1 gm of pure vincristine.

Thus India is the third largest producer in the world. Many of these items are highly labour intensive and India has a relative advantage. For example, in the manufacture of Jasmine and Rosa Otto, there is no device to pick up flowers daily and industry has to depend on human labour. Despite the diverse nature of the crops grown in the country and existence of a fast growing pharmaceutical industrial sector, the share of India in the world market, at present is estimated at 0.05 per cent, which is quite insignificant, considering the large geographical area of the country. This also was possible because of improved input in cultivation efficient management of the farm sector. In the 1st phase (1947-70) the food crop production was improved followed by high value, medicinal and aromatic crop production in the 2nd phase (1971 onwards). ICAR is now giving due emphasis in the third phase to the plantation crops (Table 3.2) as the same have remote chances of losing markets through introduction of synthetics in the near future.

Table 3.2: Export of Top 10 Fast Growing Crude Drugs Derived from Phyto-chemicals.

(Rs. crore)

S. No.	Commodity	2004-05	Growth rate
1	. Sarsaparilla	499.08	10.07
2	Galangal Rhizomes-Roots	369.20	1.81
3	Ipecac Dried Rhizomes-Roots	25.02	0.86
4	Liquorice Roots	243.53	0.39
5	Unab (Indian/ Chines Jujube)	227.50	0.03
6	Basil, Hyasop, Rose Mary	192.85	2.24
7	Cambodge Dried Fruit Rind	171.33	0.90
8	Psyllium Husk (Isabgol Husk)	162.78	154.00
9	Chirayta	113.01	0.46
10	Cascara Sagrada Bark	56.58	0.44
Totao exports of 40 items		263.08	

Up to the first phase, i.e. early seventies, two thirds of India's exports in the field of plant derivatives were from the forestry sector. By the mid-1980s, this scenario had radically changed. India is now exporting 80 percent of these materials emanating from the farm sector. The average exports of the raw materials and intermediary chemicals during the last decade were of the order Rs. 1,200 millions annually or about US$ 30 millions only. Chemexil/Pharmexcil (Bombay, now Mumbai) visualizes it will rise to Rs. 8,500 millions annually by the end of the decade. The decade of nineties will go down in the Indian history for heralding liberalization in the farm based economy. In quantity as well as value Psyllium export is 35.6 percent. It is obtained from a plant species Plantago, which is cultivated maximally in Gujarat, Rajasthan and M.P. The 2nd highest exported commodity was Senna (18.9 percent) followed by Henna (7.1 percent). Export of plant extracts constituted 31.2 percent in terms of value. The remaining exports consisted of myrobalans. Cassia tora seeds, sandalwood chips/dust, karaya gum, jojoba seeds, pepper long and pyrethrum.

The present scenario has brought liberalization in imports, reduction in duties and connected both demand and prices of local farm produce with the global market economy by developing strong international linkages. Major importers of crude drugs are Western Europe, USA and Japan. This is going to influence markets for several traditionally grown crops in India.

Seed Industry

The Seed Industry in the British period was largely confined to a few ornamental plants and vegetable crops but not even for cereals what to say of other crops. Thus, as late as in the 1950s the raising of seed crops was economically unattractive. When the ICAR wanted to rapidly multiply high yielding varieties of wheat in 1965, it had to canvass to organize a seed village in a block in Delhi state. When the farmers found that they get a highly remunerative price for seeds of dwarf wheat varieties, they developed their own rapid seed multiplication technology by dribbling seeds at wide distances for increasing the multiplication ratio to more than 1:100. Every farmer in the block village took up seed production as against traditional grain production. Assured remunerative prices and marketing opportunities encouraged farmers to take up seed farming;

From the First Five Year Plan onwards, there has been ample emphasis on seed production and the Government of India setup in 1963 a National Seeds Corporation (NSC) with technical help from the Rockefeller Foundation. Initially, NSC was set up primarily for production and distribution of seeds of hybrid maize, hybrid sorghum (Jowar) and hybrid pearl millet (Bajra). The Government of India took several steps to promote seed production industry and coordinated yield trials for yield potential assessment of new varieties through the agency of ICAR. As a part of the Seed Act, a central Variety Release Committee was also established to release high yielding varieties.

The Nucleus or Breeder's seed, which is the highest form of the seed developed by a multidisciplinary team of scientists or an agricultural institute or an agricultural university is further multiplied as foundation seed. Foundation seed is further multiplied through the agency of selected registered growers or government farms or NGOs as certified seed after proper inspections.

The US showed its concern in Global Bio-diversity Convention in 1992 to the provisions of effective IPR. The patenting of Biotechnological inventions and particularly natural genes will hamper free exchange of germ-plasm. Biotechnological industry of the developed nations is keen to strengthen patenting laws of products, processes and by products. The casualty of this trend will be global food security. Seeds provide the most effective safety net for poor farmers. Good seeds with tolerance to a range of biotic and a-biotic stress, can help small farmers to achieve goals of increasing productivity and reducing cost of production. As the role of private sector in seed industry, is increasing in India, it is also helpful for jobs in villages and for triggering economic growth strategy too. In any policy on job oriented economic growth strategy in rural areas, seed technology will occupy a pivotal position. India has potential to become one of the world leaders in seed technology and trade if right decisions are implemented soon.

Terminator Technology

The patenting of gene controlled terminator technology in

the US has added fuel to social apprehensions in India. This has recently been seen as a big threat to the farmers of the developing countries. In India most of the farmers use their home-grown seeds. If one visits the Kullu valley in HP. during Dussehra festival, good looking maize cobs will be found hanging on the door. These are the cobs from which seeds for the next sowing will be taken out. Since the grains produced from the seed based on the terminator technology will be devoid of the regenerative capacity the farmers using them will become totally dependent on the market for seeds in the next season. Majority of Indian farmers still use home grown seeds to the extent of more than 90 percent (with the exception of oil seeds, where the percentage is less) the terminator technology has great implications for the farming in India. Therefore, most of the farmers consider the use of terminator genes as unethical.· Thus the social apprehensions about this technology in the context of emerging intellectual property rights (IPR) of the World Trade Organization (WTO) have increased tremendously in India (Mishra,1999) and developing nations.

For alleviating the economic problems in rural India, technical progress has long been advocated. This approach has indeed brought some results, so much so that India has become self sufficient in food grains from a position of net importer of food grains in the fifties and sixties. In intellectual property protection, through patents, agriculture is generally excluded. In the Indian Patent Act of 1970, agriculture and horticulture have been excluded from patentability. The Trade Related Aspects of Intellectual Rights (TRIPS) agreement is unique in this regard as it explicitly includes protection of agriculture including plant varieties, under article 27. Patents shall be available for any inventions, whether products or processes in the fields of technology, provided they are new, involve an inventive step and are capable of industrial applications. Patents shall be enjoyable without discrimination as to the place of invention, the field of technology and whether products are imported or locally produced. Members may exclude from patentability inventions, the prevention within their territory of commercial exploitation. This is necessary to protect human, animal or plant life or health or to avoid serious prejudices to the environment, provided that such exclusion is not made merely because the exploitation is prohibited by domestic law.

Members may exclude from patentability plants and animals other than micro organisms and essentially biological processes for the production of plants and animals other than non-biological and microbiological processes. However, Members shall provide for the protection of plant varieties either by patents or by an effective *sui-generis* system or by any combination thereof. This is unique in that plant varieties are not patentable under laws of even industrially advanced countries with the exception of the US. For example, the European Patent convention does not approve patentability of plant and animal varieties or essentially biological process for production of plants and animals. In India, the above provision was a source of debate in the mid-Nineties when Dunkel draft on GATT was under consideration.

Even eminent and highly responsible people viewed this provision with apprehensions. Therefore, the then Director General of GATT, Peter Sutherland chose to clarify the position through the Indian Press during his visit to India. However, with the creation of the WTO, it is incumbent upon the member countries to have a legal system to provide protection of plant varieties. The legal system should be conducive to the Indian farming systems and at the same time it should protect the rights of farmers and those of plant breeders. It should also be consistent with the objectives of conservation of bio-diversity. It may be noted that for India the losses from the deals are significant, there are potential gains also, depending on how much we can exploit them. Among the important clauses pertaining to agriculture are: The value of direct export subsidies will have to be cut by 36 per cent and volume by 21 percent over the next 6 years by developed nations. It was expected that subsidies would be phased out by that time by developed nations.

Trade distortion support for farmers is to be cut by 20 percent over 6 years for developed nations and by 13.3 percent over 10 years.

Developed nations with markets closed to agriculture must open them by 3 percent, raising it gradually to a minimum of 5 percent over 6 years. Japan will open 4 percent of its imports of rice and South Korea by 1 percent only.

India is exempt from each of these regulations. If the Aggregate Measure of Support (AMS) for agriculture is more than 10 percent, it has to be phased out. For India, this varies between five and seven percent. If agriculture sector is fully liberalized, the total markets of all importing countries are expected to open up by about US$ 50 billion. Due to the unity of developing countries in Doha and Cancun discussions developed nations yielded, in Geneva meetings, to the demands to reduce their subsidies on agriculture and export to some extent. The same are good news to the poor farmers throughout the globe and would make the world trade easier.

There are several countries which are dependent for their food production on other nations. For example Saudi Arabia, Kuwait, Qatar and other middle-eastern nations have surplus oil and natural gas resources but have to import food articles from foreign countries. Therefore these nations consider that if they are able to procure agricultural lands on rent they would be able to fulfil their food requirements. They have made agreement with Indonesia for paddy production and are having eyes on Pakistan, Kazakistan, Myanmar, Philippines etc.

Patentable Agriculture in TRIPS: An interesting aspect of the TRIPS agreement is the language on provisions relating to exclusions from patentability. If we look at the language of Article 27.3(b) critically, all Member countries are free to decide whether or not to treat the plants and animals patentable. Depending on their choice Members are free to provide legal protection of plants and animals. In the US plant varieties are protected under its usual plant patent laws and also under the US Patent and Trademark laws.

The Government of India has initiated a serious thinking, on the issues of evolving a plant variety protection after considering the above mentioned features. The government has now steered a model bill for protection of Plant Varieties and Farmers Rights bill as also the Biodiversity bill passed in Parliament to ensure protection of our indigenous materials from depredations by Multinationals and the same is reported to be in final stage of action.

The UPOV Approach: It represents the views of the developed countries about the significance and modus operandi for protection of new plants varieties. In the developed nations there has been awakening for protection on new varieties for quite sometime, 50 to 70 years back. In 1930, the US created a special form of protection (limited to vegetative reproduction of varieties of plants, which precisely reproduced themselves) and called a Plant Patent. In the Netherlands, the Breeders Ordinance of 1941 granted a limited exclusive right for breeders of agriculturally important species to market the first generation of certified seed but an exclusive right to market propagating material of other species. In Germany, after many years of limited protection for breeders based upon seed certification, the Law on Protection of Varieties and the Seeds of Cultivated Plants of 1953 gave breeders the exclusive rights to produce seed of their varieties for purposes of seed trade.

The organization of the International Convention for the Protection of New Varieties of Plants (UPOV) by a Diplomatic Conference in Paris provided, for the first time, recognition of the rights of plant breeders on international basis. Thus UPOV came into existence of December 2, 1961 but was implemented only in 1968, with its headquarters based in Geneva. Since then there have been many modifications in UPOV, which was revised three times, i.e. in 1972, 1978 and 1991.

Bio-diversity and Variety Protection

According to a UNDP Human Development report of 1944 the developing world is the home of major global diversity the developed nations are the home of most technologies converting biodiversity into economic wealth. The painful outcome of the present day development path-ways is the fact that 84 percent of the world's income is going to 20 percent population. The poor 80 percent is getting only 16 percent of global annual income. Thus the rich are becoming richer and the poor are becoming poorer.

Bio-diversity is the back-bone source for development of new varieties. There are however areas of conflict between variety production and bio-diversity. Plant variety protection is governed purely by market forces, whereas bio-diversity is mainly government supported because of ever increasing loss. The global convention on bio-diversity was attended by over 150 nations in Rio de Janeiro in June 1992. Bio-diversity refers to totality of species, populations, communities and ecosystems, both wild and domesticated that constitute life of one area or of the entire planet. Others define it as a totality of genes, species and ecosystem in a region. Thus bio-diversity is composed of genetic diversity, species diversity and ecosystem diversity. Genetic diversity is the hallmark of life on earth and relates to the variety of species within a region.

Ecosystem diversity refers to variation in the ecosystem in a nation. The greater the bio-diversity in a region, the greater would be the benefits to the people. Diversity of the species and ecosystems influence productivity and services provided by the ecosystem. Diversity of species is desirable in that people can select species of their choice. Species diversity has provided food, fibres and items of medicine and health care in the old world. In India, since ancient times (around 6,000 BC.), domesticated animals and plants afforded food and fibre. Forests provided aromatic and medicinal plants besides wood. Genetic diversity in crops is of special value. It gives an insurance against crop losses due to pests and diseases and in many cases important aroma in food articles, liked by people. In present times when the possibility of evolving suitable varieties increased through genetic manipulations, the importance of genetic diversity has tremendously increased. For the purpose of seed industry, crops can be classified into three major groups.

First group consists of the self-pollinated cereals like rice and wheat. The farmers generally keep their own seed and change seeds when or a better variety becomes available. Second group is that of the cross-pollinated crops which require special methods of seed production. There is a distinction between hybridization inherent in breeding and the use of F1 hybrids to take advantage of heterosis or the hybrid vigour. In the US, the use of F1 hybrids revolutionized corn or maize production and was introduced in India also. In India, hybrid cotton was produced by hand emasculation and pollination. Thus, India became the first nation to start hybrid cotton production. The third group is vegitatively-propagated crops.

The horticultural crops like potato, colocasia, turmeric and many ornamentals are propagated by underground tuber or bulbs or corms etc. In the case of fruit trees like mango and citrus etc. buds, cuttings or grafts are used for raising orchards. It can also be used in plantation crops like coffee. Recently in all these crops there have been tremendous advances in seed production technology. Micro, mini as well as mist propagation methods have helped to accelerate multiplication of clonally propagated material. Today, the biological diversity is being eroded at a much faster speed than any time.

According to the best estimates around 10 million species live on earth and tropical forests house between 50 and 90 percent of this total. About 17 million hectares of forests are now being cleared annually and about 5 to 10 percent of species may face extinction within the next thirty years or so. About 60,000 of the world's 240,000 plant species and perhaps even higher proportion of vertebrates and insects could become extinct within the next three decades. There have been rapid losses of habitat, species and ecosystems in this century. This has been accompanied by loss in genetic diversity. With the advent and spread of Green Revolution varieties of rice, wheat, maize, potato as well as land races in many countries including India have disappeared. In 1991, the genetic similarity of Brazil's orange trees opened the way for the worst outbreak of canker disease recorded in that country. In 1970, the US farmers lost US$ 1 billion to a disease that swept through uniformly susceptible corn varieties. Similarly, the Irish potato famine of 1846, the loss of Soviet wheat crop in 1972 and the outbreak of Citrus canker in Florida in 1984 all stemmed from reduction in genetic diversity.

Ecologists and even Economists have long been advocating for initiating the steps for conservation of bio-diversity. Because of such concerns, international organizations have responded and half a dozen international conventions have taken place since 1971. In 1983, the FAO International Undertaking on Plant Genetic Resources was commissioned in Rome. In 1992, the Convention on Biological Diversity was signed as an outcome of the Earth Summit at Rio de Janeiro. In 1993, the Crucible Group was born which recommended special privileges for rural and indigenous societies for their traditional knowledge. In December 1993, the CBD became operational for ensuring implementation of, (i) conservation of Bio-diversity, (ii) sustainable use of its components and (iii) fair and equitable sharing of benefits of the use of genetic resources. The CBD resolved; "Reaffirming that States have Sovereign rights over their own biological resources and reaffirming that the States are responsible for conserving their biological diversity and for using their biological resources in a sustainable manner" (Mishra, 1999).

In India the case for bio-diversity protection with appropriate property rights to local communities has been advanced. It has been observed that India must try to promote continued cultivation of thousands of land races of rice and husbanding of hundreds of different breeds of cattle in its strategy to conserve bio-diversity. A formulation of appropriate property rights for the tribal communities in medicinal and aromatic plant resources has also been advocated as these have transnational connotations. With the legal framework for bio-diversity, the Farmers' and the local Community Rights will be entrenched. A country or a multinational desirous of using the genetic resources of another country will have to abide by the rules or prior informed consent (PIC). For proper compensation to farmers or communities, mechanisms are being evolved.

Thus plant variety protection has to fall in line with the intellectual properties contributed by biodiversity. This will entail significant changes in the existing convention on plant variety protection as continued emphasis on bio-diversity in member countries will entail larger demands on intellectual property associated with plant variety protection. The greater the use of plant genetic resources from India and developing countries, the larger will be the share of India and developing countries in benefits on account a "Farmers Right" and the rights of "Indigenous community". With increase in global population (particularly in India) the land available for cultivation is dwindling, agricultural scientists are trying to identify more productive and profitable cropping systems. Potato and other short duration crops, fit in nicely into several multiple and intercropping systems, thus increasing cropping intensity, production for exports and productivity of the land (Nagaich, 1981).

Stimulation of crop growth and development can be expected to play a major role in cropping system optimization, which is on the verge of furthering production technology and productivity in India. The new technologies developed through research should not remain thin the four walls of laboratories. In spite of the strides made in agricultural research and development, there are potentially productive eastern states of India the average yields of which are about half of the national average and much less than the global average, due to poor irrigation and infrastructure investments. This calls for urgent need to gear up extension and financial assistance activities so that the modern production technologies reach the farmers of not only low productivity states but of the other states as well.

Thus by raising the average yields of the low productivity states to the present national average, agricultural production in the country can be increased substantially. There is no doubt that agricultural, economic and demographic trends will pose a tough challenge for the countries fragile environment. On one hand, resources such as water and land will be in short supply, while on the other hand available supply will likely suffer from severe contamination due to increase in industrial and agricultural activity. Consequently, the country will have to face more cases of water and land conflicts. Economic growth can reduce some of these problems. However, previous trends indicate that economic growth is adding to this stress rather than reducing it.

Inefficient Public Distribution System (PDS)

Lester Brown of the Worldwatch Institute predicts India will have 45 MT of grains by 2030. The Indian Economic survey mentions that between 1990-91 and 1996-97, grain production went up by 1.7 percent annually, less than the rate of 1.9 percent our population is expected to grow during 1997-2002. For 35 percent, who live on or below the poverty line this prediction makes no difference. According to a World Bank report of 1993-94, they get one square meal to manage to ward off malnourishment. Due to high subsidies on food and agriculture coupled with several employment and loan programs, the country warded off famines and food crisis .After liberalization, the nation actually spent more of its expenditure 2.3 to 3.2 percent in 1990-91 to 1997-98.

After green revolution, food grains and potato production and yields doubled in last three decades, faster than in the US. Thus India's per capita availability of food grains has grown up slowly from 395 gms in 1951 to 512 in 1997. The PDS, initiated to protect small farmers and poor consumers, now gets about 20.9 million tons against 13 million tons in 1980-81. However, the states making greatest use of the PDS are not necessarily the poorest. In 1993, about 43 percent of the food grains supplied through the ration shops reached the poorest. Studies found major discrepancies in the PDS system, which is almost half of the poverty alleviation expenditure. Kerala and Andhra Pradesh are the maximum beneficiaries from PDS but not UP and Bihar, which should corner more than 26 percent of the PDS-they get only about 13 percent. PDS also failed to transfer grain from surplus to deficit states like Bihar, Orissa and MP which have high rate of poverty and hunger, resulting in a slight declining trend in calorie intake.

Even after 60 years of freedom, per capita consumption of the poorest remains below recommended levels of nutrition. A study in 1997 showed that the Central Government actually spent Rs. 4.35 to transfer income of Rs. 1.00 to the poorest. Such a poor progress at a very high cost! India's poor health records (again in UP., Bihar, Orissa and MP) indicate the inefficiency in the field of nutrition. Nearly half of the children below five are malnourished, low weight since birth due to the poor health of mothers also. Three fifths of all females and three fourths of pregnant women suffer from anaemia. One fourth of mothers dying in the globe are Indians. This puts India to shame-a country being one of the highest food producers in the world has an inefficient PDS (Shastri, Outlook, October 1998).

Indian Women and Agriculture

It is a happy coincidence that women (particularly rural/farm women) have recently attracted attention in many nations, especially in India. The nature as also the extent of involvement of farm-women in agriculture varied from region to region. Within a region also women's involvement differs widely due to ecology and farm practices. Despite these variations, there is hardly any activity in agriculture in which women are not involved. According to a census in 1991 the number of male workers in agriculture sector has increased by about 31.5 percent, whereas number of female workers increased by about 36.2 percent, probably because more males have shifted to other sectors paying higher wages. Nearly 60 percent of agricultural practices like planting of seeds, seedling-transplantation, winnowing, grain storage etc. are almost totally handled by women whereas in other operations they work with men.

In the second half of the 1990s labour force participation in rural areas is on slight decline, mainly because of women retreating to home-work and also because of partial mechanization of agriculture. At the national level about 45 percent of women were part of the labour force for 1999-2000, a decline from 49 percent in 1993-94. Out of all the states, Arunachal, Goa, Haryana, Punjab and J&K have shown largest decline. Some of the big states like U.P. and M.P., had very low decline in female labour force and some eastern states like Nagaland, Mizoram and Bihar had a rise of 12 to 33 percent. In spite of their predominant role, women did not get same importance as men, particularly in scientific education and training. They form the largest group of landless labourers, yet agricultural development and management programs are generally managed by men. Mechanization, which generally helps in heavy operations, is the responsibility of men.

Normally agricultural services still prefer males. Group discussions, meetings and training involve mostly men. Technology and credit are important factors for agricultural development but women are rarely encouraged to access to these resources for increased production. They are mostly questioned on the pretext that they are not the owners or they are not the managers of production. The on-going loaning procedures are cumbersome.

About 300 million people are malnourished in India. The effects of the green revolution are beginning to fade with agricultural production reaching a plateau. With population expected to reach nearly 1.5 billion by 2050, agricultural output is required to double. Shortages of irrigation water, higher salinity and water logging of soil will add to the problem of food scarcity. Agricultural biotechnology is likely to mitigate the problem of food security in the 21st century. For generations, improvement and selection of agriculturally important plant species has been continuously going on by of incorporating desirable characters through plant breeding. To sum up, female work force increased from 22 to 25 percent between 1991 and 2001. While the size of male work force has increased by over 10 million between 1991 and 2001, the size female work force almost doubled. Mizoram has the highest (47 percent) female work participation rate. H.P. has the highest (86 percent) percentage of female cultivators. It also has the highest (89 percent) female cultivators and female workers counted together. Bihar has the highest (63 percent) female agricultural labourers (ICAR News, January-March, 2008).

Recent Technological Improvements

A revolution in molecular biology during the past two decades has enabled genetic engineering, which possess novel characters. With the help of modern molecular biology, scientists have incorporated desirable traits through selected genes or chromosome portions. Indian scientists must jump into the super fast vehicles of genetic engineering or molecular biology to increase production to surpass population explosion in the new millennium. Recently, the US, Canada, Mexico, Australia and South Africa as well as China have developed cultivars through modern technology and are referred to as transgenic or genetically engineered crops.

Several crops like maize, potato, canola, soybean, cotton etc. have been engineered to make them insect resistant or herbicide tolerant. Thus insecticide applications are reduced to minimize pollution of ground water. As a result about half the soybean produce and about one-third of the world's maize production is from varieties genetically engineered. In, many developed nations, particularly in Europe, however there has been strong opposition to transgenic farmers, consumers, health workers and environmentalists. India also faced opposition to transgenic BT cotton in 2002. Since faith in government regulatory agencies is very high in the US, the commercial use of transgenic crops in the country was readily accepted there, although organic produce fetches very high price as compared to inorganic farming.

Among the countries that grew genetically modified crops USA is at the top, representing 74 percent of the global area, followed by Argentina (15 percent) and Canada (10 percent): The next generation of cultivars promise pest resistance, enhanced nutrition, healthy oils, more vitamins and a long shelf life. Productivity on farms is only one-fourth of what it is in non-farm areas. Rice yields are half of what they are in Vietnam and a third of what they are in China. India's cotton yields are even worse as compared to other cotton producing nations. Wheat yields are only three-fourth of China's. Only tea in India is more productive than its Asian rivals. Potato productivity not low because of short duration of the crop in India, if per day yield are considered.

In India, increase in salinity is resulting in several million acres of highly productive land losing fertility. The worst affected area lies in the Indo-Gangetic belt, which is the most important agricultural belt in the country, having approximately 35 percent of the saline area of the entire nation. This situation is likely to worsen further in the food production in the new century as none of the six most important food crops namely, wheat, rice, maize potato, sugarcane and soybean are salt tolerant. Scientists have recently developed modern technology to engineer salt tolerant varieties. It should be feasible to develop a spectrum of cultivars and trees, which tolerate high salt contents and can be irrigated with saline waters. It is important for India to engineer crops either tolerant to salinity or to acidity or to drought and heat or frost. Presence of these characters will help contribute to food security in the future, as Indian population explodes. Genetically engineered plants also offer entirely new benefits like vaccines against human diseases, protein richness or high mineral content. It is therefore, essential to strengthen variety improvement programs in the ICAR institutes and the agricultural universities adapting genetic engineering and bio-safety issues to reap the additional benefits, besides food security.

India's share of land resource is only 2.4 percent, but it sustains 18 percent and 15 percent of global human and livestock populations, respectively. Population in India has already crossed 1 billion and pressure on land is continuously increasing. About 57 percent of the total area of the country is suffering from various problems like salinity (as mentioned earlier), water or wind erosion, chemical or physical deterioration, degradation due to mining, quarrying, landslides, floods and urbanization. India has a net 51 percent cultivated area of about 142 million hectares, which is more than that of China and next only to that of the US whereas the world average of cultivated area is only 11 percent. Per capita availability of cropland is, at present, 0.14 ha. but is declining every year due to diversion of land for non-agricultural uses as well as increase in population.

This indicates a bleak future, with no scope for horizontal expansion and it calls far a serious national drive for population control. The net irrigated area (only 35 percent) has increased from 22.55 million ha. in 1950 to 55 million ha. Presently, which is highest in the world. Cropping intensity has increased slightly from 110 percent to about 133 percent. Therefore, any increase in production in future can come through only by vertical expansion, i.e. another green revolution through improved varieties, balanced input use, increasing cropping intensity by about 25 percent (using more leguminous crops) and by use of efficient farm power & farm machinery as well as prevention of pre-and post-harvest losses.

Due to high temperatures as well as due to continuous cultivation for centuries, Indian soils are low in organic matter and in fertility. Nitrogen deficiency is predominant as also, to a lesser extent, those of P and Zn etc. Erosion takes a heavy toll by washing away several billion tons of fertile top soil resulting into a heavy loss of several million tons of valuable nutrients and consequently food production is less. Therefore, an integrated and balance approach of water and nutrient management as also pesticide application has to be evolved for improving sustainability of farming. These approaches will have to be separate for each agro-climatic zone, with both short-term and long-term strategies. India, having about 18 percent of global population has about only 4 percent of water resources in the world for meeting the requirement of roughly 2.45 percent of area on the globe.

Therefore, it is evident that following natural balance Indian population should not have been what it is today. Country's total water requirement in 2050 would hardly match the estimated utilizable water resources. It is therefore, imperative that we aim at reducing water requirements through improvement in efficiency in water use. Integrated water-use management strategy will be highly critical in the present century as India moves towards sustainable agriculture, maintaining natural resources reserves. The national water policy of the government of India also emphasizes on effective and economical management of Indian water resources and has emphasized prevention of salinity increase, water harvesting, adoption of appropriate crops and cropping systems as well as recycling or reuse of poor quality waters.

High Prices and Global Food Insecurity

In the beginning of the year 2008 global insecurity of food grains rose to a high level mainly due to price rise of chemicals and fuels, because of insufficient investments in agriculture, population increases as well as diversion of food grains for ethanol production. Recently President George Bush and Foreign Secretary Condoleezza Rice gave statements that food insecurity and high prices were mainly because of policies in India and China. According to them in these nations income of middle class population increased resulting into high demands for nutritious food articles. According to India and China consumption of food grains in India and China is much less than that in the US.

The FAO report also corroborates the same story as grain consumption in the US is much more than that in India and China. In 2006-08 India consumed 3904 million tons of food grains, China consumed 7713 million tons and the US consumed 5880 million tons. Increased consumption in India was about 2.19 percent during this period whereas that in China it was 1.80 percent and in the US it was 11.81 percent. Last year about 30 million tons of maize was converted into bio-fuel in the US. Therefore, this led to increased food prices globally and many of the developing countries had to impose ban on their food grain exports mainly due to food insecurity, in some countries leading to food riots.

According to the report of the USDA for 2007, per capita consumption of food grains in the US was 946 kg in 2003. It increased to 1046 kg last year whereas in India it remained more or less stable during the same period. Not only grain consumption but milk consumption in the US also left India and China far behind. Per capita consumption of milk in the US is 78 kg whereas in India it is 36 kg and in China it is only 11kg. The same is the story about meat and poultry product consumption. In the US per capita meat consumption is about 53 kg whereas in India it is only 1.6 kg and in China about 5.9 kg. Per capita consumption of drinks in the US averages about 0.30 per day and in India it is 0.20 only.

From the report of 'World Food Program' of the UN it is evident that recently there were riots in several nations because of food shortages. Of these Mexico, Argentina, Morocco, Senegal, Guiana, Mozambique, Egypt, Yemen, Indonesia and

Bangladesh are prominent. According to the estimates of the World Bank, due to very high prices of the food grains, poor people of the developing countries have heavily cut down the expenditures on medicines, which they were earlier incurring. This has resulted into heavy malnutrition and death of people due to diseases in many nations. Stoppage of exports food grains by developed countries have led to the unprecedented famine like situation, which was neither predicted by Economists nor by Agricultural Scientists. In the FAO Annual Estimates Report it has been mentioned that up to 2017 wheat prices can go up by 60 percent, vegetable oil can become costlier by 80 percent. One of the main reasons for this is production of bio-fuel in the farm lands. Other important reasons are higher rate of consumption in developing countries and destruction of crops in many nations.

4

Indo-US Cooperation in Other Sectors

B.B. Nagaich

Trade was the earliest important link between India and the US. By 1850, at least one ship arrived in Bombay (Now Mumbai) every month. One ship, George, made 21 round trips. The main exports from the US were tobacco, naval stores, copper, pitch, rosin and pine boards etc. India in turn exported wool, oil seeds/hides, medicinal drugs, sandal wood, silk, cotton, tea, sugar, spices, indigo, ivory and salt petre. Among other things, the American sailors brought back with them were art-works and Sanskrit books. These books reached the US at a time when the country was witnessing an intellectual ferment and profoundly influenced some of the leading US thinkers of that period. Ralph Waldo Emersson read English translations of the Bhagvat Gita, Vishnu Purana, Kathopanishad and the Code of Manu and his works reflected Indian influence.

Another thinker who liked Indian philosophy was Henry David Thoreau. The list of other American luminaries, well versed with Indian sages, include Herman Melville, Walt Whitman, T.S. Eliot, George Santayana. While some American luminaries were discovering India through books, many others travelled to India covering thousands of Kilometres to see the country with their own eyes. In India, I found a race of mortals living upon the earth but not adhering to it, inhabiting cities, but not fixed to them, possessing everything but possessed by nothing (Appollonius Tyanaeus). They were Bayard Taylor, a correspondent of the New York Tribune, and Mark Twain. After his return from India Mark Twain said "the only land I ever day dream about or deeply long to see again." The last century also saw many US Missionaries visiting India. The distinguished names include Issabella Thoburn, Clara Swain, Ida Scudder, William Wanless, and Mary Reed. Margaret Wilson (the eldest daughter of President Woodrow Wilson) was so profoundly influenced by the Indian philosophy that she spent her last five years in Pondicherry, in South India. Other Americans, who have carved out a niche for themselves in India, are Margaret Sanger, Samuel Evans Stokes.

Prominent Indians in US

Amongst the Indians who made a significant impact in the US, was Swami Vivekananda, who came to attend the World Parliament of Religions in 1883 at Chicago. He lectured across the country and founded the American Vedanta Society. Paramhansa Yogananda was another person, who influenced American spiritual thoughts and whose autobiography, 'autobiography of Yogi' has gone into several editions in the US. Some of the other prominent Indians were J. Krishnamurthy and Maharishi Mahesh Yogi. The US was also visited by Rabindranath Tagore in 1912, 1916 and again in 1920. Six of his poems from Gitanjali were published in a prestigious poetry magazine, before Tagore was awarded Nobel Prize. The US was also visited by Rabindranath Tagore in 1912, 1916 and again in 1920. India and the US have had several opportunities for exchange of each other's artists along with their arts. Ruth St. Denis, a US dancer incorporated Indian dance forms and traditions in her work. Her dances, like "Radha" and "Lakme'" became famous in India.

Thereafter, the US and Indian artists - Uday Shankar, Ravi Shankar, Mahalia Jackson, Ali Akbar Khan, Zubin Mehta, Indrani Rahman, Balasaraswathi, Duke Ellington, Sonal Man Singh, Mangeshkar sisters (Lata, Asha and Usha), Michael Jackson and many others like Bismillah Khan, H.P. Chaurasia have regaled Indian audiences in both the nations. Ananda Coomaraswami did a lot more than others to explain about

India in the US through Boston Museum of Fine Arts. Through his articles, monographs and books, he did a good job of interpreting the spiritual base of the Indian art and Culture to the West. Satyajit Ray is another personality who brought a more realistic appreciation of India in the US through his cinema (movie) films.

Dalip Singh Saund, who immigrated to the US in 1920, rose to become a member of the US Congress and canvassed for the country where he was born. J.J. Singh, who came to the US in 1926, founded the India League of America and enlisted the support of prominent Americans like Albert Einstein, Henry Luce and Louis Fischer. Gobindram Wattumal, a resident of Honolulu set up the Wattumal Foundation for promoting a better Indo-US understanding by awarding scholarships and travel grants to both Indians and Americans for visiting each other's countries. Among the Indian leaders who visited the US in 1930s and 1940s to enlist US support were Lala Lajpat Rai, Dr. S. Radhakrishnan, Sarojini Naidu, Ballabhbhai Patel and Vijaylakshmi Pandit (SPAN, January 1985). Bobby Jindal and others are cementing our current relations.

The two largest and old democracies of the world have seen many ups and downs in political and trade relations. However, even much before India got its freedom from the colonial rule, there was enormous respect and sympathy for development as well as for the freedom struggle of India both at official and non official levels. As a result of the recommendations of the Famine Commission an All India Research Institute and Agricultural College was established in Pusa (Bihar) with generous donation from Henry Phipps, and American philanthropist after whom a Laboratory has been named in IARI at New Delhi. In 1926, India League of America was founded to help the freedom movement of India. Similarly there were other organizations, set up for India's independence and several articles appeared in the American newspapers to support freedom currently, there are about a dozen organizations of American Indianans helping in the development of nation of their origin.

PL-480 Programme

As and when India faced food shortage, after freedom, there has been a stream of humanitarian assistance from the US channelled through PL 480 programmes. Grain was sent to meet shortage, despite differences in perception over American "Imperialism" and Indian "Socialism" and on defence as well as security related issues. With a view to increase food production, a "grow more food campaign" was started in India. The Ford foundation and the Rockefeller Foundation worked in India to increase productivity of the cereals etc. (Randhawa, 1986). Later, the United States Aid (PL 480) joined into help in Agricultural research and production, hydroelectric projects and laid the foundation for the "green revolution" etc. (Randhawa, 1986).

The leading US non-government organizations have been the Ford Foundation, CARE-India and previously the Rockefeller Foundation (now merged with Winrock Internationals). The American Institute of Indian Studies (AIIS), a consortium of colleges and universities, is also a participant. Private voluntary organizations (PVOs) work with the US Agency for International development. Initially, US assistance was relief oriented covering education and poverty alleviation. However, with the passage of time there has been a shift towards a long-range development to make people responsible for their own future and for own society.

At the time of independence, India with a population of about 360 millions produced only 51 million tons of grains. Industry was essentially non-existent and literacy was less than 25 percent among men and 8 percent among women. The Ford Foundation gave grants during the first two decades (1952-1970) and mostly supported government programs. In the following two decades there was decline in direct support to state programs. Today, most of the Foundation grants go to the non-government organizations (NGOs). The major commitments of the Foundation can be grouped into four categories: food production, rural poverty and sustainable agriculture; family planning and population, child survival and reproductive health; education and culture, rights and governance; and fourthly planning and management.

The foundation's first programme, which began in 1952 with high hopes of transforming rural areas, was not as successful as it was expected to be. The program could not feed the exploding population and its failure resulted in India's virtual dependence on PL-480 imports for quite a while. The Foundation subsequently found NGOs full of ideas, ability to organize programs for poverty alleviation and resource management in the complex and diversified countryside. Grants were therefore, made to the Women's Association in Ahemadabad as also to Mysore resettlement and Development Agency.

In 1974, the Foundation helped set up the first women's studies research centre in a university in Bombay (Mumbai). The Foundation also founded the Centre for Women's Development Studies in New Delhi for women's employment and the Institute of Social Studies Trust began a program of research on Women's jobs in association with the University Grants Commission. The Foundation also served as an important partner in building up the private sector Birla Institute of Technology and Science, Pilani (Rajasthan). In the cultural field, Triveni Kala Sangam, New Delhi and National Centre for Performing Arts, Bombay (Mumbai) were given help. The country's first computer facility in archaeology, Deccan Postgraduate College and Research Institute, were also given special grants. In the field of humanities the Ford Foundation issued grants to the Indian institute of Public Administration, the national Council of Applied Economic Research in New Delhi and the Indian Institutes of Management in Calcutta and Bangalore.

In the areas of family planning and health, the Foundation

joined hands with J.R.D. Tata to set up a Family Planning Foundation of India. It launched the integrated child development scheme and a variety of large nutrition programs, as well as programs designed for the prevention of serious diseases like AIDS. In the eyes of many politicians, it gives a platform to the Central Intelligence Agency (CIA) to work in India. According to Devender Sharma, a commentator on agriculture etc., the Ford and Rockefeller-Foundations sought solutions to the problems suited to American interests, including industry. He asserted that the US fertilizer industry recorded a profit of about 14 billion during these years by introducing a rice variety that was heavily funded by the Rockefeller Foundation.

The other notable PVO is the Cooperative for Assistance and Relief everywhere (CARE). Its work commenced in 1950 with the signing of an agreement with the government of India. Since then CARE has provided $ 1.6 billion to the projects in India. Thus, India is the largest recipient of CARE assistance and dealt with about 9 million women and children every year. CARE has also dealt with emergency aid to the victims of the drought in 1973, the Latur earthquake in 1993 and those of the flood and cyclone in Orissa in 1996. The Mid day Meal Nutrition project has had a marked effect. CARE has objectives to improve the health and nutritional status of women and children. It provides supplemental food for over 6 million people in seven states of India. It also offers health services to about 28,000 women in Uttar Pradesh. No matter how good or bad Indo-US relations were at government level the CARE projects have not been affected by them. Although the US food assistance has been eliminated since green revolution, CARE has really assisted in building food-processing plants.

American Institute of Indian Studies (AIIS)

A group of American scholars of the leading universities under the leadership of W. Norman Brown, Professor of

Sanskrit of the Pennsylvania University formed a non-government consortium called American Institute of Indian Studies (AIIS) in 1961. It deals with entirely different kinds of development programs in India. For more than 40 years the institute has been providing fellowship supports for senior scholars and Ph.D. candidates in America and it has spread the knowledge of Indian culture through its two research centres. The consortium is aided by Ford, Melon, Carnegie and Rockefeller Foundations and has benefited more than three thousand and five hundred scholars in the fields ranging from anthropology to zoology. About 2,700 books and thousands of articles resulting from AIIS support have been given to the libraries in India. Some of these libraries are, the National Library of India in Kolkata, the Nehru Memorial Museum and Library in Delhi and the Adyar Library in Chennai. AIIS houses extensive archives of photographs and slides of India's artistic and archaeological heritage, recordings of Indian music and films of traditional rituals (Anonymous, 2004). The Indian head quarter of this institute is located in Gurgaon, outside, Delhi.

Similarly, Govindram Wattumal set up a foundation as early as in 1917 to award scholarships for better understanding between India and the United States and since then a considerable number of scholars have been benefited by the same. A large number of senior scholars have been benefited by this foundation. With the help of US educational programs in various Universities and Colleges, the number of Indian students studying in the US has increased greatly. In 1996-97 the number used to be about 30,700 and the same was about 74,600 in 2002-2003. Today, more than half a dozen of the leading US centres have programs on India and South Asia that deal with political, economic as well as strategic issues. The Indian Americans have become an important source of financial support.

Surprisingly India is one of the most pro-American countries in the World. The Pew Global Attitudes Survey

Report of January, 2005 mentions that out of the 16 nations (including USA) surveyed, about 17 percent Indians said they liked the US. Only Americans showed a more favourable view. About 83 percent Americans said they liked their country, whereas Pakistan was found to be the most anti-American.

The software engineering institute at Carnegie Mellon University gives a very high ranking to only 48 software companies in the world. Out of these about 65 percent are based in India. Over the past five years, the average annual growth rate of India's total export in services has been about 21.5 percent. Outsourcing placed by software and software-enabled services exports grew at an average of 40 percent.

Economic reforms have also begun to open up the insurance sector. Till recently, the government of India was not very keen to open insurance sector. Today, at least five big insurance corporations of the US are operating in India through joint ventures with Indian companies. During this period, the top US Financial Corporation has already signed at least 400,000 customers and has approximately invested about US$ 700 million in India (Anonymous, 2004).

In the same manner the Bank of America (BA), Enron Corporation, Amway International and other American Corporations are working to make lives better and prosperous in the future for many underprivileged Indian individuals. Corporate giants have realized that without social investments, their spending on production would not make a good social sense. They need to portray themselves as well wishers of the community they operate in.

In fact in the developing countries the budgets of the governments for poverty reduction are insufficient. Therefore, private investments on poverty reduction programs are increasing. Development agencies have realized the decreasing support from governments and are tapping more and more private companies, which are known to donate funds. The Corporations have themselves recognized that they need a positive image in areas in which they set up industries. They are therefore, becoming aware of their social responsibilities. As an illustration the Enron Corporation is embarking on long-term efforts to improve the living standards of the people of Maharashtra and many others communities in India.

CARE has joined hand with Enron Corporation in this regard for improving the economic status of low-income families. Both the organization recently initiated joint work for Konkan Integrated development (KID) in Ratnagiri district of Maharashtra and this is expected to benefit the poor masses of rural areas through jobs and strengthening of local institutions. Enron Corporation (which is pulling out from India) is a part of CARE's Corporate Council in the US. In India, CARE and Enron are using local NGOs to implement their projects. For example, fishermen are presently forced to sell their catch immediately, before it is spoiled and consequently the price is dictated by the purchasers.

Therefore, Enron-CARE team is working together to develop an infrastructure like an ice factory and cold storage so that the fishermen can store their catch for sometime and then sell the stocks at remunerative prices. Fishermen cooperatives will help the fishing communities in storage, marketing and management. Other activities include nursery management and horticultural work for landless small farmers by inducing savings and skill training for women and youth, inducement of primary education. The principal objective of these projects is to generate additional income for low-income families. Similarly, Proctor & Gamble (P&G), another of the CARE's Corporate Council member is working to promote primary school education for girls in U.P., a heavily populated state. With Enron earmarking US$ 2 millions a year, P&G US$ 100,000 per year, and the TATA Foundation contributing 25 percent of the cost for a child survival program in Bihar, it is apparent that the Corporations are getting more serious about their social responsibilities.

Amway Corporation made its entrance in India in 1995 as

Am-way India Enterprises. Under the umbrella of Amway Opportunity Foundation, it has started working in several social programs. In 1996, Amway gifted a fully equipped mobile dental clinic to the Rotary Club of Delhi to deal with the dental health care of the low-income people in and around Delhi. In 1997, the Amway joined hands with the All India Confederation of the Blind in which the Amway would sponsor the printing, production and distribution of textbooks to the blind students across the country. Recently, Amway India has bestowed a chair on entrepreneurial development at the University of Delhi, donating Rs. 3.5 millions to the Faculty of Management Studies.

Same way, the Cargil India recognized the need for good education in rural India. In a survey in the states of Karnataka and Andhra Pradesh, it found that state governments had built wide spread primary and secondary schools but paid no attention for maintaining educational aids and facilities. Therefore, the Cargil started Cargil Vidyarthi scholarship programs in villages where it produced seeds. Through this program the company helps to upgrade the identified schools with equipment. It contributes to the recruitment of teachers in specific subjects with matching contributions.

Before Rajiv Gandhi and President Reagan signed an agreement to cooperate in the field of Science and Technology in mid 1980s there were very few scattered collaborative programs on health. As an offshoot of the agreement was the development of a set of rotaviral vaccines. This is the longest-term bilateral program, the results of which will have an impact on people of both the countries. Encouraged by the findings, the 10 year programme has been given a new lease for another five years, with government as well as non-government support. Needless to mention, that thousands of infants were dying every year due to diarrhoea in developing countries.

In India alone, approximately one fourth of diarrhoeal deaths occur due to a severe form of rotaviral infection. With the development of suitable vaccines these deaths are likely to become preventable soon, as a part of Indo-US collaborative researches on Vaccine Action Program (VAP). As the program developed, YAP work was expanded to include canine rabies, HIV/AIDS, Leishmaniasis and malaria too. Several Indian institutions are participating in VAP and over 225 Indian scientists have visited various US laboratories. All India Institute of Medical Sciences (AIIMS) and Indian Institute of Sciences (IISc.) have been working on rotaviral strains with the help of VAP. The AIIMS is collaborating with Centre for Disease Control and Prevention, Atlanta, whereas IISc. is joining hands with Stanford University School of Medicine. The Biotechnology department is trying, to involve Indian and American companies for commercial production of vaccines.

Another important aspect of VAP is development of diagnostic assays for hepatitis, in which Osmania Medical College, Hyderabad, is cooperating with Colorado University, Health science Centre. Since due to development of drug resistant strains TB is also coming back, work on genes associated with virulent TB is going on. Scientists at Jawaharlal Nehru University (JNU) have been able to identify a chromosome in Leishmanias, which is responsible for drug resistance activity. At the moment there is no vaccine for Leishmania induced Kala-azar and the drugs are not effective. Therefore, the researches at JNU and the cooperating Seattle Biomedical Research Institute have a goal for the development of detection techniques and vaccine for control. VAP has an elaborate arrangement for monitoring progress, with Nobel Laureate Dr. Frederick Robbins, of the Case Western Reserve University and Dr. N.K. Ganguly, Director General of the Indian Medical research as Co-Chairmen.

The US Public Health Services (USPHS) and USAID provided the funds initially, while for the duration of extension for 5 years, up to 2002 the Starr Foundation is likely to make a grant for VAP for the third phase. However, one of the important links between the two countries is the Indians themselves living in the US, or the Americans living in India. Many of them like Drs. Hargovind Khorana and S. Chandrashekhar have not only a name for themselves but have also brought fame for both countries. In the same manner Samuel E. Stokes became the Johny apple seed of India in Kotgarh valley (H.P.). Renamed as Satyanad Stokes he distributed Delicious group of apple plants free to the local peasants and made the valley surplus in apple production. The author (B.B. Nagaich) had the opportunity to help him in this program, while working at Flowerdale Station of the Indian Agricultural Research Institute at Shimla (H.P.) India to benefit Kotgarh valley (H.P.). It is expected that the present generation of the non-resident Indians (NRIs) living in the us will build bridges of cooperation and understanding between the two nations, particularly in the post-cold war and post nuclear-detonation cum economic sanction era, resulting in better relationship between the two governments.

Microsoft in India

Marking the 10th anniversary of Microsoft's presence in India, Bill Gates, the Chairman and the chief software architect, launched the global Information technology (IT) in September 2000. He unveiled plans to set up a state-of-art laboratory in Bangalore on the development activities of the centre over the next three years. He also announced that his company would spend US$ 50 million on his Hyderabad based development centre and fund a program to take the IT to the rural areas of India through IT education initiatives. The Redmond (Washington) based software giant also tied up with India's rapidly growing software solutions provider Infosys Technologies—a Bangalore based company in a strategic global partnership. On behalf of the Bill and Melinda Gates Foundation, he announced two grants totalling US$ 30 million for underprivileged students and administered polio drops to children at a health clinic at Delhi. In November 2002, Bill Gates again visited India for 4 days and donated US$ 100 million to assist in the subcontinents battle against AIDS. Since then he has been visiting India practically every year. It may be stated that India has the second largest number of AIDS affected people.

Several agreements were signed during the visit of the Indian Prime Minister to the US in September 2000. In a MOU signed between the US Department of Energy and Indian Ministry of Power it was agreed to establish a Working Group on Energy. The MOU was signed by Deputy Secretary T.J. Glauthier and by Secretary A.K. Basu. Signing of the agreements was witnessed by Mr. Mineta, the Secretary Commerce of the US Department and Mr. Yashwant Sinha, Finance Minister of India.

Southern Energy Inc. of Atlanta (Georgia) signed a development agreement with Reliance Power Ltd., and the Power Trading Corporation of India Ltd., for the Hirma (3960 MW) power project in Orissa. This would be world's biggest power project, involving more than US$ 4.5 billion and will sell power to the electricity boards of several states in the region.

CMS Energy Corporation of Dearborn (Michigan) signed a joint development agreement with Power Trading Corporation of India and Dakshin Bharat Energy. The agreement finalized a power purchase agreement and other key agreements for the construction of the Ennore liquefied natural gas (LNG) terminal and an 1850-megawatt power plant in Tamil Nadu. The project cost was estimated to involve investment of US$ 2 billion. Power Trading Corporation is supposed to purchase all of the plant's output for subsequent sales to the consumers in the region. CMS will oversee construction, while Unocal Bharat (a co-investor) will coordinate construction of the LNG plant.

Synergies Energy Development Inc., of Maryland signed a memorandum of understanding (MOU) with the Infrastructure Development Finance Corporation Bank (Duncans India Ltd.) for financing the Srinagar hydroelectric project in Utranchal (earlier in U.P.) will provide power to three million people in northern India. This project involved an investment of nearly US$ 0.5 billion (Haniffa, India Abroad, September 22, 2000).

On August 9, 2001 the US President announced that his administration is planning to fund partially the stem cell research work, which the Indian Reliance Corporation is contemplating through its centre, costing about 100 crore Rupees (US$ 21 million approx.). That India ranks among the leading nations in this field of cell research has been well noticed. According to Professor Inder Verma, one of the leading US Geneticists, field of cell research could open new vistas for Indian biologists. He declared that embryonic cell research "is an area where Indian science can compete with the best of them because this is new, we are not behind others and our political situation and our social situation is such that people are willing to work on stem cells even from aborted fetuses."

Reliance Co. is already negotiating with the Centre for Cellular and Molecular Biology, Hyderabad. Setting up of the facility is likely to raise company's profile. However in the US, decision of Bush government to permit partial funding has been denounced as a betrayal from his stated position during election. In his 9th August announcement, Bush stated that the decision placed him at a 'difficult moral intersection.' Therefore, he cautioned the administration to proceed with great care. The 10 embryonic stem cell lines made available to the US by Reliance group (Reliance Life Sciences, Mumbai) and the Bangalore based National Centre for Biological Sciences (NCBS) have met all the eligibility requirements of the US law (India Abroad, September 14, 2001).

Recently, a group of doctors and scientists of the US formed World-India Diabetes Foundation' (WIDF), which intends to setup the Indian Institute of Diabetes (IID) in Thiruananthapuram (Kerala) where diabetes incidence is very high as compared to other states. According to WIDF plan there would be a stone-laying ceremony in November 2001, followed by a two-day conference, as informed by Dr. S. Nair, Professor of Medicine at the Mayo Clinic, and WIDF President. The state government, the Mayo Clinic and WIDF have reached an agreement for research and education on the 'silent killer.' The institute will train physicians and paramedical staff from entire country on prevention and management of diabetes.

Government has allotted land and the former ruler of Travancore has pledged about Rs.5 million (US$ 106 approx.) for establishment of the institute. The institute is being set up by NRIs, with support from people in the US, India and other parts of the world. In India diabetes is usually diagnosed at a very late stage and consequently patients develop serious complications. Type-2 diabetes mostly remains without symptoms for several years till complications like damage of kidney, heart failure and gangrene etc. prevail. Regular exercises and dietary interventions can prevent diabetes. Therefore, educating doctors, paramedics and people becomes very helpful and the institute has been proposed to meet these challenges (India Abroad September 14, 2001). The IID got a boost recently with the involvement of Ambassador-at-Large B.K. Agnihotri. The Chief Minister of Kerala (A.K. Anthony) laid the Foundation Stone for the IID in November 2001.

An agreement on the transfer of dual use high technology items to India was signed in Washington in September 2004. This signalled the 2nd phase of Strategic Partnership between India and the US. The Executive Director, India Initiative and South Asia Programme at the University of Georgia's Centre for Trade and Security said that implementation "would test out empirically the movement from the presumption of denial to the presumption of approval whereby the US industry can actually apply for these licenses--" (India Abroad, September 24, 2004). Indo-US relations comprise of expanding strategic and economic ties. The Bush Administration was prepared to make a major offer of arms sale to India. It is needless to mention that reinforcement of economic foundations of bilateral cooperation is highly desirable. The US arms deal (if any) will have many repercussions with several foreign countries like Russia, France, Britain, China, Pakistan and Israel etc.

Sorting out the controversial issues and perceptions like agricultural subsidies are very important. The US policy makers have quite a few items on their 'to do' list. The most important item is a permanent seat in the UNSC if a hand of friendship is to be extended to India. Similarly, MFN status to India, like that given to China will surely boost up the friendly relations between the two nations. Time has now come to look at India as another destination for investments. Many CEOs state, India is a 'Knowledge base', China is the 'Manufacturing base' and this myth has to go away. The US Corporations must now look at the manufacturing capacity of India and its willingness to join hands with the multinationals (Vinai Rai, 2005).

After about 15 years of discussions, India and USA ultimately signed an agreement in October 2005 for cooperating in the fields of science and technology. The agreement was signed by Kapil Sibal, Minister for Science and Technology and Condoleezza Rice, the US Secretary of State (The Hindu, October 19, 2005). The cooperation would be based on joint responsibilities and equitable contributions. India assured the US that all the efforts will be made to curb money laundering and prevent financing of terrorism. It developed a road map for major reforms in the field of financial regulations. At the joint press conference of John Snow, the US Treasury Secretary, and P. Chidambaram, the Finance Minister, Chidambaram explained the intention of the two countries to implement the recommendation of the Financial Action Task Force. The panel was created to prevent misuse of the financial regulations and both nations agreed to work together to identify and freeze the finances as well as all the assets of the terrorist organizations (The Hindu, 10th November 2005).

Similarly, US, European Union, Russia, China, Japan and South Korea, the members of the International Thermonuclear Experimental Reactor (ITER) program, while acknowledging India as a responsible nuclear state, invited it to become the seventh member of the group. The invitation recognizes that India can contribute significantly to such endeavours with its advanced nuclear technology, including in the field of fusion research. ITER is the experimental step between the modern studies of plasma physics and fusion power production of future electricity. The main facility will be built in France by 2016 and all members will participate in its construction, research and development (Daily Times, December 8, 2005).

An important outcome of September 11 was the initiation of one organization of a group of former security cum intelligence and counterterrorism officials of India, the United States and Israel to work as one group of eminent professionals for promoting greater counter terrorism cooperation amongst their native countries. This initiative was taken by a Jewish Institutions for the National Security Affairs (JINSA) located in Washington DC. Under the auspices of this institution the group has already held a few meetings and made certain recommendations for necessary action. If the governments of the three countries and other nations encourage similar non-government advisory committees or groups, a lot can be done to help maintain peace and prosperity in the globe.

In India it may appear that interest of people in Hindi is diminishing, but in the US use of Hindi is slowly increasing. The results are also apparent. About a decade ago only 25 universities were teaching Hindi but nowadays Hindi is being taught in more than 100 universities. Through 'Salam Namaste' Hindi radio program Hindi is being popularized. Indians in America are pressurizing local governments to teach Hindi in schools to their children. In New Jersey appointment of Hindi teachers have begun and soon it is expected that Devnagri script sign boards will start appearing in Indian restaurants and hotels like those in Arabic, Chinese and

Japanese scripts.

Three weeks after taking office, President Obama's administration makes its first significant contact with India by sending a special delegation on the occasion of 50th anniversary of Civil Rights leader Martin Luther King's visit to India to study teachings of Mahatma Gandhi. A US Congressional delegation, accompanied by King's eldest son, his wife and close associates, followed the footsteps of M.L. King (TNN February 8, 2009). It is believed that he inherited Gandhi's mantle as the world's most influential advocates of non-violence. He tried fasting, meditation and material dispossession.

Landmarks in Indo-US Relations

1. 1792: Appointment of Consul General of the Trade at Calcutta.
2. 1800-1900: Influence of Indian philosophy & culture on US intellectuals like Emerson, Thoreau, Melville, Whitman and Mark Twain etc.
3. 1893: Swami Vivekananda visited US and founded American Vedanta Society.
4. 1912-20: Rabindranath Tagore visited US several times and published poems in the US.
5. 1911: Lala Hardyal visited US and founded Ghadar (freedom) movement.
6. 1915: Prafulla Chandra Mukerji founded Friends of India Society.
7. 1917: Gobindram Wattumal set up Wattumal Foundation.
8. 1920: Dalip Singh Saund became a member of the US Congress.
9. 1926: J.J. Singh established India League of America for freedom of India.
10. 1931: Mahatma Gandhi chosen as "man of the year" by Time magazine.
11. 1941: President Roosevelt wrote to Churchill to concede freedom to India.

12. 1942: Louis Fisher visited India.
13. 1949: Jawaharlal Nehru paid tributes to US fathers in the US Congress Joint session.
14. 1949-60: The US supplied food grains to India under PL-480 program.
15. 1950: Establishment of the US Educational Foundation in India under Fulbright act. CARE started work in India.
16. 1959: President Eisenhower visited India and received a warm welcome.
17. 1962-63: US under the leadership of J.F. Kennedy helped India in Chinese war and Dean Rusk declared continued support.
18. 1974: Setting up of Indo- US joint Commission.
19. 1980s: US investments increased following Indian liberalization policy. Science and technology agreement signed by Rajiv Gandhi and President Reagan.
20. 1998: Bhartiya Janta Party formed a coalition government and carried out nuclear detonations. Pakistan also carried out nuclear tests, leading to imposition of economic sanctions by the US.
21. 1999: The US slid down to 5th position in the list of Foreign Direct Investors. The US directed Pakistan to vacate its aggression in Kargil in days. US Senate did not ratify CTBT.
22. 2001: Hillary Clinton the then first lady visited India. A new era was heralded in bilateral relations by President Clinton's visit to India and Vajpayee's visit to the US.
23. 2001: President G.W. Bush relaxed US economic sanctions. India provided logistic supports on terrorists training camps in Afghanistan, POK and also offered CIPRO worth US$ 1 million. Reliance Corporation of India started cooperative research work on Stem Cell culture.
24. 2002: Prime Minister Vajpayee visited the US, as also Defence, Foreign & Finance Ministers. The US Secretaries of Defence and Foreign Affairs visited India. Military

cooperation started. Bill Gates donated US$ 100 million to India for fighting against AIDS.

25. 2003: Prime Minister Vajpayee and Deputy Prime Minister Advani visited the US and had discussions with President Bush and Secretaries. Joint Indo-US exercises of army were conducted in India as well as in the US.
26. 2004-05: Prime Minister Manmohan Singh visited the US and had discussions with the President about mutual cooperation including nuclear energy.
27. 2006: President Bush visited India and signed Civil nuclear energy agreement along with others. Prime Minister Singh visited the US.
28. 2008: The Civil nuclear energy bill was made a law which would result in nuclear material and technology trade between the two countries.
29. 2009: A US Congressional delegation along with Martin Luther King III visited India on the occasion of 50th anniversary of Civil Rights leader. Richard Holebrook visited India & Af-Pak region. Secretary Hillary Clinton visited India.

"We owe a lot to the Indians, who taught us how to count, without which no worthwhile scientific discovery could have been made!" (Albert Einstein).

5

India's Foreign Relations

B.B. Nagaich

Prior to 1947, India's foreign relations were intended for safeguarding primarily British imperial interests. The Durand line was the boundary between India and Afghanistan and Mc. Mahon line the boundary between India and Tibet. The Durand line did not extend to Chitral, Hunza and Gilgit etc., which were under Kashmir princely state. In the East, Burma (now Myanmar) [separated from India in 1935] and China were the neighbours of India. Tibet extended from Ladakh to the North of Myanmar. Interestingly there was not a single army unit of Tibet or India in the 1600 mile-long frontier. In 1914 Simla (now Shimla) Conference the boundaries were demarcated between India, Tibet and China with a line called Mc. Mahon line, with free trade along this border. After 1947, India's post-independence period can be divided into three phases based on objectives of development vis-à-vis its external policy. The first phase commenced from 1947 to 1962, and was dominated by Nehru's idealism.

The Asian Relations Conference, organized by India in March, 1947, was the first significant foreign policy initiative that India took in this regard. India supported the freedom struggles of the countries in South- East Asia and Africa not only politically but also materially. In late 1949 a non-alignment conference was held in India and it emerged that the non-aligned nations would not be a party to the post war conflicts of claims of the Western powers (Jha, 1983, Jackson, 1983). The world was divided into two rival groups, the NATO and the WARSAW Pact camps.

Non-Alignment Movement (NAM)

However Nehru's views were altogether different. He wrote, "Idealism of today is the realism of tomorrow." It is the ability to know what is good for tomorrow or the next year and to fashion your-self accordingly. According to Nehru, the practical person, the realist, looks at the tip of his nose and visualizes what is good for the day, for tomorrow as also beyond. It was this vision that guided the Non-Alignment Movement (NAM) and a doctrine of 'Panchsheel', the five principles of co-existence emerged. This was the cornerstone of India's foreign policy and a source of great influence in the international matters.

The roots of NAM originated from Nehru's writings and were strengthened by friendship between Nehru, J.B. Tito and G.A. Nasser (Jha 1983). NAM helped in 3 ways the newly independent African, Asian and Latin American countries to escape from entrapment in rivalry from the rivalries between the two Superpowers, Western nations and the Communists. Secondly, it also allowed non-aligned nations to judge each and every international issue on its merit and to make their own decisions. Thirdly, it permitted the non-aligned nations a status to pursue diplomacy constructively and to act as honest mediators between hostile nations (Dennis Kux, 1993). Nehru viewed that democratic India would be better off with a socialistic economic and development model and a peaceful non-aligned country that had a destiny as a major power. According to some, the Nehru model showed the influence of dreamers and schemers rather then builders of strong India. The singular achievement of the BJP under Vajpayee (1998-2004) was that the minority government motivated Hindu nationalism to join the ideological battle against Islamic Jehad, emanating from Pakistan-Afghanistan-Saudi-Kashmir fronts and was spreading into the subcontinent (Kapur, 2006). For India, Russia's invasion of Georgia as a retaliation of Georgia's invasion of Ossetia, poses a difficult situation. The US is trying to turn India into a bulwark of "a coalition of democracies" with non-democratic Russia to the west and communist China to the north. Pushed too far, Russia is taking risk of another cold war with the West to protect its national interests (Business India September 7, 2008). What should we do? Should we again pretend to be non-aligned?

India's role in the Korean crisis and other international issues is mostly considered a model for solving conflicts. NAM, which began with only 25 founding members, now has more than 125 members. For the countries, which were liberated from colonialism, NAM is a liberating ideology. India wanted the rest of Asia and Africa to gain freedom from European colonialism. The reluctance of the US to press the Dutch and French in Indonesia and Indo-China disappointed Nehru. Indians, on the other hand, were happy with the USSR support on de-colonization. Indians also resented racial prejudice and discrimination against non-whites in South Africa as well as racial segregation in the southern US. Therefore, Nehru made South Africa India's top issue in the very first session of the UN General Assembly (Dennis Kux, 1993, Nehru, 1946).

Surprisingly, Washington had also lately displayed interest for the first time in attending the NAM summit in Durban in 2002. In these meetings James Foley of the US State Department said the US desired to engage constructively on major global issues like terrorism. In the NAM meeting at Cape Town, unilateral action, non-observance of international law and continued military occupation of Palestine and terrorism were identified as threats to global security at the ministerial meeting. They also hit out at the US global agenda. The 14th summit of the world's more than 125 developing nations met at Havana in September, 2006 to discuss terrorism, nuclear programs and development goals set by the UN for 2015 to reduce poverty. Indian Prime Minister Singh and other world leaders participated. They condemned terror in any form. India advocated moderate actions, mid-path courses and not extreme actions advocated by countries like Iran and

Venezuela. He also mentioned the peace process opening transportation between India and Pakistan.

Liberating Philosophy

Even small nations could take a policy stand without having any fear of the repercussions. For countries that were earlier under colonial rule for long time and were still dependent economically on their former rulers NAM was the best choice. The main objectives of the NAM were: 1. Strengthening of the United Nations, 2. Anti-colonialism and Anti-racialism, 3. Peaceful settlement of disputes, 4. Disarmament and arms control and 5. Economic independence and cooperation for mutual benefits. India's other foreign policy contributions are mainly in the area of disarmament, inspired by Mahatma Gandhi. Gandhi was horrified by the atomic bombings in Japan. He believed that the nuclear arsenals would bring mass devastations. In his article in Harijan, he wrote, "I regard the employment of the atom bomb for he wholesome destruction of men, women and children as the most diabolic use of science."

For Indian Foreign policy he proposed a commitment to freedom based on democracy and a pledge to encourage reason and impulses of peace in international affairs. Gandhi was of the opinion that "Democracy is not a state in which people act like sheep. Under democracy liberty of opinion and action is jealousy guarded. I am not pleading for India to practice non-violence being fully aware of its power". The presumption was the since India had no expansionist designs, it would not face any threats. This was supported by the fact that since India takes no sides with any power block and wants to be friendly and cooperative with all notions, power block equations should not adversely affect it. Another thought was that establishment of the UN provided both a moral and procedural basis for conflict resolution through mutual negotiations and peaceful means, India did not need a large military with sophisticated arms as it would have no tension.

Some of Mahatma Gandhi's ideas pioneered by Nehru later became a part of the international arms control and continue to be widely debated even now. As early as 1948, at the third session of the General Assembly of the UN, India proposed a resolution of the "peaceful uses of atomic energy" for human welfare. In 1954, Nehru sent a message (Standstill Agreement) to the Secretary General which became the basis for the Partial Test Ban Treaty and later the Comprehensive Test Ban Treaty (CTBT). In 1948 an atomic energy Commission was set up in India for working on nuclear energy for welfare of people by peaceful means. Nehru had no ambiguity about India's nuclear program. In 1957 India openly announced that it would not use atomic energy for evil purposes and has been using it since then for constructive purposes only leading to human welfare (Chari et al., 1996). After the 1998 detonations, it has again unilaterally announced a No First Use (NFU) policy and is ready to sign CTBT etc., if they are not discriminatory (Matin Zuberi, 1999). India is also ready to destroy its nuclear arsenals if the other nuclear haves are prepared to do so.

In the post-independence period India developed friendly relations with both Western nations and the Communist States. For economic development through 5-year plans India did not plan for a large defence forces initially. Looking at the size of its borders and the attitude of its neighbours, India should have a very large military with ultra-modern equipment, but Nehru continued to articulate morally superior policies of non-alignment and disarmament. However, Nehru's idealism and faith were shaken in 1948 after Kashmir was invaded by Pakistan. Under the advice of Lord Mountbatten, the first Governor General of India, Nehru referred the matter to the Security Council under chapter VI dealing with the settlement of disputes and not under chapter VII dealing with aggression (Chibber, 1998; Chopra, 1990).

Mountbatten's military advice was particularly directed against any advance beyond Uri, which the Indian army had captured in the middle of November 1947. Unfortunately, Nehru did not realize that to expect the UN to live up to the ideals of the charter was unrealistic. In fact, Nehru's mistake of taking the Kashmir issue to the UN Security Council against the wishes of the Indian army and some other senior political leaders continued to plague India even today, more than sixty years after independence. The UN Security Council resolution required (a) immediate cease-fire, (b) the total withdrawal of "all" Pakistani nationals (including military and paramilitary personals) from the region of Jammu & Kashmir, while permitting India to retain her troops in Kashmir to maintain law and order and (c) finally a plebiscite "only" after (a) and (b) were complied with (UNCIP Resolution, 13 August, 1948). But since Pakistan never complied with part (b) of the resolution i.e. it did not withdraw from POK/G.K. etc. plebiscite could not be held.

What India was defending in Kashmir was not only the land but it was trying to preserve secularism, which is the basis of Indian democracy. India did not accept partition on the ground of religion (Chibber, 1998; Chopra, 1990; Ganguly, 1999; Grover, 1995; Lamb, 1967). It cannot accept the demand to secede the Kashmir valley on the basis of religion. India has more than 125 million Muslims whereas the Srinagar valley has only about 4 million. This is not an issue of religion but an issue of secularism and development. Pakistan's argument of ethnic pluralism is not appealing. It later ignored religion and suppressed its own nationals, resurgent Muslim Bengalis, thus undermining its own irrational demand of Kashmir. The East Bengal (Pakistan) crisis showed fragility of Islamabad's philosophy of religious pluralism.

Thus, the current Pakistan's rhetoric lacks credibility because there have been several elections (including the last one in 2008 and 2009) in Indian Kashmir and people have freedom to elect their own democratic representatives to the State Assembly but similar opportunity was never given to the Janta of POK/GK, which has been resented by the masses of that region. To keep people of GK/POK ignorant Pakistan did not spread modern education there. As a result for every 14 males only 3 females are educated. There is no TV or radio station in that region despite more than 60 years of Islamabad's rule. Further, the nomination of all the members of the Kashmiri Nationalist Party intended to be nominated in the state assembly in July, 2001 were cancelled because this party did not agree for making their state as part of Pakistan. According to the Friday Times, residents of Gilgit-Balistan desire complete freedom from Pakistan, which has gifted about 5200 sq. km. area to China without their consent.

Terrorism in Jammu and Kashmir

To hide the above facts Islamabad has waged an undeclared war by fomenting terrorism in the Indian Jammu & Kashmir (Nayar, 1998). Islamabad refused permission to the world famous Mori International to survey GK because only a few days before the results of an earlier survey were declared, which showed that the majority of residents from that area desired to live in India (INS, London, 2nd June, 2002). One of the objectives of terrorism is to prevent J&K citizens from elections/ voting. Just before elections ISI organizes crimes to attempt to deter people from participating. In 2002 about 600 people including political leaders were killed. In an article on 'Jehadi iceberg' B. Raman, the former Head of the Counter-terrorism department of government of India, asked how many hours have government of India and the state governments devoted to this task despite the fact that India has been one of the worst victims of Jehadi terrorism.

He gave three main reasons for continuity of terrorism. 1. There is deterioration and lack of coordination in the preventive and investigative people of the security agencies. 2. Despite reports of task forces on revamping the intelligence apparatus and internal security management set up, there is no improvement in our counter-terrorism capability. 3. Despite periodic claims of the government about success of the security agencies in neutralizing dozens of Jehadi militants and ISI modules dozens more continue to operate undetected. After 9/11, the US political parties devoted 1/4th of their sittings to improve counter-terrorism ability and worked out a consensus on how to improve/ strengthen it (India abroad September 5, 2003).

The second or the final shock of Nehru's idealism was much stronger and perhaps responsible for his death. He had a sincere belief that India and China, the two Asian giants, were waking up and would remain friendly. In fact he described a Hindi slogan of Hindi- Chini Bhai-Bhai or the brotherhood of Indian and Chinese. In spite of Kashmir's invasion, because Nehru and his defence Minister Krishna Menon believed in friendly co-existence with China, they did not strengthen and equip the Indian army properly, particularly for a mountain war. Later China became unhappy with India because India did not agree to play the tune of China in Indo-China war and over China's occupying Tibet.

Also, India did not expel the Tibetan leader Dalai Lama, who in 1959 formed a government in exile in Dharamshala in India. As a friendly neighbour India also helped Tibetan refugees to settle in India, who (in thousands) flee Chinese rule every year. For instance, even in 2006 October 75 refugees were making a secret trek across the border on a mountain slope (19000-ft. high Nanpa La Pass), Chinese border guards opened fire without warning. Out of these only 41 survived and managed to reach India to get shelter (Seattle Times October 24, 2006). As a result of such actions, China had long back claimed a big Indian area as its own and crossed the British period international boundary line called Mc. Mahon line (agreed in 1914 in Shimla) to capture Indian Territory (Hoffman, 1990). As mentioned earlier, the United States helped India by transporting India's war materials and supplies but Russia (considered as an ally of India) remained neutral.

The shock the humiliating defeat demonstrated the weakness of Nehru's idealism. In concrete terms, it demonstrated the weakness of idealism and gave way to the policy of power with principles, followed by L.B. Shastri, Indira Gandhi, Rajiv Gandhi and Vajpayee. Immediately after the 1962 war, the second phase (1962-1990) began, which entailed the pursuit of power with principles. In 1971 there was a big departure in India's policy in the form of a treaty of peace and friendship signed by Prime Minister Indira Gandhi with the USSR (Jha, 1983). The United States of America and its Western allies viewed this agreement as India's compromising non-aligned principles, but for India it was a clear demonstration of annoyance with the US over its policy of favouring Pakistan against Indian interests (Cohen, 1985; 1987; Dixit, 1998).

Despite personal likings, Nixon's desire was to have a good relationship both with India and Pakistan, continuing substantial aids and large peace Core programs in India. Although Nixon supported a strong military relationship with Pakistan as Vice-President, he had no plans to revive the same as President. In August 1969, his official meetings with Indira Gandhi at News Delhi lacked warmth. The discussions, mainly on Vietnam and Pakistan lacked interest and animation. Following an international outcry regarding the refugee crisis in East Pakistan (now Bangladesh), and the flood of refugees numbering in millions, India intervened by helping Mukti Bahini (Liberation Force) of East Bengal and subsequently independent Bangladesh came into existence much against the wishes of the then West Pakistan and its supporters.

Even the US Consul General in Dacca urged the US government to show concern for human rights violations in East Pakistan. Some claim that Indira Gandhi made a last minute concession at Shimla for several reasons. Firstly she agreed that an imposed solution based on a military victory may lead to Pakistan's permanent enmity with India. Secondly both the US and USSR brought pressure on Indira Gandhi to reach a mutually accepted settlement. Thirdly Bhutto had taken with him to Shimla a number of leaders including Arbab

S.K. Khalil, Ghous Baksh Bizenjo, Mohammad Yunus, who had worked with Nehru. She held them in high esteem (Humayun Khan & Parthasarthy, 2004). President Nixon and Henry Kissinger had claimed that if they were given sufficient time the US could get Yahya Khan to concede self-determination for East Pakistan, either provincial autonomy or full freedom (Kissinger, 1994; Thornton, 1992).

This provided an ideological basis to the infuriated Pakistan for attempting to create disturbances first in Punjab (where it failed) and later in Indian Kashmir (J&K) by providing training to Islamic militants and arming them. India was in need of defence equipment including aircraft. Russia was willing to supply the same and a breakthrough was achieved by a rupee system of barter trade. Russia needed tea, textiles, leather goods, tobacco and coffee in return. This rupee trade became a significant factor for friendly ties between India and Russia. India's disillusionment with the United States reached a peak when President Nixon and Secretary Henry Kissinger sent the Seventh Fleet (with nuclear powered aircraft carrier) called Enterprise into the Indian Ocean as a deterrent to India (Dennix Kux, 1993; Gupta, 1977).

In 1965 India made a distinction between non-proliferation and the universal disarmament in its proposals to the UN and promised its support for total disarmament on the basis of non-proliferation. Just about a year after Nehru's death, India suggested a treaty, which separated vertical proliferation from horizontal proliferation (Chari, 1995). Subsequently, later in 1968, India refused to sign the Nuclear Non-Proliferation treaty. India carried out nuclear tests in 1974 (10years after China) to culminate a decade long confrontation with nuclear power nations. In 1998 it again carried out a series of nuclear tests as a minimum deterrent. From the Indian perspective this was consistent with its disarmament policy because of the unwillingness of the nuclear powers to provide adequate security assurances to India against possible Chinese nuclear arsenal elimination program (Noorani, 1967). The Indian national psyche was deeply scarred by the Chinese attack of 1962. Therefore, Prime Minister Shastri was convinced by Dr. Homi Bhabha and allowed continuity of a nuclear program, resulting in the 1974 Pokhran I and later in 1998 Pokhran 2 nuclear tests.

End of Cold War

The third or the modern phase (1990 onwards) has faced the break-up of the USSR and with it the end of the cold war era. The NAM is now assuming a more constructive and economic cooperation role on the basis of equality and mutual benefits. India's continued economic reforms have resulted in self-confidence and more openness to foreign investments and imports. Although the United States has been India's main partner in commerce & trade by investing huge sums in India, the staunch US backing of Pakistan and China is a hurdle in Indo-American friendly ties (Harrison & Geoffery, 1993). The US authorities knowing that Pakistan and China both attacked India and that Pakistan, which failed to get sympathy in Indian Punjab, is continuously promoting terrorism in J&K and other parts of India. It (US) continues to supply modern weapons and monetary support in some form to Pakistan. China is a nuclear power that is unfriendly to India and has supplied M-11 and Hatf missiles etc. as well as the associated technology to Pakistan in spite of its 1994 agreement with the US not to do so. China is not returning the occupied Indian territory but on the top of it is alleging that India is occupying Chinese area.

Therefore, it is crystal clear that Pakistan and China are teaming up against India and are carrying out deals secretly. The US itself has alleged that China has stolen vital US nuclear technology and has been helping Pakistan's nuclear programs but it has continuously encouraged both of these countries. Therefore, the US continued leanings toward China and Pakistan are detrimental to an Indo-US friendly relationship. Under the present circumstances there are 3 main stands in India's foreign policy. First, India is desirous of emerging as a major economic power. It realizes that in the 21st century, power shall not flow growth rate in India of about 10 percent per year for the next ten years, growth rate can bring more influence in the international arena than UN resolutions. Second, India will work for sustained nuclear and missile control regimes. Third, most Indians are of the view that one of the principal reasons for India's limited influence in the international system is the relationship with Pakistan. If India can get rid of the Pakistan load, there is no limit to India's influence, as proposed in former Prime Minister, I.K. Gujral's doctrine. Gujral liberalized visa policies for Pakistani visitors and extended the MFN treatment to Pakistani imports (Dixit 1995, 1998).

The statement of the US Assistant Secretary that President Clinton will ask Congress to end all discriminatory laws against Pakistan, start assistance on military training, including the Pressler Amendment, did increase resentment in India. Apparently the US desired to favour Pakistan as an important and strategic country knowing fully well the game the China-Pakistan team was playing against India. Besides imposing economic sanctions in 1998 the US made several Indian scientists leave its territory, particularly those dealing with energy programs. Several institutions working on nuclear energy, missile technology and military matters have been blacklisted. According to the report of the Heritage Foundation both China and Pakistan forced Indian nuclear detonations. China prepared the blue prints for Pakistan, starting from nuclear bombs to missiles, with the help of which nuclear bombs can be used. These programs were apparently funded by Saudi Arabia. To treat the uranium, magnetic rings were supplied by China to Pakistan.

Besides these, missiles and other weaponry were given and the scientists were trained in nuclear related projects. Additionally, Chinese missiles have been deployed in Tibet. Arms are being deployed by China in Myanmar. In the light of all this and consequent to the Ghauri missile tests, India was alarmed and was left with no alternative but to carry out minimum deterrent nuclear tests for its own security as mentioned by Frank Pallone, the US Congressman and Senator Sherrod Brown. It was a big surprise, Nuclear powers, including the US which has itself carried out twelve hundred nuclear tests and has a stockpile of eight thousand seven hundred nuclear bombs are opposing Indian nuclear programs, for which India has unilaterally offered "No First Use" policy voluntarily against Pakistan or any other non-nuclear nation (Ganguly, 1999; Matin Zuberi, 1999).

The US did not impose any economic sanctions against China, which has carried out more than forty-five nuclear tests and has a store of four hundred and fifty nuclear weapons. On the other hand President Clinton visited China, signed agreements for supplying nuclear technology and weaponry. He went on further and declared it a leader in Asia. By Clinton's post nuclear move to resume lending to Pakistan while keeping a ban on India, had been referred by Prime Minister Vajpayee discriminatory and created an unhelpful atmosphere in India. Therefore problems have got enhanced for a smooth dialogue with the US. However the role that was played by President Clinton during 1999 Kargil-conflict, by asking Pakistan to vacate aggression, had been greatly appreciated by Indians.

In an article in 'Atomic Scientist' the President of the Institute Energy and Environmental Research had stated that even if India had not carried out its nuclear tests in 1998, it could not have escaped economic sanctions because of its not signing discriminatory CTBT.

After Vajpayee became Prime Minister for the second time he decided to improve relations with neighbouring countries displaying goodwill along with toughness. In February 1999 he opted for a travel by road to Pakistan by himself riding the first bus (Hindustan Times, February 21, 1999) and signed Lahore Declaration with Nawaz Sharif and later a similar declaration was signed with Bangladesh too. However, Nawaz

Sharif had something else in mind, as had his predecessors. Pakistan infiltrated its army with plain clothed soldiers with extremists over a 25 km. wide and 150 km. long territory in Kargil sector, just after Lahore Agreement. Therefore, India had to retaliate with operation 'Vijay' to flush out the infiltrators and recover the territory after 74 days fierce fighting in the hills. Analysts felt that India, after the 1999 elections, must enter into mutual dialogue with Pakistan to avoid any nuclear brinkmanship. However, the day Vajpayee took over as Prime minister (third time), there was a swift military coup in Pakistan and General P. Musharraf, the main architect of the Kargil conflict took over Pakistan. He suspended the Constitution and dissolved the Parliament.

In summary, India would view the US as more friendly if it did not unduly favour Pakistan and China, if it did not criticize India for its nuclear and missile programs and if it did not put pressure on other countries to refrain from transferring advance technology to India. From an Indian point of view there is need to undertake a series of diplomatic initiatives to put across India's views to foreign powers and the international corporate world. High-level delegations should target nations like France, UK, Russia, Canada, Germany, Japan, Korea, South Africa, Australia, Holland, Norway, Sweden, Israel, Arabian and NAM countries. India also needs to engage China in dialogue to clear the air for resuming border talks and improve relations, luckily it was done. The US has also responded favourably by signing a civil nuclear energy program in 2006 and finalizing it in 2008 but not with Pakistan despite its keen desire. Similarly France and Russia have also agreements with India on civil nuclear energy programs.

In the present competitive era, the US should show better understanding of India's domestic problems and poverty in relation to trade policies. Mutual economic relations however are governing largely by India's handling of the security and trade issues. The present economic reforms and liberalization policy of India, unless pursued vigorously, are unlikely to attract US business/direct investment as much as that attracted by China. One of the difficult issues before the world's two largest democracies is the nuclear question. With both India and Pakistan becoming nuclear powers, the issues of non-proliferation and missile development have become important bilateral problems. Washington now desires to induce New Delhi and Islamabad to renounce their nuclear programs. Clinton had a desire to take this to take back this as gift during his March visit to India and Pakistan in the last year of his presidency but unfortunately it did not happen then and did not happen during the visit of the Indian Prime Minister and Pakistan's Chief Executive in September 2000. A nuclear Islamabad has achieved strategic parity with India. This is a great achievement for Pakistan because it could not have hoped to achieve parity with conventional weapons. For about 60 years, Indo-US relations have been rocky. The clash, which developed in the Cold War, are now over as the Cold War ended more than a decade ago (Harrison Geoffrey, 1993; Sandy Gordon, 1995).

Top Level Visits to Herald a New Era

The 5 day visit of the President Clinton to South Asia in March 2000 was the only visit made by a US president in 24 years. This trip had enhanced New Delhi's status as a reliable partner with Washington, at least for trade and commerce. For the first time both democracies agreed officially to prepare a common economic program for increasing corporation. This had a special significance after the imposition of economic sanctions by the US for Pokhran-II nuclear tests (Venkataraman, 1998; Gupta, 2000). President Clinton changing his views, expressed opinion that until Pakistan stopped cross-border terrorism and honoured the present LOC, India may not have any talks with Pakistan. India and the US signed agreements, which would act as a foundation for improvement in mutual relations in important fields including energy, science and technology, industry and environment etc. However, on nuclear issues the bilateral relations remained the same as they were before. No assurance was given by India on signing CTBT. President Clinton also visited cities of Agra, Hyderabad, Bangalore, Mumbai and State of Rajasthan and received unprecedented welcome and affection.

A leading think tank in the US, in the post-mortem had said it "heralded India's centrality to US policy in South Asia, and a new economic emphasis on US-Indian relations." The Centre of Strategic and International Studies (CSIS), in a report titled " President Clinton's South Asia Trip: Beginning of a Long Road," argued that " if India emerged as a key player in the US policy toward South Asia, Pakistan is a key problem." The report mentioned "the contrast with the Indian extravaganza was devastating" vis-à-vis Clinton's "sombre, five hour stop in Pakistan". It said the longer term outlook depended on whether New Delhi and Islamabad "inject some new substance into their hitherto sterile bilateral dialogue. It also depends on whether the Pakistan government is willing or able to disciple militant groups" (India Abroad, April 28th, 2000). India's Prime Minister Vajpayee, during his visit to US in September 2000, asked the US for understanding of India's policy of nuclear-weapons program in what Congressional leaders hailed as an historic speech. "We both share a commitment to ultimately eliminating nuclear weapons," Vajpayee said in an address to a joint session of Congress. "India understands your concerns...We wish you to understand our security concerns," he stated.

The comments indicated a main disagreement on India's nuclear tests in 1998 and it's not signing discriminatory CTBT. Vajpayee desired the two democracies to unite against poverty, terrorism and hunger. Members of the Congress praised his assertions that India and the US have embarked on "A new beginning in our relations." "This truly illustrates India's growing importance to the United States," Speaker Dennis Hastert, said. The US government welcomed closer ties but was also concerned with India's decision to develop nuclear weapons as also not signing the CTBT (which has already been turned down by its Senate). On the fringes of Vajpayee's visit, the US signed a number of agreements with India's Public and Private sectors, which were presided jointly by Norman Mineta and Yashwant Sinha. Among the agreements signed were US Export Import Bank (Ex-Im) pledges of US$ 900 million to help Indian business purchase US goods and services and the US Agency for International Development (USAID) documents pledging support for urban development. The Indo-US commercial dialogue is an implementation of the "Vision Statement" signed by Clinton and Vajpayee in March 2000 and seeks to identify and revise policies restricting the Indo-US trade growth.

The images that lingered from Clinton's visit to the Indian Subcontinent in March 2000 were contrasting; the president being showered with flowers in India whereas arriving grimly in a heavily guarded camouflaged plane in Pakistan. In September the Chiefs of both India and Pakistan government visited the US. The contrasts were again sharp: Vajpayee was cheered by Congress and feted on the White House lawn, while Musharraf was forced to delay his flight because of a bomb threat. US officials stated they will "work with" the Pak military government on such contentious issues as Islamic terrorism and the Indo-Pak dispute over Kashmir. Clinton declared, "It is not only India's democracy, but India's manner of achieving democracy that will forever inspire America. Our challenge is to turn our common bond into common achievements" (Seattle Times, September 16th 2000). "There was very little Pakistan could do to keep itself from being over shadowed" by Vajpayee's visit, wrote columnist Tahir Mirza in the Dawn Newspaper.

He suggested that Musharraf made things worse by "engaging in a war of words with Indians over Kashmir" and by "ridiculing the concepts of democracy and secularism" on his visit to the US. Musharaff also renewed his call for mediation in Kashmir and blamed India for all the woes of South Asia. The US diplomat, Arthur Davis, who was the US ambassador and also advised the US mission to the UN, said: "the economy of Pakistan is sinking, yet the focus of military leadership remains stronger than ever over Kashmir. Pakistan's janta continues to concentrate all its resources on funding and fuelling terrorism in Kashmir on the one hand while, on the other, dashing domestic hopes for a return to democratic and secular society." Davis said: "declaring Pakistan a terrorist state would encourage the people of Pakistan to remove the military war mongers who have deprived them of sustainable development" (Washington Post, September 8, 2004).

For the first time the US Foreign Secretary, in an interview to two news channels stated that Islamabad government and some Pakistani organizations have close friendly relations with terrorists and the US is going to take serious action against Pakistan for the same (Hindustan, August 9, 2008). President Bush further improved Indo-US relations by military cooperation and civil nuclear energy deal.

In October 2000, Russia and India revived the warmth of their strategic partnership but said they were not seeking to create a new military-political alliance. The declaration signed by Atal Behari Vajpayee and Vladimir Putin binds the two countries to a joint approach on fighting international terrorism, defence issues and nuclear energy. The two countries also agreed not to participate in any military-political alliance, associations or armed conflict directed against each other. Vajpayee emphasized that India, which has gone nuclear owing to threats from Pakistan and China, was not forming strategic alliance with Russia.

Taliban Movement in Afghanistan

Since both countries were wrestling with armed Islamic insurgency, the two heads of the government referred to the concerns about the radical Islamic agenda of the military regime of Pakistan which has become a safe heaven for terrorist organizations and their mentors attacking India and the ruling Taliban movement in Afghanistan. They said their agencies would work closely to combat international terrorism (Seattle Times, October 4, 2000). Recent agreement to manufacture Sukhoi-30 in India and a proposal to set up a factory the manufacture of MIG aircraft parts are examples in this direction, for which a large deal has been made between the two closely cooperating nations. After Russian President's arrival from China, Prime Minister Vajpayee favoured further extension of strategic alliance between the two nations. They discussed the joint anti-terror efforts and also looked at the new axis with China (India Journal, December 6, 2002).

Later both nations signed an agreement for developing fighter jet planes and other high-tech weapons. Russia also gave a proposal to India for making a single seat fighter plane like SU-30 MKI (Agencies January 30, 2003). In the Security Conference in Munich, Russian Defence Minster Sargai Ivanov said Pak Madarsas are affiliated to the terrorist training camps. Therefore, he did not like to meet Pak President during his visit to Russia. According to him several extremist organizations are encouraging Muslim youths to become terrorists through their published literature. Russia is therefore, making an air base in Kant, Kirgiz (Amar Ujala, February 11, 2003). Russian Foreign Minister Igor Ivanov said Russia too is unhappy with Pak sponsored cross-border terrorism and instead of believing in statements Russia would like to see Pakistani work (Press June 17, 2003). President Putin had discussions with Manmohan Singh and 11 agreements were signed for closer cooperation. Similarly, China and India are trying to improve their mutual ties as indicated by high level visits in 2001 and 2002 as well as by starting direct flights between New Delhi and Beijing.

Total value of several ongoing Indo-Russian projects/ purchases and new projects is estimated over US$ 10 billion. India is purchasing 347 more T-90 battle tanks and 40 more

Sukhoi 'air dominance' fighters, apart from 80 more Mi-17 medium lift helicopters from Russia. Several ongoing naval projects include Rs. 5,514 crore deal for three more Talwar class stealth fighters; Rs. 6,900 crore deal for aircraft carrier Admiral Gorshkov, along with its complimentary helicopters. In addition there is a Rs. 865 crore deal of upgrading submarines with Klub-5 cruise missiles. Moreover in 2008-09 nuclear powered Akula-II submarines are to be leased for 10 years from Russia at a cost of Rs. 2,600 crore. Sailors for these submarines are already being trained in Russia. Some irritants have however, surfaced in the Indo-Russian military ties. 1. Delivery schedules are not being strictly followed by Russia. 2. Russia is showing an increasing propensity to ask for higher rates on the pretext of weakening dollar. 3. China has become a major client of Russia. Therefore, India has become suspicious of deep links between China and Pakistan.

Indo-US Military Cooperation

The envisaged military-to-military ties received a fillip with Indian Ambassador Lalit Man Singh's visit to Hawaii to meet the top officials of the US Pacific Command and later by observing joint exercises in Anchorage, Alaska. During this visit of Ambassador of L.M. Singh in 2001, it was decided to resurrect army cooperation, which had been lying dormant after India's Pokhran-II nuclear tests. Indo-US joint military exercises were later carried out in several places in India and the US and the proposals to sell radars etc. to India came about. The largest joint exercise between India and the US navy was held off the Kochi coast (H.Q. of India's Southern Command) in 2003. The previous four exercises were held in 1992, 1995, 1996 and 2001.

After Pokhran-II tests (1998) joint exercises were not held and restarted only in 2001. The USS Sides, exclusively deployed for operation 'Enduring Freedom' had arrived on Kochi coast. In 2003 India's INS Godavri had docked in Washington DC coast as a symbol of cooperation. Under the name 'cope India' the US Pacific Command reached Gwalior to practice 10 joint military exercises with Indian Air Force (AP February 26, 2004). In all, India and the US had 120 joint exercises between 2002 and 2006. As per Indo-US agreement to supply modern military equipment the US supplied two 'Fire Finder' radars. These radars can in no time find the place from where the rockets are being fired. By the end of 2006 10 more such radars were to be supplied (Amar Ujala, July 11, 2003). Soldiers from 5 nations including the US are getting 6 months training in Mizoram forests to fight against terrorists (IANS February 4, 2005). Pranab Mukerji, Indian Defence Minister and Donald Rumsfeld, the US Defence Secretary signed a 10-year 'Framework for US-India Defence Relationship', which obligated the two countries to prevent the spread of WMD and established a joint defence procurement and production group to increase cooperation and missile defence (Agencies June 30, 2005).

In the new millennium Indian and US forces held a number of joint exercises, which rapidly acquired a routine and substantive nature. The most important 14 exercises were:

1. Exercise Balance Iroquois in May 2002 of Indian parachute brigade and US special force at Agra.
2. Exercise Yudh Abhyas at CIJWS, Vairangte in May 2002.
3. Exercise Geronimo Thrust, a mountain warfare in Alaska in 2002.
4. Exercise Malabar in 2002, joint naval practices off India's Kochi coast in the Arabian Sea.
5. Exercise Cope India 2002, an air transport practice of Indian Air force and US Air Force at Agra.
6. Cooperative Cope Thunder in June 2003 involving 7 organizations.
7. US-Indian special forces, near India-China border in September 2003.
8. Exercise Malabar in October 2003 with US nuclear submarine, a missile destroyer and a cruiser.
9. Exercise Cope India 2004, an air combat training with

USAF F-15C and Indian fighter planes, Gwalior.

10. Cooperative Cope Thunder 2004, with Jaguars, IL-76, IL-78 tanker aircraft in July 2004 in Alaska.
11. Exercise Malabar 2004, with US guided missile cruiser, guided missile frigate, attack submarine, P-3C maritime patrol and reconnaissance aircraft in October.
12. The two nations conducted the biggest exercises near Ranikhet in Utranchal in January, 2005 to open the doors to high technology transfers. One company of the US army also conducted joint exercise with a thrust on insurgency.
13. A 12-day joint exercise of Indo-US navies at Kochi began on September 13, 2005. The exercise, called Salvex, focused on diving and salvage operations, training and professional discussions.
14. Besides the above exercises there were many others organized later either in India or USA. In the one carried out in the desert of Nevada Indian special air force called Garur Commando Force took hold of one air field within two hours after destroying radar very quickly (Agencies August 20, 2008).

Although the US arms sale to India has not been quite as fast, India purchased a dozen Fire-finder counter-battery radar sets. India is also sourcing electronic sensors for border management from the US. Aircraft self-protection systems and Israeli Phalco early warning system are some important acquisitions since 2004. Lockheed Martin has also offered to sell its superior fighter aircrafts and also to set up production lines in India, which are still in consideration by Indian government. The US and Indian army Chiefs met on September 8, 2006 at New Delhi. The US army Chief of Staff General Peter J. Schoomaker discussed with Indian Army Chief at the army head quarters in Delhi to further strengthen the growing military relationship with India. The Indian Navy took charge of the American warship Trenton. The 17,000 ton INS carrier vessel commissioned as INS Jalashva, is the second largest ship in the Navy and the first American warship to join Indian Navy Fleet. Officials said Indo-US defence trade stood at US$ 287 million but they are expecting a big jump in arms sales with Navy, Special Forces and the Air Force (Deccan Herald, December 10, 2005).

After attack on USS Cole in Aden in 2000 and 9/11 terror strikes in 2001, the US has been promoting steps like Public Security Initiative (PSI) and Container Security Initiative throughout the globe. Despite having world's best navy, with over a dozen aircraft carriers, the US recognizes that it alone cannot ensure maritime security. Therefore, India and the US are already finalizing a Maritime Cooperation Framework (MCF) to enhance security, prevent piracy and other transactional crimes at Sea as well as address emerging threats. For this purpose US Chief of naval operations, Admiral Michael G. Mullen visited India in April, 2007.

Will nuclear 123 equal IAF 126? This is the most important question in the minds of Indian intellectuals. Will finally agreed 123 Agreement for civil nuclear Indo-US cooperation give American fighters the required thrust to go ahead of other competitors in securing the IAF project to acquire 126 multipurpose combat aircraft. The IAF gigantic deal may amount to Rs. 42,000 crore (US$ 10.4 billion). For this purpose, Lockheed Martin made a presentation in July on the ongoing F-35 project, indicating this G-5 fighter could fulfil India's fighter jet needs after induction of 126 combat aircraft in the next decade. India needs G-5 fighters beyond visual range combat capabilities, reduced radar tracking signature and supersonic cruising ability.

Besides joint military or navy exercises, India and the US came closer in 2007 to discuss the massive build up and modernization of China's military and expanding arc of influence in Asia-Pacific region. At the same time India desires to be viewed as a neutral nation rather than a counterweight to China or a supporter of containment of China being an 'axis of democracy'.

After Afghanistan retaliatory attacks, India and several

other nations recommended the US 'no military strikes' on Iraq. India believed efforts must be made to avoid conflict and settle the alleged issue of weapons of mass-destruction by mutual discussions and peaceful means, the way US likes India to treat Pakistan on cross-border terrorism issue. "Any military conflict in that area is going to be disastrous from our (India) point of view," said Foreign Minister Yaswant Sinha in a debate in Lok Sabha on Middle East situation in December, 2002. Prime Minister Vajpayee had earlier expressed similar views, a few days earlier, while speaking to the reporters in Kuala Lumpur during the meetings of NAM nations. He said to get involved actively in bilateral issues would amount to denouncing of the NAM philosophy. B. Raman, a panellist in the conference organized by US-India Political Action Committee and the Director of Tropical Studies Institute, said "When no body was willing to help us (India) against state-sponsored terrorism by Pakistan after Mumbai (bomb) blasts, Saddam Husain's Iraq helped us," (Aziz Haniffa, 2003). The Indian government decision to send its troops to Iraq only under a UN mandate came as a surprise and shock. The US had counted on it as a sure deal and did not expect rejection of the request because both President Bush and Secretary Rumsfeld had asked the Deputy Prime Minister for the Indian troops. Explaining why Washington took New Delhi's support for granted when India had opposed the pre-emptive strike on Iraq, a senior Administrator said, "We were so upset with French and Germans we hardly noticed the noise coming from Delhi" (Aziz Haniffa, 2003).

Even former president Gerald Ford said in an interview in July 2004, about a year after launching invasion, that Iraq war was not justified. I would not have gone to war, he said. In a four hour interview he very strongly disagreed with President Bush's justifications for invading Iraq and said he would have pushed alternatives like vigorous sanctions etc. He also criticized Vice President Dick Chenny and Defence Secretary Donald Rumsfeld. "Rumsfeld and Chenny and the president made a big mistake in justifying going into war." On the 2nd anniversary of the US attack on Iraq there were several demonstrations throughout the world. Even in US, U.K., Turkey, Japan, Egypt, Australia and Pakistan people protested. Despite elections in January, 2005, normalcy could not be restored and suicide attacks or sectarian violence incidences are generally in the news. World is clearly divided on this issue. Iraq war has now lasted longer than the US involvement in the war that President Bush's father was involved in. The conflict in Iraq has raged for about five years and about 4,500 military deaths have occurred. US increased its forces to achieve peace but it is still not in sight despite elected Iraqi government's best efforts.

More than six decades of active relations between India and the US have had several ups and downs. The clash of interests, which became prominent in the Cold War, should now end after the cold war. Let us hope the estranged democracies have learnt the lessons from the past. Although the problems of the past are out of sight now, they are definitely not out of mind. Luckily a good progress has been made during 2000 to 2008 by top level visits, joint military exercises and civil nuclear energy agreement. Like Indian Prime Ministers Rajiv Gandhi and Atal Bihari Vajpayee the US President Obama also has a dream of ending nuclear weapons from the globe. He said in Prague that the US has responsibility of ending nuclear weapons and if he seriously works for the same, he is likely to achieve significant results (April 6, 2009). As a first step talks on reduction of nuclear arms have been proposed between Russia and the US.

The US Foreign Secretary Condoleezza Rice visited India and Pakistan in 2005 and expressed resentment on India-Pakistan-Iran gas pipe line. She also avoided replying questions on F-16 fighter plane supply to Pakistan and on support to India for permanent seat in the UN Security Council. Recently, the US also refused visa to an elected Chief Minister of Gujarat, an Indian State. The facts indicate a possibility of pressurizing Pakistan on gas pipe line from Iran, which would make Indo-US relations again rocky. In support of UN mandate and world opinion on Iran nuclear issue, India did not push forward tripartite Iran- India gas pipeline despite energy shortage but Pakistan hastened its agreement with its nuclear partner Iran with a view to render economical help because UN and many other nations are putting sanctions on it. If the US and India desire to forge more constructive mutual ties in the new millennium, views of the French President Jacques Chirac must be kept in mind. In his year-end interviews to media, he had several years earlier articulated that unlike the previous century, the new millennium would be multi-polar. In addition to the US, "China, India and Europe will be great powers in the next century," he had said. In early 2006, he visited India and signed a nuclear technology cooperation agreement for civil purposes. Russian President Putin also signed agreement with India in 2007 to help build four more atomic plants.

A few days later President Bush also came to South Asia and signed a civil nuclear energy agreement with India and did not agree with the request of Pakistan for a similar agreement with that country. It is therefore, apparent that the US has realized the necessity of overcoming the energy shortage in India for civil purposes. If we look at the rhetoric of US-India relations, economic, energy and security domains have been fundamentally transformed. Passed by the US Congress and signed by the President on December 18, 2006, the bill has now become an act and now the US companies are free to trade with India on civil nuclear energy programs. A series of separate deals between India and the US will make the deal operational. Some senior US politicians are viewing it as a 'historic mistake'. India signed a deal with IAEA and secured approval of the 45-nation Nuclear Suppliers Group (NSG) to allow nuclear trade with India.

While signing the India-US Peaceful Energy Act at a special White House ceremony, President Bush had hailed it as an important achievement for the world and hoped to get India's cooperation for NPT, which it had been avoiding to sign because of its discriminatory nature. Indian Prime Minister Singh accepted that there were certain areas of concern, clarification for the same will be sought from the US to maintain India's nuclear 'swaraj'. India would not accept any legal binding on nuclear testing and there is no question of signing CTBT. He added there was no reason for opposition leader, L.K. Advani to worry about India losing its nuclear 'swaraj'. Earlier Sitaram Yechury and Shahid Siddiqui also had expressed similar concerns.

The Henry Hyde Act passed into law in 2006, christened as the 123 Agreement, in reference to section 123 of the American Atomic Energy Act 1950 is more about the overall strategic Indo-US relationships, rather than exclusive access to sensitive technology. For India the core issue is not so much purely civilian use of nuclear energy but overwhelming strategic objective of preservation and maintenance of nation's indigenous nuclear weapon program. The final agreement will now allow India to carry out reprocessing spent fuel from the reactors but requires a new facility for that purpose as per IAEA standards. However, former Chairman of the Atomic Energy Commission, P.K. Iyengar, is of the opinion that government should not sign 123 Agreement because its part 2.1 is highly objectionable.

Although on October 16, 2007 Prime Minister Singh had told the US President Bush that his government would not be able to hold negotiations with IAEA soon, negotiations were made. On the issue of nuclear deal Indian public seems to be on the side of the UPA government as shown by a June 2008 survey. It appears public does not agree with the left parties and 80 percent surveyed people have clearly given verdict by yes. Only 20 percent people did consider left parties to be right. It would be honest to admit that the Indo-US nuclear deal is a 3-in-1 document comprising a civil nuclear energy cooperation agreement, de facto NPT and CTBT. The deal has been approved both by the IAEA and the NSG. Whichever way one looks at the deal, honest or deceitful agreement, it certainly is a very significant historical agreement.

All the three factors seem to range against the ruling party in India. In politics or in any other sphere of life, one wins if one dares. If one dithers or delays one is bound to get defeat. After approval by the NSG, Condoleezza Rice pressed US Congress to approve the deal. Fortunately the nuke deal has been finally approved by the US Congress. A few days earlier the House Representatives had already passed the same. With this deal (signed by the President as law on October 9, 2008) the ban on India to trade nuclear technology or material would go. In the White House ceremony President Bush said, "Even though the US and India are separated by half the globe, we are natural partners...into the 21st Century", indicating better relations between the two nations. He also stated that India was granted advance consent for reprocessing the fuel. On October 11, the US and India put the final seal in New Delhi, making the deal "legally-binding" for both nations. For India it is the first step for cooperation with the world on civil nuke programme.

However Indian government's priority is to produce more electricity as quickly as it can. Following waver granted by NSG France became the first nation to sign a civil nuclear energy pact with India the very next day. This pact will be the basis of wide ranging mutual cooperation for research, including reactors, fuel supply, safety, radiation and environment protection as well as nuclear fuel cycle management. Indian Security Adviser MK Narayanan told reporters, "The world needs India as India needs the world..." Pakistan, which opposed the deal, now demands a similar deal from the US, Prime Minister YS Gilani said to reporters (AP October 3, 2008).

6

US Perspective of India

B.B. Nagaich

The US President, Harry S. Truman, was among those who welcomed the freedom of India from the British colonialism. Although both India and the US desired their mutual relations to be extremely friendly, unfortunately, they have not been always so. At times the relations have been cordial, but most of the time they have been indifferent or estranged (Dennis Kux, 1993; Garry, 1992; Gould, 1992; Gupta, 1977; Limaye, 1993). For India the year 1947 had been very painful and also very happy bringing it freedom from British rule. The tragedy was in the mass killings, which were followed by partition and the movement of about 15 million people from one area to another. For the US it was the beginning of the Marshall plan, massive economic assistance to rebuild Western Europe after World War II, and to protect it from the USSR and the dreaded communism (Gupta, 1977).

With the onset of the cold war, Indian Prime Minister Pandit Nehru adopted a policy of non-alignment (Jackson, 1983; Jha, 1983; Nehru, 1948; Sandy Gordon, 1995). After Nehru brought Kashmir issue to the United Nations, the US became active for the first time in the affairs of the Indian sub-continent (Siddhu, 1998, Sinha, 1998; Harrison et al., 1993). Not considering the merger of Kashmir with India, by Maharaja Hari Singh as proper, Truman did not agree with India's position on Kashmir and after the rejection of Truman's proposal in 1949 by India, the US concluded that India wished to grab all of Kashmir on the basis of Hari Singh's merger of Kashmir with India (Dennis Kux, 1993, Dixit, 1998; Cohen 1987, 1998).

The then Secretary of State, Dean Acheson, referred to Nehru as one of the most difficult men he had to deal with. Kashmir had merged into India, but the Secretary of State could not reconcile with the fact, and hence did not view invasion by Pakistan as an aggression. In his opinion, he was not ignoring the British government declaration of independence to India, Pakistan and the princely states. US pressure in support of the UN proposal for complete withdrawal of Pakistani and Indian forces from Kashmir and to hand over Kashmir administration to the UN for plebiscite irked Nehru, who was disappointed by the treatment of aggressor and the aggrieved as equal. Nehru, therefore, did not agree to hand over the administration of Kashmir to the UN for plebiscite. Ultimately the UN sent an Australian jurist, Sir Owen Dixon to settle the issue. He suggested partition of the valley of Srinagar, leaving Jammu to India or some other means of allocating the valley rather than over all plebiscite. He also recommended the UN not to pursue the mediation, letting the two countries settle the issue themselves.

This laid the foundation for an estranged Indo-US relationship. Although Nehru admired the US, he disliked its military based foreign policy and its capitalism. By 1950 North Korea invaded South Korea, and the US committed 5000,000 troops. Supporting the UN (Nehru, 1950), India took almost a neutral position and played an important role in the cease-fire agreement and management of the prisoners of war in South Korea (Alan, 1969; Dixit, 1998; Gupta, 1977). In Kashmir, where Indian soldiers shed their blood against Pakistan, the US attitude badly upset the government of India. However, in Korea, where the US soldiers were shedding their blood against North Korea and Chinese communist forces, the Indian's near neutral attitude badly upset the US government. Thus India and the US both wanted aggression punished and basic principles of international morality upheld but only when they were themselves affected (Dennis Kux, 1993; Ganguly, 1986).

India sent medical teams and appointed its top soldier, General K.S. Thimaya, to head its Custodial Force to see that the POWs could freely express their views and no one was sent home against his wishes. Thimaya's strict neutrality in official and unofficial contacts annoyed China more than the US but was highly appreciated by others. India's Defence Minister, Krishna Menon, became prominent internationally in 1954. He made statements in the UN over the Kashmir Issue, which irritated the US authorities, and which they interpreted as signifying that India was moving towards the USSR (Immerson, 1999). Nehru's prestige as a leader of the developing countries helped India to gain a position of weight in the international affairs. Chester Bowles, the US Ambassador to India, improved the image of the US in India and gained sympathy of the US government for India. Consequently, the US began economic assistance to India. In 1953 Dwight D. Eisenhower became President of the US. He strongly advocated the containment of communism. Prime Minister Nehru had a good relationship with Chou En-Lai of China. After visiting India and Pakistan in 1953, the US Secretary of State John Foster Dulles, became a strong supporter of Pakistan (Immerson, 1999). He believed that a Pakistan armed and economically aided by the US could fight communists.

CENTO and SEATO Defence Pacts

Consequently, despite Indian opposition, the CENTO and SEATO defence pacts were formed, Pakistan was enlisted as a member of both the pacts and in 1954 military aid was provided to Pakistan (Barnds, 1972). The Middle East and Pakistan were thought to be more important than India, as Pakistan agreed to the flights of the U-2 aircraft against Russia from the airfields near Peshawar. To please India, the US rebuffed Pakistan's attempts to have the US ally with it in CENTO and SEATO against India. However, India remained angry because it considered that the US had brought the cold war to South Asia also and had strengthened Pakistan (Gupta, 1977). This resulted in better Indo-USSR relationship. The Soviets began to side with India on Kashmir and other matters. Consequently Nehru, who had been outspoken about the Suez Canal issue, kept his own counsel in regards to the events in Hungary. India was adversely commented upon in the West as the Prime Minister spoke against the British-US moves in favour of Egypt but not for Hungary against the USSR.

During his visit to the US in 1956 Nehru regarded Eisenhower as a strong supporter of peace. Eisenhower appreciated Nehru's anti colonial feelings and his desire to promote democracy and economic standards. With bilateral relations improving and with increased economic aid to India, Eisenhower received a big welcome in 1959 when he visited the nation. However, it was soon neutralized by the non-endorsement of the Indian stand on Kashmir in the UN. India's taking back Goa from the Portuguese by military intervention also adversely affected the Indo-US relationship.

Mutual goodwill further increased when John F. Kennedy became the US President in 1961. He praised the "soaring idealism" of Pandit Nehru and argued that US foreign policy had earlier over emphasized military ties to pay less attention to the non-aligned nations. An initiative by President Kennedy to sideline the Kashmir debate in the UN did not get much notice in India (Dennis Kux, 1993; Gupta, 1997; Gary Hess, 1992). To avoid the issue surfacing again, Kennedy in January 1962 proposed that Eugene Black (former World Bank President, who had good contacts with Nehru and Ayub and had successfully mediated the Indus water dispute) to visit India and Pakistan to promote the Kashmir settlement. Black seemed a logical choice for mediating in Kashmir imbroglio.

Pakistan accepted the proposal but India refused. In 1962 when the Indo-Chinese border dispute over the Mc Mahon line became a war, the Kennedy administration moved quickly to help India despite the Cuban missiles crisis (Hoffman, 1990). At the end of war Nehru removed Menon from the defence ministry as he was considered responsible for the debacle. After the Indo-China war Nehru also agreed to discussions with Pakistan concerning Kashmir settlement. However six rounds of talks ended in a failure. In spite of Pakistan's opposition, Kennedy administration made it clear that it intended to help India. The President announced, "Let's not be penny wise about India; let's not let get them into the position where they feel that they can't cope with the Chicoms and the Paks on top of their problems." President Kennedy told the President of India, a month later in June 1963, that the US was prepared to move in the direction of helping India.

The Kennedy government called for a tripling of the US development lending provided in 1960. By the end of 1961, the first two dozens Peace Corps volunteers also reached India. This team later grew to several hundred volunteers whose program supplemented India's rural development work and was highly appreciated by the Indians. In December 1961 the Indian army moved in Goa and the Portuguese surrendered without a fight. The US vociferously disapproved that of all the countries, India resorted the use of force against the US desire to delay the action for a few months to give diplomacy a chance and solve the problem peacefully.

After Kennedy was assassinated, Lyndon B. Johnson took over the implemented agricultural policies, after making some changes. Not sharing his predecessor's views, he suspended military and economic aid both to India and Pakistan because of their war over Kashmir, but later resumed economic aid to Islamabad due to friendship with Ayub Khan. After Indira Gandhi became Prime Minister of India, she visited Washington in 1966 to meet President Johnson. However, following Johnson's tough stance on food aid and his urging devaluation of the Indian currency, Indira Gandhi became closer to the USSR and vehemently criticized the US Vietnam policy.

After the 1965 Indo-Pak war, the US supported the Russian mediation at Tashkent and strenuous efforts were made to prevent USSR influence in the sub-continent. During 1967 and 1968 the US and USSR both pressured India to adhere to Nehru's policy of NPT (Kapur, 1971). New Delhi however, refused because neither country would guarantee against a Chinese nuclear threat and also because NPT was an unequal arrangement between nuclear haves and have-nots. The have-nots neither moved towards disarmament nor placed their own nuclear facilities under international safeguards.

When Richard Nixon became President, US policy favoured Pakistan more and more (Harrison and Subramanyam, 1989; Maroof Raza, 1996; Palmer, 1984). In 1969 Nixon's discussions with Yahya Khan were more substantive then those with India. Previously Pakistan's close ties with China had caused great tension in the US but now Nixon asked Yahya Khan to convey to China his interest in opening a dialogue with China (Thomas, 1992). In 1971, with Pakistan playing a key role in arranging the US secretary of State Henry Kissinger's secret visit to China, Nixon carefully avoided criticizing President Yahya Khan's brutality and suppression of East Pakistan, which ultimately became an independent nation, Bangladesh (Kennedy, 1971).

US on East Pakistan (now Bangladesh)

At the end of 1971, during her official visit to Washington, Indira Gandhi rebuffed Nixon's bargaining for time to settle the East Pakistan (now Bangladesh) problem. Nixon and Kissinger were of the opinion that if they were given sufficient time they could have persuaded Yahya Khan for conceding self-determination for East Pakistan, either full freedom or provincial autonomy without blood-shed (Vinod, 1991; Venkataramani and Arya, 1996; Thornton, 1992). This was because she lacked confidence in Nixon. When war broke out between Bangladesh guerrilla forces called the Mukti Bahini (liberation force) and Pakistan army in December, Nixon and Kissinger declared that India intended to attack West Pakistan despite disagreements from the South Asia specialists. Because of this fear Nixon sent the 7th Fleet aircraft carrier Enterprise to the Bay of Bengal in the Indian Ocean to boost Pakistan's morale (Kissinger, 1994). Nixon in a private letter rebuked Indira Gandhi for having spurned his efforts to find a peaceful solution of the crisis.

He also warned Moscow through a variety of channels to call off its "Indian friends". Vietnam became another cause of tension after Delhi desiring to raise the level of its mission in Hanoi. The US cautioned India that this would result in no more US aid. Therefore, India deferred it, as it wanted US assistance, although the levels of the aid were declining. Another bilateral problem had a unique origin. In 1969 the USSR proceeded to start a cultural centre in Trivandrum, where the communists were in power. The building collapsed and New Delhi refused further construction work of the centre and also told USIS to shut down its five centres already running in Lucknow, Patna, Hyderabad, Bangalore and Trivandrum. Additional pinprick came at the end of the UN Golden Jubilee. Several heads of governments including India, Pakistan and the US etc attended the celebrations.

Yahya Khan and several others accepted President Nixon's invitation for dinner at the White House but Mrs. Gandhi turned it down. Nixon also told Yahya Khan, "Nobody has occupied the White House who is friendlier to Pakistan than me." The Indians also opposed a small naval communication facility on Diego Garcia and supported the Indian Ocean as a peace zone (Joshi, 1991). Thus Indo-US relations were damaged, the damage being maximal and long lasting. The relations improved somewhat after Daniel Patrick Moynihan was appointed as Ambassador to India in 1973.

However, in 1974 India lost more US friends when India exploded a nuclear device. Canada, which closely cooperated with India on its nuclear program, reacted very strongly by cutting of all help on nuclear projects; Canada was particularly annoyed because the plutonium used in the test was produced in the reactor supplied by Canada for peaceful purposes.

Emergency declaration by India in 1975 led the US to believe India to be another dictatorship and the Indo-US relations remained in the doldrums because of Mrs. Gandhi's frequent sniping at the US. Moynihan was able to negotiate a rupee package worth US$ 2.2 billion. Although Nixon, never regarded as a friend of India, deserved part of the credit because of his support to ambassador Moynihan on this issue in 1974.

In October 1974 Henry Kissinger attempted to repair the damages in relationship by staying at Delhi for 3 days but did not succeed although during his stay Kissinger and Y.B. Chavan signed an agreement to establish the Indo-US Joint Commission (Moynihan, 1978; Dennis Kux, 1993). Ambassador William Saxbe's frankness and diplomacy upset the Indians. Mrs. Indira Gandhi continued her allegation periodically about foreign elements trying to destabilize India to divert attention from domestic problems. She obviously referred to the CIA, Moynihan pointed out in his book that as President of the Congress party she herself received money from the CIA to help out the Communist government in Kerala in the 1950s and that was why she was suspicious of the CIA.

In 1977 Morarji Desai became India's Prime Minister and the relations improved slightly. The next US President, Jimmy Carter, responded favourably to India, downplaying the ties with Pakistan where a military dictator Zia-ul-Haq ruled. With US supplying nuclear fuel (the supply of which was delayed during Ford's presidency) for the Tarapore power reactors the relations became cordial. Prime Minister Desai visited Washington in 1977 and President Carter was given a deserving welcome in New Delhi in 1978. Just after the US was defeated in Vietnam the global balance seemed to tilt towards Soviet Russia. In 1979, Russia intervened militarily to replace the Afghan leader with another of their choice (Yousaf and Adkins, 1993). Speedily, cold war returned and Pakistan, bordering Afghanistan, became a front line country. One year later, President Zia-ul-Haq received US$ 3.2 billion in assistance. Pakistan and the US cooperated and supplied an aid to Afghani burgeonists for fighting against the Russian supported government, much against the wishes of India. In 1980 India whitewashed, in the UN General Assembly, a debate of the Soviet Union action in Afghanistan, annoying President Carter, who helped India in spite of differences over nuclear non-proliferation (Mohite, 1995; Prajapati, 1998).

In 1981 after Ronald Reagan became President the US considered India to be a Soviet camp follower and gave Pakistan much more aid (Harrison and Subramanyam, 1989). Thus Pakistan became the fourth biggest aid receiver after Israel, Egypt and Turkey. Surprisingly, however, Indo-US relations improved when Indira Gandhi felt that India should improve relations with the US as her country required an access to the advanced US technology not only in the defence sector but also across the economic spectrum (Gandhi, 1981). She met with Reagan in Cancun, Mexico in 1981, and in 1982 she visited the US. However, India's refusal to grant a visa for George Griffin, assigned to the US Embassy in New Delhi, made matters worse. A serious dispute arose over a US$ 5.8 billion loan sought by India to which the US was opposed initially but later abstained on instructions from President Reagan (Sharma and Sharma, 1997; Wolpert, 1982).

In 1984 Rajiv Gandhi succeeded his mother as Prime Minister and continued the foreign policy inherited from his grandfather and also mother. Both India and the US wanted to get out from impasse of the US tied with Islamabad and India with Moscow. About a month after Rajiv Gandhi took over as the Prime Minister, the US and India reached an agreement on technology MOU. In June 1985 he visited the US and as a well-informed, pragmatic young leader was liked by Americans. However, the US found it very difficult for security reasons to accommodate India's desire to get the Cray X MP-24 super computer and GE 404 engine from Washington.

Improvement in the Indo-US relations continued, although

India's opposition to the US supplying arms to Pakistan and the US dislike for India's friendly ties with the USSR remained as they were. In 1990 the US President George HW Bush implemented the Pressler Amendment to cut off aid to Pakistan because of Islamabad's refusal to roll back its uranium enrichment program. During the Gulf war India permitted refuelling of the US military aircraft quietly although India had friendly relations with Iraq, which was the major supplier of oil to India and unlike other Arab States backed India on Kashmir. India also condemned Zionism. Robert Gates, the US deputy National Security Adviser, was received in India in a friendlier manner than in Pakistan (Sharma and Sharma, 1997; Sidhu, 1998; Thornton, 1990). Alleged human rights violation in Punjab began to draw criticism in the US Congress. Active lobbying by supporters of the separatist movement and references by Amnesty International stirred interest in the US.

Washington however, did not give a favourable response to India in terms of defence and security cooperation (Ohajunwa, 1992). In fact the US opposed increased economic assistance on the pretext of alleged human rights violations and missile development programs. When India asked for the Cray X MP-22 instead of 14 (which the US had offered) it resulted in unhappiness. In June 1989 the Bush Administration issued the first Super 301 watch list. In this paper Japan, India and Brazil were mentioned as trade offenders. There were three complaints against India. The first complaint was against foreign investment. The second complaint concerned insurance. The third and the most important dispute related to the so-called IPR and patent protection. This release further incensed New Delhi. In 1988 and afterwards, the Communist countries in East Europe started collapsing. With the collapse of the USSR, the United States emerged as the sole super power (Thornton, 1990; Srinivasan, 1995; Sandy Gordon, 1995). After Bill Clinton's taking over as President, the US remained indifferent to India. Although the political relations between India and the US remained at a stand still, economic relations began to improve (Sharma and Bakshi, 1992).

Indo-US ties entered a new phase in May 1994 after the visit of the Prime Minister Narsimha Rao to the US. Despite differences over many issues, the two countries announced a frame work for building a new partnership. The Prime Minister made it very clear that India will not make a change in the traditional foreign policy, emphasizing the non-discriminatory global framework of nuclear-non-proliferation. In a joint conference on 19th May, President Clinton mentioned the differences between the two countries but agreed with Rao that "in the context of our common interest and common values, we believe that they can be managed in a constructive way and can still allow this relationship to grow and strengthen." An important part of the meeting was the effort to free Indo-US mutual relations from Pakistan or Russian ties. It was also agreed to continue discussions on the issues of Kashmir, non-proliferation, human rights and international trade.

Besides discussing the production of fissile materials, the US was anxious to know the Indian thinking on global and regional levels (Rana, 1994; Sondhi, 1998). The categorical endorsement of the Shimla Pact as the basis for resolving the Kashmir imbroglio redressed the expressions of Robin Raphael. Clinton said, "We have evidence that private parties are aiding and abetting militancy in the valley. Ultimately, it is for India and Pakistan to sort out the Kashmir problem through dialogue." The decline in the Indo-US ties during the first part of Clinton's presidency was mainly because of the suggestions on India's human rights in Punjab and Kashmir. The 27th December 1993 letter from President Clinton on human rights in India were viewed as unwarranted interference in India's internal affairs. Indian thought that the US was practicing double standards, treating China with kid-gloves because of its possibility as a potential economic market.

The visit of Bill Richardson (Ambassador to UN and personal envoy of the President) in April 1998 seemed to have lifted the Indo-US ties out of stagnation. Advani and Richardson discussed the most concerned issues, terrorism, national security and the wide-ranging Indo-US relations. After the discussions Richardson conceded, "This is a voice which ought to be heard from the national Press club in Washington D.C." After the meeting with Vajpayee, he was of the opinion that the US administration should not try to equate New Delhi and Islamabad.

After Prime Minister Narsimha Rao adopted economic reforms and opened the Indian markets, a liberalization policy continued and the US became the largest foreign investor in India. While the US investment of US$ 500 million annually is less than the US investment in China or South East Asia, it is still huge when compared with the investments earlier in this decade. The US has given undue importance to non-proliferation or the missiles development etc. in India whereas its achievements of institutional democracy and progress in varied conditions have not been given proper recognition.

On the Indian side, the reaction to the Brown Amendment and the absence of US action with regards to China's supplying M-11 and Hatf missiles and other weaponry to Pakistan increased prevalence of anti-American feelings in India. The teaming up of China with Pakistan against India and President Clinton's efforts for making China the main power in Asia annoyed India further.

Consequently, New Delhi strengthened its military and increased its readiness along the Kashmir and other borders. Pakistan too responded similarly. India is working on its own whereas Pakistan is getting help from North Korea and China etc. Chinese help in Pakistan's nuclear projects irked India, which ultimately carried out a series of quick nuclear detonations in May 1998. However this opened up a nuclear conflict between New Delhi and Islamabad as well as diverted the much-required resources for developmental activities in the region for acquiring weapons of mass destruction (Joshi, 2000; Gupta, 2000; Venkataraman, 1998). Therefore, the US had no other alternative but to impose economic sanctions (Glenn and Symington Amendments), withhold loans, aid, blacklist laboratories and institutions helping in the nuclear programs and military matters (Annexure 13). In 2001 President G.W. Bush waved off these sanctions, after terrorist attacks in the US.

Looking forward to the continued expanding economic Indo-US ties provided good hopes for a closer bilateral relationship. The prospects of more Indo-US cooperation were much better before the Indian nuclear tests in May 1998. If New Delhi and Washington both make genuine efforts to understand each other's reasoning, chances are the world's two largest democracies can have a much better relationship than at present. With this hope Strobes Talbott and Jaswant Singh met about 14 times to understand each other's problems. The last official meeting was held in January 2000, in which they agreed on many issues.

The US had set five bench-marks for India and Pakistan for normalizing relations - (a) signing the CTBT,(b) pending the conclusion of the FMCT join an interim multilateral moratorium on the production of fissile material to be agreed to by all seven countries which have conducted nuclear tests, (c) defining strategic restraint or a defence posture which outlines a finite strategic version, (d) tightening export controls on sensitive materials and technologies, and (e) initiating direct, high level frequent dialogue between India and Pakistan (Chari, 1997; Dinshaw Mistry, 1998; Gupta 2000; Joshi, 2000; Subramanyam, 1998). The US arms control advocates took the position that India's declaratory approach was full of strategic tentativeness. They were looking forward to India finishing its Strategic Defence Review and proclaim a policy that would be reassuring to US security interests.

After infiltration of Pakistan's army in the Kargil sector in 1999 President Clinton called Nawaz Sharif to Washington on July 4, 1999 and asked him to vacate its aggression in the area within a few days. US army general Henry Shelton was later sent to Islamabad for discussions with Pakistani leaders and army officials. Simultaneously, a White House representative was sent to New Delhi to explain US views on the Kargil conflict. Eventually Pakistan agreed and vacated the remaining Kargil-sector area it had occupied illegally (Nanda, 1999; Behl, 2000; Joshi, 2000; Vohra, 2000). Three months later General Pervez Musharraf, the main architect of the Kargil incursions, staged a swift military coup in Pakistan. He suspended the Constitution and dissolved the parliament, only a few hours after Vajpayee took over as Prime Minister of India.

Religious Freedom in India

In September 1999 the US showed its displeasure with the ruling party, BJP, the Rashtriya Swayamsevak Sangh (RSS), and other Hindu organizations for their opposition to Christianity. The displeasure was the result of a global survey on religious freedom conducted by the US State Department on the mandate of the US Congress. It had been suggested that Robert Seiple, Ambassador at large, who ran the International Religious Freedom office in the State Department, visit India and study the problem on the spot. The government of India expressed strong Indian public opinion when it immediately made it clear to Washington that Seiple was not welcome. The US ignorance of the Indian scene and its insensitivity to Indian feelings seemed to be truly appalling. India has always been the land of religious freedom giving shelter to people speaking different languages and following different faiths. Christianity came to India long before it went to Europe.

The Syrian Christians were a harmonious part of the Indian society for over 1500 years. But India always resented conversions by the Portuguese as well as by Pakistanis, by force, and by the British, through state patronage. Indians allowed the missionaries thrown out from neighbouring countries to work in India but did not like conversions by giving temptations or by the use of force. The Constituent

Assembly of India gave citizens the freedom to preach and propagate religion but the same did not happen in Islamic Pakistan, where Hindu and other minorities were kept like slaves and converted by force. Despite the facts stated above there had been some attacks on Christians and their churches, which created concerns. Deendar Anjuman, an unknown organization based in Pakistan, which had a centre in Hyderabad was found to be responsible for attacks on Christians in Karnataka. The outlawed Deendar Anjuman denied it.

It is however, said that these attacks were organized really to show that the minorities in India are not safe and orthodox Hindu organizations like RSS and Bajrang Dal are behind the same. On the other hand in September 2002, Vishwa Hindu Parishad (VHP) from South India appealed to the Central Government to stop Christian and Muslim missionaries from forcing conversions. With funds from their headquarters in the US, several Evangelical and Pentecostal churches are converting Hindus to Christianity. This was supported by the fact that the New York Times correspondent, who covered the pope's visit, summarized apparently divergent directions of the Pontiff's messages. "The pope came to India with two agendas. He preached ardently for religious tolerance for all faiths, but also instructed his own to convert new followers. To even the mildest leaders of other religions, the two messages do not easily mix" (The New York Times, November 7, 1999).

According to the VHP, Muslims are similarly touring in Tamil Nadu and Karnataka to press poor Hindus to become Muslims, luring them with jobs in Gulf countries (George Iype, India Abroad, September 20, 2002). However it may be noted here that in June 2001 in Gopalganj (Bangladesh), where Christians are in good numbers, there was a bomb explosion in a church killing 10 people and injuring more than a dozen. Earlier in April a similar bomb explosion was reportedly caused in Bangladesh by some orthodox Muslim organizations. Later extremist Muslims carried out several attacks on Christians and minorities. In Pakistan on October at Bahawalpur 18 Christians were killed in St. Dominic's church by Muslims, followed by killings in Islamabad and in Karachi where 36 people were killed.

Therefore, hundreds of Christians and minorities protested (Seattle Times, September 26, 2002). Police arrested four people in connection with a grenade attack on a Church on the occasion of Christmas. In this attack three people died and 15 were injured. Out of arrested people, one is a Maulvi, who issued a Fatwa for the death of Christians (Agencies, December 27, 2002). These facts indicate the thinking of fundamentalist Muslims in S. Asia and they would like to see that secular India is also blamed and that is why they had attacked churches in India too.

In Quetta 4 Hindus were killed after tying the hands of 6 people in a wine shop and spraying with bullets (Amar Ujala, January 10, 2003). Again in Quetta a few months later, 3 Sunnis entered the Shiite mosque during Namaz. Two suicide squad personals blew themselves to kill others. The third sprayed people with bullets and left 32 dead and several others injured (Agencies 5th July, 2003). A couple of months after, more Shiites were killed. Therefore, the US human rights report pointed out that in Uzbekistan, Pakistan and China human rights were violated last year. In Pakistan Ladies and minorities were not treated properly. Crimes increased particularly against Hindus and Christians. They carried out false encounters, associated in rapes and did not register cases against officers (Agencies Washington, March 5, 2003). Similarly, Asma Jahangir, human rights specialist of the UN stated that in Okara (Punjab) a farmer Amir Ali died due to excessive use of force on May 11, when farmers were protesting peacefully (Agencies, May 17, 2003).

Three International Organizations pleaded against Musharraf, who is suppressing the freedom of Press in Pakistan. In the reports of Green Press and Internews it has been mentioned that more than 50 cases are there in which basic rights were suppressed (Agencies, May 13, 2003). On the contrary, a judge in Orissa (India) sentenced to death a Hindu hardliner, Dara Singh, and 12 others to life imprisonment for the murder of an Australian missionary and his two sons (India Abroad October 3, 2003). The accused were annoyed because of allurement of poor Hindus to convert to Christianity. Continuity of allured conversions was being protested by several Hindu and non-Christian organizations, particularly VHP in 2008.

However, killing of VHP leader Swami Laxmananda Saraswati and four of his disciples led to a flare up of violence in Orissa and later in Karnataka for conversions, particularly by an organization called the New Life Fellowship. Mob vandalized churches or prayer halls, houses and government vehicles etc. There were road blocks and death of human beings with mob seeking revenge for killings of VHP personals. Taking serious view of the communal violence the Indian Prime Minister offered to provide assistance to the family members of the persons who have lost their lives or have been incapacitated (PTI September 3, 2008). Political or religious murders of Christians (as suspected murders) or vandalizing any worship place is unacceptable in any part of India.

The 'International Religious Freedom Report 2003' of the US State department has also focused on Christian related issues in anti-conversion law passed by the Gujarat and Tamil Nadu state assemblies. It is suspected that this law is for continual institutionalization of Hindutva (Times News Network December 21, 2003). The state officials however do not agree with the apprehensions. They mentioned that monetary allurement or forced conversion of poor people is to be prevented. Some changes in the text books were made on the recommendation of the NCERT for correcting the historical errors; which crept in during British rule. The US issued a report on religious freedom in the globe and did not mention anything about India but did mention the name of

Gujarat Chief Minister Narendra Modi for his acts in the 2002 riots, for which he was not allowed to enter US. This report also mentions that minorities in Pakistan do not enjoy any protection from the government and the Taliban terrorists carry out violence frequently. Therefore the UASCIRF report terms Pakistan a 'religion incited violence' country.

At the end of 1999, after delivering the inaugural address at the South Asia Institute of the John Hopkins School for Advanced International Studies, Karl Inderfurth, Assistant Secretary of State, replying to the question on Kashmir, said, "There is no question that this issue is fundamentally important for the long-term stability in the region." He further said that the United States' position on Kashmir "is that we believe that this issue must be resolved between India and Pakistan, taking into account the wishes of the Kashmiri people." He noted that the US does not want to propose a solution but can play a role to facilitate whatever bilateral effort is going on. According to him, one of the negatives in the region was the recent conflict in the Kargil, "The crisis between the two nuclear-capable states dealt a severe blow to the Efforts of Prime Minister Atal Bihari Vajpayee and Nawaz Sharif towards reconciliation that they started at the Lahore Summit last February."

The US envoy William B. Milan, while addressing a gathering at the Punjab club on December 2, 1999, hinted at the rescheduling of Pakistan's US$ 32 billion foreign debt or writing them off for helping Islamabad in overcoming the current economic crisis and putting the national economy on track (Nation 3/12). He also said the US was against terrorism, not Islam. Some Americans feared Islam as an enemy of the US and some Muslims considered the US as their enemy but they all confuse Islam with terrorism. The US however, is not at all confused. It has been at war with terrorism, or with criminals and not with any religion. However, it is the fear of nuclear proliferation and the terror of a nuclear war that is keeping the US engaged with India and Pakistan, as was already announced by President Clinton. He went further and declared Kashmir as the most dangerous issue in the World. If given a choice the US would like to make Kashmir independent. However, neither India nor Pakistan would like to accept that. President Clinton, in his 1999 report, has listed fighting terrorism among his administration's top priorities for 2000. "We are grateful that the hijacking was resolved with no additional loss of life," the US spokesman James Folly said. He also said, "We will work with other governments to see that those responsible are brought to justice."

Senior US Congressman Gary L. Ackerman has lauded the Vajpayee government for securing the release of hostages of Indian Airlines Flight 814, and urged Washington to work with India and Israel to wipe out international terrorism. "I take this opportunity to call upon the State department to conduct a speedy, time bound review of various violent Kashmiri outfits operating out of Pakistan and Afghanistan. I also urge that the role of Pakistan's military janta and the illegal Taliban regime in supporting these outfits be simultaneously reviewed," Ackerman said. Leading House of representative member Frank Pallone has said he would draft a legislation calling on the State department to declare Pakistan a terrorist State if the department failed to do so on its own. He also said that "now is the time" for the US and other major nations to declare Pakistan "a state sponsor of terrorism." For the first time the US Foreign Secretary in an interview to two news channel accepted that Islamabad government and some of their organizations have close friendly relations with terrorists and the US government is thinking of some strong action against Islamabad (Hindustan, August 9, 2008).

The new tilt in Washington is also reflected in the resolution sponsored by congressman, Benjamin Gilman, who desired better Indo-US ties. The resolution submitted during Vajpayee's visit included: China's hegemonic ambitions, Islamic terrorism spilling out of Afghanistan and Pakistan, the narco leadership in Burma, and China's illegal occupation of Tibet, as serious concerns to both United States and India.

Gilman added that the US and India "must develop a closer military and intelligence relationship to confront our mutual enemies."

The economic aspect of the visits of the US President and Indian Prime Minister in the year 2000 is perhaps more important than political relations. If India and the US are to move forward politically in the years ahead, the economic aspect is what is going to give the required momentum. Politicians and bureaucrats come and go, but the economic links move forward beyond personalities.

In November 2000 the Indian Prime Minister announced a unilateral first halt of terrorist combing operations of the Indian army during the holy month of Ramazan to avoid bloodshed (Amar Ujala, December 23, 2000) and despite the hostile attitude of LET, he extended the peace plan for another month and again third time (Agencies, January 23, 2001). Pakistan also responded with reduction in shelling and bombing on the LOC. This peace plan of Vajpayee was appreciated by the US, Britain and Russia as well as by other nations. The US warned Pakistan to contain LET from killings and threats. Bruce Riedel the Director of the South Asian department informed that the US was against attack in Red Fort and the threats given to bombard Prime Minister's office by LET. In particular, he said, "We think that threat (made against Vajpayee) is reprehensible" (Agencies Washington, December 30, 2000).

In an interview given to Financial Times, Deputy Secretary Richard Armitage reconfirmed that the US is not interested in mediating on the Kashmir issue but is certainly interested in Indo-Pakistan talks, as stated earlier by different US authorities. The US can help in the matter (Agencies, June 25, 2002).

A Wake up Call to a Giant

President George Bush said in a statement that we are at war and for that he called for an active military response to

September 11, 2001 terrorists' attacks on the World Trade Centre in New York followed by an attack on the Pentagon, Washington and later a crash of another hijacked plane in Pennsylvania state. These attacks resulted into huge monetary losses and human life. The President identified Osama bin Laden as "The prime suspect". He said retaliation would go far beyond the ringleader. He told the US troops to "get ready." "We will find those who did it; we will smoke them out of their holes; we will get them running and we will bring them to justice." "We will not only deal with those who dare attack America, we will deal with those who harbour them and feed them and house them." Afterwards, army and diplomatic preparations were made to achieve the objectives.

In the meantime an anthrax scare started and for sometime it appeared as if a widespread bio-terror attack had occurred and there would be a shortage of CIPRO, the most effective antibiotic in treating anthrax. Many friendly nations, including India, promised to help by supplying CIPRO. The US froze the assets of Jaish-e-Mohamad, Harkatul-Mujahideen, along with Lashkar-e-Toiba, after they were put on the watch-list. Pakistan has been made as one of the important key players and not only sanctions were lifted completely but the debt payments too were rescheduled. Colin Powell announced economic and military cooperation between Islamabad and Washington.

However, thousands of militant Pakistanis have gone to Afghanistan to fight along with Taliban since US air strikes began. Ustad Farooq, one of the 22 members of Harkat-ul-Mujahideen who died in a US air strike was buried in Karachi as about 3000 mourned (Seattle Times, October 26, 2001). Harkat-ul-Mujahideen and other terrorist organizations also fight in Indian Kashmir too. The simmering anti-US sentiment in Pakistan found a deadly outlet on October 28 when 21 people were killed in 2 terrorist attacks and thousands of Pakistanis lined up to cross over to Afghanistan to join Taliban. Four extremists stormed into a Roman Catholic

Church and sprayed bullets, killing 18 Christians, including children and women. Later also, they killed many Christians, including Americans, Australians and French. Such killings were repeated again' and again in other Islamic Asian nations, like Indonesia, Philippines, Yemen, etc.

Discussing the issue of terrorist camps in GK/POK the US Secretary of Defence Donald Rumsfeld told George Fernandes, the Indian Defence Minister that the current war against terrorism will not end with Afghanistan. "This (war against terror) is much bigger than Afghanistan." He also spoke of strengthening Indo-US military-to-military ties, which could include training and exchange of personnel. "President George W Bush and I have been unambiguous that we will be pursuing terrorist networks wherever we find them," Rumsfeld said (Express News Service, Delhi, November 5, 2001). The Congressional Research Service (CRS) informed that India, US and other allies had been put on target by Islamic extremists and warned that Gulam Kashmir would become a safe heaven for terrorist and suggested the vigil should be strengthened on LOC.

A year after the start of the Afghan war, Defence Secretary Donald Rumsfeld pledged that the US would track down Bin Laden and other leaders of the Al-Qaida network. He further said he was not frustrated that Laden and top Taliban leaders were on the loose. They have learned how to conceal themselves from US surveillance. At a ceremony at US Command H.Q., General Tommy Franks said the US was committed to remaining in Afghanistan to ensure that Al-Qaida and the Taliban forces were rooted out. New Al-Qaida strikes may be imminent on US soil or overseas, CIA Director George Tenet warned as he defended his agency's counter terrorism efforts to lawmakers (AP October 19, 2002). These comments came during a session as FBI Director Robert Mueller and the National Security Agency Chief Michael Hayden were answering questions from the House and Senate Intelligence Committees.

In a US programme "Seeds of Peace" 2002, there were about 166 youth members including youths from India and Pakistan. A 14-year old Munir, resident of Lahore, said he was initially hostile to Indians. However, slowly this feeling disappeared and now he has several friends in India and all over the world. This program was started with the idea that youths from different nations would meet and understand each other better.

After a break of several decades, the US has agreed to start selling arms to India. India has signed an agreement to buy 8 modern radar systems. The US has also agreed to sell unmanned air-craft and ground sensors etc. The US now does not have the bitterness it had in 1971 or in 1998. In 1971, it had sent its seventh fleet into Indian Ocean in support of Pakistan (Anonymous, 2004). A few years back Indo-US joint exercises were held near Agra, Anchorage and Kochi and in 2004 at Gwalior. The Deputy Secretary R. Armitage, while addressing the press in Washington, stated that fair elections in J&K could help solve the Kashmir imbroglio. Therefore, they should not be disturbed as quoted by Pakistan Daily 'The News'. This comment clearly indicated suggestion for Pakistan to keep away from them.

US Senators Frank Pallone, Garry Ackerman and Representative Jim Mc Dermott, while participating in a Federation of Indian Chamber of Commerce & Industry (FICCI) meeting in New Delhi, on 'Indo-US closer cooperation', objected to the US supply of sophisticated arms to Pakistan. They said India must be assessed separately and not as India versus Pakistan. Representative Mc Dermott said India has no intention of attacking Pakistan despite the fact that the latter is supporting cross-border terrorism. Later, Senator Joseph Biden, the Chairman of the Foreign Relations Committee indicated that if India agrees to accept LOC as the international boundary Pakistan must agree for the same and stop cross-border terrorism. Bidden was speaking in the meeting organized by the Federation of the Indian Chamber of

Commerce and Industry (FICCI) in Washington (INS June 19, 2002).

According to CIA sources Pakistan has taken the place of Afghanistan for Al-Qaida. Bin Laden's associates have built up close ties with LET, JEM and other local terrorist organizations and are resting. Thus, it has become a safe heaven for them and in the ceremony at the US Command H.Q., Gen. Tommy Franks said the US was committed to remaining in Afghanistan to ensure that Al-Qaida and the Taliban forces were rooted out (AP, October 7, 2002). New Al-Qaida strikes may be imminent on US soil or overseas, CIA Director George Tenet warned as he defended his agency's counter terrorism efforts to lawmakers (AP, October 18, 2002).

The software engineering institute at Carnegie Mellon University gives its top quality ranking to only 48 software companies in the world. About two-third of these companies are based in India. With many Fortune 500 companies opting for a back-office centre in India, the service sector is the fastest growing component of India's GDP. Economic reforms have also begun to open up the insurance sector, which India was reluctant to open earlier. Therefore, at least 5 large US corporations are operating as joint ventures with Indian companies (Anonymous, 2004).

In November 2001, President Bush and Prime Minister Vajpayee reviewed a most ambitious economic dialogue. It focuses on strengthening of official Indo-US interaction in four broad aspects of trade, i.e. environment, finance, energy and commerce. With President Bush coming in White House, the 'Vision' agreement signed earlier between, Clinton and Vajpayee, got a big boost. Bilateral trade, less than US$ 8 billon in 1994, jumped to over US$ 18 billion in 2003. US direct investment also rose to record high of US$ 3.6 billion. Working together NY City Transit and the Delhi Metro charted a road map to attain ISO 14001. NYCT believes it gave Delhi Metro the technology to work as a model network to be emulated by mass transit systems throughout the world

(Anonymous, 2004).

American knowledge of India is shaped by American Institute of Indian Studies (AIIS) which engages scholars to teach and carry out research about India. The Indian H.Q. of AIIS is located in Gurgaon (Near Delhi airport). For more than forty years, AIIS has provided fellowship support to more than 3500 senior American scholars and Doctoral candidates. In recent years the number of Indian students in the US has risen steadily from about 31,000 in 1997 to about 75,000 in 2003 (Anonymous, 2004).

According to American intelligence sources Pakistan has taken the place of Afghanistan for Al-Qaida. Bin Laden's associates have built up close ties with LET, JEM and other local terrorist organizations. Thus, it has become a safe haven for them and terrorists are roaming about freely everywhere. Bin Laden is most likely somewhere in West Pakistan bordering Afghanistan or in Iran. The surviving Al-Qaida terrorists have become more dangerous and united (Agencies, June 17, 2002). This has become apparent after the audiotape praising recent terrorism in Bali, Yemen and Moscow surfaced through al-Jazira network. The discovery of secret nuclear program of North Korea with the help of Pakistan and possibility of Bin Laden being alive in Pakistan-Iran region have given reasons to many to doubt the credibility of Pakistan as a responsible member of the anti-terrorism alliance. They think Islamabad is playing the game of 'hunt with the hunter and run with the rabbit'.

Contrary to the desire of many Senators and Representatives, both the CIA and the FBI urged Bush to limit US pressure on Pakistan to force a return to democracy, halting infiltration in J&K and non-interference in their elections. According to them Musharraf has become more important than ever to kill al-Qaida leaders in Afghanistan, North West Frontier Province or Karachi. Musharraf is also not listening to US for terrorism in J&K. Hence the US is now not likely to stick to assurances given to India from time to time (Haniffa-India Abroad, September 27, 2002).

Besides many European and African nations, India also did not agree with the pre-emptive strikes on Iraq on the issue of weapons of mass destruction. It recommended the US to employ mutual discussions for solving the problem. After the end of major war, the US desired India and other countries to send troops to Iraq. The Indian government decision to send the troops only on the UN mandate gave the US a great shock as the US was sure of the Indian troops. Both President Bush and Secretary of Defence Rumsfeld had earlier requested Indian Deputy Prime Minister to help with its troops and they expected India would agree to it. In any case the US and its allies invaded Iraq and captured Saddam Hussein to ultimately execute him on December 30, 2006, after he was sentenced for the same, about two months earlier.

Recently the US agreed to supply F-16 fighter planes to Pakistan for, which it has been pressing for long time. According to Pak foreign minister this is the indication of Pak diplomacy. To India also it has agreed to sell F-16/ F-18 and also its improved versions along with transfer of technology too, besides agreeing for civil nuclear energy production program. Therefore in the words of many what Nixon did to Pakistan and China, Bush is trying to do for India. According to G. Parthasarthy, the former Ambassador, India must cooperate with the US in obtaining arsenal technology, nuclear energy and space programs.

However, many experts think that too much diversion in arms and armaments is not in the interest of any country. India has already been using Mirages, MIGs and Sukhois. On supply of spares and after Sale supports, any fresh US sanction could mean India holding a US$ 3 billion dud. "The US track record is abominable. What if it holds back spare parts at a critical stage (via sanctions)?" (Tipnis, A.Y., former Air Chief). However, Indian Government is already considering proposal as per statement of the Indian Defence Minister Lockheed Martin, the manufacturer of F-16 etc. is keen to supply fighters to India. Chief of Indian Navy, Admiral Arun Prakash stated that F-35 is more useful to the Indian Navy and not F-18 (Agencies July 12, 2005). Indian Navy took charge of the American warship Trenton. The INS carrier vessel was commissioned as Jalashva and is the 2nd largest ship to join the Indian fleet.

Indo-US Nuclear Deal

Reversing many decades of US policies, Congress passed a long-stalled pact giving access to India with American nuclear technology. The same was earlier passed by the House of Representative and the Senators voted unanimously in favour of the deal, which was finalized by President Bush during a visit in March, 2006. They say that opening India's nuclear industry to US$ 100 billion in potential sales from abroad will help cement a relationship that may also serve as a hedge against the growing clout of China in Asia. Sanjay Puri, chairman of the US-India Political Action Committee, said some estimates had placed the potential value of the deal at US$ 30 billion in the US and India alone. Further, it also could add 10,000 to 15,000 jobs in the US. Under the agreement, India would be free to expand its nuclear weapons arsenals but for the first time it would allow international inspections of its 14 civilian reactors out of a total of 22.

The implications of the nuclear deal are being debated in India (Koshi, 2006). According to the Indian opposition leaders this deal would make India a client of the US. The deal, which has been finally confirmed by the President on 18th December, 2006, in a White House ceremony is very expensive in the eyes of many, whereas some authorities are happy that India decided to become a US-nuclear Associate to help NPT. President Bush hailed it as an important achievement for the world. In India Prime Minister Singh informed the parliament that there were some areas of concern in the deal, clarification of which will be sought from Washington and nuclear 'swaraj' (freedom) would be maintained. He said there was no reason for the opposition leader, L.K. Advani and other leaders to worry about India losing its nuclear 'swaraj' by accepting any legal binding on nuclear testing or signing CTBT. Recently two Senators have written to the Secretary of State, Rice about improvement in Indo-Iran military ties. This bogey has been useful for the opponents in the US as they are for opposition in India too. A few months ago, the US asked India to limit its economic relations with 'nuclear outlaw' Iran, but Pakistan agreed to the deal of Iran (its nuclear associate) gas pipeline to help it economically at a time when UN as well as many nations are imposing economic sanctions on Iran.

The agreement will allow India to carry out reprocessing spent fuel from the reactors on the civil side but requires it to develop a new facility for that purpose and subject to IAEA safeguards. IAEA and NSG both have approved the deal. The reprocessing had raised concerns in the US about opportunities to produce weapons-grade plutonium for India's military arsenal. Similar to that in 2006 the USIBC had once again become active for persuading the US Congress to approve the deal. India did not agree for not carrying out any nuclear test but made suitable changes in the text. The US ambassador to New Delhi David Mulford said, "The US and India stand shoulder to shoulder in their desire for a clean exception and we will continue to work with our Indian partners to persuade the Nuclear Suppliers Group countries that such an exemption is in the international community's best interest."

After the agreement was endorsed by the NSG on September 6, 2008 the Secretary of State pressed Congress to approve the nuclear deal with India (AP September 6, 2008). The US Congress completed final approval of the deal. With this deal India will get access to civil nuclear technology, material and fuel. The US House of Representatives already passed the agreement a few days ago. President Bush signed the historic nuke agreement (HR 7081) on 9th October into law. President said there were no changes in fuel supply commitments mentioned in 123 act. According to him "This agreement sends a signal to the world—democracy and responsible behaviour will find a friend in USA." He said, "Even though the US and India are separated by half the globe, we are natural partners—into the 21st Century." Prime Minister Singh stated that the nuke deal will help India to liberate itself from "the constraints of technology denial of 34 years." Foreign Minister Mukherji and Condoleezza Rice put a final seal in New Delhi on October 11 and made the accord binding for both countries.

Indo-US Maritime Security

With India not happy in joining Proliferation Security Initiatives (PSI), the US desires India to join 'Thousand Ship Navy' (TSN) concept. The US Chief of naval operations, Admiral Michael G. Mullen, discussed this concept with Indian navy Chief, Admiral Suresh Mehta and others at Delhi. This concept involves navies of like minded nations coming together to enhance security on high Seas. India agrees with the proposal but has to get a nod from Parliament. However both the nations are already finalizing MCF. Admiral Mullen's visit in April, 2007 provided apex-level discussions. The US is also keen to get more 'access and berthing' at Indian naval bases. After 2000 attack on USS Cole and 2001 terror attacks, the US has clearly understood the value of cooperative security, particularly in maritime cases. TSN is just a brand name, involving 500, 1,000 or even 10,000 ships, forming a voluntary global partnership to tackle maritime challenges like WMDs, gun running, piracy, illegal immigration and slavery as well as terrorism etc (TNN, April 20, 2007).

INS Jalashwa has joined Indian navy in Norfolk (Virginia). The Indian Ambassador, Ronen Sen was also present on this occasion. This is first American ship to join Indian navy. It was earlier called USM Trenton. With this India has become one of those countries which have ships with landing platform-dock. With INS Jalshwa India will have the capability to transfer large number of soldiers and armaments to other places.

The US also agreed to lease two P-3C reconnaissance aircrafts, built by Lockheed Martin, to India and informed the Congress of a US$ 133 million military sale for logistic support of the deal including training, test equipment and spare parts. These aircrafts would replace the Navy's Soviet IL-38 May aircrafts which are reaching the end of their operational service life (Hindustan Times, November 16, 2005).

India was also included as a member in an important multinational energy program called International Thermonuclear Experimental Reactor (ITER) to acknowledge its being a responsible nuclear state possessing advanced technology. This decision was from the six member countries - USA, European Union, Russia, China, Japan and South Korea. The decision recognizes the capability of India to contribute significantly in such endeavours, including in the field of fusion research. According to the spokesperson of the External Affairs Ministry ITER is the trial step in the modern studies of plasma physics and future electricity producing power plants. In 2007 India and the US came together to discuss China's massive military build up and modernization as well as its expanding arc of influence in Asia-Pacific region. India desires to be a neutral nation rather than a counterweight to China.

President Obama said in Prague (where he is establishing anti-missile system) that since US is the only nation which used nuclear arms it has a responsibility to free the globe from weapons of mass destruction. Reportedly, he intends to make strong efforts in this direction and try to involve all the nuclear nations in destroying nuclear arms. He also said that if Iran does not pose nuclear threat there would be no need for anti missile system. While giving interview to Dawn T.V., Obama said that both India and Pakistan are good friends of the US and his administration would like to help in Indo-Pak mutual talks. During Hillary Clinton's 5 days visit to India in July 2009, she tried to emphasize that Pakistan was taking a serious view of global terrorism and due to Indo-Pak differences, Islamabad's attention was being diverted from Afghanistan and therefore India should remain patient about Mumbai attack culprits because Pakistan is a responsible nation in her eyes.

7

Indian Perspective of US

B.B. Nagaich

Technically, Indo-US relations started in 1792 with appointment of Benjamin Joy as United States Consul General in Calcutta by the President George Washington. During Franklin Roosevelt's presidency, India's participation on the side of the Allies in World War II was considered important by the US, although a very popular leader, Subhash Chandra Bose or Neta Ji as he is called in India, had friendly relations with Japan. Roosevelt's three confidants were entrusted with the job of resolving the Indian freedom issue, but they could not do much because Winston Churchill had his own prejudices against India and he was not prepared to listen to anybody against his ideas. Unfortunately for India, President Roosevelt died before India became independent and from 1946 to 1952 President Truman guided the American foreign policy. India's leading freedom fighter, Pandit Jawaharlal Nehru was at the helm of affairs and during his Prime Ministerial period, he dealt with four US Presidents. During his earlier part of the tenure, Pandit Nehru had high hopes for continued good relations with the US. Due to his liberal and socialistic views, he presumed America would appreciate his ideology and support Indian policy for friendly mutual relations (Nehru, 1946). Many of his predictions in international matters were not understood in US at that time but the some of them were acted upon later.

Nehru's refusal to take sides in the cold war and his assertions to remain non-aligned created doubt in the US (Jackson, 1983; Dennis Kux, 1993). Secretary of State judged Nehru as theoretical or unrealistic and did not know how to deal with him, as he did not expect India to be so self-assured and insisting on self-respect, particularly in a situation when it required additional food articles as well as technological and financial help. The confrontation over Kashmir and Britain's patronization of Pakistan did affect the US foreign policy as the same was based on British perceptions and recommendations. After the election of D.D. Eisenhower as President, Indo-US relations became complex and economic assistance started. Although Pandit Nehru's personal relations were very good with President Eisenhower, this friendly feeling was adversely affected by Dulles doctrine. Secretary J.F. Dulles was of the view that those who were not with the US were against the US. Thus, he considered India a satellite of USSR (Immerson, 1999).

Indo-US Trade and Economic Relations

Except for the unwillingness of the US to finance India's Bokaro Steel Plant (which was ultimately funded by Russia), trade and economic relations expanded between and 1953 and 1990 (Cohen, 1998; Dennis Kux, 1993; Dixit, 1998; Jain, 1987). Indo-US technological cooperation in heavy industry and nuclear power commenced during this period. The contributions of the Ambassador Chester Bowles were the main factor for better bilateral relations. To a great extent, Nehru had views similar to Eisenhower on disarmament and nuclear issues and accordingly he supported Eisenhower's atoms for peace policy and partial test ban treaty. To some extent relations improved on bilateral issues, but significant differences emerged on domestic security as well on international matters. India did not favour military alliances like NATO, SEATO and Baghdad pacts. It also criticized strongly the US defence supply to Pakistan, stated to be for containing the Chinese communism (Barnds, 1972; Cohen, 1987; Gould and Ganguly, 1992; Gupta, 1977). The US, not only supplied military material to Pakistan, against resentment in India, it concluded a Defence Assistance Agreement to provide necessary equipment and services etc. and in return got the base facilities in Peshawar, on 19th May, 1954. Later a mutual Security Pact was also signed in 1959. With this pact the US confirmed full support to Islamabad and hostility to India.

The US treated India and Pakistan as equals when Pakistan invaded Kashmir (legally merged with India) and complicated matters further by not recognizing Kashmir as an integral part of India. Efforts to have closer ties with the USSR and China and the founding of the non-alignment movement indicated to the US that India was becoming part of the Russian block. India's suggestion that the mainland China should be included as a veto power in the UN angered the US (later this not only came to pass but the same China, which was to be contained has been given the status of the most favoured nation) (Dennis Kux, 1993; Cohen, 2001). India's remaining silent on the Soviet invasion of Hungary in 1956 (as gratitude to Russia for its help on the Kashmir Issue) while criticizing the Anglo-French invasion of Suez Canal finally convinced, the US and its western allies that India's claim being non-aligned nation were only tactical and that, in fact India was considered aligned with the Soviets for ever (Jackson, 1983; Kennedy, 1988; Nayar, 1992; Harrison and Subramanyam, 1989).

On the economic front, despite the misgivings the US emerged as the major trading country and continued food and monetary assistance. Education and cultural exchanges also increased. For higher studies the US academic institutions started replacing British and German institutions. Eisenhower was the first US President to visit India in 1959 and received an over whelming welcome from Indians. His visit was a great success but was soon neutralized by non-endorsement of the Indian stand on Kashmir in the UN; Krishna Menon and India's taking back Goa from Portuguese were mentioned as the main reasons for stance of the US (Azad, 1960; Chopra, 1990; Dennis Kux, 1993; Ganguly, 1999; Morgenthau, 1967).

John F. Kennedy's becoming President raised hopes in

India of positive and fruitful relations. Closer ties were temporarily established and aid increased. Among the first issues confronting Kennedy administration was the Congo crisis, in which India supplied the largest contingent of soldiers (Alan James, 1969). Therefore, President modified US policy to place more emphasis on using UN to ensure freedom for Congo, seeking Indian help (see message from Kennedy transmitted in State Department telegram on 18th February and the reply of Prime Minister through telegram to the State department on February 20, 1961).

In December 1961, on provocation and threats of Portuguese troop movements, Indian forces seized Goa from Portuguese (who surrendered without much of a fight). According to analysts this should have been done long ago. Since the US had good relations with Portugal, it made them very unhappy with India. After the Chinese, because of their unhappiness with India concerning the Tibet issue, crossed the Mc Mahon line in 1962 (British period international boundary) to capture Indian territory, Kennedy acted swiftly for India's defence assistance and asked Pakistan to refrain from becoming a party to this war, whereas Russians stayed neutral (Hoffman, 1990).

To some this generosity of assistance in defence had a secret motive of containing Chinese communism and making India too a partner in this program. Whatever the reasons were, the positive impact was neutralized by the US government deciding to ask India to compromise on Kashmir with Pakistan. Ambassador Averell Hariman's diplomacy to New Delhi made India feel that there was no room for goodwill and assistance in international matters. India's equivocal stand on the Cuban missile crisis added fuel to the fire. These strained relations continued into 1990. India and the US were both strong democracies but relations between them were dominated by fundamental differences in their strategies on security matters. India's non-aligned foreign policy was considered deleterious to the US interests and plans. India's socialism and economy were deterrents for substantial economic and technical cooperation. Finally, Indian doctrine on disarmament issues did not fully conform to the US philosophy (Chari, et al 1996; Bramha Chellany, 1990; Cohen, 1991; Sandy Gordon, 1995).

Although President Lyndon Johnson suspended military supplies to Pakistan during the Indo-Pak war of 1965, the use of earlier supplied American weapons by Pakistan angered India. This was the main reason that the US attempts to mediate in the war did not succeed. The US asked the USSR to act as mediator, resulting in the Tashkent Agreement. Relations with the US suffered because of Johnson's PL480 policy and devaluation of the Indian currency. Another factor was the revelation of funding of cultural and educational programs by the CIA. Feeling tricked and betrayed intellectuals, supported by the Communists, led an anti-US crusade to tarnish the US image in India (Jha, 1983). Prime Minister Indira Gandhi inherited the strained relations.

During her period as the Prime Minister (1966-1984) she dealt with four US Presidents, Lyndon Johnson, Richard Nixon, Gerald Ford and Ronald Reagan. Indo-US relations were very friendly during the periods of Johnson and Reagan but cool or indifferent during the periods of Nixon and Ford. By and large, economic, educational and cultural relations remained normal. Political and military strategies continued to affect relations adversely. The US's turning a 'blind eye' toward Pakistan's efforts at acquiring a nuclear capability and continued military aid to Islamabad bypassing 'Symington Amendment' despite violation of the US non-proliferation Act (of 1978), had a direct bearing on India's security (Bose, 1994). India therefore opposed the Nuclear Non-Proliferation Treaty on the basis of its being discriminatory in nature, which angered the US. Further, the underground nuclear explosion of Pokhran in 1974 led to India being called a spoiler of the US initiated Nuclear Non-Proliferation and the Comprehensive Test Ban Treaty (CTBT).

In 1971 the East Pakistan crisis, which indirectly resulted in India-Pakistan conflict brought Indo-US relation to their lowest level. There were indirect threats by the US through sending its nuclear powered 7th fleet aircraft carrier, called Enterprise, in the Bay of Bengal, clearly to boost the morale of Pakistani forces, which were killing and looting the innocent Bengalis to suppress their freedom struggle. This was disliked by not only Indians but also by many Americans and NAM nations. The 1971 meetings between Nixon and Indira Gandhi were therefore dominated by their mutual dislike of one another.

However, India learnt another lesson of international politics as the US stand in this crisis was completely in contradiction to its commitment to human rights and the democracy. The whole world was very well aware of the brutality and suppression of the human rights of the majority of populace of now Bangladesh (earlier East Pakistan) and the US role brought down its own prestige (Kennedy, 1971). Later, the US realized the reality of the situation and desired to revive the normalcy in 1974 by acknowledging India's importance and its role in South Asian region by establishing an Indo-US joint commission to improve bilateral relations. Dislike for Prime Minister Indira Gandhi's domestic policies again became a barrier for improvement of friendly ties. By then the Indian "Green revolution", for which the US organizations also helped a lot, increased food production. However, there was another positive point when the US agreed to utilize its accumulated PL-480 funds for development in India. Mainly because of the efforts of Ambassador David Moynihan, these funds were ultimately absorbed and written off. As a result relations again became cordial (Moynihan, 1978).

In 1977 when Morarji Desai became Prime Minister, more or less the same time Jimmy Carter assumed the US Presidency, Desai's rightist leanings and inclination towards free market economy brought a temporary improvement of relations. Desai visited the US in 1977 and Carter reciprocated soon after. However, because of India's refusal to agree to the Non-Proliferation Treaty, Carter's visit could not make a positive impact in the relationship (Vinod, 1991; Wallace, 1985). During Reagan's Presidency, Indo-US relations were plagued by Afghanistan crisis. The US was opposed to the Soviet influence in the Afghan government and resisted it through Pakistan and mujahideen.

Although India did not support Russian moves, due to its large considerations, it did not oppose the same (Yousaf & Adkins, 1993). Surprisingly, during this period, the US emerged as India's biggest trading partner, in spite of the differences in views on the Non-proliferation treaty and military issues. Indo-US cooperation in the sector of peaceful uses of atomic energy and exploration of outer space accelerated. Interestingly, with better understanding between the Prime Minister Indira Gandhi and President Reagan the bilateral relations improved. Prime Minister Gandhi's meeting with President Reagan in Mexico and in the US helped in the reduction of tension and in furthering the cooperation between the two largest democracies. Due to Pak-US alliance over Afghanistan, USA was channelling arms through Pakistan, overlooking the Pressler amendment it sent F-16 aircraft to Pakistan (Vinod, 1991; Wolpert, 1982).

To balance, India had to buy military aircraft from England and France etc. India had to plan also for anti-Chinese contingencies particularly for naval and air forces by purchasing submarines and maritime patrol aircrafts like P-3C. Air Force had to buy multi-role aircrafts and upgrade air defence systems. Army was still tasked primarily for dealing with Pakistan and the terrorists it supported. Therefore it was prepared to fight intense & short wars for dealing with terrorism and possible nuclear threats. Thus Afghan war not only resulted in guerrilla war in Kashmir but it also enhanced the purchase of military hardware in the region (Karan Singh, 1982; Bramha Singh, 1998; Sinha, 1994).

In 1984, when Rajiv Gandhi took over as Prime Minister, he had the advantage of friendly relations between the two nations and the same progressed further. Prime Minister Rajiv Gandhi visited the US twice and was received warmly. During this period, technological cooperation increased, Rajiv Gandhi said at a Press Conference on 5th June, "We do not intend making nuclear weapons and we will hold ourselves back from developing a nuclear weapon. But the fact is, if Pakistan does have a nuclear weapon, it is going to cause very serious problems for us" (Statesman, 6th June, 1988). The end of the Gulf war and disintegration of the USSR changed the international situation. Prime Minister Narsimha Rao adjusted himself to fundamental changes in economic trends. Rao laid the basis for friendly ties with the US during his discussions with George H.W. Bush during 1992. It was accepted that there were basic differences on disarmament and strategies, and agreed that if these could not be resolved attempts should be made to keep them under control (Gould and Ganguly, 1992; Harrison and Geoffrey, 1993).

New Sore Points

Besides Kashmir and certain international matters, the important sore points in Indo-US relations are mainly the nuclear energy issues, UN composition and terrorism.

Nuclear Issues: As far as the nuclear energy and the missiles are concerned, the US and certain other Western nations blame India for thwarting nuclear non-proliferation agreements. However the agreements have an inherent flaw. These allow some countries to continue use of their technology and arsenals while denying others like India, Pakistan, Israel, and South Africa that right. It is time for the US and other nuclear powers to realize that treaties like NPT and CTBT are discriminatory and therefore may not be agreed to by some nations. India and Pakistan are the two sons of old India or Hindustan. They are aware of the danger of using nuclear weapons against each other because of their geographic contiguity. Their cultural, ethnic language links, past history as well as economics make them conscious of each others sensitiveness more than far apart nations like the US and USSR, which are ideologically opposed to each other. India has set an example to the P-5 and other nations by unilaterally declaring no-nuclear-first strike (Chari, 1995 & 1997; Chari et al., 1996; Cohen, 1997; Gupta, 2000; Kapur, 1971; Subramanyam, 1986). If Pakistan agrees to do likewise, there would be no question of India-Pakistan using their nuclear arsenals against each other.

This feeling has already been echoed in the Lahore declaration of 1999. "We shall take immediate steps to reduce the risk of accidental or unauthorized use of nuclear weapons and discuss concepts and doctrines with a view to elaborating measures for confidence building in nuclear and conventional fields," read the Lahore declaration (of eight measures) issued at the end of Vajpayee's two-day visit to Pakistan. As agreed both nations have to inform each other about their missile tests, 1 day in advance. If the nuclear nations follow a hands-off policy with regard to South Asian nations or do not take sides for or against India or Pakistan, these countries would resolve their problems and also work for greater economic cooperation.

The South Asian Association for Regional Cooperation (SAARC) has already been sponsored by them to achieve some of these objectives. Since the Cold War has ended, there is no need for nuclear weaponry. Therefore, it is time to agree to elimination of nuclear arms within a suitable period, under international supervision without discrimination. The need of the day is a nuclear weapon free world. Jawaharlal Nehru once said, "The only alternative to total nuclear disarmament in the nuclear and space age today is total mutual destruction." In 1988, India again proposed a nuclear weapon free and non-violent world order, which was not been taken favourably by any of the P-5 nations (Gandhi, 1988).

Therefore after the 1998 nuclear tests in India, Prime

Minister Vajpayee pronounced a nuclear doctrine, and his special emissary, the External Affairs Minister Jaswant Singh had a series of 14 meetings with the US Deputy Secretary of State to solve many issues (Cohen, 2001). Indian government views can be summed up as a balance of rights and obligations in disarmament and non-proliferation. India's emerging nuclear doctrine has two elements, minimum deterrence and no-first-use (NFU) policy (Matin Zuberi, 1999). The NFU policy underlines self-restraints and operated very effectively under mutual deterrence. Pakistan, unfortunately, has not adopted NFU policy so far (Weisman and Khosney, 1981; Venkataraman, 1998; Sondhi, 1998; Sunderji, 1993; Specter, 1988; Sharif, 1994).

NFU and the minimum deterrence require maintenance of a limited number of weaponry and delivery systems as well as controls to prevent a nuclear arms race. Since the minimum nuclear deterrence also does not envisage a nuclear engagement, nuclear weapons are not delivered to commanders in the field. India has already established its good intentions by unilateral declarations like NFU, voluntary moratorium on nuclear tests and promising to sign a non-discriminatory CTBT. It has also expressed its availability for discussing fissile material and accession to the Chemical Weapons Convention (CWC). What is now needed is a new nuclear weapon convention for global disarmament by a time bound plan to eliminate nuclear arsenals. However, the US decision to take India to the World Trade Organization's arbitration procedure, the disagreements on CTBT and the proposed Fissile Material Cut Off Treaty (FMCT) all reflect the serious differences in ideologies.

Adding fuel to fire were the 1998 Pokhran-II nuclear tests and missiles development, the necessity of which could not be understood in Washington. For these tests the US imposed economic sanctions, thrown out several Indian scientists and blacklisted more than 200 scientific institutions. As a result there has been considerable deterioration in our relations, which were already strained. The request of President Clinton to his Russian counterpart, during Moscow summit on 1st September 1998, to stop military aid to India was rebuffed and not agreed to by Russia. The same has elicited a sharp reaction from New Delhi. Elaborating on the theme, the Indian Defence Minister George Fernandes said, "The assumption that the bomb is safe in the hands of nuclear weapon states and dangerous for the people of South Asia is exaggerated and not acceptable." He added, "It does not suit Mr. Clinton, whose country is the only one in history to have used a nuclear weapon, to make such observations."

The US, which has been trying to destroy the weapons of mass destruction throughout the world, is now preparing to develop weapons of the next generation. Senate has lifted the ban on nuclear arsenals and allotted funds so that small atomic bombs can be prepared to blast the underground bunkers (Seattle Times, September 21, 2003). Later, President Bush improved Indo-US relations by lifting the economic sanctions, military cooperation and by signing civil nuclear deal, which he finally signed on October 9, 2008. Like Rajiv Gandhi and A.B. Vajpayee President Obama fixed a clear responsibility of the US to end the dangerous inheritance of the cold war era, in the form of nuclear weapons of mass destruction.

Passed by the US Congress during the lame duck session, Indo-US civil nuclear deal, will allow Washington to restore civil nuclear relations with New Delhi. President Bush had signed the Act on December 18, 2006 in a ceremony at White House, hailing it as a major achievement, the accord for which he and Prime Minister Singh had earlier signed in 2005. A separate agreement with IAEA made the Act operational. IAEA approval was obtained in August, 2008 and the approval of 45-nation Nuclear Supplier Group (NSG) was endorsed on September 6.

After this the Secretary of State Condoleezza Rice pressed the Congress to approve the deal. In India Prime Minister Singh assured the parliament, on the same day, i.e. December

18, that the country has not become the 'client' of the US as considered by several opposition parties and the nuclear freedom will be maintained by not accepting any legal binding on nuclear testing or by signing CTBT. Whichever way one looks at the deal, whether honest agreement or otherwise, it is a great political albatross. The nuclear deal is a three-in-one agreement, comprising of a civil energy document with de facto NPT or CTBT agreements. Like that in 2006 the USIBC had once again started a move in Washington DC for persuading the US Congress to approve the deal. Ron Sommers the Chairman of the USIBC said that American companies are interested in joining hands with Indian companies in this regard.

The final agreement forged during five rounds of discussions, will allow India to carry out reprocessing of spent fuel from the reactors on the civilian side but India has to develop a new facility for this purpose and subject to IAEA safeguards. After President signed the legislation on October 8, 2008 in White House, the US Secretary of State went to New Delhi and along with Indian Foreign Minister signed the accord on October 11, 2008 to make it a binding for both nations. In 2007, Russia also signed agreement to help build four more atomic plants in India independent of Indo-US civil nuclear energy agreement.

UN Security Council

With respect to the composition and conduct of the UN Security Council, there is considerable disagreement. The Council is no longer representative of the changed number of UN members. At inception, there were only 61 members and 11 Security Council members. Now there are 190 plus members but only 15 Security Council members-an increase of 260 and 36 percent, respectively (Thakur, 2000). The overwhelming majority is from the developing world, which now finds itself quite under represented in the Council. Europe is over-represented, Asia under-represented, Africa and Latin

America not represented altogether. The Council seems to have become a tool in the hands of P-5 nations, led by the US, misusing its authority under article 25 of the UN charter, and in the process losing credibility.

Therefore, the Council needs to be restructured to make it really representative, democratic and transparent. Without this its function as a guardian of international peace and security cannot be discharged effectively. The Security Council has virtually surrendered its decision making to the extra-constitutional body called the P-5. These nations hold closed door meetings, excluding other elected members, and yet claim their decisions to be those of the Council. This is exemplified by condemnations by the UN of Indian and Pakistani nuclear tests in May 1998. The P-5 met in Geneva on July 4 and their joint communication was made the basis of the resolution of the Council. The Council also chose to disregard the Indian request to state its case of Pokhran 2 under article 31 of the charter but later allowed Pakistan to state its case. Similarly in November 1950 China was also allowed to state its case on Korean War. It is noteworthy that over a period of 50 years the Council never even chose to discuss the threat to the international security posed by the nuclear testing and stockpiling by the P-5 nations.

It has been considered by some that since the US was unhappy with India for disturbing its plan for nuclear non-proliferation, it influenced the Security Council, through P-5, to condemn India for nuclear testing and to deny India's request to present its case. The US imposed sanctions on India for nuclear tests, but even prior was intent on punishing India for its stance against NPT and CTBT. Similarly punishing Yugoslavia by NATO (without prior approval of the UN) in 1999 and later showed US desire to do what it likes with or without Council's stamp. The UN and the US have been struggling to learn to coexist in a world in which there is only one superpower and only one international organization. The UN cannot embark upon any venture without the consent of the US. There is wisdom and virtue in imposing the international discipline and moderating influence of the UN upon the exercise of American power. The anger of the majority has been reflected in not electing US on the Human Rights Commission of the UN.

In 1945, when the UN Charter was finalized, the world was Eurocentric, with hardly any Afro-Asian countries independent, and with Latin America shadowed by its elder giant on the North (Thakur, 2000). At that time, China was engulfed in a civil war and ruled by the US backed Chiang Kai-Shek. Later, with US determination to prevent a repeat of Pearl Harbour by keeping Japan under check, the US proposed China for the Security Council membership. China was thus the only non-Western nation of the P-5.

Therefore, the composition of the Council has never been democratic or truly representative. The present Council is considered by many as a legacy of the Colonialism. Veto power is undesirable and should either be replaced with a decision making process by absolute majority or be vested in at least 11 permanent member nations, representing all the 5 continents. The question of restructuring the Council has been on the agenda of General assembly since 1979. Enhanced membership of the UN merited the expansion of Security Council both in the category of its permanent and non-permanent members.

The expanded Council should have balanced continental and regional representation. There should be no distinction between old and new permanent members in terms of equal responsibilities and equal power. India's reaction to the suggestions regarding Germany and Japan joining as Council's permanent members in advance of others was negative because important countries in Asia, Africa and South America would have no representation or unduly low representation. Inaugurating a two-day Inter-Parliamentary Union (IPU) Conference of Presiding Officers of National Parliaments at New York on August 30, 2000, Najma Heptulla, President of

Inter-Parliamentary Union, said, "Security Council should be broad-based and further strengthened to reflect the present global scenario. Its composition must reflect global political reality." She added that the Council "must be democratized."

The summit drew legislators from 153 countries. "The United Nations and Parliamentarians the world over will have to have more interactions in view of the new economic architecture to insure that poor people are not marginalized further," she said (India Abroad, September 15, 2000). During his September, 2003 visit to the US, Prime Minister Vajpayee emphasized restructuring of the international political, security and economic institutions established nearly 60 years ago, based on today's realities and future needs (India Abroad, October 3, 2003). Developing nations have been pressing for the Council's expansion on the basis of equitable regional representation. Brazil, Nigeria and India have been strong candidates for permanent seats, but the US and some other P-5 nations favour Germany, Japan, South Africa, and other nations.

The Indian candidacy is based on the roles it has been playing and could play in the maintenance of international peace and security being a large and functional democracy. This peace keeping activity continued right up to the present time with the Indian forces operating in Cambodia, Mozambique, Angola, Somalia, Sierra Leone, Ruanda, Burundi, Haiti, Congo, Gaza, Lebanon, Cyprus and Middle East etc. (Alan James, 1969; Gupta, 2000; Thakur, 2000). India's deep concern in economic prosperity of the developing countries resulted in its playing a leading role in establishment of UNCTAD, the G-77, the ECOSOC, the UNIDO and other specialized agencies of the UN. India represents (excluding China) more people and technocrats than the population of the entire current membership of the council.

It occupies a strategic position and serves as a bridge between East and Central Asia. It has been the sponsor as well as the leader of NAM and has made contributions to strengthening the UN system and disarmament. In fact UN owes India about US$ 100 million for its peace keeping activities (Agencies UN, April 5, 2001). Despite India's strong case as an economic and military power, as well as the urgent need to restructure the council, nothing is likely to happen because no change is possible without the concurrence of the P-5.

Recently Secretary Condoleezza Rice visited India and Pakistan to express resentment on Iran-Pakistan-India gas pipeline but kept mum on the issue of India's candidature for Security Council's permanent seat. The P-5 nations, in spite of public posture on the need for a change, will prefer to maintain the status quo so that they can continue to make the UN Security Council subservient to themselves. Recently Russia, Britain and France as well as many others expressed desire to see India as a permanent member of the Security Council whereas Pakistan and its allies are not eager to see India in the Security Council where it could exercise a veto on Kashmir issue. One of the Congressman from American Samoa said India being the 4th economy of the world, based on its purchasing power, deserves to be a permanent member of the Security Council and also of the G-8 council (Subramanyam, 2005).

The US Ambassador Mumford at New Delhi stated in January, 2005 that UN Reforms Report has been received in Washington but no action on India's claim has been taken, although former Deputy Secretary Strobes Talbott advocated evolving a formula to include India as a permanent member of the Security Council (Agencies February 4, 2005). In an opinion poll by Amar Ujala 89 percent of the Indians considered that the US is for its selfish reasons not supporting India for Security Council. About 9 percent think otherwise and 2 percent are not sure (January 23, 2005). China proposed the role for India on a unanimous decision and not by voting. G-4 and India on the other hand, advocating a quick action by voting so that expansion is not delayed un-necessarily

(Agencies, April 9, 2005).

While participating in the 60th anniversary of Indian freedom, Kim Hovels, In- Charge of Commonwealth, stated in Durban Court that Britain will support Indian efforts for the permanent seat of the Security Council of the UN. In January 2008, President of France recommended India to be elected on the permanent seat of the UN. For agreement on the new proposal to expand UN developing countries did not favour the proposed formula because the same was did not specify the number of additional permanent members in the Council. Fast developing economy has begun to show its effects on international relations too. Foreign Minister of Australia has stated in June 2008 that, in association with India, it desires to build an organization of Pacific and Asian nations. He also pleaded for a permanent seat for India in the Security Council.

US Policy on Terrorism

In relation to terrorism, US policy is considered by India to be discriminatory. Speaking at a public meeting in his constituency, L.K. Advani, the Home Minister of India, said, "For you, American citizens anywhere are not expendable. Are Indians expendable? We are victims of terrorism and Pakistan is waging a proxy war. Are we not expected to take steps for the security for the nation and its citizens?" Analysts view the US strikes in Sudan, Afghanistan, and elsewhere as justified. In spite of tons of information on Pakistan's support for terrorism in North-western India, to the US there is no positive proof of Pakistan's involvement in terrorism. This is so despite the fact that the US has declared Harkat-ul-Ansar, Jaishe-e-Mohammad and Lashkar-e-Toiba of Pakistan to be terrorist groups and banned them. Recently it has also put Hizbul Mujahideen and Jamai-ul-Mujahideen on the watch list of terrorists (Amar Ujala May 3, 2003).

J.N. Dixit, the former foreign secretary of India, said, "The US is expressing views on the basis of its interests and we are reacting on the basis of our own interests." Vajpayee , the

Indian Prime Minister, and L.K. Advani, Home Minister, noted with regard to 1998 US strikes in Afghanistan and Sudan that the US can unilaterally act against terrorists who target American interests, namely the embassies in East Africa, while India is asked to refrain from doing so in its interest (Joshi, 2000; Mohan, 2000; Mohite, 1995; Raza, 1996). The Undersccretary of State, Thomas Pickering, and the Assistant Secretary of State for South Asian Affairs, Karl F. Inderfurth, had no clear answers and both denied any such double standard. To them India and Pakistan presented a very different case. Hence, India should not adopt the tactics used by the US to protect its interests. Analysts in the US, on the other hand, commented on the Indian government's double standard. To them the Indian government seemed to be concerned about the attack on Sudan, while it appeared to be discretely pleased with the strikes on terrorist bases in Afghanistan.

India has for more than a decade been saying that terrorists infiltrating Kashmir were being trained, armed and monetarily, supported by Pakistan at bases in G.K. or POK and in Afghanistan. Indian intelligence agencies provided reams of evidence to the US. However, the same has not been taken very seriously by the US administration (Bhattacharya, 1994; Chibber, 1998; Dixit, 1995; Ganguly, 1991; Gupta, 1996).

Compounding US reluctance were warnings by Pakistan that the US action against it would drive it into the hands of anti American extremists. The major factor that has so far saved Pakistan from being listed as a sponsor of international terrorism is a sentiment prevailing in the US that such action would be a kind of betrayal of an old friend who had stood by Washington and supported its war against Russia in Afghanistan, while India remained neutral. Although the Indian stand on the 1998 strikes by the US may not have been very clear, the Ministry of External Affairs has persistently condemned terrorism throughout the world. Clearly there is a need for effective international cooperation to identify and take strong actions against those responsible for international terrorism.

Both the US and the Soviets are now thinking to cooperate internationally on terrorism. London based Asia Pacific Foundation disclosed in its report that Pak English papers criticized murder of journalist Daniel Pearl whereas Urdu papers tried their best to justify it because of policies of the US (INS London, March 17, 2002). Prime Minister Vajpayee's statement on the US strikes apparently justified them. He was, however, critical of the partisan view taken by the US and reminded the country of its history of support to Taliban (the past ruling group in Afghanistan, which got enormous US financial support and armament through Pakistan), who were protecting Osama bin Laden, a Saudi millionaire responsible for US embassy bombings.

The Indian Home Minister, Advani, also questioned Thomas Pickering's stand that while Washington can eliminate terrorist threats on foreign soil, the same could not be applied to the Indian sub-continent. It may also be added that while India may be able to justify a policy of "hot pursuit" of terrorists across the national border, it would be unwise to act. Such action could provide the needed opportunity to Pakistan, its Islamic supporters and the patronizing nations to provoke a retaliatory action. This was the reason why India did not chase Pakistani infiltrators in 1999 Kargil conflict beyond LOC. Now America has agreed that Islamabad government and some of its organizations have close friendly relations with militants.

This was stated by the Foreign Secretary Condoleezza Rice in an interview to "The Politics" and "Yahoo News". ISI has been clearly mentioned to be playing an important role in the same and the US is now thinking of some serious action in the matter. She also stated that Islamabad has understood that besides neighbours Pakistan itself is also in danger. In order to fight terrorism one must disrespect the demands as well as the threats of terrorists and must not yield to their attacks. A country like India, which is going to become a strong world power, should act on such policies and act strongly against terror like Israel and the US. But for such actions we need a strong government which can send the message to the public not by words but by deeds.

According to the Press Trust of India, Taliban militia in Afghanistan have shifted, in 2001-02, a large number of terrorist bases run by Inter-Services Intelligence (ISI) to GK of Pakistan because of fear of fresh missile strikes by the US. The ISI commanders had issued strict orders asking the terrorists to go underground and lie low. This had been corroborated by the dissident Afghanis. The daughter-in-law of the founder of JKLF told that Pakistan has merged many camps into one camp only. These camps have been sent to Gilgit-Balistan areas, where Pakistanis are normally not allowed to go. The top leader of the JKLF repented to take the route of militancy (Agency January 20, 2004).

A large number of freshly trained terrorists of, the US banned Harkat-UL-Ansar (renamed as Harkat UI-Mujahideen) and the Laskar-e-Toiba, having a wide network in Jammu and Kashmir, were also told to flee from the camps. On October 15th 2001, Indian troops had to shell Pak army posts killing 12 terrorists, who were trying to cross over LOC in Mendhar and Akhnoor sectors, a defence spokesman said (Times of India, October 16, 2001). Michael Krepon, Chairman emeritus of the Stimson Centre said the timing of attacks to coincide with Powell's visit was significant. "I suspect New Delhi was sending Washington a message that its forbearance would be rather limited in the event of future provocations and would act whether the US and Pakistan were involved in the war in Afghanistan or not," he said.

Sumit Ganguly, Professor at the University of Texas University (now at Indiana) warned, "We stand at an important juncture in Indo-US relations. If the US does not honestly address India's legitimate concerns in Kashmir, yet another critical opportunity to place Indo-US relations on a secure footing will have been irretrievably lost" (India Abroad,

October 26, 2001). According to western military sources, the ISI has trained about 300,000 terrorists. Of these, about 90,000 were thought to have been killed in various operations in Afghanistan, J&K, Bosnia, Egypt, Algeria, and Pakistan. Western experts estimated that about 60,000 terrorists were helping Taliban with the backing of the Pakistani army, helped by the US. Somewhere between 30,000 and 40,000 terrorists from the nucleus of the Arab dominated International Islamic Brigade are bluntly advocating anti-American moves in Islamic countries, which has been confirmed by Bin Laden's declaration of holy war against India, Israel, Russia and the US. Pakistan (using American aid given for Afghanistan refugees) has deployed some and kept the rest for operations in India, where local militants have given up.

This apprehension became a fact in the Kargil conflict of 1999 (Behl, 2000; Mohan, 2000; Nanda, 1999; Nayar, 1998). The Harkat-ul-Ansar and the JKLF linked with Pakistan have carried out several operations against Indian troops and civilian targets in J&K and in neighbouring states, particularly targeting Pandits, the majority of whom have been forced to run away from the state. Mirvaiz Umar, former chairman of Huriat Conference, declared Pak terrorist organizations as thieves, who have used Kashmir issue for collecting money for their advantage. He is the 2nd leader to give such comments. First was Abdul Ghani Lone, who was murdered during 2002 elections in J&K. The terrorists include Arab war veterans and Afghans, who use machine guns, mortars, explosives and rockets. According to the US State department reports, Harkat-ul-Ansar (now Mujahideen) collects donations from Saudi Arabia, Gulf and Islamic countries. A considerable amount of the US money intended for the welfare of Afghanistan refugees coming to Pakistan flowed into hands of terrorists, it is alleged. Recently, the US has started showing some understanding about the cross-border terrorism from Pakistan, POK and Afghanistan, after it has suffered several_terrorist-attacks in the mainland as well as outside in other countries, particularly after September 11 terrorist attacks on World Trade Centre and the Pentagon, in which about 4400 people died or were missing, including more than 350 persons of Indian origin.

With the international movement towards free market economies there are now opportunities for expanding economic and the technological cooperation. After end of the cold war and India's increasing technology-and defence-needs, there is feasibility for cooperation for peace and stability in South Asia. President Clinton was fortunate in having Ambassadors like Thomas Pickering and Frank Wisner in Delhi and Strobes Talbott as Defence Secretary in Washington. They played important roles in maintaining friendly Indo-US ties. India's economic policy of liberalization has given momentum to bilateral relations. Indo-US trade, which stood once at more than US$ 5 billion per year, was down to a fifth place. The US investments in the core sector also started increasing.

During 1999 Kargil conflict the US declared Pakistan responsible for the conflict and pressurized it to vacate illegally occupied Indian territory within a few days and not in few weeks. The US army general, Henry Shelton, also visited Islamabad in same connection. These US actions were appreciated by the Indians. However, it is to be seen in which direction the Indo-US mutual relations travel in the near future. The chances were for the betterment but were shadowed with abundant economic and military aid to Pakistan (supporting terrorism), as indicated by Jim Hoagland (Agencies, June 13, 2003).

The US has responded to the Indian concern about cross-border terrorism, and the need for checking this menace on global basis. The US sent its top expert, Michael Sheehan, to coordinate responses to international insurgency actions. Sheehan met with senior officials of Ministry of External affairs, Home Ministry etc. India feels that both Pakistan and Afghanistan have become the main breeding grounds for

Islamic fundamentalism and insurgency. India has allowed opening of an office of the Federal Bureau of Investigation (FBI) in New Delhi.

However, it has been alleged by some that this is the first step for large-scale activities of the CIA in India. The military coup, staged on October 12, 1999 therefore became very important in the world scenario, particularly for India. General Musharraf, the coup leader, was the main architecture of the Kargil conflict. He suspended the elected Parliament and the constitution on the plea that the former government was very corrupt and could not improve the economy of the country. A few days after throwing out Nawaz Sharif, General Musharraf offered several gestures to the international community. He promised nuclear restraint, a departure from the previous government's repeated threats to test new missiles and use nuclear arsenals, if necessary. Pakistan followed India in 1998 by testing nuclear devices and proclaimed itself a nuclear-weapon state. After 74 days war with India, the Pakistani forces and the supported Mujahideens, who had earlier infiltrated in the Kargil sector of NW Indian hills, had to go back to Pakistani side of the LOC (Nanda, 1999; Behl, 2000; Joshi, 2000; Malik and Kapur, 1998; Mohan, 2000).

Even after the guns were silent the Pakistan instigated terrorists continued their nefarious activities in J&K. But on 18th October 1999, on one hand, Pakistan's troops began moving back from the Indian border to ease the conflict with India to gain financial support from the US. On the other hand, the Chief Executive declared continuity of the moral and material support to Mujahideens and others creating terrorism in J&K. First, he banned five organizations to show international community that he wished to stop support to terrorism.

However, later he released more than 800 terrorists from outlawed groups under a new formula (Press, March 17, 2002). The CE (who later managed to become President) vowed to usher an era of true and strong democracy before handing over power to the civilians. Pak media reported that in October, 2002 elections Political parties will not take part directly and to keep power in his control the President will nominate Prime Minister (Agencies Islamabad, April 13, 2002). History created by Ayub, Yahya and Zia shows that all military rulers also made a similar start yet they ended up in prolonging their stay in power. The agenda they have set for themselves were not radically different from Musharraf's agenda. The conclusions should not elude anyone as the CE already visited Iran, China, Arab States etc. to seek their cooperation for military regime. Pak officials have said, "when the crunch comes, it is really these states that support us in many ways." This is especially true given the attitude of Commonwealth, European Union and the US, which have shown impatience with military regimes in Islamabad.

Hatred Begets Hatred

"Those who take the sword shall perish by the sword!" said Lord Jesus. In both Kargil conflict and the IA plane hijack incidents in India, Pakistan lost to the powers of evil. The greatest damage is the hatred shown afresh in the two nations. More-diversion of funds for making/ purchasing arms, more hostility leads to the poor of both nations suffer consequently. Pakistan swears by Islam and India by secularism. A by-product of the conflict was the communal divide of the Indian subcontinent (Azad, 1960; Hodson, 1969). India has been tolerating Muslims, making them even as the Presidents of the Indian Union. The Muslim population in India is more than the Muslim population in Pakistan. Whereas percentage of Hindus and other minorities in Pakistan is now one-tenth of what was at the time of birth of Pakistan in 1947. The minorities in that country are officially the second rate citizens and cannot hope to rise to top positions in any field (Newsline February 10, 2001). Pakistani citizens are more concerned with demolition of a Hindu religious building (converted to Babri mosque) in India but not in the Hindu temples demolished in Pakistan, minorities being killed or driven out from the country or from the Srinagar valley in Kashmir (Priti Jairath, Jalandhar, December 7, 2000) or the destruction of Budha statues and Sikh Gurudwaras by Taliban.

To ease tension the Indian Prime Minister initiated bus diplomacy in February 1999 with the Pakistani Prime Minister and Lahore Declarations were signed. The army Chiefs of Pakistan abstained. ISI and the Pak army instigated the terrorists to cross LOC in the Kargil sector and occupy strategic areas. This resulted in a military conflict in 1999 summer in which Pakistanis were pushed back on their side of the LOC. Since the other side of the LOC is also Indian area illegally occupied by Pakistan in 1947, India could have crossed the border but it did not. India had long back given the MFN status to Pakistan but the same has not been reciprocated to India so far. By adding religion to Politics Pakistan has destroyed its social harmony. The same way it is adding politics to trade and damaging its economy.

By increasing trade and having peaceful relations with India it is likely to gain more than India. This ground reality is not being understood by Islamabad. On the other hand, Pakistan has tried its best to obstruct 2002 elections in J&K state, in which more than 600 innocent lives have been lost. President Musharraf had earlier termed these elections as farce. The US leaders as well as from some other democratic nations asked Pakistan to stay away from them but these wishes were not heeded to. Election Commission of India had issued 28 special passes to 28 diplomats to witness these elections, in which about 47 percent population participated actively, despite hurdles created by terrorist. Again in 2004 and 2008 despite calls from militants and separatists not to participate in elections, people turned out in large numbers to elect a new government. In the light of above it is not clear will Pakistan ever like to co-exist peacefully with India. Information Minister Sheikh Rashid has stated that India is hoarding biological and chemical weapons, besides nuclear arsenals (Agencies, Delhi, April 9, 2003).

The allegation has been denied by India. Pakistan refused to take part in the fair being organized for the past more than 300 years at the border by Hindus, Muslims and Sikhs to celebrate saving the life of 4 lakh people. Earlier Pakistan used to participate in the Chamaliyal Mela. This year they prevented Pakistanis to participate in the same (Amar Ujala June 26, 2003). Similarly, Pakistan has denied lifting the ban on Indian TV channels despite progress towards normalcy of relations (IANS Islamabad July 8, 2003). For resuming flights between the two countries, Pakistan asked for a guarantee for not stopping flights, in future under any circumstances and the flights could not be started. Ultimately, Pakistan agreed to resume flights between the two nations.

On the other hand, to reduce tensions, India decided to pull out thousands of its troops from Pak border but not from the LOC. Matching the move made by India, Pak authorities also announced withdrawal of troops. India has completed the movement and Pakistan has also followed the suit. As a result of the new peace process declared by the Indian Prime Minister in 2003 in Kashmir, some results have started coming in but a lot remains to be done (Amar Ujala, April 19, 2003). In May, 2008 the peace process was however broken twice by the Pak forces in Bengalarh (Jammu), Sambha and Kupwara to help entry of terrorists. Indian forces however did not retaliate because they wanted to continue peace and they have sent message for flag meeting with Pak forces. Indo-Pak Chamber of Commerce and Industry submitted its recommendation to the Indian Prime Minister.

It has been suggested that these recommendations should be applied in different ways and mutual trade development should not be held in ransom to some disagreement. Foreign Minister Yashwant Sinha suggested Pakistan should take a lesson from Sino-India model. He said India does not want to avoid talks on Kashmir but certainly wants not to hold the progress on other important matters in ransom (Amar Ujala,

July 10, 2003). On his visit for SAARC summit at Islamabad, Prime Minister Vajpayee asserted, "If we could put violence, terrorism and hostility behind us, I can see no obstacle to establishment of a climate of friendship and cordiality in which we can discuss and resolve all our outstanding bilateral issues, including J&K" (PTI, January 3, 2004). In the meeting of February, 2005 between Commerce and Industry representative a commitment was made to increase trade between the two countries.

India and Pakistan agreed to initiate talks on boundary in Sir Creek region, confidence building measures in the nuclear fields and the gas pipe line from Iran via Pakistan. Pakistani Prime Minister Shaukat Aziz appealed to World Bank on Baglihar dam construction by India. But Indian government thinks this will not affect ongoing peace process (Amar Ujala, January 28, 2005). India is continuing withdrawal of some of some of its troops from J&K. Bus service was started from Srinagar to Mujaffarabad. On January 20, Pakistan carried out mortar shelling on 2 Indian posts at a time when Pak students were visiting India for promoting friendship. During cease-fire Pakistan also constructed underground bunkers, border posts and roads even in disputed lands. National Intelligence Council of the US in its report (Mapping Global Future) mentioned that Pakistan is capable of using nuclear power in the event of any war with India (Agencies, January 17, 2005).

This is the reason why Pakistan was keen to obtain F-16 fighters planes capable of carrying nuclear arsenals. According to many analysts whenever India acted seriously for peace in Kashmir, Pakistan's Jehadi personals or supporting army or ISI created bloodshed right from the period of Nehru to Vajpayee and Manmohan Singh. However, many separatist leaders are getting fed up with militancy in J&K. In January, 2007 Huriat Chief Mirwaiz expressed his unhappiness with terrorism in J&K and suggested to terrorists giving up arms to stop death and destruction in the interest of the nation. As a part of confidence building measures the decision taken last recently trading began for the first time across the LOC in Kashmir in October 2008. This trade not only raises the hopes for reduction of tension between the two countries but also reduces illegal trade.

8

Kashmir Factor in Indo-US-Pak Relations

Jayant Kumar and B.B. Nagaich

According to 2007 US Congress Report on 'global terror' India is the worst sufferer from terrorism as it lost about 2,300 Indian citizens in different parts of the country. For better comprehension of the Pakistan supported terrorism in India a look at the history of Kashmir is useful. This historical backdrop helps in placing the present problem in the right perspective. The issue is not merely an Indo-Pak problem but with an international ramifications. This has come about because of the inapt handling of the situation by the Indian government at the Centre & State and the needless involvement of the UN in the issue.

The region of Jammu & Kashmir, comprising of Leh-Ladakh, Jammu and Srinagar valley, east of the river Indus and north of the river Ravi in the undivided sub-continent have always been like a paradise, distinct from the rest of the sub-continental Indo-Gangetic plains. The region has now changed from being a paradise to a death-trap for the innocent residents and tourists. It is now riddled with violence and terror. Foreign mercenaries are now active; militants from Pakistan, Afghanistan, Sudan and elsewhere have fought against Indians (Kashmiris & others) in security forces. Should peace be established before a permanent solution is found? Where should we go from here or what should we do now are the questions frequently asked? One thing is sure. The most vulnerable states are those with pluralistic open societies that do not mind dissent. Earlier, terrorism used to be the problem of developing nations. Today it is entire World's problem.

Even Pakistan, which is an important terrorism-sponsoring nation, is not free from militancy. If we keep quiet after noting terrorism elsewhere, we will have to regret it some day because it is going to affect us also very soon.

Historical Background

Emperor Ashok, who ruled India during the 3rd century BC, extended his rule into Kashmir and is known to have established the city of Srinagar. During his period, Buddhism took roots among the population, which was predominantly Hindu. Later Jammu & Kashmir formed part of the Kanishkan Empire. Subsequently, the State thrived under illustrious rulers like Lalitaditya and Avanit Varman in the 8th and 9th centuries. Owing to decadence and turmoil, in the 14th century, Muslims came into power. While the early Muslim rulers were tolerant, some of the subsequent rulers indulged in mass conversion of people and forced a large number of Pandits to flee the Valley. In 1814, Maharaja Ranjit Singh invaded Kashmir. He took over the area by 1819 and ruled it. Kashmir was then sold to Maharaja Gulab Singh in 1846, ushering Dogra rule, which lasted till 1947.

The Muslims, who were majority in Srinagar Valley (but a minority in Jammu and Leh-Ladakh), were unhappy and felt no say in the matters. Consequently some of them launched a movement in 1931 for securing their demands and the Dogra ruler conceded a number of them. Some well known leaders like Sheikh Mohammad Abdullah, Bakshi Ghulam Mohammad Sadiq and Mirza Afzal Beg came into prominence during the movement. Their fight for liberation from autocratic rule received the support from the national leaders like Mahatma Gandhi, Jawaharlal Nehru, Maulana Azad and Sardar Patel. However, Mir Waiz Mohammad Yusuf Shah revived the Muslim Conference in 1941, an organization, which had first originated with limited support from some fundamentalists. In 1946 Jinnah visited Kashmir and tried to persuade Kashmiris to join the proposed state of Pakistan but was rebuffed. In 1947, at the time of partition, Maharaja Hari Singh took time to decide the issue of accession, in accordance with the Indian Independence Act. Instead of waiting, Pakistan decided to annex the state by force.

The Pakistani Attack

On the night of 20th October 1947, Pakistan (encouraged by Liaquat Ali) invaded J&K using tribals from N.W. Frontier Province, ex-soldiers, deserters from State Forces and Pakistan Army (Akbar, 1985; Chibber, 1998; Chopra, 1990; Ganguly, 1991). Realizing that Pakistan posed a serious threat to Srinagar, the Maharaja sent the Kashmir Prime Minister to Delhi and sought military assistance from India. The then Governor General of India, Lord Mountbatten advised him to get the Maharaja Hari Singh to sign the accession papers first, which was done on October 26 with the help of Sheikh Abdullah. Indian troops were then sent on October 27 to repel the aggressors. In order to better manage the affairs of the State an interim administration was set up. Sheikh Abdullah was appointed the Chairman of the emergency administration (Mahajan, 1963).

A local Kashmiri resistance force, the J&K militia, working in conjunction with Indian troops saved Srinagar in time and subsequently cleared out a major part of J & K from the control of the invaders. It is interesting to note that the US Charge d'Affairs, in Pakistan, Lewis visited NWFP at this time. Anglo-American newspapers glorified the raiders (Chopra, 1990). While the operation to clear the invaders out of J&K was in progress India also appealed to the United Nations on the December 30, 1947 to intervene and to force Pakistan to vacate its aggression. After protracted debates in the UN, two mutually acceptable resolutions were adapted on August 13, 1948 (Chopra, 1990). A cease-fire came into being on January 1, 1949, which envisaged three steps to be taken in sequence as follows:

1. First, Pakistan should withdraw its all of its forces from

J&K.

2. Second, India to withdraw its additional forces and maintain only requisite strength for safe guarding law and order.
3. Thirdly, the future status of the State was to be determined in accordance with the will of the people.

On July 27, 1949 an agreement known as the Karachi Agreement was signed between the two sides under the aegis of the UN Commission for India and Pakistan, delineating a cease-fire line (LOC). Pakistan so far has not implemented the first part of the UN resolution, upon which hinged the implementation of the other two parts. Instead it built up its forces further in the occupied Kashmir, instigating militancy in the Indian side of the J&K as well as in the Punjab and neighbouring states. Further, it also kept raking up the issue in every forum of the world that India is not permitting self-determination in J&K (Chibber, 1998; Chopra, 1990). Successful twists in colouring the issue on communal lines also continued unabated by Pakistan (Dixit, 1995; Ganguly, 1993, 1999). At this point of time, it joined the West sponsored CENTO and SEATO pacts and received support from Western nations, particularly USA and some Islamic countries.

Democracy in J&K

Despite the non-implementation of the UN resolutions, the Indian leadership continued to encourage democracy in J&K, like in other states in the country and decided to form a Constituent Assembly to act according to the wishes of the masses in different parts of the state. Article 370, defining the special relationship of the State with the Centre was also included in the national constitution. Elections were held to the Constituent Assembly and a constitution was framed for the state. The Constituent Assembly ratified accession on February 6, 1954 as per wishes of the masses. The state constitution was adopted on November 17, 1956, based on which the elections were held several times and Kashmiris elected governments of their choice (Gupta, 1996; Lamb, 1967; Nayyar, 1992). Whereas no elections were ever held in the Pak occupied Kashmir (so called Azad Kashmir/ Gulam Kashmir) and no mentionable development took place there. To keep people ignorant and uneducated, colleges, radio and TV stations have not been started in the region. About 14 percent of males and only 3 percent females are educated in P.O.K/G.K.

Accordingly, the masses there are highly naturally highly dissatisfied and demonstrations and violence are not uncommon in the region. Till today the people of Pak occupied Kashmir (POK) have neither the Pakistani citizenship nor have been given the right to elect their own government like their Indian counterpart. In June 2001, there were demonstrations under the leadership of Sardar Showkat Ali Kashmiri in front of the office of the UN Human Rights Commission in Geneva because about 2 million people of POK/GK were not given the right to vote in their Assembly elections. Earlier 80 nomination papers of the Nationalist party candidates were rejected because this party had not agreed to merger of POK in Pakistan. On the other hand a number of seats have been kept vacant in J&K Assembly for the representatives of POK to be elected, whenever this area also merges with India (Prajapati, 1998; Salman, 1994). European Union in its report on Jammu & Kashmir has alleged human rights violation in POK. Foreign Affairs Committee of the EU has shown its worry on torturing people after arresting them without valid reasons. EU Parliamentarian B.E. Nicholson has prepared the report on Gilgit-Balistan showing human rights violation in that region. He was hoping to submit the report on violation of birth right in POK & Gilgit-Balistan areas in the EU Parliament in May, 2007.

In the past, India and Pakistan have tried to outwit each other without looking at possible solutions. President Musharraf was obsessed with the right of self-determination, which he used as a tool to show that he was championing the cause of Kashmiris. Later, he stunned the Pakistanis, who thought that self-determination will deliver Kashmir into Islamabad's hands, by his statement that instead of such exercise other solutions be explored. India, when confronted with this suggestion asked Pakistan to indulge in self-introspection. It recommended to Pakistan to first "practice before preaching" democracy, which became very common in the speeches of former Prime Minister Vajpayee. He was naturally reminding Pakistan, 'if you talk of J&K, we will talk of POK' (Joshi, 2004).

Political Developments in J&K

Maharaja Hari Singh left the state in June, 1949 and his son Yuvraj Karan Singh was elected Sadar-e-Riyasat and appointed as the constitutional Head. The relationship of the state with the rest of the country was further discussed and an agreement called Delhi Agreement was passed by the Parliament on July 27, 1952. This was also approved by the State Constituent Assembly on August 19, 1952. On August 9, 1953 Bakshi Ghulam Mohammad took over as the Chief Minister and worked for the greater integration of the state with the rest of India. Later Khwaja Shamsuddin became the Chief Minister and in his period the sacred Relic of the Hazratbal shrine was found missing. There was considerable turmoil in the Srinagar valley. Fortunately the relic was found. Ghulam Mohammad Sadiq took over from Shamsuddin and followed liberal policies and worked for the emotional integration of J&K with rest of the country. Even the National Conference was converted into Indian National Conference. In 2008 elections extremists did not want to participate and asked people to shun elections. But more than 65 percent turned out to vote and elected National Conference President Omar Abdullah for becoming Chief Minister. His grand father and father both remained Chief Ministers of J&K. These facts show that despite warning from separatists Kashmiri public still believes in pluralistic Indian democracy.

Second War in J&K

During 1962 Indo-China war, Pakistan brought pressure on its allies, to bring about settlement of Kashmir issue with India. Pakistan demanded considerable additional territory including Srinagar valley and a plebiscite thereafter. India was prepared to consider stabilization on the cease-fire line and a No War Pact with Pakistan. Despite six meetings having taken place between Zulfikar Ali Bhutto and Sardar Swaran Singh during 1962-63 no results could be arrived at.

In 1965, Pakistan launched yet another aggression on Kashmir initiated by infiltrating a large number of forces. As a result India also carried out counter offensive moves. A cease-fire came about on September 23, 1965. The Tashkent Agreement was arrived at on January 10, 1966. On the demise of Prime Minister Shastri at Tashkent, after signing the agreement, Indira Gandhi succeeded him (Dixit, 1998; Gandhi, 1988; Grover, 1995; Maroof Raza, 1996). During 1966-71, Pakistan continued unabated the subversive activities in J&K and persistently raised the issue of self-determination. However, during this period, owing to a feeling of total neglect by Bengalis in East Pakistan, serious agitation took place there under Sheikh Mujibur-Rehman, the undisputed leader of East Pakistan. West Pakistan retaliated by repression, leading to a liberation struggle by the Bengalis in 1971.

During this period Pakistan also took the irrational step of bombing Indian airfields, followed by large scale infiltration in J&K and attack by regular forces along the borders. India retaliated on a massive scale, resulting in the liberation of Bangladesh and some loss of territory of Pakistan on the Western front. This was followed by the Shimla Pacts on July 2, 1972, but again, after the return of nearly 95,000 prisoners and the territory captured on the Western front by India, Pakistan never observed the Shimla agreement and returned back to its policy of fomenting law and order problems in J&K etc. (Ganguly, 1993; Hoffman, 1990). Islamabad encouraged separatists to threaten people from participating in elections.

Even in 2008 polls extremists tried that people should not vote but not listening to them more than 65% people caste their votes, neglecting the call made by extremists. The same happened in 2009 elections for Parliament.

Preparation for Terrorism in J&K

At one stage, it was considered that religion would not play an important role in political affairs. However, it did not prove to be true. Today no government can ignore religion. India began as a secular nation in 1947. But then, the three time Prime Minister Vajpayee had to accede to the pressure of all religious groups of all shades, Hindus, Buddhists, Sikhs, Muslims and Christians. Israel started as a secular country but Prime Minister Ariel Sharon had to go with hat in hand to the religious parties for support so that he could maintain a majority in the Knesset. In Pakistan President Musharraf had to go in hand in hand with Islamic fundamentalists.

To a truly religious person extremism found defeat in the traditions that extremists are trying to preserve, neglecting compassion, which all the religions highlight as primary virtue. Thus the root causes of extremism are hopelessness, despair and nihilism. We cannot appreciate fundamentalists because they threaten our values and they do not accept us because we threaten their most sacred values. In 1972, after Sayid Mir Qasim became the Chief Minister of J&K a conciliatory policy to restore full normalcy was adopted. After about three years, he stepped down in the larger interest of the state and Sheikh Abdullah took over as Chief Minister again. There was an all round development till his demise in September 1982. In the May 1983 elections Farookh Abdullah received an impressive majority and formed the government.

However, he looked to the opposition for support and attended opposition conclaves. After one year he lost the majority and his brother-in-law Ghulam Mohammad Shah was appointed as the Chief Minister. He also was dismissed in 1986 because of his failure to maintain law and order. Taking advantage of the unstable conditions in the state, Pakistan intensified its nefarious activities, including violence. About a decade ago Pandits numbered about 500,000 out of about 8 million Kashmiris, a small but well educated and successful minority. And they have since been persecuted so ferociously by extremists or by infiltrating guerillas that only a few remained in their homes. The displaced Pandits moved to Jammu region, Delhi and to other countries, including the US.

It was felt in the wake of this ethnic cleansing that all nationalists, secular and democratic forces should be brought together to combat fundamentalism and secessionist tendencies. The Congress party and the National Conference once again got together and Farookh formed an alliance government in 1986. The opposition within the State also got together and formed Muslim United Front (MUF). In the 1987 elections Farrokh got a considerable majority in the state legislative Assembly. However, on instigation and support from Pakistan, the MUF resorted to a violent agitation to topple down the elected government.

The involvement of the Pakistani Administration through sponsored terrorist outfits is laid bare by lucid accounts given by Khurshid Ahmad Magre, Nisar Ahmad Magre, Abdul Ghani Butt, Firdos Ahmad Mir, Sikandar and Sajjad Ahmad Mir (then only 18-19 years old). These individuals recounted incidences of how terrorists lured Kashmiri youth, forced them to go to Pakistan for training and made them walk several days without enough food. They threatened to kill these youth in case of non-submissiveness and treated them like animals till they were freed by the 19th Dagger Division (AP July 4, 2001). A good account of terrorism initiation in the valley is given by Chopra, 1990.

Pakistan's Doctrine of Proxy War

In order to take advantage of the disturbances in the state Pakistan evolved a new strategy of alluring disgruntled youth to Pakistan, training them and pushing them back to J&K, with the aim of stepping up militancy in the region and resting the state from India. It was expected that the people would rise in rebellion against the Union of India. When militancy gained momentum, they were expected to rise to liberate Kashmir, thereby avenging the creation of Bangladesh. Towards this end, Pakistan organized and supported some militant groups such as Jammu and Kashmir Liberation Front (JKLF) under Amanullah Khan, who was encouraged to have his head quarters in Rawalpindi.

Subsequently after JKLF started demanding independence, Pakistan switched its support to Hizbul Mujahideen (HU), a fundamentalist and fanatic pro-Pakistan group, which demanded merger of the state with Pakistan. Later other groups came into prominence such as Harkat-ul-Ansar (HUA) and Lashkar-e-Toiba (LET), which had their roots in Jamait-e-Islami (JEI), the rabid fanatic organization based in Pakistan. Initially when some trained militants infiltrated back in India and were apprehended, it was treated as a routine affair, as the strategy was not yet clear. However, with more militants coming in and indulging in terrorism, killings, kidnappings, blackouts and intimidation etc. the strategy began to unfold. Concurrent with terrorist acts, considerable propaganda was let loose against India (Nayyar, 1998; Salman, 1994; Grover, 1995).

Since 1980s Islamabad has waged proxy war unremittingly but New Delhi has not been able to shed its blinkers what to say of the start of a concrete counteraction. New Delhi is still debating as to how to respond to the doctrine of proxy war. Failure to advance from sound bites to action has turned India into a veritable target for daring attacks that US analyst Ashley Tellis told Congress, "India has become the sponge that protects us all". Pakistan's ability to wage a proxy terror war owes a lot to India's own failings. While Pak is a quasi-failed nation, India has yet to come of age – still to learn statecraft.

Efforts were also made in the 1980s to propagate Islamic fundamentalism, which is different from the Kashmiri culture.

The National Conference-Congress coalition government of Farookh tried to combat militancy on the security and political fronts. The state police however, could not match the highly trained motivated militants and additional forces were badly needed in the state. As Parliament elections were announced in the country, additional forces were provided only in December, after the elections. By then the situation had deteriorated further as militancy had almost touched its peak. First the Governor of the state resigned and later Farookh and his government resigned. This created chaos and President's rule had to be imposed.

Disillusionment with Pakistan

While many Muslim Kashmiris shared condemnation of India, they began to distance themselves from Pakistan. Political leaders from Pakistan deny giving support to terrorism but money does originate from Islamic nations like Saudi Arabia, Pakistan and Iran etc. funnelled through Islamabad to pay mercenaries from Pakistan, Afghanistan, Libya and Chechnya, who infiltrate Indian J&K for waging Jehad. Yasin Malik, a JKLF militant, who spent four years in a Delhi jail and was later released, did not apologize and did not boast for his past work but hoped to see Kashmir as an independent country, away from Pakistan.

Another Kashmiri militancy leader Maqbool Butt, the man behind the first hijacking of an Indian plane in 1971 was thoroughly disillusioned with Pakistan, as evident from his letters written in jail prior to his death in 1976.The hijackers were initially given a hero's welcome by Z.A. Bhutto but later arrested within 24 hours. In April 1973, Butt wrote to his daughter Azra, "The Pakistani (ruling) click had never had an interest in freedom for Kashmiris. They only talk and they should not be trusted." His letters written from jails had been compiled into a book by Mohammad Saeed Asad titled 'Shaoor-e-Farda' (understanding to tomorrow). In a letter concerning massacre of Bengalis by the Pakistani army, Butt wrote, "that those very Pakistani rulers, who felt nothing in gunning down their own country men, were now punishing Kashmiris".

When he became convinced that Pakistan could not be trusted he returned to Kashmir and was later arrested and hanged (Chopra, 1990). He and many others were trained for hijacking by a Pakistan air force pilot in Rawalpindi. Another shock to Butt was an offer of money to him from POK puppet President Abdul Quayyum Khan "if he joined Pakistan People's Party." Butt's associate Hashim Qureshi was first received as a hero and later jailed in Pakistan after alleging to be working for Indian Border Security Force. On release from jail in Pakistan, Hashim went to live in Holland as he was frustrated with Pakistan. He returned to India nearly 30 years after on December 29, 2000 to surrender to face trial. He was one of the founders of JKLF in 1982. He appreciated Prime Minter Vajpayee's peace invitations. He hated violence in J&K and invited residents of POK/GK to liberate themselves from the clutches of Pakistan (Agencies, December 29, 2000).

Frustrated by the ill effects of cross-border terrorism three farmers of the village Marodh of Tehsil Surankot of the District Poonch, namely Nazir Husain, Mohammad Ilias and Nazir Hisamuddin, moved from J&K to as far as Bundelkhand in U.P. in search of employment to live in peace. To help the Indian army they gave their houses to be used against terrorism in the border village. They recounted experiences of how during snowfall militants from across the border come to their village and demand free boarding and lodging by force. These farmers, after handing over their houses to the Indian army moved in winters from their village in search of work in far away peaceful areas. They also informed that many of their relations have been killed by terrorists because of their opposition to terrorism. The Indian government gives innocent victims of terrorism money as compensation ranging from Rs. 50,000 to Rs. 100,000.

According to them the Indian army tries to be helpful and

remains on duty for 24 hours (personal interviews to B.B. N.). In January 2007, Huriat Chief Mirwaiz fed up with militancy in J&K suggested giving up arms by terrorists to stop death and destruction and work for development. Every time elections are announced in J&K the separatists and terrorists give a warning to people and asking them for not participating in elections. Sometimes local political parties abstain from elections. However these warnings were never heeded by the majority. In 2008 & 2009 elections a record number of turn out was reported from different places and in general above 65 percent people voted to elect National Conference as majority party to form the government.

Conversion of Terrorism into a Movement

With the seeds sown all through the late, seventies and eighties, the winter of 1989 saw unprecedented levels of violence in Srinagar valley. Fundamentalists filled the narrow lanes and streets of Srinagar shouting anti-Indian holy war slogans, as they converged on the UN observer's office to hand over their demands for independence. In October 1947 the Kashmiris sought India's help and acceded to it to protect their Kashmiri identity from the ravages of the raiders, but not to lose it in the vast Indian 'ocean'. Every attempt at forcing them closer to the rest of India, constitutionally and administratively, only widened the emotional gulf between Delhi and Srinagar because of the brainwashing from pro-Pakistani extremists. When even the ballot could not satisfy their valued Kashmiriyat the bullet was used as another option. The civil war in Afghanistan and the semi-insurgency in Punjab were inspiring examples just across the gate, while the withdrawal of the IPKF convinced them that they could do what the Tamil Tigers have done. There followed the collapse of the Soviet Union. Their Muslim cousins in Central Asia and Azerbaijan achieved independence from Moscow almost effortlessly. With the end of the Cold War arms too could be had for a song and Pakistan was there to help every anti-Indian movement, be it in Punjab or in J&K or in the strife torn north east. All these events formed a perfect backdrop for the unfolding of the insurgency movement in the Valley. Kashmiris demanded a change and believed that they would be able to get it. Thus began the era of militancy and terrorism.

In its first phase Kashmiri militancy was mostly indigenous, their aim was independence and their organized wing was the JKLF. Pakistan found in this movement another opportunity to embarrass India. Therefore, arms, assistance, and encouragement continued to pour from across the LOC and the ordinary Kashmiri, euphoric with his expectations and ignorance, defied the authorities. They thought in terms of independence within a couple of years. But, they were calculating without taking into account the massive power of the Indian State. While troops were rushed in to choke all expressions of dissent, hardly anything was done to provide the frightened Kashmiri Pandits with the required security. Instead, their mass evacuation was arranged. This is the sole instance in history of the community loyal to the government be moved away from their homes and hearts and that too from state capital itself.

The twin operation of operation and evacuation had the expected results. Slowly Kashmiris turned increasingly to religious orthodoxy and looked at Pakistan for solace, support, and sympathy. If brutal oppression drove the movement underground and destroyed the space for any dialogue, the operation evacuation, tantamount to ethnic cleansing, of the Pandits completely communalized it. As popular participation fell because of frustration, the space vacated by Pandits came to be occupied by an increasing number of trained guerillas and religious fanatics from Pakistan and POK/GK and even Afghanistan (Yousaf and Adkins, 1993). Thus began the second phase. The so-called foreign militants were not Kashmiris and shared neither their liberal ethos nor their Kashmiriyat dreams. They were loyal to Pakistan and were extreme religious fanatics. With the strings of purse and arms in their hands they began calling the shots, while the locals gradually fell back to their roles as guides & informers and were forced to provide shelter and food. As Islamiyat replaced Kashmiriyat, militancy restricted so far to the Valley began receiving a warmer response from the non-Kashmiri Muslims of Poonch, Rajauri and Doda (Nayyar, 1998; Nanda, 1999).

As radical Islam became the public face of militancy in the state even a large number of Kashmiris took shelter behind the Namaz, the Burkha, and anti-modern demonstrations. An Islamic militant group called Lashkar-e-Jabbar carried out two acid attacks unveiled Muslim women in J&K in August 2001 and gave September 1 as a deadline for women to adhere to Islamic dress codes. The idea is to impose Sheriat laws in the state following in the steps of the Taliban. The secular regionalism surrendered before the Jehad or holy wars, acting on instructions from Pakistan. The official media too helped in communalizing the issue by harping on the number of Hindus forced out of the valley without even mentioning the number of Muslims who too had to share a similar fate. In the vitiated atmosphere a few Pandit families, who were staying on in the Valley or had just returned, were mercilessly exterminated.

The next phase began with the large-scale use of the surrendered militants to confront their former comrades and frightened the country side. These renegades were the new terror of the Kashmiris, worst than what they had faced in the hands of paramilitary forces during cordon, search and interrogation. All of them were used extensively to force elections on an unwilling population only to install a puppet government. Even that government could not restrain the arms of indiscriminate oppression nor could it ensure development and security. By then militancy had spread even to the three districts of Hindu majority Jammu division. The people there had reasons to be frustrated with the new National Conference government, but the virtual elimination of the Congress as a force left them with hardly any alternative. Jammu political life too had been communalized by then, and the BJP with its ideology was ill-suited to meet the emotional needs of the neglected backward Muslims of these outlined districts.

So, again the Pakistan sponsored militants who stepped into that vacuum, arms in hand, gave the locals both confidence and a cause. Ethno-cultural similarities enabled their patrons across the LOC to enter and operate in these forested districts, south of the Pir Panjal range. Besides, the massive presence of the armed forces in the Valley made it very difficult for terrorists to carry out operations there. So in the summer and autumn of 1998, they shifted their attention to the northern belt of Jammu division, and over half-a-dozen mass murders of the Hindus were carried out, in Poonch, Chamba and in neighbouring Himachal Pradesh. The government responded by arming members of the minority (Hindus) and forming village defence committees (VDC) to meet the surprise attacks. But arming only one community, when the atmosphere is tense, is fraught with many problems and prompted the Muslims to fall back on the local Muslims as their source of confidence and strength. As a result, the militants received not only shelter and food but also the required information about the movements of security forces and the activities of prominent Hindus in Poonch, Rajauri and Doda districts (Mohan, 2000; Gupta, 1996).

To kill a large number of civilians to attract world attention, the ISI trained terrorists were putting time bombs in scooters/ motorbikes and leaving them in crowded places in different cities. When the first bomb exploded, people out of curiosity came to watch what has happened. These innocent bystanders became fodder for a second bomb that would explode killing many more people in the crowd of onlookers, who came to watch the first explosion. Besides arms the terrorists were being given second hand white ambassador cars, which are normally used by Ministers and senior government officers, to run away without being checked by police. Fortunately, cross border-terrorism saw a slight decline during the recent two years but in the first quarter of the year

2008 ISI took a decision to increase the amount given to the militants for substantially stepping up terror in India. Long time has passed after Bangalore, Ahemdabad and Jaipur bomb blasts. If we add the list of terror attacks in India the list would become very long. However nothing has changed.

The capacity of the majority community to bear these attacks is immense. Generally it is said that Indian democracy is very liberal. In such a situation control of terrorism becomes very difficult. Neither one can make strong laws nor use strong methods. POTA was formulated during BJP government's rule but the same was abolished by the next government. To deal with terror one must not agree to militant's demands nor should bother for their threats or attacks. Such attacks can neither change political set up nor can change the foreign policy. Therefore India must take very strong measures to fight terrorism. But for such a policy we need a government which by its deeds can convey the message to every body. After several terror attacks in many cities including New Delhi and Mumbai the UPA government has started thinking to have some strong regulation to control terrorism and after 26/11 Mumbai attacks it had to bring an act called Unlawful Act Prevention Act (UAPA) and create a National Investigation Agency (NIA). The longest engagement between terrorists and the Indian security forces continued on 8th day in thick jungle area of Poonch in strong bunkers in which 7 persons died including 4 extremists (Hindustan January 9, 2009). Mohammad Omar Madni, working for LET, having knowledge of six languages was arrested from Delhi on June 6. He had lots foreign currency and fake Indian rupees, Nepali citizen card and armaments to hand over blast materials to one of his team member.

Lashkar-SIMMI Partnership

In Aurangabad, about 200 miles east of Mumbai, police ceased dozens of AK-47 rifles and crates of explosives. The arrest resulted from apprehension of suspected Lashkar operatives in Mumbai with 2 pounds of explosives. SIMMI and LET have apparently united by a wild-eyed cause of bringing the Indian subcontinent under Muslim domination. They want Saudi type Wahabi Islam and reject notion of majority "polytheist infidel" Hindus outnumbering Muslims. LET-SIMMI partnership has been growing and they have collaborated in bomb blasting of temples in Jammu, Gujarat, Varanasi and markets in New Delhi or trains & hotels in Mumbai, Hyderabad or Ajmer Sharif shrine and other places, killing thousands of people. Thousands of armed guerrillas are believed to have attended LET's training camps in POK/GK. Intelligence revealed SIMMI has about 500 hard-core members and more than 25,000 sympathizers, who shelter culprits. Al-Qaida and Taliban are anxious and trying to take advantage of 'Muslim-sentiments'.

The threat from Al-Qaida and Taliban to India deepened with reports coming in that about 300 Jehadi fighters, including some from Kashmiri groups, coming together for a secret gathering in Rawalpindi that serves as headquarters to Pakistani army. The groups launched long ago with Pakistani army's support to fight in Kashmir, agreed in June, 2008 meeting to resolve their differences and commit more fighters to Afghanistan too (TNN & Agencies). Because India invested heavily in Afghan reconstruction program along with the US is against Taliban desire and consequently Taliban retaliated with attack on India embassy in Kabul, which killed one diplomat, the defence attaché, two ITBP guards and several dozens of other people. The leader of SIMI or its cooperator Indian Mujahideen (created with the help of HUJI), Mufti Abu Bashar was arrested in Ajamgarh for planning along with several others for planning 2008 Ahemdabad bomb blasts at a cost of about Rs 85 thousand only. For Jaipur blasts also three SIMI workers from Kota were found responsible and arrested (PT August 18, 2008).

The Chief of SIMI Safdar Nagori and his brother Karimuddin planned Jaipur and Hyderbad bomb blasts

(Hindustan, August 20, 2008). In September, 08 beginning there were series of blasts again in a New Delhi market, killing 20 people and injuring about a hundred. Indian Mujahideen (IM)-SIMI activists were arrested for September 13 Delhi blasts. The mastermind Atif Ameen Alias Bashir had planned other bombings also. LET leader Abu Al Kama too was arrested. It was found that LET-HUJI had provided help to SIMI-IM in UP blasts of several cities. A few days after the blasts in an international seminar on counterterrorism Afghanistan, France and India all criticized the role of ISI for encouraging terrorism in the neighbouring nations. Despite arrest of 4 terrorist leaders and mastermind there was another bomb blast in New Delhi killing 4 people and injuring 25 others, only two weeks after the second bomb blast in New Delhi (Times of India, September 27, 2008).

Thus it is the 4th blast in New Delhi in recent years. On October 2, 2008, four back-to-back terror strikes in Agartala (Tripura, in Eastern India) left at least four people dead and about 90 others injured. Security officials said that they suspected Harkat-ul-Jehad-e-Islami (HUJI), a Bangladeshi terrorist organization to be responsible for the same. October 30 (2008) 13 serial blast's death toll in Assam rose to 86. Chief Minister and the Intelligence Officers said the needle of suspicion for blast in different cities point out to insurgent groups based in Pakistan and Huji from Bangladesh, cooperating with IM.

If we agree with the views of American Foreign Policy Department, since 2007 fight between Pak forces and terrorists led to Al-Qaida joining hands with other militants to organize terror in the US and European nations (Agencies, May 2, 2008). According to Dale Daily, the Coordinator of US Department of Foreign Affairs Al-Qaida had become very week after September 11, 2001 attack but to completely destroy this organization all the nations will have to work jointly to continue military actions.

A more recent development was the mass-killings of

Sikhs, Christians and Buddhists in Hindu majority areas, to give an impression that staunch Hindu organizations like RSS and Bajrang Dal are involved. According to Home Ministry sources, an organization Deendar Anjuman, run from Pakistan, has been organizing a series of killings of Christians in Karnataka. Later, Deendar Anjuman denied its involvement in the case. However, after confirmation of the involvement, this association has been banned. Recently there have been similar attacks on Christian churches in Bangladesh also.

For funding all these activities the ISI is using either the counterfeits printed in Pakistan or the money collected from the sale of narcotics and drugs. In Peshawar a full-fledged facility has been set up for printing counterfeit Indian currency and is being supplied through various persons code-named as "Safaris". The ISI has now opened two more fronts in Kathmandu and Dhaka to supplement its activities from Pakistan (Daruwalla, 2000). Vakil Juvaid, whose parents moved from the Hamirpur district of U.P. to Karachi (called Mohajirs by Hakikis) at the time of partition has also confirmed many of these facts. He also stated, in an interview to B.B. Nagaich, that RAW is generally blamed for most of the crimes in Pakistan. On September 8, 2006, there were series of 3 explosions in a Muslim Majority town (Malegaon), killing about 37 people at Friday Namaz and injuring more than 100 persons. The intelligence gathered evidence that these blasts were made by LET-SIMMI with an objective to encourage Hindu-Muslim communal rift and violence in the country. Fortunately, they did not succeed.

Kargil Sector War

During the second week of May 1999, a little after the Lahore Declarations, the Indian surveillance team learnt about the presence of Pakistani infiltrators and soldiers on the hills on the Indian side of the LOC, which was under the supervision of the 52nd Infantry Brigade. It is now clear that while the Lahore agreement was being signed, infiltrators were already going to the borders. The Indian army therefore started 'operation Vijay' to throw out the militants illegally occupying 150 kms. long by 25 kms. wide Indian territory in the Kargil sector. When the Indian army estimated the strength of the intruders to be more than 500 to 600 (which ultimately turned out to be more than 1500), it deployed its air force to speed up the operations, first to push the militants away and safeguard Srinagar-Leh highway. Initially the Pakistan army, using Stinger missiles (SAMs), was able to destroy MIGs 27 and M-17 helicopters on the LOC.

Later, it cleared the entire area including Tiger Hill (18000feet high). On June 15, President Clinton asked Pakistan to honour the LOC. The US General went to Islamabad and a White House representative visited New Delhi in the last week of June. Nawaz Sharif was called to Washington on the 4th of July and in no uncertain terms was asked to withdraw his forces and all the supported Mujahideens from the Kargil sector in a few days. India allowed the invaders to vacate illegally occupied territory by the 16th of July and stopped military action on them till the deadline. The invaders first resisted but later obliged Nawaz Sharif reluctantly and accepted his instructions to vacate the Indian territory.

To sum up, this undeclared war continued for 74 days and more than 20,000 Indian troopers were involved in the operation. About 300 guns had to be employed by India and about 5,000 shells were fired each day. In this fierce fighting in excess of 700 soldiers/ officers were killed and about the same number were injured. Nearly 20 troopers are missing. On the Pakistani side it is estimated that about 700 soldiers/ officers were killed and a much larger number of personals were injured. This war cost India about 20,000 million rupees. Whether it was due to the international pressure or the internal economic factors or the fear of nuclear conflict or all of them combined, Pakistan did exercise restraint by calling back its sponsored invasion, when about 90 per cent of the area was already recovered. However, it is obvious that the conflict is in the state of temporary abatement.

The possibility of recurrence of massive violence of Kargil type has already been threatened by the Pakistan Prime Minister. If India and Pakistan fail to start the peace negotiations in the near future the possibility of violence exists, as General Pervez Musharraf, who hatched the Kargil conflict, has imposed a military rule in Pakistan, dissolved Parliament and the frustrated Mujahideens and fundamentalists are looking for an opportunity to avenge the humiliation. The opposition parties were already trying to throw out Nawaz Sharif. They were organizing demonstrations against government, who, under the guidance of General Musharraf allowed illegal occupation of Indian territory.

When troops of the 15 Corps and thousands of soldiers from other areas were sent forward to rugged heights of Kargil, the task of fighting the insurgents was left to only a few battalions of the RR, BSF and the CRPF. All eyes were turned north of Zojila and the militants had a relatively easy time, both in the Srinagar valley and in Jammu division. But the situation has not yet been reversed even though guns have officially fallen silent. Pakistan is still continuing its subversive activities in India and has declared continuity of support for insurgency in India. In POK/GK Afghan Mujahideens are being settled on the border for this purpose (Behl, 2000; Ganguly, 1999; Joshi, 2000; Nanda, 2001). Pakistan continues to pump huge sums of money in J&K for funding terrorists and secessionists. To sustain militancy, it has also shot down the Indian plan for an extradition treaty (PTI August 29 and September 6, 2004).

In fact, since August-September, 1999 the third phase of militancy has begun with increasing attacks, mainly, on security forces and the VDCs. There attacks and ambushes are no longer restricted to a lone soldier or small patrol- parties, but are usually directed at their camps and administrative centres, not always close to the LOC, but often deep inside

Indian territory in Bandipur, Badgam and Pulwama. With obvious local support they can penetrate considerable distances even with rocket-launchers, attack the security forces and then disappear in nearby forests. The GOC of the Victor Force responsible for fighting militancy in the Valley had words of praise for the militants, suspected to be Pak regulars in plain cloths, for their high degree of efficiency and fanatical determination. Probably, during the Kargil conflict, they could discover some new chinks in Indian armour and are now making full use of these. The Myth of the Mujahideens that was so carefully built up by the Pak authorities is inspiring them to scale greater heights in their fight against Indian forces.

Meanwhile, the populace of Leh revealed their dislike for Muslims by refusing to accommodate the Muslim refugees from the Kargil sector. Social divisions and tensions, political extremism, absence of any dialogue, and cynicism about democratic methods are the food for militancy separatism to grow. One has to fight not only militants but militancy too. Counting the heads of dead or capture terrorists leads one nowhere. Recently, Bin Laden has urged Mujahideens to start a Jehad or holy war against India as well as against the US. According to the reports published by media Bin Laden has been able to raise a brigade of about 35,000 trained fighters. "This is war against infidels", Bin Laden declared. The hijacking of an Indian Airlines aircraft on December 23 1999, carrying 162 passengers from Kathmandu to New Delhi, showcases the long drawn cross-border terrorism. The aircraft landed in Kandahar (Afghanistan), where extremist Talibans had their stronghold. The Prime suspect was Lashkar-e-Toiba, which had carried out many explosions in Kashmir and had been attacking military posts. It may be mentioned here that one Pak embassy diplomat has been involved in getting arms to the hijackers. The diplomat using immunity passed unchecked through security to hand over the bag containing arms to the hijackers in the waiting hall at Kathmandu airport.

Now, more than twenty years have passed since the start of the militancy, thousands on both sides have been killed, trillions of rupees have been wasted, but the struggle with the instigated extremists still continues. Only its nature and modes of operations have undergone considerable change under the pressure of circumstances. During the last decade Pakistan has become the hub country for Muslim fundamentalism. It appears Islamic fundamentalists, supported by some Muslim countries and billionaires are working for an Islamic belt from Turkey to Indonesia and Malaysia. In their opinion India is an obstacle in their way. Therefore, they do not observe family planning to increase their population. Already there have been some problems recently in the Muslim dominated areas in Russia, Indonesia, Philippines and China, because of which these nations did not encourage Pakistan on escalating the Kargil conflict and General Musharraf as well as Nawaz Sharif had to return empty handed from China during the second half of June 1999. Similarly, as Israelis and Palestinians battled for several days in 2000 on the issue of holy sites in Jerusalem, angry crowds in Muslim nations took to streets for what they called the "Jerusalem war". At Cairo University, students burnt down Israeli and the US flags.

The issue has broken out even in pro-American Arab nations like Kuwait, Oman, the UAE, Yemen and Qatar. In Bahrain, demonstrators chanted "death to America", and protests were reported even in Saudi Arabia, a strong US ally. "The Al-Aqsa uprising is transforming the struggle. It now pivots around Islamic-Mid-east," a senior US official in Washington said on the condition of anonymity. Spreading to non-Arab Islamic nations, demonstrations were also held in Iran, Pakistan and Indonesia. On October 14 a Muslim cleric with ties to Yemen said that Islamic Army of Aden-Abyan, connected to terrorist Bin Laden, was behind the bombing of the USS Cole in Yemen earlier in October 2000. Similarly, Bin Laden was once again the prime suspect in arranging hijacking of 4 US planes and crashing them on the World Trade Centre and Pentagon on September 11, 2001, which resulted in a huge monetary loss as well as suffering and death of about 4,500 innocent people. In the same manner, Bin Laden's followers had planned to explode the US embassy, involving Sudanese, Indian and Yemen extremists in June-July, as informed by Ajay Raj Sharma, the Police Commissioner of Delhi. This group included some experts on explosive too. Three of them have been caught by Delhi Police with IED, Mobile phone, Timer and batteries and are facing trials in India (Agencies, June 16, 2001).

Terrorism during 1999-2001

Subversives and extremists carried out daring attacks with terrorists picking legislatures, security forces and army establishments as special targets. In the light of Wandhama, Surankot, Chapnari, Kalaham, Rajauri-Udhampur, Chittisinghpora, Doda Anantnag and other massacres, the home ministry held review meetings on J&K in which issues of law & order and development in the state were discussed in details. A special package was formulated after discussions between Central and state governments. Despite the spurt in terrorism and killing of pilgrims, Amarnath Yatras were decided to be continued and so were the elections. Separatists carried out agitations not to give land on rent to Yatris and consequently the 3 months lease was withdrawn and counter agitations in Jammu region started in August 2008.

To put pressure on the State and Central governments separatists again became active and threatened the State legislators and parliamentarians to resign. To disturb the 2002 elections Al Jihad, Huriat and the Talibans were pressured by ISI to create problems and mass killings. Musharraf called the elections a farce. The Indian Election Commission issued special passes to diplomats to witness these and later elections. The Pak paper "The News" quoted that Deputy Secretary Richard Armitage said fair elections could help in solving the Kashmir imbroglio and advised Pakistan not to disturb them.

Again in 2008, extremists were working against the upcoming elections. Police had to fire tear-gas shell to deter the protesters in Srinagar. Government forces fired tear-gas and swung batons to disperse extremists protesting elections in Kashmir. About a decade back hijacking of the Indian Airlines plane on December 23, 1999 by five Pak nationals was supposed to be a part of "operation Ramadan" planned jointly by Harkat-ul-Mujahideen, Lashkar-e-Toiba and Al-Badr under the supervision of ISI (Daruwalla, 2000). The sources, quoting from reports from various places in Pakistan and POK/GK, said these outfits also floated a " Jehad-e-Kashmir fund", which has been banned by military regime in August 2001 after the Agra Summit (Press Karachi, August 20, 2001).

There was no disagreement in India on declaration of Pakistan as a terrorist state. In 1993, the US had threatened Pakistan that it would be included in the list of terrorism sponsoring nations following shooting of shooting of CIA personals on the gate of its headquarters in Langley, bombing of the World Trade Centre and killing CIA worker in Pakistan. When Mrs. Bhutto returned to power, Washington not only gave up the threat but even tilted towards Pakistan on the Kashmir issue. Subsequently even the kidnapping and killing of 5 foreigners by Al Faran (part of Harkat-ul-Ansar) did not bring any change in the US policy, although it had proscribed Harkat-ul-Anbsar a terrorist organization. Surprisingly, Washington did not even warn Islamabad that permitting operations of the group on its soil would lead to Pakistan being declared a terrorist state.

The activities of the Saudi financier O.B. Laden raised concerns about terrorism especially after the bombing of the US embassies in Nairobi Dar-e-Salam. After US missile attacks on Laden's headquarters and execution of death sentence on Mir Kansi, Washington looked away from insurgency of Islamabad. Therefore, it is clear that if Washington does not declare Pakistan a terrorist state it is not because of lack of information. Quick about turn in US policy toward Musharraf's government shows that Pakistan's hold on the US decision-making in South Asian matters is very strong. This is also borne out by the comments of the US spokesman in response to Indian allegations of Islamabad's involvement in hijacking of IC 814 plane. Although Pakistan had been operating a proxy war for more than 19 years, Indian government have failed to evolve a comprehensive strategy to deal with cross-border terrorism and the US has remained indifferent to Indian appeals against Pakistan and China. If India has any illusion that Pakistan will be designated as a State sponsor of International terrorism by US Administration, it will remain an illusion, despite all the evidence that India has provided or may provide to Washington over the years. The National Security Council Official, Harry Thomas, said, "It is a stretch to say the government of Pakistan is a state sponsor of International terrorism."

The recent terrorism report, which was significantly tougher on Pakistan than in previous years, mentioned, "Pakistan's military government headed by General Pervez Musharraf, continued previous Pakistani government support of the Kashmir insurgency, and Kashmiri militant groups continued to operate in Pakistan, raising funds and recruiting new cadres" (India Abroad August 20, 2001). Michael Sheehan Coordinator for counter-terrorism acknowledged that the US was facing tough questions as to how US could draw a distinction between Pakistan's links to terrorist organizations, while not designating it a terrorist State (India Abroad May 2000).

Indian Defence Minister talking to media on 5th January 2000, stated Washington is overlooking Pakistan's support to terrorism and said India would mobilize World opinion to declare Pakistan a terrorist state. "When it comes to Bin Laden, the US fires not one but scores of missiles with high precision technology that it possesses...What the US and the world need to realize that terrorism understands no borders. Therefore, to aim at Bin Laden and overlook what is happening across the borders in India at the hands of Pakistan is not addressing the problem," he said. Though Pakistan repeatedly claims to oppose terrorism, it harbours several training camps for insurgents of several nations, preparing thousands of them to spread pan Islamic movement (Chopra, 1990). These prominent training camps were Markaz-e-Abul bin Masood in Muzzafrabad, Markaz-ul Kura in Chilabandi, Markaz-e-Aska in Kotli, Markaz-e-Toiba in Kunhar and Garhi-Habibullah in Balkot. The first camp has capacity to accommodate 2,000 militants at a time, while the second could train 1,000. The last three can host 500, 500 and 300 insurgents, respectively. Apart from Kashmiris, Sri Lankan Tamil Tigers (LTTE), Chechens, Bangladeshis, Egyptians, Afghans, Sudanese and British Muslims have been trained. The camps, which produce thousands of trained and motivated insurgents, are frequently visited by Bin Laden for special indoctrination sessions.

The funding of these operations mainly comes from West Asian countries, some funds are raised by Maulvis in Pakistan in the name of Jehad. The Jehad issues in different parts of the globe are raised in Friday congregations in mosques in many countries including Pakistan, USA, Britain and Algeria etc. (Mohan, 2000; Nanda, 1999; Joshi, 2000). President Bush assured Vajpayee that the US would pressure Pakistan to eschew cross-border terrorism and push a peaceful election in J&K (India abroad September 20, 2002). Earlier Richard Boucher had dismissed demand to declare Pakistan a State sponsor of terrorism, overlooking continuous killings of innocent people in J&K to disturb 2002 elections in the region. Christina Rocca, the Assistant Secretary of Foreign Affairs, while speaking to the subcommittee on South Asia and Pacific-rim nations, stated that in view of the Indo-Pak tension the terrorism in Kashmir should be stopped completely. She pleaded for talks between India and Pakistan. A couple of years back, Washington has put Hizbul Mujahideen and Jamait-ul-Mujahideen on watch list of terrorists. Lately, three more organizations namely Sipah-e-Saheb (Army of Prophet Mohammad), Tahriq-e- Jafaria and Tanjim-e- Nifaj also came into limelight. According to the American security sources Indian nuclear installations are in danger as the Pak militants are keeping a close watch on them. Terrorist activities, in different parts of country, from 2001 onward are listed below:

1. October 1, 2001- Srinagar- 35 killed
2. December 13, 2001- New Delhi- 12 people killed
3. September 13, 2002- Gandhinagar- 39 killed
4. March 13, 2003- Mumbai- 11 killed
5. May 14, 2003- Jammu- 30 killed
6. August 15, 2003- Dhimaji (Assam) 16 children killed
7. August 25, 2003- Mumbai- 60 killed
8. October 29, 2005-New Delhi- 65 killed
9. December 28, 2005-Bangalore- retired professor killed
10. March 7, 2006- Varanasi 23 killed
11. May 21, 2006- Srinagar- seven killed
12. May 25, 2006- Srinagar- 4 killed
13. July 11, 2006- Mumbai- 180 people killed
14. July 11, 2006-Srinagar- 8 persons killed
15. September 8, 2006- Malegaon- 38 killed
16. February 18, 2007- Panipat- 68 killed
17. May 18, 2007- Hyderabad- 16 killed
18. August 25, 2007- Hyderabad- 42 killed
19. October 11, 2007- Ajmer- 2 killed
20. October 11, 2007- Varanasi, Faizabad & Lucknow- 13 killed
21. May 13, 2008- Jaipur 68 killed
22. July 25, 2008- Bangalore- 2 killed
23. July 26, 2008- Ahemdabad- 49 persons killed
24. September 13, 2008- New Delhi- killing 20 people
25. September 27, 2008- New Delhi- 3 killed
26. October 30, 2008- 6 cities in Assam- 86 killed
27. November 26, 2008- Mumbai- 190 killed including Pak terrorist.

Whole world is saying that Pak terrorists are involved but

Islamabad was attempting to prove that Pakistan was not involved and the sole survivor M.A. Amir Kasab is not Pakistani, despite Kasab's, father's and Nawaj Sharif's statements of Pakistan's involvement and souring of Indo-Pak relations. Due to unrelenting global pressure and un-refutable evidence, Pakistan accepted after 79 days that 26/11 was plotted from its soil and perpetrators were from LET aligned with ISI. ISI chief was invited by India to come and assist in the investigations, akin to the police inviting mafia to help crime solving. It is well known that Kabul embassy and Mumbai attacks are the actions encouraged by ISI. 26/11 VoIP calls were traced to a Pak colonel and a major general Sahab. Later, Kasab accepted all the charges and gave details of Pakistani training.

You Help, We Kill

You help and we kill has been the recent policy applied by the Pakistan sponsored terrorists. India has been the worst victim of terror having lost more than 50,000 lives since 1994. After October 8 tremors in POK/GK, where international help poured in, India also sent plane loads of blankets, medicines woollen jackets, tents and tarpaulins etc. to the land of terrorist training camps. Pakistan asked for helicopters without pilots to which India disagreed but opened 5 relief camps on the LOC, where affected people can seek cover for relief and medical aid. Free telephone lines were also opened for talking with relations on either side. However, Pakistan wanted to open entire LOC possibly with the intension of making it easy for terrorists to enter India before the passes close. They know that at many places barbed wire fence on the LOC has got destroyed in earthquake and opening of the full LOC would be good for terrorism.

Despite all these relief measures the terrorist vowed to continue their militancy in India. Since many security personals killed several terrorists on LOC, they diverted their militancy to soft spots in Delhi during the Diwali festival

(October 2005) by serial bomb-blasting in three places, which resulted in destruction of property, loss of 30 lives with about a hundred injured. Later the same was repeated in a temple in Varanasi and twice in Hyderabad. These clearly show that despite India's help in terrorist dominated POK/GK, the Pak ISI and their sponsored militants intend to continue their nefarious activities. It is suspected that the Dawood gang may be behind these bomb blasts, as it has a well-oiled network of trained militants to handle sophisticated explosives and the local help of SIMI insurgents.

In May 2008 Harkat-ul- Jehadi Islami created serial blasts in the tourist city of Jaipur in a Hindu temple in which about 90 people were killed and 130 injured. In October, 08 Pakistan (Balochistan area) was again hit by a quake and despite national and international help a terrorist group has taken a lead in building temporary houses for the survivors. Therefore, the US and India both are skeptical of the help reaching proper persons and affected valleys. In the earlier quake the Indian government was consequently in a quandary whether to continue or to stop relief material from being sent to Pakistan as the same was being handled either by Pak soldiers or the POK officials. At that time LET had gone to POK/GK on the suggestion of Aiman-al-Jawahiri, as stated by JKLF leader Amanullah Khan. This fact is well known and the Intelligence agencies were therefore, warning that our money and relief materials were reaching the hands of terrorists and were used against us to destroy and kill innocents.

ISI Counterfeiting Indian Currency

To provide funds for various subversive activities in India, Islamabad's ISI has set up a full-fledged facility at Peshawar an additional unit in Kashmir for printing counterfeit Indian currency and those are being supplied under the code name 'Savaris'. A counterfeit racket was uncovered following traps set in Samjhauta express (a train running between India and Pakistan) and also in the Pakistan High Commission office based at New Delhi. The lady, who had gone to seek a visa from the High Commission, became a prey to one of these conduits in December, 1999. The sources said she had accepted a bag from a stranger at Lahore railway station for delivery at Delhi on being paid a certain amount.

According to the interrogation reports on her arrest it was found that the bag contained more than 3 Lakh rupees in counterfeit Indian currency in concealed pockets. Nepal is also being used for supply of fake Indian notes to terrorists. It may be recalled that a racket in paddling fake Indian currency of very high denomination for which Aslam Saboor was deported from Nepal was also detected. Later Nepal police arrested three more persons and recently a worker of the Pakistani embassy with fake high denomination currency notes of India. According to Agencies reports the Nepal police once again arrested a clerk of the Pakistan embassy Shiraz Ahmad Shiraz, one day before SAARC meetings in 2002 with fake Indian currency and US dollars.

The state of U.P. has become an important centre for the sale of these counterfeits and several persons have been arrested there (Times News Network, August 2, 2002). Similar operations have also begun from Dhaka, Dubai, Hong Kong but the attempts of sending counterfeits through Dawood Ibraheim's gang have been busted by Delhi police. Although Islamabad continues to deny any presence of Dawood Ibraheim in Pakistan, intelligence agencies have evidence of his running a high quality counterfeit printing press near the Pak-Afghan border for supply of fake currency to India through Dubai (Times News Network December 21, 2003). Kashmir police disclosed that ISI makes available funds to Hizbul Mujahideen and Jamait-ul-Mujahideen through Britain and they arrested three individuals, Imtiaj Bajaj, Gulam Hasan and Abid Husain in this connection.

In February 2005 a Huriat leader, Sheikh Abdul Aziz was arrested by Delhi police for bringing counterfeits and foreign currency from the Pakistan High Commission. Even now counterfeit currency production and poppy cultivation by ISI are going on but the routes of supply keep changing. Earlier fake currency notes were coming from Quetta (Pakistan), Bangkok (Thailand). Later they started coming from Nepal, Bangladesh and now thru Kabul. They have also recruited many locals to carry out distribution of counterfeit currency distribution in India. U.P. is their favourite state for fake currency distribution. Several people working for distribution of currency have been arrested from many towns in this state. Ladies and rural area residents are generally the agents. It has come to notice that they offer 35 percent share for counterfeit currency distribution (Hindustan, August 12, 2008). Mohammad Anshad coming from Dubai was arrested with counterfeit currency notes worth Rs. 75 lakh at Karipur International airport on August 16, 2008.

Make Proxy War Expensive

From its birth, Pakistan has been trapped in its hate India campaign as suggested by Nalapat. It began its covert war against India in 1949 when Nehru (not taking a lesson from Prithvi Raj Chohan's act of setting free invader Mohammad Ghori) agreed to a cease-fire that allowed Pakistan to retain POK. The advance of Indian troops would have enabled them to take back the entire Kashmir within 2 to 3 weeks. However, he allowed himself to be manipulated by the then Indian Commander in Chief and sought UN intervention based on the assessment of the Indian army authorities among others. It is Islamabad's thinking of the inability of India to deliver a deserving blow that has inspired Pakistan to repeat its forays against India. A majority of Indians feel that forgiving Pakistan could one day lead to vivisection of India. In 1949 gifting of GK/POK land was followed by concessions over Kutch in 1965. Close on the heels of this was the diplomatic retreat at Tashkent in 1966, surrendering captured strategic areas. Similarly, the Shimla Pact (1972) returning more than 94,000 Pak troopers and important land at the cost of huge economic loss, followed by Kargil conflict (1999) at the expense of over 500 lives and more than 2500 crore of rupees are such examples. Soon after the guns fell silent on the Kargil sector, ISI increased cross-border terrorism and masterminded the hijacking of IAC flight from Kathmandu, a move to bury the immediate prospects of peace in Kashmir.

Pakistan is likely to continue the policy of its proxy war on India till such time as it is made to believe that India will retaliate seriously. Only when Pakistan is convinced that India will retaliate with force to its mischief, will ISI put a stop to its subversive activities and terrorism in India. In the hijacking incidence, Islamabad and its Taliban allies were aware that the India government would not use force against them. Therefore, were able to get three insurgents released instead of one, which they had originally demanded. The soft attitude of Indian rulers ruined years of principled opposition to a regime linked with narcotics and terror. The built in hostility may some day lead to tempting Islamabad to use nuclear devices. Atal Behari Vajpayee's government's tough talk has proved to be mere rhetoric especially after the hijacking. This has resulted in the intensification of proxy war. In an age when Pakistan has been given not only nuclear devices but also the delivery systems, India should not practice Nehruvian peace policy. Unless Pakistan is made to realize how the expenses of its proxy war will rise to become unbearable, the aggression is bound to continue with increased vigour.

As long as Islamabad gives moral and material support to terrorism and sends desperados to India, its border need to feel the heat of Indian military weapons and it should know the possibility of hot pursuits, like those of the US, Turkey and Israel. Indian minority enthusiasts state that if the covert war has to be fought back along with the conventional responses, help should flow to the Northern Alliance in Afghanistan as well as to the suppressed and oppressed sections of the society in Gilgit-Balistan. Simultaneously, the full-scale development of both nuclear deterrence and also carrier systems need to be undertaken to prevent any adventure of nuclear weapons from Pakistan for which they have already given threats. India needs to convince Pakistan that after more than 60 years of patience it now means business (Subramanyam, 1998; Nayyar, 1998; Joshi, 2000).

Special Counter-militancy Units

To counter terrorism more effectively, it has been decided to take steps including an additional unified headquarter for areas north of Zojila pass. Specialized battalions trained in waging counter-insurgency (CI) would be raised. Additional forces would be deployed on LOC and in disturbed areas. It was also decided to divide the CI grid into 49 sectors as part of the 3-tier command. Unified command is needed not only at the state level but down to the sector. Shortly after the Kargil war, ISI created suicide squads meant to attack army and security installations. A decision was taken to launch a special operation with the help of retired soldiers and members of VDCs with CI grids and to provide them with sophisticated arms and modern communication equipment. Special programs to supplement border area development projects and the basic minimum service activities are also to be launched. Special funds shall be provided for border roads too to make communication faster. Some of the analysts, however, feel that the "unified command" is old wine in a new bottle (Chibber, 1998; Joshi, 2000; Behl, 2000; Nanda, 2001).

A Soft State Incapable of Hard Decisions

The leadership in all parties had shown distaste for hard decisions. Privatization and disinvestments are words that are uttered by one and all in every Parliament session. The intentions are clear and honourable. The implementation is almost nonexistent. On the security front, the BJP-led coalition earlier showed unusual strength in exercising the nuclear option, by allowing Pokhran II nuclear tests in 1998. A couple of years later the same government surrendered to the hijackers of the IAC Kathmandu-Delhi flight and it became clear that the so-called strong government has also started shying away from necessary tough decisions. The next government also followed the suit. For several years Pakistan has trained, funded, armed and even given sanctuary to terrorists who ravaged J&K. Number of policemen is very low. Similarly our laws are very soft and their implementation is also not very efficient. Further we do not have modern weapons to control militancy. All these reasons encourage terrorism. On the top, Pakistan encouraged the terrorists to kill thousands of innocent Indian citizens and security personals. They have ethnically cleansed the Srinagar valley of Hindus and now they are trying to do the same to the Sikhs, Christians and Buddhists. Now they have shifted their emphasis to the Jammu region and temples and busy places to kill Hindus and try to create religious riots in different parts, leaving no part of India unscathed.

The ISI has established secret facilities in many Indian cities with local Muslim organizations and has been smuggling or printing counterfeit Indian currency to partly meet the expenses incurred in terrorism. Several experts disagree with the futility of dealing with terrorists as a simple domestic law and order problem. They have suggested that cross-border terrorism can only be effectively tackled by cross-border pursuits, by attacks on training camps, shelters and bombing of supply routes. The US bombed Sudan and Afghanistan to destroy certain terrorist camps. Turkey had to resort to military action in Iraqi Kurdistan against insurgents. Israel also took similar action several times, whenever necessary. But in India, the political leadership, in the ruling party or in the opposition, cannot take hard decisions.

The Bold decision by Indira Gandhi to send Indian troops to East Bengal in 1971 was an exception, possibly she had a good majority government of a single party and also because most of the parties were in favour of an action like that. Therefore, a very bold action was taken that time (India

Abroad, September 15, 2000). Actually there are five main reasons for weak India security. 1. As compared to the total population the number of policemen is very low. India has only 126 policemen on one lakh people. In addition some sections of the society are sympathetic to the terrorists or are indifferent to terrorism. 2. Our security forces are not geared to tackling counter-terrorism measures efficiently. 3. Modern weapons are lacking or insufficient in quantity, which makes counter terrorism measures inefficient. 4. Till now we do neither have a proper data on terrorism nor have a centralized agency like FBI to tackle the same. Therefore coordination between different agencies becomes difficult. It becomes much more complicated in J&K because of a special status of Kashmir. 5. We do not have strong laws like those in UK or US to deal with terrorist. Anti-terror law (POTA) that we had, has been abolished by the UPA government on the excuse of its misuse of against the minority community.

It is difficult to implement even the week law that we have. Public is suffering because of politics to attract votes. Religious extremists brainwash the youths and show them dreams of Sheriat laws. Such organizations are getting monetary aid from certain Islamic nations. People sympathetic to SIMI do not hesitate to carry out anti-social anti-national activities. Due to religious brainwashing minority youth has begun to believe that Bin Laden was not behind 9/11 activities in the US but to blame Muslims Israel had carried out these terror attacks with the help of its security agency Mosad.

Several years back Prime Minister Vajpayee voluntarily offered the peace for the holy month of Ramzan (Ramadan) in 2000-01 against terrorists working in Kashmir so that the public might carry out Rozas in peace. Later Pakistan also supported this proposal by reducing firing and shelling on the LOC. Vajpayee took a bold step of extending the same twice (Agencies, January 23, 2001). To undermine India's continuation of its unilateral cease-fire offer, surprised Pakistan guided the militants to selectively target Hindus and

Sikhs. This led to India's stopping cease-fire in February, 2001. Later, Musharraf and Manmohan Singh restarted peace process and several CBMs were taken. To further the peace process India and Pakistan exchanged list of nuclear sites on January 1, 2007 for preventing attacks on each other's nuclear installations. They also agreed to exchange similar lists each year on 1st January for the same reason. This cease fire was broken by Pakistan army three times in May 2008 to infiltrate terrorists, before Indian and Pak Foreign Secretaries met in Islamabad. On October 21, 2008 trading across LOC in Kashmir began for the first time in 6 decades raising hopes of reducing tension in the region.

POTA was withdrawn by the Congress-led UPA government for protection of the minorities but nothing has been mentioned for protection of both majority and minority from terror attacks from within or cross-borders. After 26/11 NIA and an act (UAPA) for dealing with terrorists have been created in 2008. Terrorism is threatening our sovereignty and integrity but we are simply treating it as a law and order problem to become a sponge that protects others. No other country has lost as many people as India, even then our country has weak laws to fight terrorism. We have agreed with the UN and many other countries to strengthen internal laws to fight terrorism. The US has 'Patriot Act', England and Pakistan have new strong terror laws which make even hijacking punishable by death but India has only weak laws and those too take years to award punishment. Even after award of punishment by the judiciary action takes long time or is even not executed. Therefore, India needs to apply judicial reforms proposed by 'Malimath Committee'. For this we need a strong government which can convey its message to public not by words but by its deeds. Such a government can only implement strong laws to fight terrorism and it would be true respect to those who have lost their lives due to terrorism.

In the northern Kashmir Gandarbal area Shabbir Malik died while fighting with terrorists. He was a member of the security force but the procession consisted of the local people, who were having tears in their eyes and were beating their chests shouting slogans in favour of India. This indicated that Kashmiris are also learning the facts about terrorism. This shows a strong desire for peace and beginning of hatred against separatists.

Global War on Terrorism

Next to India where over 50,000 people have died in terrorism since 1994, Israel, the US and Russia are the three countries which have suffered the most due to terrorism. Unlike India, the US considered terrorism before 9/11 mainly as a threat to the US interests abroad. Each country has some separate groups of terrorists but their bases are either in Arab nations, Pakistan, POK or Afghanistan. One thing that stands out is the fact that the terrorists originated from the least globalized and least open corners of the world, i.e. Saudi Arabia, Yemen, Afghanistan and Pakistan; countries that tend to remain closed door with the least trading in ideas, pluralism and tolerance (Friedman, 2002). Russia has lost more than 300 people in bomb explosion, which have destroyed many residential buildings/ accommodations in Moscow and other cities. According to the Russian government sources the hot beds of terrorism are in Chechnya and Dagestan. They further stated that it was the handiwork of Pakistan and Afghanistan trained insurgents.

Bin Laden (earlier US favourite) is considered as the main architect behind the scene. Taking the situation seriously, Russia launched a combined air and land attack mainly on Chechnya to flush out the disgruntled elements. Bin Laden gave a press statement on September 17th 1999 stating that India and the US are two more countries against which Jehad should be declared. The Press release issued from Jalalabad mentioned that Mujahideens should target these two imperialist nations, as they are infidels/Kafir states and the biggest enemies of Islam. It further stated Laden is ready to help the Kashmiri Mujahideens and did help them during the 1999 Kargil war. It is well known that Bin Laden was able to procure Stinger missiles, the Russian SAM 7 surface to air missiles and huge stocks of sophisticated smaller weapons that were supplied to Taliban by the CIA. Over and above when he had the support of Pakistan, why should he or the holy war fighters worry about the arms or money, as there is enough flourishing business with ISI in drug trade and counterfeit currency. Recently Defence Secretary, Robert Gates, said to MSNBC news that all major terrorist networks have found safe haven in Pakistan and are creating problems in war against terror. These organizations like Al-Qaida, Taliban, Haqqani, Hekmatyar group and other affiliated networks are separate but work together.

Therefore, the farsightedness of Prime Minister Vajpayee and diplomacy of Jaswant Singh had been utilized for taking up initiatives to forge concerted action to fight international terrorism, violence, religious extremism and narcotics trafficking. In September 1999 India and the US began high level consultations for countering cross-border terrorism across the globe, which were later supported by many other nations. Michael Sheehan, the US Coordinator for Counter terrorism, met several Indian officials and defined parameters for mutual cooperation to prevent terrorist attacks. The US is anxious to evolve an international legal framework to deal with terrorists. This also covers international extraditions of the suspected persons and the right to prosecute them in third countries. India and the US also discussed terrorism in J&K and spread of extremist violence from Afghanistan to Central Asia. All actions across the globe seem to spread from Afghanistan and Pakistan.

The US reprimanded Pakistan over its support for terrorists in J&K and asked to hand over Dawood, Masood Azhar and Tiger Memon etc. to India (Agencies November 8, 2001). However Pakistan is not doing the same. Instead Islamabad freed Hafiz Mohammad Sayid of Lashkar-e-Toiba and others, who are on the list of 20 culprits wanted by India, involved in attacks on the Indian Parliament on December 13, 2001, on American Centre etc. (Agencies Islamabad, January 4, 2002). It is now an open secret that terrorism could not have survived so long without active support from Islamabad. In September 1999 the issue of international terrorism was discussed between Jaswant Singh and his Russian counterpart Igor Ivanov. During the deliberations of the UN India was the 47th country to sign the International Convention for Suppression of Terrorist Bombings. The agreement enables the countries to either prosecute or extradite those alleged to have carried out bombings. Despite attempts to curb terrorism internationally, Al- Qaida has publicly announced on Al-Jazeera television network the adoption of the Kashmir issue to their list of grievances that include the US presence in Saudi Arabia, the Palestine issue and the situation in Iraq.

On September 11, 2001 four planes were hijacked in the US. Two hit the twin towers of the World Trade Centre, third hit Pentagon and the fourth crashed in a field in Pennsylvania. In these terrorist attacks about 4,500 people are considered dead or missing. Once again Bin Laden was the prime suspect. The US started retaliatory attacks on October 7 on Afghanistan after it did not surrender Bin Laden and leading terrorists of Al-Qaida under operations 'Enduring Freedom' and 'Anaconda' etc. In this war, the US had to face the sting of its own missiles turned against it. It had supplied about 2000 Stingers in 1980s to the Mujahideens fighting against USSR. Indian authorities believe, Pakistan kept a good number for its use and gave some to China and North Korea to explore the technology. India gave intelligence information, accumulated over the years, to the US on terrorist training camps in Afghanistan and Pakistan.

Though the US was more concerned with specific information about Bin Laden and his outfits only, Indian intelligence insisted that the violence in Kashmir and other parts of the world, including the US, were inter-related. The

US had its own yardstick for Pakistani cooperation in war on terror, to India's irritation. According to India, Pakistan is the main patron of the Taliban regime. In 1996, Islamabad gave Taliban regime aid worth Rs. 300 million and in 1997 & 1998 US$ 30 million. In addition, it supplied men and materials. Out of every 10,000 active Taliban, 1,700 personals were Pakistanis, getting paid from the abovementioned funds (India Abroad, September 28, 2001). Many other countries too promised support to 'Enduring Freedom'.

Pakistani atomic scientist Basruddin Mahmood, who had connections with Bin Laden, was busy in preparing helium balloons to fill anthrax bacteria to create devastations in Washington and New York. As reported in 'Economist' Mahmood is a member of the banned Usmah Tamir-e-Now (UTN). CIA alone had funnelled more than US$ 5 billion through Pakistan's ISI. The very forces reared by the US came back to haunt them (India Abroad September 21, 2001). The US froze the assets of Jaish-e-Mohammad and two other organizations after they were put on Watch-list, as the car bombing from suspected Muslim militants killed 40 people in Kashmir on October 1, 2001(Hindustan Times October 14, 2001). Burial of eight bodies of Harkat-ul-Mujahideen terrorists in Pakistan, killed in US strikes in Afghanistan confirmed the nexus between Pakistani organizations and their mentors in Afghanistan. Return of the bodies for burial in Pakistan shows their citizenship and the state support.

It confirms what was being said by India all along about Pakistani support and sustenance to terrorism (Seattle Times October 26, 2001). It had been estimated that there were about 70 per cent Pakistanis in Taliban, about 25 per cent Arabs (including African and other nationals) and the rest Afghans. During bombarding in Afghanistan Jaish-e-Mohammad was recruiting in Pakistan to fight alongside with Taliban. More than 3,000 Pakistanis were released from Afghan jails since the Taliban was ousted in 2001 (The News Tribune, September 13, 2004). Under the cover of the US bombarding, Northern

Alliance captured area after area and the Taliban either ran away or were killed or captured. POWs from Afghanistan had disclosed that Islamabad directed 400 terrorists to gather at Palindri (GK/POK) for infiltration in India. Such terrorism in the name of Jehad must be prevented said former Prime Minister of POK/GK Saradar Abdul Qayuum. Early in the winter of 2004-05 Bin Laden and his entourage were hiding in a mountain along the Afghanistan-Pakistan border. A sentry posted by them spotted a US patrol and radioed an alert. Bin Laden fell back in a mountain hideaway. Since then he seems to have disappeared into thin air, near Queta.

On December 22nd under the leadership of Hamid Karzai an interim government consisting of 20 members took over peacefully. Britain and India opened their embassies after a long time and started helping rebuild Afghanistan. Ever since the Karzai government came into power it has been trying to develop Afghanistan. In November 2004 Karzai was elected President and began modernizing Afghanistan. But with help from across borders the militants have been regrouping to create problems for the Afghan government and the American forces. For the past 2 years in southern provinces, Karzai government barely controls outside district head quarters. Lately a senior British Commander in southern Afghanistan stated that he had asked the US Special Forces to leave from his area of operations because the civilian casualties they had caused was making it difficult for allied forces to win over local population.

Hardcore Taliban from lawless tribal areas of Pakistan have now regrouped to create more problems. Pakistan has signed an agreement recently not to interfere. To what extent Pakistanis had hated the US attack became clear from the fact that the Pak cricketers refused to drink Pepsi because this drink was manufactured by an American company (Guardian December 8, 2001). Similar was the response from the public in Pakistan. They have demonstrated frequently in favour of Bin Laden. They have even shown their respect by giving him a special title when Salman Rushdie was honoured in Britain. The US had been helping Pakistan with money and military hardware, which has occasionally been objected to even by US Senators and Congressmen. Indian Foreign Minister visited Kabul to help the Afghan National Army by presenting 49 vehicles. Karzai arrived in India on a 3-day visit to further bolster mutual ties (PTI, January 25, 2005). Top Commander of the US army, Lt. Gen. Karl Eikenberry said, "We need more in terms of resources, for road building, counter-narcotics, good governance, a just justice system". Jim Dobbins, Bush's ex-envoy to Kabul also agrees that resources are only about 30 per cent of what they ought to be. Many analysts believe the US has created another Kashmir.

Even President Bush had to agree that Musharraf has allowed the Taliban to set up head quarter near Quetta through the deal giving militants free rein in North Waziristan. A team of UCLA geographers, after study of satellite imagery, reported Bin Laden is in one of the three large compounds in Parachinar town in Pakistani Kurram Agency (TNN February 18, 2009). About thirty NGOs and Social Institutions have mentioned that joint action committee organized a rally against Pakistan government support to help terrorists and Taliban in April, 2007 and also later. In an interview given to New York Times Karzai has stated that due to arrests of Taliban by US and British forces and due to wrong behaviour with them Taliban is refusing to surrender. He also said that real danger is because of Pakistan becoming a shelter place for Al-Qaida as well as Taliban. On the occasion of 16th annual day of the fall of Communist regime in Afghanistan Karzai was given a salute with 21 guns and just after the gun salute he was fired from all sides but due to prompt action by the security forces he and American General were safe although 11 parliamentarians were injured, 4 died including 3 terrorists. According to a report from Europol 203 suspected terrorists were arrested in Britain in 2007 and 30 were caught in France. Thus 30 percent more terrorists were caught in U.K. as compared to other years and it appears that this country has become a base for terrorists outside Pakistan.

President Bush secretly approved US military raids inside its anti-terrorists ally Pakistan. President Bush acted through classified orders and gave leeway to its forces to cross from outposts in Afghanistan into tribal areas along the Pakistan border. Pakistani government has very little control of these areas and extremists have found a safe haven here and have been hiding comfortably since long (AP September 12, 2008). Earlier President Bush had stated that if intelligence reports presence of Osama in Pakistan, the US will send its forces in Pakistan for attacking Bin Laden.

On 24th February 2007 a report of last two year-surveys conducted internationally by the University of Maryland showed that 1. Only 46 percent US nationals and Europeans reject terrorism. 2.24 percent of the surveyed people had said terror attacks were sometimes justified. 3. 86 percent Pakistanis, 81 percent Bangladeshis and 74 percent Indonesians said they reject terrorism. 4. The survey also said that 50 percent Westerners associated Islam and Muslims with terrorism, as was the report of the Christian Science Monitor too.

Indo-US Differences on Terrorism

The US was happy with Islamabad's cooperation by handing over Ramzi Youssuf in 1995 to the US for the 1993 World Trade Centre bombing. Similarly, it was also pleased with Pakistan for the joint investigations of the murder of four US oil executives in Karachi in 1998. Thus Pakistan appeared on the US watch list but not on the list of state sponsors. Whereas India asked the US to declare Pakistan a state sponsor of international terrorism in 1991 because it had been supporting violence by Kashmiri militants, earlier Sikh separatists in Punjab and later in other nations too. New Delhi desired that Islamabad must end militant infiltration across the LOC in Kashmir. However Washington was considering

Pakistan's support to militancy as a part of a tit-for-tat program and also a result of regional conflict. Therefore, the US had been repeatedly stating the reduction of Indo-Pak tensions for ending terrorism against India and also for averting the war between the two nuclear states.

The Clinton administration wanted to conduct dialogues on Indo-Pak tensions with India and Pakistan. However, India was reluctant. Later, Bush administration also adopted the same approach after Indian Parliament was attacked by Pak-sponsored terrorists in December 2001, which resulted in massive deployment of the military on the border. For the first time Foreign Secretary Condoleezza Rice said in an interview to "Yahoo News" and "The Politics" that Pakistan government and some of their organizations have friendly and close relations with terrorists and the US is going to take strong steps against Pakistan (Hindustan, August 9, 2008). Same way India's antagonistic attitude on US views on Iran's and Iraq's support for international terrorism made Washington unhappy. While USA declared both Iran and Iraq as sponsors of terrorism, India remained cordial to both of them. In 1993, the US described Iran supported Hezbullah in Lebanon as a great threat to USA and Western nations, India was expanding its trade and energy ties with Iran.

In 2004-05 Washington became unhappy with the proposed Iran-Pakistan-India gas line to solve energy needs. Bush administration reported "...the last thing we would want to see is Iran getting more revenue to fund its nuclear weapons program." The threat perceptions of United States and India were also diverging on Iraq. The US viewed Iraq as sponsor of terrorism but India considered Iraq not responsible for international terrorism. In fact India did not send troops to join US forces in Iraq because after Mumbai bombings in 1990s, Saddam Husain alone offered to help India track down the terrorists who carried out bombings (Nayak, 2007). Indian officials repeatedly indicated terrorism in Kashmir sponsored by Pakistan, a US ally on terror war, as one of the reasons for not sending the troops to topple Saddam Husain. The other but more important reason was that the attack was not approved by the UN. It is thus clear that both India and the US pushed for tight global controls on terrorism but their reasons for doing it differed. It may also be mentioned that even Pakistan, for its own reasons, did not send troops in Iraq to help US forces.

The US regards North Korea-Iran-Iraq as axis of evil whereas India considers China-Pakistan- North Korea team as axis of evil.

Attack on the Seat of Democracy

On December 13, 2001 a five-member suicide squad of Pak nationals attacked the heavily guarded Indian Parliament at New Delhi, which was then in session. However, Parliament security personals managed to kill all the attackers. Twelve security men paid with their lives. Within 3 days Delhi police disclosed the details of this attack, which was carried out jointly by Lashkar-e-Toiba and Jaish-e-Mohammad. The ISI had planned the attack in February, 2001 and given to the terrorists information about security details of the Parliament building. The leader of the attack was Mohammad Afzal, who was one of the five killed on the spot. On December 17, four persons associated with the ISI were arrested in Delhi along with RDX. The promoter of the attack, Tariq Tanvir, who had enlisted suicide attackers for the mission, was also arrested in Delhi.

After being declared terrorist organizations both Jaish-e-Mohammad and Lashkar-e-Toiba have renamed them selves as Al Furkan and Paswan-e-Ahla Hadid respectively to escape penalties. NWFP based Balkot mosque is the main base along with other centres in Gulam Kashmir for training Jaish-e-Mohammad terrorists as reported by New York Times. In all, there are about 6,000 training centres/religious Madarsas for teaching extremism. Of all Deobandh has the biggest number of Madarsas above 2,000. They have 166,000 students from Afghanistan alone.

India asked Pakistan to hand over 20 terrorists/culprits, including Daud (the 4th most wanted criminal of the Forbes list). The refusal of Pakistan to hand over culprits on the pretext of insufficient evidence infuriated the Indian government, which has since then supplied more evidence but did not succeed. The US was also treated similarly by Taliban in the beginning and it had to begin attacking Afghanistan. Therefore, the Indian High Commission staff in Pakistan was reduced to half. The Indian High Commissioner was recalled. In addition the High Commissioner of Islamabad was sent back and Pakistan Airways was forbidden from flying over Indian territory. In addition, train and bus services between the two nations was also stopped.

To prevent Kargil type infiltration in Indian states bordering Pakistan, forces have been deployed along with missiles, wherever necessary to deter cross-border infiltration. India has also been refusing to open talks with Islamabad unless it stops helping the terrorists against India. Meanwhile, a US journalist Daniel Pearl, based in Mumbai, was kidnapped and killed in Pakistan and Musharraf blamed India for this act, although the facts proved otherwise. Even Pakistan's own police contradicted his allegations. The Pak police later arrested the main culprit, Omar Sheikh from Lahore. Similarly Musharraf also alleged that India carried out fresh nuclear tests, with regard to which he was rebuffed by both India and the US. Less than three weeks after the attack on American Centre based in Kolkata, Dubai based Aftab Ansari (alias Farhan Malik) was arrested and handed over to the CBI. He admitted huge earnings through kidnappings etc. for terrorism and funding Jehadis, chiefly with the help of O. Sheikh, one of the three persons released by India following 1999 hijacking of the IC 814 plane (Times News Network February 12, 2002).

In the light of the foregoing it is apparent that on one hand Pakistan is helping the international terrorists and on the other hand it is helping the US to get monetary benefits in the name of 'Enduring Freedom'. Islamabad is not interested in stopping terrorist training camps. In fact it is shifting these camps from mainland to GK/POK to justify the term 'Freedom Fight', which he (Musharraf) has been using for terrorism in J&K. According to Harbans Nagoke of Jammu Dainik Jagran (April 22, 2002), Musharraf, who has been trying to hasten economic aid to terrorists, allowed mosques, after prayers, to solicit donations for Jehad and rich extremists and certain industrialists have come forward in the name of Islam. In J&K, Hindus as well as minorities are being frequently targeted. Some TV channels and other media are also helping in this matter.

At the Kathmandu SAARC meetings on January 5, 2002 all seven nations condemned terrorism in all forms. The SAARC nations also highlighted the proposal of the UN in which action against terrorism was made compulsory. At the same time the US again declared cross-border terrorism sponsored by Pakistan undesirable and asked Musharraf to take strong action against terrorist groups. Assistant Secretary Victoria Clark said that no terrorist is a freedom fighter and cannot be excused. Foreign Secretary Colin Power stated, in an interview to the BBC, that Musharraf has already taken action but that a lot more is to be done. He also said that he appreciates India's patience in this connection. Salauddin Khalid, from Chagai Baluchistan, boasted of killing 50 Northern Alliance troopers in Jabul-us-Sheraj. Commander Salami, the prison warden told Rakesh Sinha of the Indian Express (December 29, 2001) in Doab in Panjshir valley that the prisoners included Pakistani, Chinese, Burmese, Iraqi and Yemeni. If they are released they will return to Pakistan to go to Kashmir. Former members of the Taliban organized Shura-e-Farkan, based in Gulam Kashmir, with about a thousand Pakistanis, who were taken out from Kunduz city during the US bombing. They also wish to keep Jehad alive in India. Western media quoted that 3500 to 5000 troopers were taken out safely by day and night operations of Pakistan (INS, Delhi January 29, 2002). Bin Laden and Al Jowhari were seen in

Pakistan according to the Chief of Afghanistan Intelligence Service, Hazrat Uddin (Agencies, N.Y., May 5, 2002).

Former ruler Mohammad Zahir Shah came to Afghanistan to get a warm welcome and started reconstruction of the nation. Hamid Karzai was made the President, after escaping an attack. It is suspected that Gulbuddin Hikmatyar, who is presently living in Iran and who has waged Jehad against Karzai, may be behind the attack on Karzai. India, US, Britain and Japan are continuously helping in rebuilding of Afghanistan. India started renovating Habibiya and other schools, supplied buses, telephone network and built roads. Indian doctors are working in several hospitals, including Indira Gandhi Institute of Child Health. India is also training administrators, health workers, policemen, lawyers, judges and airways workers etc. Unfortunately, security situation in the countryside is deteriorating, especially in the south and southwest which are under the influence of Taliban or Al-Qaida. Several technical persons working from the countries trying to rebuild Afghanistan were kidnapped or killed. Even schools giving modern education were not spared. They were destroyed. There were attacks on security personals also. The United Nation's Anti-drug Chief said that proceeds from Afghan opium production are being used to finance terrorist groups. The country's drug trade was about US$ 3.1 billion business in 2005 and 2006.

A year after the Afghan war started, Donald Rumsfeld pledged to track down Bin Laden and other terrorist leaders, if they are alive. He said he was not frustrated because Laden and Taliban top leaders are loose and they have learned to hide themselves from the US surveillance. At a ceremony at US Central Command Headquarter in Tampa, General Tommy Franks stated the US is committed to remain in Afghanistan to ensure that Al-Qaida and Taliban forces are rooted out. Afghan Officials said they want the US forces to stay till the situation is stable enough. Afghan national military is to be trained, said Foreign Minister Abdullah and there is no timetable for the same. Fighting in Afghanistan has gone on for more than 5 years. It is continuing as the Taliban is resurging with the help from cross borders and is challenging the Central government.

Terrorism on the Increase

During past few years terror increased significantly throughout the globe. A balance has therefore to be struck soon to protect the world from terrorism without violating the civil rights of peace loving people of the religion of terrorists. According to the FBI Director Robert Mueller, "The overwhelming majority of Muslims in the US and around the world are peaceful, law-abiding citizens. A small number of Muslims, however, are members of radical fundamentalist sects sworn to destruction of the US," he said in a speech at Stanford University. "This presents a dilemma for those charged with protecting against the next attack." Since the terror attacks in 2001, the US has detained more than 1,000 people.

The disclosure that North Korea has a nuclear weapons program (earlier stated by Karl Inderfurth also), helped by Pakistan in exchange of missiles, has created big problem and a bad precedence. Six nation talks were going on to stop North Korea's nuclear program but they did not succeed. There was no agreement in these talks till December 22, 2006. Drawing encouragement from this program, Iran is also developing its nuclear facilities and missile development. The US alleged Jemmah Islamiyah's involvement in bombing in Bali, Indonesia. Its leader Abu Baker Bashir was already a suspect in a series of church bombings in December 2000. Abu Sayyaf, who has a link to Al-Qaida, is the most likely suspect with regard to the October 2000 bombings in Philippine cities. Earlier there were some bombings in 2000 in many places in Manila. Fatur Rehman admitted to have planned them. He also showed the police a buried stash of 1.2 tons of TNT for attacks in Singapore. During this period, India had several problems in J&K, Delhi, Mumbai, Kolkata and Hyderabad and many other places. Afghanistan, Israel, Nepal, Sri Lanka, Pakistan and Russia had their own similar problems. On October 26, 2002 Russian troops burst into a Moscow theatre, freeing over 600 hostages held by Chechen rebels and killing their leader.

All these go to show that the international terrorist network, though loose, is increasing in coordination with local units and help from some Islamic nations. New Al-Qaida strikes may be imminent on US soil or elsewhere, CIA Director George Tenet warned during his defence of agency's counter-terrorism efforts to lawmakers (AP October 8, 2002). The Chief of the Defence Intelligence Department, Kamal Davar that India has already supplied information to the US on terrorist training camps in Pakistan but nothing has been done so far. According to him the US is perhaps silent because of its present priorities but would come back later to attend to this issue after it is free from Afghanistan and Iraq problems (AP, March 14, 2003). About 4 years ago, an audiotape of Bin Laden surfaced through Al Jazira network. Some suspect his whereabouts are known to ISI. The week end hostage-crises in the city of Khobar (Saudi Arabia) were a reminder of how vulnerable the world became to terrorism. The terrible events suggest that Al-Qaida expanded its hit list to include as many non-westerners as possible. Indians were targeted because of Kashmir issue (HT January 6, 2004). The best thing would be in asking the moderate Islamic clerics to preach the detainees and their family members to think of human welfare of all the people in the world and not only of Sunnis, Shias etc. or Muslims only.

To ease the tension, India withdrew troops from the border and Pakistan followed pulling back its troops too. About a year back both countries had deployed the troops, which were put on alert. So far, a pull back move on the LOC is not there. In 2003, a peace-process was again started by Prime Minister Vajpayee. Consequently, there was considerable normalization of relations between the two nations, posting of High Commissioners followed by exchanges of visits by journalists, students, artists and parliamentarians etc. but increased incidents of terrorism did create tensions. On one hand the Indo-Pak peace process is continuing, but on the other hand Indian prisoners are being tortured in Pak prisons. This was confirmed by Kundan Gadia, who was released recently along with 35 other prisoners. He had gone from Orissa to the Rajasthan border to find work and was caught by Pak police on the suspicion of spying. He returned after 6 years (Amar Ujala, September 7, 2004). For the first time terrorists, killed near the Lotus temple in Delhi possessed cyanide pens and Pakistan manufactured ARGS hand grenades (PTI, December 8, 2003). The peace process has been bolstered by the present Prime Minister, Manmohan Singh through Confidence Building Measures.

"New Delhi's concerns about Pakistan's tolerance at a minimum, (and) of terrorists attacks on Indian soil remain a dominant theme in relations, and risk derailing rapprochement," Department of Homeland Security report warns. The report also mentions the possibility of a nuclear Indo-Pak conflict despite improved relations. Notwithstanding better Indo-Pakistan relations, the US apprehends a terror attack on a high profile target. Such a case could prompt India to "punish Islamabad for its continued support to Pakistan-based militants" (Indo-Asian News Service, Karachi, January 21, 2007). Turkish Islamic Party, an Islamic terrorist organization, has issued a new video claiming that Chinese Communist government is not treating Muslims well. The video is in Turkish language, which is spoken by some people in western China. It states that for family planning many Muslim women were forced to carry out abortions. The video also told Muslims to stay away from Beijing Olympics (Press Trust, August 9, 2008).

Some Facts about Al-Qaida and Terrorism

Major General Randhir Singh of the Indian army informed that some Al-Qaida terrorists were hiding for some time in the thick jungles of the Surankot area of J&K (Agencies, August 10, 2002). According to Michael Chandler, the Head of a finance group of the UN, a number of new camps were recently activated in Pakistan border near Khyber Pass. He said the Al-Qaida network was a big threat to the global peace and security. According to a report from Morocco, when Bin Laden came to know that the CIA was tapping his satellite phone, his body guard, Abdulla Tabraq alias Abul Umar rescued him by getting hold Laden's cell phone and using it. Thus he fooled the US intelligence agencies and got himself arrested to give time to Bin Laden to run away and escape (Agencies, January 22, 2003).

According to the 9/11 Commission Bin Laden never severed his links with Pakistan or Afghanistan where he trained terrorists for J&K and other Islamic insurgencies, even when he moved to Sudan (IANS June 17, 2004). J.A. Bukhari, Pakistan's crime investigation Chief said several dozens of Al-Qaida outfits are hiding in Karachi and plan terrorism from here (Agencies, July 17, 2004). Attacks in Britain and US were planned by Al-Qaida as informed by the arrested outfits from London (Agencies, August 6, 2004). FBI was keeping a watch on 2 Maulvis, who were arrested from a mosque in US for purchasing missiles for terrorism (Agencies, August 7, 2004). As per information provided by the US intelligence services Al-Qaida had planned attacks on big leaders too. This message was given by Bin Laden (Washington Time, August 11, 2004).

Italian police captured Pakistanis, along with blast materials, detonators and forged documents. These persons were suspected to be the members of the International Islamic Force (AP, February 1, 2003). Colin Powell, Secretary Foreign Affairs stated that Iraq utilized its embassy in Islamabad for maintaining relations with Al-Qaida from 1990s to 2001 (Agencies, February 8, 2003). Russian top officials have stated that despite joining in the war on global terrorism, Pakistan is encouraging extremists and terrorist organizations in Afghanistan and India etc. to carry out terrorist activities

(Press, February 11, 2003). CIA claimed that with the arrest of Khalid Sheikh Mohammad, the senior leader of Al-Qaida, the terrorist organization suffered a great setback (Agencies Islamabad, March 17, 2003).

According to the Wall Street Journal, Pakistan President Musharraf was giving contrasting statements about Bin Laden. He ultimately agreed that Laden possibly came to Pakistan, because of fear of American Forces (Amar Ujala, March 25, 2003). From the sources in Washington and Kabul, it is apparent that Mullah Omar, the supreme Taliban leader who headed the repressive Islamist regime ousted by the US-led forces five years ago is hiding in the Pakistani City of Quetta. A senior Afghan intelligence officer said, "Every single bomber or I.E.D. in one way or another is linked to Pakistan." Same way Al-Qaida top leaders are also suspected to be taking shelter in Pakistan, as per information of anti-terror specialist, Peter Burgen. According to a Science Journal of Atomic Energy, Pakistani scientists Bashir-ud-din Mahmud and Chaudhary Abul Majid had several meetings with Al-Qaida officials and Bin Laden to transfer nuclear technology. Both of these scientists are founders of Umar Tamir-e-naw (UTN) (Amar Ujala, April 7, 2003). To fight against US-led pre-emptive attacks on Iraq, the international Muslim forum has invited people to register as volunteers. About 1200 Bangladeshis came forward to offer their services for suicide squads called 'Mritunjai Dasta', as per information of a newspaper Star, published in Dhaka (Amar Ujala, April 8, 2003). Osama Bin Laden, in an audiotape found in north-eastern Pakistan, pleaded with the Muslims for International Islamic movement to form suicide squads to attack Islamic governments favouring attack on Iraq (Agencies April 9, 2003).

On September 9, 2007, he again issued a similar statement and requested Muslim youth to join Jehad. This attracted Islamic militants to carry out blasts in Morocco and Riyadh. Pak newspaper Friday Times, based on a petition filed by a senior advocate, Dr. A. Basit, mentioned that before the September 11 attacks, the person who was purchasing his land for an Al-Qaida university was a link of Al-Qaida and Toiba. After the attack that person disappeared because intelligence agencies were after him (Amar Ujala, April 16, 2003). According to US officials, Pakistan village-camps on the border of Afghanistan have turned into places to shelter Al-Qaida terrorists. This was indicated by e-mails and websites (New York Agencies March 6, 2003). Accepting the presence of Al-Qaida, the newspaper 'The Nation' pointed out that during the last month 6 Al-Qaida men were arrested with a large quantity of blast material. In the editorial, it was mentioned that foreign terrorists come to Pakistan through several routes. Former Prime Minister of Afghanistan, Gulbuddin Hikmatiyar, earlier a favourite of the US, while living in Pakistan, appealed to the Muslim community to start Jehad against the US. He was declared a terrorist (Agencies, May 11, 2003). According to the US army sources North Korea supplied missiles worth 580 million dollars to Islamic nations like Pakistan, Iran, Libya, Syria, Egypt and Yemen. The officer, who did not want to be named, said North Korea was also involved in narcotics and counterfeit US currency trade (AP May 14, 2003).

In a blast in Casablanca (Morocco) at least 40 people were reported dead along with 10 Fedayeen members. Terrorists had aimed a Jewish community Centre and two buildings of Western nations (Agencies, May 18, 2003). A terrorists attack by International Islamic Front of Bin Laden in Riyadh, gave a great shock to the monarchy of the country. A week earlier the Saudi police had forfeited a large quantity of arms and also cash after a long encounter with the terrorists. Asia Times Online had earlier indicated that Islamic Front Network was being led by the right hand of Bin Laden, Aiman al-Jowahri, who was supposed to have blessed the attack (IANS May 16, 2003). According to American official sources, the senior leaders of Al-Qaida, including Said-ul-Adil and Bin Laden's son, Abu Mohammad Masri, have taken shelter in Pakistan and Iran. According to a team of geographers from UCLA Bin Laden has been hiding since 2001 in one of the three large compounds in Parachinar town of Pakistan (TNN February 18, 2009). Possibly Said-ul-Adil was responsible for recent attacks in Riyadh. About 33 persons were arrested in that case. Such attacks are carried out to show that Al-Qaida is still active.

A very large number of Al-Qaida members are resting in Pakistan on the border of Afghanistan. Al-Qaida has increased admission to its cadres and was developing blasting materials, which would not be detected during security checks for air travel, as per the Pak newspaper, 'Dawn' (Agencies May 30, 2003). It was presumed that Abu Gaith, the Al-Qaida spokesman, was arrested in Iran as per the Arab newspaper, 'Ashrak Al Avast' (Amar Ujala, May 31, 2003). A legal appeal board in Pakistan ordered release of Dr. Ahmad Javed Khwaza and his brother Ahmad Navid, who were jailed for their close relations with terrorist organizations like Al-Qaida (Amar Ujala, June 1, 2003). Communicating the reality of bitter truth, the Home Minister Advani stated that Pakistan has become a hub for terrorism and a place for sheltering Al-Qaida, Talibans and other militants. After being defeated several times Islamabad is still aiming to capture Kashmir. Although India has the second largest population of Muslims, next only to Indonesia, there is not a single Indian who is an Al-Qaida member because India is a pluralistic democracy, where every body is free to express and to pray according to ones desire.

Newsweek indicated that Al-Qaida terrorists had prepared a scheme for blasting the Brooklyn bridge of New York, blowing up airplanes through suicide squads and destroying railway trains. This information was based on the statement of the project chief, Khalid Sheikh Mohammad, who had recruited a licensed Ohio truck driver, Limon Faris. Faris was supposed to look for more terrorists and to drive a truck with blast materials to the airport for enacting the scheme (AFP

June 2003). The CIA reported the two Pak scientists were working with Al-Qaida (earlier reported in a science journal in April, 2003). Pakistan was denying it but the CIA found that Bashiruddin Mahmood and Abdul Majid were really involved with Al-Qaida and this organization had chemical, biological and nuclear weapons (Terrorist CBRN: materials and Effects, May 2003).

Dr. Abdul Kadir Khan, father of the Pakistani nuclear program, is also involved in proliferation. US media gave this information based on a brochure with 'Rawalpindi P.B. No.502' address and Dr. Khan's photo printed on it. Musharraf had made him Science Adviser, after his retirement. In the report the item which is most serious is about giving training. Khan's network closed in 2003 when the US, U.K. and Italy intercepted Libya bound ship, carrying tools for manufacture of the enriched uranium. The suicide blast in a Shiite mosque in Quetta, Pakistan, which occurred on Friday, was alleged by Prime Minister Jamali to be perpetrated by India. India denied this. The President of the Shia Conference and local Shia leaders, on the other hand, said that the Fedayeen attack was carried out by an Al-Qaida group (not Indian) and the dead bodies were of Al-Qaida members (Amar Ujala, July 8, 2003). As per the Chicago Tribune, Afghan and US officials in Afghanistan suspect that Islamabad once again is lending support or at least turning a blind eye to Taliban forces inside its borders.

According to New York Times, a document filed at a detention hearing for 19 Pakistani students and other immigrants detained by Canadian security officials for possible ties to terrorism cited a "pattern of fraudulent document use to obtain or maintain immigrant status" by men (Seattle Times 24th August, 2003). Iran's peaceful nuclear program suffered a blow when the inspectors discovered Pakistani enriched uranium at the Natanz facility (Seattle Times August 27, 2003). Villagers of North-western Pakistan know that they are suspected of giving shelters to Taliban guerillas and Al-Qaida fugitives, who has been launching raids in Afghanistan. However, in the presence of Pak soldiers standing nearby, the villagers deny the allegations. US officials said they suspect Al-Qaida is operating there. It was difficult to say whether the villagers would give different answers if Pak soldiers were not there. Sambhal Khan, however did say that, "The Taliban are our brothers but they have been given a bad name" (Seattle times August 28, 2003).

Thinking in the US is that terrorists in Pakistan are helping Al-Qaida. According to them these terrorists are the same persons who were creating violence in Indian J&K. Now they have an eye on the NATO forces in Afghanistan. According to a senior officer of National Security organization Pakistan terrorists came in close contact with Al-Qaida in the year 2006 and are training them to work in the US and Europe. During tight security in China for Olympics a series of bomb blasting and firings eight people were killed in the Muslim majority region in western China. These incidents happened in the Kuka town in Shinziang. During the same period an American tourist was killed in Beijing. He was a relation of an Olympian. About 15 militants targeted a government building. Therefore security forces had to take preventive measures and seven terrorists were killed. It is considered that the terrorists desire to create a Muslim South East.

The CIA claimed again that with Chinese help Pakistan is quickly developing weapons. Since 1998, Pakistan has been busy preparing nuclear arsenal and procuring machinery for them. In 1996 China promised not to help any country develop mass destruction weapons but it is helping Pakistan with materials and technology. It is also mentioned that Russia and India are also working together on several projects on missiles, tanks, submarines etc. According to a report from Washington (Reuters), Pak is building a new nuclear reactor that could produce enough plutonium for 40 to 50 nuclear weapons a year. This is a major expansion of its nuclear program and could prompt an intensified arms race in South Asia.

In Quetta, Pakistan four Hindus were killed when unknown gunmen tied six people in a shop and sprayed them with bullets. Four of them died on the spot and two were seriously injured (Amar Ujala February 10, 2003). The Indian army reported a mass murder of 24 Kashmiri Pandits in the Srinagar valley by the involvement of Jaishe Mohammad and Lashkar-e-Toiba terrorist organizations in March, 2003. This way, Kashmiri Pandits have been forced out of the Valley. About three years ago, there was a large scale admission in Muridke (POK) training camp for later attack in J&K, as informed by London media. This Al-Qaida associated camp is located in a 190 acre plot with tall barbed wire fence and with trees all around. Despite this, Prime Minister Jamali said, in an interview to CCTV 1, that Pakistan never supported terrorism (Agencies London March 31, 2003). President Musharraf asserted that Delhi should avoid construction of a fence on LOC (PTI December 13, 2004). Such requests, from Islamabad, were taken by the J&K state government as evidence of desire to continue funding terrorists to sustain militancy. The Pakistani government signed a peace accord with Islamic rebels, who are closely allied with Afghan Taliban movement, having effective control of the Waziristan border. The deal demands Pak troops will stop their military campaign in this region, which has left more than 350 soldiers dead, along with hundreds of militants and scores of civilians. White House officials did not confirm the reports but doubted Pakistan would give Bin Laden a free rein.

The Deputy spokesman of foreign affairs in Washington said that Khan Research Laboratory was blacklisted along with North Korea's Chhangwang Ciniyog Corporation due to nuclear proliferation from Pakistan. Musharraf, on the other hand, expressed his dissatisfaction to Colin Powell (Agencies April 3, 2003). Just before the visit of Richard Armitage to India and Pakistan, the CIA Director informed the Senate Intelligence Committee that Pakistan was continuing its support of terrorist organization. Consequently tension is mounting and some serious attack like that on Indian parliament is likely to occur (Agencies Washington April 25, 2003). One of the leading terrorists, Kari Abdul Hai was arrested in Pakistan. He was involved in several killings and was giving training to Islamic terrorists in Afghanistan. He was also one in the group responsible for kidnapping and killing Daniel Pearl, a Wall Street Journal reporter (Amar Ujala May 21, 2003). Several times Musharraf had to accept Pakistan's sponsorship of terrorism in the name of freedom fight. However, it is for the first time that a senior minister accepted it. Khurshid Mahmud Kasuri said that terrorists are neither slaves of Pakistan nor Pakistan posses "Aladin Chirag" which on rubbing would finish terrorism. We do, however, have some influence on terrorists because for the past fifty years we have given them diplomatic and moral support (Amar Ujala, June 4, 2003).

The Chief of the Joint Army Intelligence Services, Lt. Col. Kamal Davar stated that hundreds of terrorists were waiting at the LOC to enter J&K. With the opening of the Passes militants not only enter through Pir Panjal in north Kashmir but they have also started entering into southern areas. There are several training camps in POK/GK. But due to international pressure Musharraf has started criticizing terrorism and offering peace talks. In Quetta (Baluchistan), three Sunni terrorists entered a Shiite mosque during prayer (Namaz) and showered people with bombs and bullets. As a result, at least 32 people were killed and many others injured. Two terrorists blew themselves up with bombs to kill others and the third sprayed Namzis with bullets (Agencies Islamabad June 5, 2003). Iran's Chief delegate to the UN atomic agency warned the US and other nations that nuclear tensions could be aggravated if they put too much pressure on Iran to open its programs to inspectors.

An audiotape by an Al-Qaida spokesman vowed attacks on Americans everywhere and so devastating that Washington would forget the horror of the September 11 attacks. The tape was broadcast by an Arabic TV channel Al Arabia (Seattle Times, September 8, 2003). From the above it is quite clear that Pakistan has become a hub for terrorism and also nuclear proliferating nation, not only in the region but also elsewhere. Only people of Islamic origin (mainly Sunnis) are welcome in Pakistan. Thus in the eyes of many, North Korea, China and Pakistan are, in reality, the new axis of evil nations. Paul Rogers, a Professor of peace studies at the University of Bradford (England) said that while US-led anti-terrorism wars succeeded to prevent many terrorist attacks, Al-Qaida linked violence has killed about 400 people and injured almost 1000 in two years. Military successes in Afghanistan and Iraq have failed to crush Al-Qaida structure or stem its recruitment. The terrorists have spread out and are hiding (Seattle Times September 9, 2003).

Although Islamabad denies the presence of Dawood Ibraheim in Pakistan, intelligence agencies claimed they have hard evidence of his running a counterfeit printing press in Pakistan near the Afghanistan border (TNN December 21, 2003). The first video image of Osama Bin Laden in nearly two years was broadcast on Al-Jazira TV on September 10, the eve of the 9/11 attacks. He was shown walking through rocky terrain with his top aids. A speaker identified as Bin Laden praised the "great damage to the enemy". On a second tape, a voice said to be that of Aiman Al-Jowahri threatened more attacks on Americans and called on Iraqi guerillas to 'bury' US troops.

The backdrop in the video resembled the border area between Afghanistan and Pakistan, where Bin Laden is hiding. Another tape of his appeared in 2006 on Pak TV blaming the US on atrocities and boasting that the US would not be able to capture him alive. Hundred of Al-Qaida suspects escaped into Pakistan (a hub for terrorism) and Bin Laden is suspected to be one of them. Now Al-Qaida is carrying out propaganda amongst Islamic youth with western rap music in English. In these videos Bin Laden has been praised and Muslims are asked to carry out Jehad. It says become martyr and show the path to more Muslims. The worst disaster in 2004, which was carried out by Chechen terrorists, was the death of more than 350 people, most of whom were hostage school children. Before this there were bomb blasts in trains in Russia and Spain, Killing a large number of people. Israel and Egypt blamed Al-Qaida for attacking two Sinai resorts on October 7, 2004 which killed about 35 persons.

Dodging the US military in Afghanistan after 2001 attacks, Al-Qaida command reconstituted itself in the Pakistani rugged tribal-border areas, near Peshawar. In the first few years many senior leaders were captured but in the last 18 months or so no major personality has been killed or captured. Therefore, on 7th September 2007 Bin Laden again surfaced and in a 26 minutes videotape-speech his important apparent message was 'we have survived'. Counterterrorism officials did not grasp the resurrection of Al-Qaida command but from their hideouts in Pakistan, the command Deputies did order attacks in a Tunisian synagogue, a British bank in Istanbul, London transit system and many other failed plots like flights from Britain in 2006 etc. A third tape from Bin Laden appeared on 20th September 2007. Joining him on this tape was Ayman-al-Zowahiri. Bin Laden called on Pakistanis to wage a holy war to overthrow Musharraf for his alliance with the US against Islamic militants. The tape sought to galvanize Muslim militants (Seattle times September 21, 2007).

In Punjab, police captured 5 terrorists, including two from Pakistan. They had a large amount of arms and counterfeit Indian currency for starting terrorism in State (Agencies September 6, 2004). The ongoing arrests of Al-Qaida suspects from the houses of MMA leaders, the MMA's pro-Al-Qaida's instances against the US strengthen the notion that the MMA of Pakistan and Al-Qaida are two sides of the same coin (Hindustan Times, August 27, 2004). There were suspected Al-Qaida linked attacks in a Sinai resort and in a Hilton hotel in Egypt (AP October 10, 2004). Attacks in Egypt, Britain and

Turkey in 2005 indicated that the terrorists are still active and definitely being supported by some nations/ organizations, and most of the times finger are pointed at Pakistan. Due to its controversial foreign policy and military utilization, England has become a strong place for Islamic terrorism.

Terrorists are being recruited there and this fact has been accepted by their home ministry. Evidence has been collected to show that the conspiracy to blow up the planes flying from London for USA is pointing out totally to Pakistan. Abdul Rauf, father of the main conspirator (Rashid Rauf) had been arrested from the airport, who was trying to run away from the country (Amar Ujala, August 19, 2006). Investigations into the bomb blasts in a mosque in Hyderabad confirmed the role of a terrorist Shahid alias Bilal. A Pakistan trained terrorist named Sheikh Sameer to whom Bilal had handed over cell-phone-operated IED was arrested while trying to sneak into India from Bangladesh, told investigators that the mastermind is holed up in Pakistan (TOI, May 23, 2007).

Two synchronized terrorism-explosions in 2 popular spots in Hyderabad in August 2007 killed at least 30 people and wounding more than 60 others. Similarly on October 11, 2007 blast at Ajmer Sharif Sufi shrine killed two persons and wounded about 20. Terror outfits like LET are against Sufi Islam and are the prime suspect in Ajmer blast. Three days after Ajmer blasts, there were blasts in Shrinagar cinema of Ludhiana, killing seven persons and severely injuring about thirty persons. On June 22, unknown armed militants surrounded a church in Peshawar (NWFP) in Pakistan and killed at least 25 people, including two padres who were busy praying. Earlier Christian colony people were being threatened and were asked to vacate the area. In 2008 also several Indian cities had to face terror bomb blasts, killing people and injuring innocent persons. Jaipur, Ahemdabad and Bangalore bomb blasts were planned in Karachi Intelligence Bureau claimed that Rasul Khan Parti and Mohammad Sufia Ahmad Patangia were the main planners.

Basically both are the residents of Hyderabad (India) and had recruited many youths before running away to Pakistan. Materials were also purchased in India for making bombs. There were repeated infiltration bids by terrorists from Pakistan in September-October, 2008. Pakistan denied Indian protests. Repeated infiltration (Intelligence) of BSF stated on October 3, 2008. On 26/11 there were series of blasts in Mumbai Railway Station, Taj Palace hotel and other places killing about 200 people (particularly from Israel, US and U.K.) and doing a great damage to the historical Taj hotel. Terrorists, from Pakistan were killed in 2 days by Commandos, excepting Kasab, who was captured alive to get the information. Terrorists started from Karachi and reached Mumbai by sea route. Their aim was to kill around 5,000 persons and carry out heavy damage to property.

Consequently tension between India and Pakistan increased. Not only regular forces on Indian border were increased by Islamabad but also reconnaissance flights were increased. India is also keeping an eye over these activities by Pakistan. Amir Kasab, from Faridkot, has disclosed his identity. Former Prime Minister Sharif has confirmed involvement of Pakistan but Islamabad is trying hard to disprove its involvement. Dawn and The news have accepted these facts of Pakistani involvement. Later Lashkar accepted the responsibility of blasts. This attack attracted attention from people around the globe and condemned Pakistan, from where terrorism spread in the entire world. The US however is not prepared to call Pakistan a terrorism supporting nation, although it agrees to Pakistan's involvement and suggested giving serious punishment to the people playing a role in the 26/11 blasts. Entire world opinion is for punishing guilty persons. India again demanded extraditing the terror culprits again, which Pakistan is not agreeing, despite the fact that SAARC convention article 3 of 1987 says, "If a contracting state which makes...consider this convention as the basis for extradition..."

As per report from Dawn, Washington told Islamabad to hand over Lashkar commander Zaki-ur-Rehman Lakhvi and Yusuf Muzammil to India. Despite India's repeated demand to hand over 20 culprits, no one in right mind will expect Zardari to hand them over for terrorism committed on Indian soil. Not only that would drastically undermine Zardari's position in already perilous situation, but Pakistan's military will not allow it (Hindustan Times, December 11, 2008). Both FBI of USA and Indian government submitted strong evidence suggested that 26/11 attacks were planned and were carried out by Pakistanis. India submitted 5 proofs, i.e. the statement of Kasab (the only terrorist caught alive); discussions between terrorists and their bosses in Pakistan; GPS records and details of telephones of terrorists; made in Pakistan arms & equipment etc. recovered from terrorists as well as miscellaneous stuff, made in Pakistan, recovered from Kuber boat (snatched from Indians). The whole world is now eagerly waiting for Pakistani actions on these evidences (Hindustan, January 5 and 6, 2009). For the first time, five weeks after the attacks, Pak Officials accepted that Kasab is their citizen but to protect LET they told Dawn News that terrorists themselves had planned attacks without involvement of any organization.

Later they demanded pointed answers to thirty questions and India government supplied them and is waiting to know what action Pakistan is proposing to take on culprits. On the other hand Senator Joseph Lieberman has asked Islamabad to it should stop all the terrorist training camps and must punish the persons associated with in 26/11 Mumbai attacks. He also said Pak government as well as everybody knows who are the persons involved in these attacks and wherefrom they came (Agencies, January 9, 2009). After several weeks of trial, Kasab accepted all the charges and disclosed lots of information in the court.

Concerted earnest efforts by citizens and the governments must be made towards secularism and wide concept to achieve stabilization of democracy. Swami Vivekanand had said,

"Religion is not in doctrines, in dogmas, nor in intellectual argumentation; it is being and becoming, it is realization." We Indians more or less have understood it since ages. Would the polity now follow the suit? Will the so called rogue nations realize it?

9

Nuclear Issues and Regional Security

B.B. Nagaich and Jayant Kumar

Just after one year of independence Prime Minister Nehru arranged to propose in the General Assembly of the United Nations a resolution on the "Peaceful Uses of Atomic Energy" for the welfare of human beings. In 1954, he wrote to the Secretary General the policies for restricting nuclear arsenals, which became the foundation for the partial test ban treaty. This was the first step towards a total disarmament and later the Comprehensive Test Ban Treaty (CTBT). In 1948 an atomic energy commission was set up in India under the leadership of Dr. Homi Bhabha for harnessing nuclear energy for human welfare through peaceful means. In 1957 India voluntarily announced that it would not use nuclear energy for evil purposes and has been using it ever since for constructive purposes only (Babu, 1994). Unfortunately, none of the Superpowers took lessons from Indian example and kept on expanding their nuclear stockpiles, disregarding the hazards created by the same (Gandhi, 1988).

China's 1964 Nuclear Test

India's interests in the military applications of nuclear energy gained momentum after China's 1964 nuclear test. The explosion caused great alarm in India because of the humiliating defeat it had suffered in 1962 Sino-Indian conflict. The Jan Sangh, precursor of BJP, had raised demand for production of nuclear weapons in Parliament in 1962, nearly 2 years before the Chinese nuclear test (Koshi, 2006). A fruitless search for guarantee added fuel to the fire. The effectiveness of the nuclear security umbrella depends not on the spirit in which protected powers accept it, but on the national interest of the country, which offers it. The compromises reached during the negotiations on NPT led to security pledges by the US, USSR and U.K. as mentioned in the Security Council Resolution 255 of June 19, 1968. A joint US-USSR guarantee was also sought by India, but without abandoning its non-aligned policy. Now the problem was the incompatibility in basic interests of the two super powers to deter China on political and military considerations (Noorani, 1967). This dichotomy led India to carry out its nuclear test in the year 1974 about 10 years after China exploded its nuclear weapon. K.C. Pant the then Defence Minister desired nuclear weapons for strategic purposes, but India did not develop weapons. In May 1998, with five nuclear tests in quick succession, with simultaneous testing of a fission device, a low yield fission devise and a thermonuclear device India demonstrated an unprecedented event in the nuclear history. The subsequent sub-kiloton tests yielded additional data for simulation purposes (Koshi, 2006).

The India government missed the opportunity to undertake nuclear tests in 1995. Doing so then, along with French and Chinese explosions, could have considerably lessened the international political and economic fall out. Unfortunately, the Bhartiya Janata Party (BJP) had to take this step, when its political standing was fragile in the coalition government. Although these tests have drawn criticism from some political parties, the BJP's stand on nuclear arsenal production has been overwhelmingly appreciated not only by the Indian masses but also intellectuals as well as many other countries (Kapur, 2006).

Scoreboard of Nuclear Tests by P-5

The first nuclear (atom) bomb was dropped by the US on Hiroshima on 6th August 1945 followed by bombing of Nagasaki a few days later. With this beginning of nuclear bombs on the globe, there are seven declared nuclear powers today, i.e. the US, Russia, U.K., France, China, India and Pakistan. There are at least 3 more countries, i.e. Israel (undeclared), North Korea (declared) and Iran ready as nuclear powers. Another two are likely to become nuclear powers in the immediate future. The first five nuclear powers have exploded more than 2,000 nuclear devices so far. It has been estimated that these explosions yielded about 630 megatons. They have polluted oceans, made several islands radioactive, poisoned marine life and spread incurable diseases. The scoreboard of these tests carried out by P-5 nations by 1995, and warheads were as follows:

(a) USA: One explosion every 18 days—10,925
about 15 percent retired
(b) USSR: One explosion every 2 days—20,000
about 40 percent retired
(c) France: One explosion every 6 days—450
(d) China: One explosion every 264 days—400
(e) Britain: One explosion every 331 days—185

France and China conducted nuclear tests as late as 1996 just as the CTBT was being finalized. As of May 1998, the US possesses about 20,000 nuclear warheads, Russia 22,000, France 500, U.K. 380 and China 450. Even if SALT and START treaties were implemented the US would retain 10,000 warheads till the year 2007, Russia would have retained 11,000 and there would be no change in the numbers or quality of nuclear arsenals of the three other nuclear power nations. The U.K. and France need not have become nuclear power States, which they did despite having a guaranteed nuclear security umbrella provided by the US as NATO leader. India did not get a similar security umbrella either from the US or Russia as it belonged to no power group.

Therefore, it had to work its way up because of hostile environment in the region (Noorani, 1967). Israel's non-declared nuclear power weapon status has occurred despite security guarantees of the US, U.K., France. Thus Israel became nuclear weapon power with support mainly from the

US. Pakistan was supported by China and North Korea, the missile. South Africa's nuclear weapon status was sustained and supported till Dr. Nelson Mandela came to power. Recently North Korea, the missile-proliferating nation, exploded its nuclear devices and thus its aspirations became a reality with the help of proliferating nation Pakistan. Six nations North Korean talks ended on December 22, 2006 without any agreement. In February 2007 these talks brought some hope. North Korea agreed to shut down its nuclear reactor at Yongbyon.

It has also promised to allow international inspections within 60 days. In return North Korea is to receive 50,000 tons of fuel oil from the US, China, Russia and South Korea to run electric power plants. If North Korea permanently stops the reactor, it will be donated additional 950,000 tons of oil. But in 2009 North Korea has again restarted its nuclear program. Some weapons experts are however skeptical that Syria has been in league with North Korea to build a secret nuclear program. Following US stopping exports of military hardware in 1985, Harvard educated Benazir Bhutto finalized a missile deal with North Korea. Islamabad's black marketing lead scientist Dr. A.Q. Khan, visited North Korea about a dozen times in the next 6 years. Although Pak President Musharraf denied knowing anything about it, former senior Officials confirmed occurrence of these visits with the knowledge and approval of military leadership.

Pakistan agreed to provide second-rate P-1 centrifuge technology to North Korea in exchange for missiles. North Korean scientists received nuclear training at Khan Research Lab., the main nuclear training centre of Pakistan. Pakistan supplied nuclear technology not only to North Korea but also Libya and Iran etc. North Korea, disregarding the international pressure, carried out ICBM test on April 5, 2009. According to German government's information Gotthard Lerch joined Dr. Khan's group in a secret plan to manufacture and supply to Libya a plant to enrich uranium. The project however collapsed following a tip to British and American intelligence. They raided a German freighter (BBC China) in October 2003 in Italy, with large amount of nuclear goods bound for Libya. Subsequently, Col. M. Gadaffi agreed to give up all weapons of mass destruction in exchange for an end to economic sanctions.

China's Assistance to Pakistan for Nuclear Weapons

After 1970s it became well known that China was actively assisting Pakistan to acquire nuclear weapons. India had carried out a total of six test explosions in 1974 and in 1998, whereas Pakistan carried out retaliatory explosions (also six) in 1998 only. It may be recalled that Z.A. Bhutto was the progenitor of Pakistan's nuclear program as he was also the minister for atomic energy, in addition to the charge of Foreign Ministry (Weisman & Khosney, 1981). According to many experts, Israel also has got about 100 nuclear bombs, more than double the amount India has. India today is roughly where the US was in 1952, technologically. India has unilaterally declared moratoriums since May 1998 and also declared its No First Use Policy.

Although India has finalized and announced its deterrent nuclear policy recently, Pakistan has yet to declare its policy. Pakistan's nuclear perceptions largely depend on its historical prejudices and differences with India. Pakistan has been pursuing both the plutonium and uranium routes to its nuclear weaponry. It is stated by many that China provided Pakistan with design and material for manufacturing a nuclear bomb. A Sino-US accord was signed in July 1985. China gave to Pakistan details of nuclear weapon and helped building a centrifuge uranium enrichment plant (Specter, 1988). India was from the very beginning concerned about the US-China pact since deal had waved all the conditions that were imposed on India's Tarapore Agreement. China refused all international inspections and also refused commitment for processing spent fuel. The US agreed to these conditions. Thus, the US action exposed the selective implementation of non-proliferation policy. Richard K. Betts, a noted analyst, branded these actions as the US double standards (Bose, 1994). India has been advocating elimination of nuclear weapons and for a complete disarmament without discrimination.

Following a thermonuclear test in March 1954 that exposed hundreds of Japanese to radioactive fall out, a proposal for abolition of nuclear weapons and also for reduction of conventional forces was submitted by India to the UN, which was first opposed by Soviet Russia and favoured by the US. Later, the US delegate withdrew by saying, "it is our view that if the armed forces and military expenses were brought down to too low a level, then instead of prospects of peace being improved, real danger of war is increased." Thus disarmament was considered a danger to peace? If more armaments, nuclear or otherwise, will ensure peace why decry India, Pakistan or any other country becoming nuclear or developing missiles etc. New Delhi was particularly active in promoting a complete test ban up to 1980s, when it promoted the treaty (in May 1984) as a part of six-nation initiative on nuclear arms control by the leaders of Argentina, Greece, India, Mexico, Sweden and Tanzania. In 1985, the six countries called upon the P-5 to conclude at the earliest a treaty on nuclear test ban, which would lead to ending of the modernization of nuclear arsenals (Sharma, 1999).

Non-Proliferating Treaty (NPT)

One of the measures the P-5 brought into force through the UN was the Non-Proliferating Treaty (NPT) in March 1970. Most of the UN members became a party to the NPT. However, France and China, initially; India, Israel, Pakistan, South Africa did not sign NPT. Under article 1, the P-5 undertook a solemn obligation not to transfer nuclear weapons. Under article 3, each of the non-nuclear weapon state (and not nuclear weapon states) signatory to NPT accept safeguards set forth in the agreement including inspection, verification etc. by

International Atomic Energy Agency (IAEA). Under article 6, nuclear weapon states were obliged to pursue negotiations for cessation of nuclear arms race at an early date for complete disarmament (Babu, 1994; Sharma, 1999).

Thus, while non-nuclear states cannot manufacture or acquire nuclear weapons, there is no corresponding obligation on the nuclear powers not to manufacture nuclear arsenals under NPT, meaning thereby expansion of the nuclear stockpile by the P-5 will not be called proliferation. In other words, the 'haves' can have more and the 'have-nots' can have nothing. Further the non-nuclear nations will be subject to inspections and verifications by the IAEA but not the P-5. Therefore, India, which had its technology and had been using it for peaceful purposes (Kapur, 1971), rejected the NPT because of the abovementioned discriminations and even, carried out its first nuclear test in 1974. The India nuclear test led to the US to believe that nuclear proliferation is likely to be hastened. Jimmy Carter made non-proliferation the centrepiece of his foreign policy and South Asia became the target of technology denials and sanctions. This concern was partly "hear no evil", and "speak no evil" policy for Pakistan's weapons program (Cohen, 1999 & 2001). India's refusal to sign the NPT provoked the US authorities.

The US government refused to supply the nuclear fuel for Tarapore reactor, though under the terms of agreement the US was committed to supply the fuel for thirty years. As far as India was concerned it caused no breach of 'plow-share' programme. In 1974 when India detonated its Pokhran-I nuclear device to probe the depth of sand in Rajasthan to find out the depth of water level in desert there was an outcry in the US. It adopted a delaying tactics in supplying enriched uranium. As per agreement India could not approach any other nation for fuel till 1993, when the plow-share program was to be over. The US on the other hand repeatedly warned India of the consequences of not signing the NPT. India put 3 conditions for fulfilling the US proposal. 1. The P-5 should negotiate NPT. 2. They should accept full scope safeguards, which would end production of nuclear weapon grade materials. 3. The P-5 must take significant steps toward a total nuclear disarmament (Sethna, 1977; Sharma, 1999).

In May 1998, after supply of missiles by China/North Korea to Pakistan and Islamabad's Ghauri missile tests, India carried out further minimum deterrent tests, although originally it was India, which had given idea for disarmament long back. In 1999 both India and Pakistan have test fired the improved versions of their missiles, like P-5 nations, who desired only horizontal non-proliferation through CTBT. Confronted by the new US intelligence, North Korea followed by Iran also admitted their clandestine nuclear programs (helped by Pakistan) continuing for the past several years and expressed their unwillingness to stop them. In fact North Korea had issued a threat that Japan would be turned into a 'nuclear sea of fire' if the US were to launch an attack against the North Korea (LA Times September 24, 2004). Only a few days later Choe Su Hon, a Minister announced that North Korea has turned plutonium into weapons for deterrent purposes. He blamed the US for designating his country as part of 'axis of evil' and a target of pre-emptive nuclear strikes (Seattle times September 28, 2004).

After getting the information that the US is deputing missiles in South Korea and other neighbours, North Korea has threatened that if his country is attacked by the US his nation will give a much more dangerous reply. The US considered that Pakistan was a major supplier of critical equipment to North Korea (New York Times October 18, 2002). North Korea, in turn, had been giving missiles and technology to Pakistan. Pakistan has also supplied technology and critical material to Iran too.

Evil Axis of China-Pakistan-North Korea

Therefore, many consider 'China-Pakistan-North Korea' as the real axis of evil and the triad 'threatening world peace'.

But the great surprise was what prevented Bush Administration from slapping punitive sanctions on Islamabad for its role in Proliferation not only to North Korea but also to Iran and some other countries too. Iran is supposed to have funded development of North Korea's Nodong missile. North Korea became annoyed with its criticism in the UN on rocket test carried out on April 5, 2009 and threatened with nuclear test and military action. The question, which is generally asked, is what prompted India and Pakistan to declare themselves nuclear powers? The first Pokhran test of India in 1974 was most likely a protest against a discriminatory NPT. The NPT prohibited nuclear test in atmosphere and under water. It allowed underground testing by nuclear powers.

The CTBT extended the prohibition to the underground tests also, but not before the nuclear powers had carried out all their tests. In the documents containing aims and objectives of the nuclear non-proliferation and disarmament it has been mentioned that, "pending the entry into force of a Comprehensive Test Ban Treaty, the nuclear weapon States should exercise 'utmost restraint' (emphasis applied) in carrying out further tests" (Bose, 1994). However, not withstanding the declarations, on May 15, 1995 China conducted its 42nd test and on August 17 its 43rd nuclear test. French announced its series of eight tests from September 1995 to May 1996.

These examples of 'utmost restraints' by the nuclear powers showed the fate of the CTBT, yet to come into force. The US also carried out the so-called sub-critical nuclear tests of its stockpile. No wonder India and other countries declined to join CTBT. China supplied nuclear technology and material to Pakistan, which carried out Ghauri and Gaznavi missile tests, causing a serious concern to India and leaving it no option but to carry out its underground deterrent tests. During the period between the 1994 and 1997 CTBT was formulated. The discriminatory elements in the CTBT were the following:

1. It legitimized existing P-5.

2. It allowed them to retain or improve their weapons.
3. It did not stipulate any time bound program to destroy their stockpile.
4. It imposed a permanent ban on security options but also on their peaceful potentialities.

In addition to these, the US has put several limitations. Besides CTBT, FMCT was being evolved to extend discriminatory restriction nuclear-capable developing nations and on transfer and development of dual use technologies by developing countries.

The above-mentioned facts as well as deteriorating regional security environment around India starting from Diego Garcia up to Pakistan and the straits of Hormuz and China forced Vajpayee's government to convert potentiality to reality in the field of nuclear arsenals and missile development (Bose, 1994; Chari, 1997; Sharma, 1999). Pakistan had already threatened several times to use nuclear weapons and missiles against India. Islamabad's relations with either her nuclear powers like China and the US were important facts, which New Delhi could not afford to ignore. Tests became necessary for laying the foundation to develop a deployable deterrent capacity against security threats. This way, India broke out of the straight jacket of punitive and discriminatory stipulations, which could have become operational under CTBT by the end of 1999.

These stipulations would have been further compounded by the FMCT coming up for discussions in the Disarmament Conference (Cohen, 1991; Sondhi, 1998; Sunderji, 1993). Between 1972 and 1974, Pakistan had persuaded Libya and Saudi Arabia etc. to fund its nuclear weapon program (Weisman and Khosney, 1981; Gupta, 2000; Specter, 1988). A Pakistani nuclear device was reportedly (Dixit, 1998) tested at a Chinese testing site at Lop Nor in Sinkiang in 1987. By 1992, both Dr. Abdul Kadir Khan and Sahryar Khan had confirmed Pakistan's nuclear capability. By 1995-96 Pak political leaders threatened India with a nuclear attack, if India took military action against Pakistani intrusion in J&K. In 1987 itself, Pakistan conveyed a nuclear threat to India at the time of operation in BRASTACKS. The then Minister of State communicated this threat to the Indian Ambassador. The Indian journalist Kuldeep Nayyar was also communicated a similar warning by Dr. A. Kadir Khan (Nayyar, 1992).

In January, 1990 Foreign Minister Sahibzada Yakub Khan visited New Delhi and literally gave an ultimatum to Prime Minister V.P. Singh and the Foreign Minister I.K. Gujral. The Prime Minister enquired from the Air Chief whether nuclear weapon carrying aircraft can be successfully intercepted. Air Chief replied that the best option to India was to acquire a nuclear deterrent of its own. In 1990 the US imposed Pressler Amendment clearly implying that Islamabad possessed nuclear capability. I. Choudhuri Khan, who came to settle in the US (via Canada), told the FBI that China and Iran helped Pakistan to develop nuclear weapon and Saudi Arabia gave financial help (Agencies, N.Y. July 1, 1999).

In the light of the above and China's continued supplies of nuclear know how and materials to Pakistan, India had no option but to go nuclear. Pakistan availed the opportunity to test fire its nuclear material in retaliation to India and India got the blame for spoiling the US-led CTBT, not ratified by it (US) so far. Apparently, the P-5 really desired not disarmament but only horizontal non-proliferation. In fact in mid 2001 defence specialist of the Republican Party, Frank Gophni, predicted that the Bush administration would continue to test its nuclear weapons and not reduce arsenals to the extent desired by many (Agencies Washington May 9, 2001). The US, which is working to destroy the weapons of mass destruction from the globe, is preparing to develop the weapons of the next generation. The Senate panel has given its approval to remove the ban for research on small atomic bombs to destroy the underground bunkers, which cannot be destroyed otherwise with normal bombs. The experts have expressed their worries because with the development of these bombs, their use will increase and other nations will also develop the same (Agencies May 12, 2003). The US Senate approved energy budget for 2004 for studies into a new generation of nuclear weapons for use on the battlefield, involving more than 21million dollars for nuclear arsenals (Seattle Times September 21, 2003). Forty two governments urged the P-5 and nuclear aspirants to extend moratorium on nuclear tests. The twelve nations not ratifying the pact are China, Columbia, North Korea, Congo, Egypt, India, Indonesia, Iran, Israel, Pakistan, US and Vietnam.

There was a great apprehension in the minds of Indian intellectuals that the superpowers may squeeze India with their political clout and economic pressures, and that some may even try to activate the issue of Kashmir in the UN to embarrass India and also to appease Pakistan. It may also be mentioned that in the 1972 Shimla agreement both India and Pakistan had agreed to resolve their bilateral disputes by direct negotiations. Bilateral agreements have their sanctity and should not be brushed aside by one party nor interfered with by a third nation. India has a record of solving bilateral issues by mutual talks, as illustrated by the recent agreement with Bangladesh on sharing of Ganges water as well as other treaties with neighbouring countries like Nepal and Sri Lanka. Even with Pakistan it made an agreement to share Sindh river water in the past. While many military powers are reducing their army, some of India's neighbours are increasing them. The slapping of economic sanctions by the US and others, withholding loan or aids, blacklisting laboratories or institutions, sending back scientists and not issuing visas for attending seminars did not browbeat India to change its policies. The US had imposed sanctions against 69 countries but none had collapsed because of sanctions. If the US withheld loans for the ongoing programs, it is its own investment incurred already that suffered too.

Therefore, it had to eventually exempt projects already under execution or it had to exempt the deals, which were likely to benefit the US interests also. Already England and France had declined to join imposing sanctions. In fact in early 2006 the French President came to India and signed a nuclear cooperation deal. Many senators and important congressmen, like Representative Phil Crane, criticized the imposing of sanctions. According to him sanctions led to Washington acquiring a dubious reputation of an unreliable supplier. Meanwhile Japanese and Europeans moved in quickly and became alternate suppliers. The agricultural suppliers suffered the most. Above all, India had the resilience to take on the sanctions and economize its spending. It is also self–sufficient in basic necessities and in fact, if it desires to retaliate it could throw out most of the US multinationals, as witnessed in the past with Coca Cola.

Till recently, there was a famous slogan, "be Indian and buy Indian". No right thinking country could afford to ignore the vast present and potential market of India. The middle class Indian consumers are more than 250 millions, equal to the total US population. Many US multinationals were already carrying out trade successfully in India and the US could not afford to neglect the fate of its MNCs. Therefore, sanctions were ultimately relaxed by President Bush. He came to India in March 2006 and signed nuclear technology agreement for civil purposes. Bush-Manmohan Singh nuclear agreement was appreciated by Britain, France and Russia but China and Pakistan were critics of the same. This shows that the US has begun to realize the necessity for nuclear energy for India to overcome its shortage as also that India is a responsible nuclear power.

In 2003, the US Director of Policy Planning, Michael Reiss had said, "not only North Korea but also India, Pakistan and Israel should be stripped of their nuclear weapons." (PTI, February 12, 2003). He implied with the exception of P-5 the NPT should be made universal and as if the P-5 are not in the universe or the other nations' residents cannot be benefited by the nuclear energy programs.

Some of the P-5 nations advance the argument that India, by carrying out 1998 nuclear tests, has opened up nuclear conflict between India and Pakistan. They think the dangers have been enhanced by Pakistan's retaliatory tests, forgetting that Pakistan was already getting ready for possessing nuclear capability with the help of China and North Korea etc. On the contrary, in the history of world after the second war, there is ample testimony to nuclear deterrence. Although regional wars have been fought fairly frequently, the fear of nuclear destruction has prevented a third world war. The availability of nuclear arsenals with the enemy is one of the strongest deterrents against the aggressor. The nuclear capability of India as well as that of Pakistan is bound to prevent misadventure by any of these nations. The nuclear capability is likely to force both nations to negotiate to find solutions to their bilateral issues, provided no other power interferes.

Some authorities propound the argument that the timing of nuclear explosions in the Indian sub-continent was not proper because of nuclear powers coercing both countries to become parties to become parties to the NPT and CTBT. However, others suggest that it would not have been in the interest of India to delay demonstration of its nuclear capability. The decision to conduct nuclear tests was wise and courageous, though late. By and large Indians were happy with the Indian tests and also those of Pakistan because the same were the attempts to break the monopoly of the P-5 nations. This way we can emphasize to achieve "Action Plan for Ushering in a Nuclear-Weapon-Free and Non-violent World", proposed by late Rajiv Gandhi in 1988.

The only fear India has from Pakistan's nuclear arsenals is that some day they may inadvertently get released and land in the hands of terrorists. After breaking the monopoly of the P-5, the question remains whether India would join its advantages, which would be resisted by the super powers. However, after working for a long time for a phased elimination of nuclear weapons, it would not be proper for India to leave its policy and join the nuclear club for increasing the nuclear stockpiles. In the light of these facts, India has voluntarily declared moratorium on nuclear detonations and unilaterally promised Pakistan as well as non-nuclear nations not to first use its nuclear weapons. It had also expressed its desire to sign a non-discriminatory CTBT and was prepared to discuss Fissile material cut-off Treaty (FMCT) as well as accession to the Chemical Weapon Convention (CWC).

Nuclear-weapon-free-non-violent-world

It is time for India and other like minded nations to purse Rajiv Gandhi's proposal on disarmament, fixing 2010 for complete elimination of all nuclear weaponry to bring about creation of a nuclear-weapon-free-non-violent-world. However, The US itself could not get CTBT ratified by its Senate on October 13, 1999 it started the song of CTBT thru its former democratic Senator Allen Tasher to round up India Pakistan and Israel as a part of its 'Threat Reduction program'(PT, Washington, June 9, 2009). Besides US, India, Pakistan, Israel, China, Egypt, Indonesia, Iran and North Korea have not signed CTBT. On account of missiles and warheads retiring, Russia and the US have quietly proposed to cut back their arsenals to fewer than 1000 long-range weapons. The US is interested in keeping the level of total warheads to the level of 2,000 to 2,500, to bolster the new threats from China and North Korea etc.

It is also not certain whether a huge nuclear arsenal, particularly the one that the US has to test, will deter a new generation of potential nuclear rivals, i.e. India and Pakistan, rogue nations such as North Korea, Iran and Iraq, or terrorists seeking the weapons of mass destruction. Retired General George L. Butler says that if anything, the US is feeding their nuclear appetites, "when we have no palpable threat still declare nuclear weapons the cornerstone of our national security...is it wonder the President calls on other nuclear nations to denuclearize are going to be ignored" General

Butler asks. In 2009 President Obama and Russian President Medvedev agreed to cut back nuclear arms to replace Start-1, which ended in December, 2008. Russian expect that the US will present a written agreement for cutting back the nukes in the next meet.

The discussion so far has been on India's attempts for peaceful uses of nuclear energy. The present capacity of India's nuclear power is insignificant, only 2720 MW. Therefore, the government plans to set up new nuclear power stations to increase power generation in the country, with the hope of reducing the power shortage. Russia, France and also the US, have shown interest in helping the program. According to government sources, the present capacity is expected to increase to 3,940 MW by 2007, the end of the tenth five year plan, and to 9100 by 20012, the end of the eleventh five year plan.

During past decade, India invested more in nuclear weapons and missiles than in conventional weapons. India explored the acquisition of theatre missile defence (TMD) from the US and Israel. By acquiring TMD, it may join the Missile Technology Control Regime (MTCR). Missile defence is too expensive for Pakistan but thinks Indian TMD would neutralize Pakistan's nuclear deterrence. This can also open the door for an arms race in the region. China (Pakistan's close ally) thinks that missile defences may minimize its deterrence. Now coming to other uses, one main foundation stone for nuclear deterrents is thermonuclear weapon stockpile. The second is reliable long-range missiles able to carry hydrogen bomb loads. Intercontinental ballistic missiles (ICBMs) are the most economical, effective and potent instrument to carry nuclear arsenals to places of strikes. India has also been working steadily on the same for its own security despite threats from Super powers.

Therefore, India should seriously explore, on top priority, to at least partially militarize the India Space Research Organization's (ISRO) space launch capabilities (Krishnan,

1994). With ISRO readying its liquid fuel indigenously, cryogenic rocket system to put a geostationary satellite in orbit was initiated in 1999-2000. The ICBM technology is, in fact, already operational. All that is required is for the satellite pay load to be replaced with megaton nuclear/ thermonuclear warheads atop the ISRO rockets to make the ICBM force ready. The technology is needed to put multipurpose satellites in precise orbits over the equator or the poles require the rockets to keep to equally precise trajectories.

Moreover, the mid-course correction and terminal guidance paraphernalia developed for ICBM use can be transferred to improve the accuracy of the long and intermediate range ballistic missiles (IRBM), Lakchya, Bramhastra, Prithvi, SSM-150, Prithvi ASM 250, Agni series, Akash and Sagarika. With cooperation of China and North Korea, Pakistan is well ahead of India in missile development. Though Agni 1 and 2 were inducted by armed forces, it will take time for improved versions to be inducted. Sagarika is a submarine launched ballistic missile. Such missiles are available only with P-5 Nations. For very long period this synergy was unnecessarily sacrificed to keep the military and civilians sensitive technology programs separated. But this was, perhaps, necessitated as the US inspired missile technology control regime (MTCR) kicked in with venom a few years back.

Today that pretence should be shrugged off. In any case, the sooner it is, the quicker the country will derive substantial security benefits from the significant national investments in the dual use of the space infrastructure. Western analysts have pondered the likely nuclear force design for a "middle power" like India and concluded that, taking into account its various resources and the threats, the nation will be on par with China, U.K. and France. Many of these exercises, however, fixated on an Indo-Pak nuclear fracas and have stressed nuclear strike aircraft and nuclear tipped short-range surface–surface missiles. This limits their relevance somewhat for India as

India's strategic and threat compass includes lots more besides Pakistan (Kapur, 2006). On October 21, 2008 India launched its 2-year mission 'Chandryan' for mapping not only the surface of the moon, but what lies beneath. The mapping instruments are a joint project with NASA. According to many specialists, missile capability of Pakistan is better than that of India, mainly because of Chinese help. India's objective to have a "nuclear weapon triad" program to construct indigenous nuclear submarines was completed with the launch of INS Arihant on July 27, 2009. India now has nuclear deterrents from air, land and sea routes. Although delayed by a year and half India received 3 Awacs (Early warning and control system) from Israel in May 2009 to keep an eye over 400 sq. km. area. Two more are expected in 2010.

Nuclear Proliferation by Pakistan

The Nation reported that two chief scientists of the Kahuta Research Laboratory, who worked under Abdul Q. Khan, Pakistan's father of its nuclear program were arrested for transfer of nuclear technology (Agencies February 11, 12, 13 2004). On February 3, Dr. Khan accepted his role in black & white. Former Prime Minister Benazir Bhutto stated that during her tenure several senior officers asked to permit sale of nuclear technology but she refused (Agencies London February 25, 2004). As per a Kuala Lumpur police report there were several sales of nuclear material from Pakistan to Libya, Iran and Egypt (Agencies February 22, 2004; IAEA January 29, 2005). According to the US Centre for Strategic and International Studies and the CIA, Pakistan has become a nuclear material supplier and a dangerous nation (INS December 16, 2003; Agencies April 18, 2004). Two Pentagon officials disclosed that 14 years ago Pakistan had threatened to supply nuclear technology to Iran.

It appears Pakistan started supplying technology in 1985. This may be the main reason why Pakistan did not sign NPT and CTBT. The surprise however is that despite the above information and the world opinion the US has given Pakistan the status of non- NATO ally of the US, giving it benefits in economic and military matters. Musharraf detailed information about the relationship between A.Q. Khan and North Korea. He revealed the North Korea was possibly employing Dr. Khan and used Pakistani nuclear equipment. The same modern Pakistani technology is being used by Iran for its own nuclear program. In May-June 2008 Khan alleged that his earlier confession was not genuine but coerced by Musharraf's men. Defamed nuclear scientist Dr. Khan was freed, under the pressure of more than 100 Jehadi groups, in February, 2009. Khan's associate Dr. Mehmood had admitted that Bin Laden had acquired fissile material. Khan had taken responsibility of nuclear secrets in 2004 and he was put under house arrest to be freed ultimately in 2009.

This move has been criticized in India, the US, U.K., France and other powers and intellectuals all over the world are suspecting that with the release of disgraced A.Q. nuke proliferation is likely to restart soon. According to a recent statement of army chief, Mike Mullen, he asked Islamabad to strengthen the security of nuclear arms instead of increasing the amount. However, a few days before Mullen' statement, Secretary Hillary Clinton had said that Pakistan has made satisfactory arrangements for the security of nukes. One day before this statement CIA Chief had stated that America does not know the whereabouts of Pakistani nukes. All these statements create confusion. Mullen had stated before Senate committee that there is a lot to be done about security of Pakistani nukes and about increase in the amount of Pakistani nuclear arms.

Unlike biological and Chemicals weapons of mass destruction, which have been outlawed by international treaties, nuclear weapons are important for national securities (Gupta, 2000; Joshi, 2000; Dhar, 2000, Nanda, 2001). Possession of nuclear weapons on a selective basis was legitimized through extension of the NPT in 1995. Thus nuclear weapons States will continue to depend on nuclear weapons, adopting policies to use them even in a non-nuclear context. This amounts to virtual abandoning of nuclear disarmament and virtual denials to abolish the deadliest weapons of mass destruction. Today, and for the foreseeable future, this power will rest mainly in the hands of the US and partly in the hands of the Russia-China block. The rest of the world can keep making noises at the periphery, but it will not make any difference. Only when the US is persuaded and agrees to reverse direction will the world will also reverse direction. On April 6, 2001 the Indian Prime Minister Vajpayee invited the P-5 to agree to destroy their nuclear arsenals and unilaterally offered to be the first to destroy nuclear warheads if other nuclear powers agree to do so. Speaking on the 26th hundred anniversary of Jainism, he said that India has always been in favour of a complete ban of nuclear arms but it is mainly the P-5 which forced it to go nuclear. Unfortunately, no other country has so far responded favourably to his proposal.

Security in the Region

USA: The US, long time back, devised a "Regional Security Strategy or system" to be able to response to any crisis in the globe. Under this strategy, it has co-opted regional strategic partners or allies and share responsibility to overcome any critical situation. Due to its good economy it is able to bear the financial losses, if any. The US is now considering China as a future major power, after the break up of the USSR, and has engaged it as a regional cooperator or strategic partner in South and South East Asia. US is spending seven times more money than China on defence and China is spending more than three times its budget on defence preparations than India. President Clinton has accorded the 'most favoured nation' status to China for increasing trade relations, obviously considering it as a booming market and a powerful nation. It is easier to deal with a dictatorial regime, not constrained with democratic or political interference, as in India or in any other democratic nation.

The so-called 'human rights' rhetoric intended for pleasing the US Congressmen are related to a very low priority for the sake of strategic partnership, although the republican Senate leadership has been seething over the Clintons administration's apathy in this connection. Senator Jesse Helms, Chairman of the Senate Foreign Relations Committee and Senate Majority Leader Trent Lott have been angry over the State Department's indifferent attitude to the recent revelations by the intelligence community. Earlier, the US viewed India as a Soviet surrogate or ally (Srinivasan, 1995; Malik and Kapur, 1998; Immerson, 1999). In the new scenario, it does regard India an important nation in the region mainly for economic reasons. The US Pacific Command does have some on-going Indo-US military cooperation for the name-sake. However, the US never considered India as a counterweight against China or as a strategic partner.

Recently there have been some changes due to Global war on terrorism. In the eyes of the US, India's democratic system or its achievements, for having close relations, were never considered important. The condemnation by the US of the India's 1998 nuclear tests, followed by imposition of economic sanctions, was not only even-handed, but actually with a hidden tilt towards China and Pakistan. Sino-Indian-Pak relationships with USA were discriminatory by giving by more importance to China as compared to India, or equating India with Pakistan, apart from having acquiesced in the Chinese or Israeli nuclear programs while pressing India to give up its nuclear option (Carnegie study group report on US-Indian relations, 1993). Since Pakistan has been an old blind military supporter of the US, it views Pakistan with continuous strategic regional interests (Dennis Kux, 1993; Cohen 1998; Sunderji, 1993).

Pakistan provides access to oil-rich areas of Central Asia and it also allows airfields near Peshawar to be used for U-2 or other planes for spying against Russia, Iran and Afghanistan (Gupta, 1977; Sunderji, 1993). Therefore, the US has always been supporting Pakistan's view on Kashmir and many other Princely states merged into India and are its integral parts as per freedom act passed by Britain. Kashmir is high on the US agenda, not merely because of the US affinity with Pakistan, but also because of the US strategic interests in the region (Gupta, 1977). The US has openly suggested 'third party' intervention by China, much to the chagrin of India.

On third December 1998, President Clinton, during discussions with Nawaz Sharif in Washington declared that US wants to see Kashmir issue to be resolved, "but (we) can be of help only if both parties (India and Pakistan) agreed". Prior to this, while talking to the Pakistani media he said, "But there is no way the US can inject itself into the dispute unless both ask us to do that". This shows the internal desire for mediation despite the fact that as per Shimla agreement both India and Pakistan had agreed to solve bilateral issues by mutual discussions. In view of that any request for mediation by third party should be rebuffed immediately. However, six years back during the visit of Prime Minister Vajpayee to the US on September 2000 Clinton commented on the summit-eve that he believed the US "can play positive role to a peaceful solution of the Kashmir dispute...".

This again worried the Indian delegation, given New Delhi's categorical stand against third-party mediation in Kashmir. On September 13 Clinton's key adviser on South Asia, Bruce Riedel, told journalists that both India Pakistan should use the President's 'presence and experience' to help alleviate the situation. Therefore, it is crystal clear that the US is keen to get involved as a mediator in Kashmir dispute to fulfil its hidden desire. Recently Secretary of State Colin Powell too had spoken about Washington's good offices to help India and Pakistan to resolve their differences. India does not want to hear of it whereas Pakistan has been clamouring for it. During Powell's later visit to South Asia in the beginning of 2002, he said the US was not keen for mediation in Kashmir issue. He suggested that India and Pakistan should work in the direction of normalizing relations. This has also been confirmed by President Bush during his 2006 visit to Afghanistan, India and Pakistan. Bush Administration sees India as a natural partner, after China rising, and Europe and Japan declining. It saw that lectures on nuclear non-proliferation and sanctions did not stop India.

Therefore, it had to agree that India is a rising and responsible global power. It did not sell or trade nuclear technology. Therefore, the US is willing to make India a member of nuclear club. Its Senate and the House had already approved civil energy agreement signed between India and the US and now it has been signed by the President as an Act. It was expected that by the end of 2nd term of President Bush all the formalities will be completed and the treaty will start functioning. The agreement forged during several rounds of negotiations required India to develop a new facility dedicated for reprocessing of the spent fuel subject to International Atomic Energy Agency safeguards. Whichever way one looks at the deal, honest or otherwise, it has important consequences, particularly for India. In any sphere of life one wins only if one does not vacillate. If one delays unnecessarily, defeat is inevitable.

Should US Now Support Pakistan?

Many Senators and Congressmen have said in the past that the US should stop helping Pakistan. This was not agreed to and monetary as well as military aids were continued. Recent information regarding North Korea's secret enrichment of uranium for nuclear arsenal program, which it had promised to stop in 1994, shows the danger of believing a liar nation. The fact that Pakistan gave nuclear technology and possibly uranium too to North Korea should shatter the US faith in Islamabad as a responsible nation for non-proliferation as also a well meaning member of the counter-terrorism coalition.

Pakistan is one of the most dangerous nations but the US neither understands the countries in the coalition nor has the policy for containing them. Appeasement through monetary aid is not very effective. Pakistan is the centre from where nuclear technology, Islamic militancy, counterfeiting currency and drug trafficking are going on. Non-Muslims are not treated properly and slaughtered at will. Musharraf was pretending to move forward democracy. Huge sums of the US money are being poured for different programs, although there is no effective monitoring how it is being utilized. Washington is neither telling the truth about Musharraf's lies nor is holding him accountable.

The US policy has been to appease Pakistan with money, which it needed badly. In Pakistan, even US diplomats have limited term of about a year or two, without family members accompanying them. Elections rigged by Musharraf, after amending constitution to favour him, must not be praised or treated as a step towards democracy. Not allowing political parties in election led to fundamentalist Islamic coalition, which favours introduction of orthodox Islamic Sheriat. The sanctions, imposed earlier on military cooperation, were lifted and joint exercises held, despite protests from Congressmen. Even Clinton administration suspected clandestine barter arrangement between Pakistan and North Korea but did nothing. New York Times had identified the foul play on October 17, 2001.

Pyongyang sent missiles and its technology to Islamabad, which in turn gave nuclear technology and possibly uranium. The intelligence officials described the incidence as a slap to Washington. The Pakistani plane used for secret pay-load purposes was the US built C-130, part of the military force that Musharraf had told President Bush would be devoted to hunt down the Al-Qaida terrorists. In addition, the shipment occurred at a time the Bush administration was hailing Pakistan's cooperation in the war on terrorism (N.Y. Times, November 24, 2002). It appears these nation helped Iran too to develop nuclear and missiles programs. Iran helped Islamabad against New Delhi in the OIC etc. Colin Powell, Foreign Secretary, said, on a TV program, that Musharraf has informed him Pakistan is no longer in this trade. After this statement, he kept silent and did not want to discuss this issue. However if one goes in the past, Musharraf's lies become apparent. Bush administration, for getting Musharraf's help against Al-Qaida, has been tolerating it and continued supporting Islamabad.

It is well-known that Musharraf pledged to stop cross-border terrorism. He not only broke this pledge but even lied about discussing it with President Bush in their September meeting in New York. Earlier he had mentioned that India had carried out a new nuclear test, which proved to be wrong. He had also stated India's involvement in Daniel Pearls' case. Therefore, there is no reason to hope that the truth of helping or not helping would be told correctly now. He does not have to pay the price for his lies about stopping terrorism in Kashmir or cooperating fully in crushing Al-Qaida. Therefore why should he change his approach, which has been continuously been rewarded and also protected by the US (Jim Hoagland, Seattle Post-Intelligencer, October 24, 2002 etc).

The US has on August 11, 2003, officially given the go ahead for Israel to sell the Phalcon airborne radar system to India, which it had been preventing so far. This was on India's threatening military action against Islamabad after terrorists struck at the Indian Parliament. By this time the US had already rained dollars on Pakistan and given enough military supplies to it. After mid-term elections in 2006, the Democrats majority new House is showing willingness to stop huge economic and military help to Musharraf government because of its not being able to control assistance from Pakistan and safe haven to Taliban and Al-Qaida (Amar Ujala, March 2, 2007). According to the New York Times Website the US has spent 100 million dollars during the past 6 years in secretly guarding Pakistan's nuclear weapons.

China: President Clinton's visit to China has been the

most encouraging factor for the Chinese government, which has been given the strategic partnership status and bestowed with regional responsibility. At present, modernization of Chinese armed forces is among the four key areas of the policy. China is already a medium nuclear power, duly recognized by the US, having successfully fired long-range missiles recently. It is trying to expand military bases around India's borders and the Seas. It has developed the airfields of Akyab in cooperation with Myanmar and the facility in the Coco islands are clear indication of their new strategy for establishing its military striking ability out side their own country. It may be mentioned, China is unhappy with India for allowing Dalai Lama to stay in India and have his government in exile. It has ongoing border dispute with India, and has condemned Indian nuclear tests but has shown sympathy with Pakistan's nuclear capabilities because both China and North Korea have supplied missile technology and nuclear materials to Pakistan. China had even criticized Bush signing an agreement with Manmohan Singh on civil nuclear cooperation. China has always been viewing India as a rival and had made friendship with Pakistan (Hoffman, 1990).

Geopolitical importance of GK/POK has to be seen in the context of the fact that Kashmir occupies a strategic position because of its closeness to the international boundaries of China, USSR, Afghanistan and Pakistan. Therefore, question of building strategic roads like Karakorum highway, which passes through POK, has to be examined. In 1978, President Zia-ul-Haq inaugurated this 800-km all weather highway, linking Sinkiang with Havelian railroad 96 km north of Islamabad. By constructing roads in Kashmir (POK part, gifted by Pakistan to China, after illegally occupying it) China has made it clear what its strategic interests are in this region. Since 1988 militant Sunni Muslims have started moving in POK and consequently local Shia Muslims have alleged that this is a deliberate action to increase Sunni population over Shia, particularly in Skardu sector. It is therefore, likely that

China would support Pakistan in conflicts with India, unless by doing so its own interests are affected adversely, as happened during May 1999 Kargil war (Nanda, 1999) when it did not help Pakistan due to its internal problems created by Chinese Muslim citizens.

It is well-known that China has been providing military aid, nuclear technology and missiles to Pakistan for long time, despite the agreement not to do so. The US intelligence disclosed the same several years ago and India also provided the evidence but Clinton's administration has been showing apathy to it on one pretext or the other. Some analysts feel that it was with the consent of the US that China supplied complete M-11 ballistic missiles etc. to Pakistan and that is why Washington had to take apathy in this matter to possibly prepare it as its strong supporter and enemy of India. After China's friendly relations with the US and Pakistan, India has been put in a difficult situation as far as its national security is concerned and India is preparing itself to face the challenges. Recently, both Russia and China have lowered the "use" for threshold for nuclear arsenals.

The hardening stance can be traced to anxiety over Kosovo, when Yugoslavia was attacked by NATO and forced to secede territory. The shift in NATO doctrine from defence to intervening anywhere has led to signals from Moscow and Beijing that interference in their provinces like Chechnya, Tibet or Taiwan may lead to deployment of nuclear arsenals. Despite opposition to the continuity of ICBMs tests China has in December 2000 tested DF-31, which has a long range of 5,000 kilometres. This is the second test of the DF-31. The first was carried out in 4th November 2000. Thus all the important Indian cities are in the range of Chinese missiles (Agencies, May 31, 2001). Therefore, India had to continue improvement of Agni missiles resulting into Agni-2, which was first test fired in January 2001. Its range is up to only 2200 kilometres (Agencies January 17, 2001). A few years back India had to develop a Light Combat Aircraft, which was successfully tested (2nd time) in Bangalore to improve its arm-forces.

According to Ye Zhengjia China and India did not make much progress in 13 rounds of talks on border issues. According to him, Mc Mahon line was illegally thrust upon China by the British Imperialists (India Abroad, August 31, 2001). After a very long time, the Chinese Prime Minister visited India in 2002 and signed several agreements as well as agreed to keep working together to fight terrorism. As a result a joint panel was formed in the field of science and technology. A flight between New Delhi and Beijing was started from March 31, 2002. Afterwards the visits of dignitaries from both countries started for mutual discussions and there were improvements in relations. In January 2008 Prime Minister Singh visited China on a similar mission.

Pakistan: Pakistan has always been considering itself as equal to India, not taking into account its size, population, resources and diversity of India. It had already in possession covert nuclear capability since 1980s and threatened India. The Chagai nuclear tests in 1998 have given Pakistan an opportunity to increase its prestige and the role in international politics. These tests have been welcome in Muslim world, which is annoyed with Israel and USA. In US the Muslims see Patron of Israel. Therefore, these nuclear bombs were termed Islamic bombs by many. The Islamic countries, especially Iran, Saudi Arabia, Kuwait and Libya, will like to woo Pakistan for its nuclear technology and military alliances. Several Arabian nations have been giving monetary help to Pakistan for armaments and made it feasible to acquire weapons at a faster rate with Petro-dollars. North Korea and China assisted with technology and the US with silent patronization (Venkataraman, 1998; Venkataramani & Arya, 1996; Mohan, 2000).

Several experts fear that Pakistan's nuclear arsenals or the know-how is likely to be passed on to Islamic fundamentalists. The emerging situation may be exploited by Pakistan to internationalize the Kashmir imbroglio, disregarding Simla Pact and Lahore Declarations. It has already started stating that the issue cannot be solved bilaterally and China or the US should mediate, to which President G W Bush had disagreed. Because of the India opposition for mediation, the US at one stage desired China to intervene as a 'third party', knowing fully well the border dispute between India and China. For similar reasons India had to once again disagree for appointment of special Ambassador. India stated in 2008 that countries in the region should solve their problems bilaterally. Pakistan is continuing its active ISI involvement in India's north-western states (Daruwalla, 2000) and recently in north-eastern states too as a serious endeavour to take a revenge on India in retaliation for India's help for freedom of Bangladesh (Joshi, 2000; Mohite, 1995; Mohan, 2000).

The US silence over Pakistan's support for terrorism in J&K serves Pakistan's strategic aims better and encourages it to adopt openly hostile attitude towards India. Consequently, in May 1999 India had to fight a war with Pakistan to throw back its forces and supported insurgents in Kargil sector, where they had penetrated up to 25 km. inside (Nanda, 1999 & 2001). It was the same storey as had happened in Kashmir in 1947. Thus the US encouragement to Pakistan and China enhances the estranged relations between the US and India. Looking at the size of Pakistan and its borders as well as that of India, the ratio of military strength of the two countries in early nineties, as given below in table 4 is revealing (Chopra, 1990 and others). While Indian per capita defence expenditure was about US$ 10 in 1997, Pakistan was spending about US$ 26. While India financed 19 soldiers per 10,000 citizens, Pakistan was supporting 49 soldiers per 10,000 people, despite the fact when Islamabad had been getting lot of free arms and armaments from the US from time to time.

Accordingly a much heavier expenditure on army in Pakistan increased the race between the two countries. On the top of it, in 2002, Pakistan test fired Ghauri, Gaznavi, Abdali

(Hatf-3) and Babur (Hatf-7) missiles {all named after Muslim invaders attacking India} to increase the range of attacks, against the wishes of international community. Pakistan's economy was in bad shape and the US decided not to oppose IMF's loan of US$ 226 million. Maleha Lodhi, Pakistna's Ambassador to the US, virtually said this was like a straw thrown at a drowning man, indicating anger in Pakistan over the US economic sanctions after the Chagai nuclear detonations. Despite poor economy of Pakistan, Admiral Tahir, at the conclusion of Pakistan's naval exercises in Arab Sea in 2001, stated that their navy is better than Indian navy (based on the geographical area of the two nations). Even then Pakistan has to arm its army with atomic weapons to achieve further superiority over India.

Consequently, French aided Agosta 90-B or Hashmat submarine fitted with 4 torpedo tubes were procured (Press Islamabad February 22, 2001). Luckily, shortage of money has been overcome with recent monetary aids and military supplies from the US for fighting global terrorism. With dollar rains, Islamabad has started looking for purchase of superior arms and fighters like F-16 and missiles like Shahin-2 (Agencies, April 1, 2005). Some of the senior US politicians have however, objected to military supplies. The most serious problem is whether Pak nuclear material/technology has already been supplied to Bin Laden or other terrorists because Abdul Q. Khan and S.B. Mahmood met Bin Laden and Lashkar outfits several times (Agencies April 4, 2005), although Pakistan has been denying it. In May 2009 Pakistan conducted cruise missile test quietly and is now purifying Thorium & Plutonium for development of more dangerous nukes.

According to the report of American Congressional Research Service for 2008 it has about 60 nuclear weapons and is constantly increasing the weapon delivery system. Because of Chinese and North Korean help Pakistan is slightly ahead of India in missile defence.

Table 9.1: Comparative Military Strength of India and Pakistan: Approximately about 2 Decades Ago

Military Power	India	Pakistan	Ratio
Troops	1,280,000	560,000	2.3:1
Paramilitary Men	672,000	165,000	4.1
Tanks	3,500	2,800	1.4:1
Artillery	5,320	2,500	2:1
Aircraft	856	461	2:1
Nuclear bombs (year 2000)	80	25	3.6:1
Annual budget (expenditure)	3 percent	18 percent	1:6

According to an interview of Dennis Kux (Former Ambassador to India and Pakistan) on CNN and the report of the Centre for Strategic Studies (CSIS) in 2001, India has in regular and nuclear warfare about double the strength, sometimes even more. In addition, because of geographical advantage India can divide Pakistan into two parts in the event of a war (AFP, December 30, 2001). Islamabad has taken full advantage of the US financial support for the so-called war on terrorism in Afghanistan. According to the Congressional Research Service report Pakistan figures right on the top with US$ 5.1 billion in agreements to buy arms in 2006. This amount works out to be about 4.5 percent of the GDP. India was placed second with US$ 3.5 billion, spending about 2.5 percent of its GDP on defence, a trend witnessed since 1991-92. The depleted air force and also navy are risky for the national security of India. IAF needs about 40 squadrons but it has only 30-32 squadrons with many more old MIGs lined up for retirement. Both Pakistan and China are boosting their defence arrangements. For example, Pakistan is getting 36 more F-16s from the US and 250 JF-17 'Thunder' fighters from China. While as per CAG report to Parliament India is likely to increase its air force only in 2012.

Vajpayee's government stepped up production of its Prithvi, Agni and other missiles, along with acquisition of US-Israeli Arrow-2 missile defence equipment with the accompanying Green Pine radar system as well as Russia's S-300 V theatre missile defence material. The government also asked for the Patriot missile (PAC-3) equipment. India was developing reliable missile defence on Western border to deal with Pakistan.

The Role India Can Play

India's renunciation of the nuclear option is yet not on the cards. With nuclear options open, India should be able to press the point that unless there are moves towards elimination, the NPT will remain a dream. This prediction has become true as North Korea and Iran are another two nations, which are declaring themselves as nuclear power nations and very soon another two or three are going to declare the same in the near future. May be NPT will provide a motivation to the nuclear powers to work towards elimination as a goal within a time frame. India's relations with China and China's approach to disarmament are fundamental to India's position for resolution of the issues. There is a possibility that CTBT may fail because India and some other nations have not yet agreed to it, which would be one of the best for India. In such a situation, India could represent the views of the developing nations in the "nuclear club". That India would have assumed the role of a spoiler would be rather uncharitable, given the unhesitating acceptance of the Chemical weapons Convention that adequately indicates India's desire for complete disarmament. Further, the roles of spoiler have now been taken by North Korea and by Iran. India should continue to be a model for restraints (unilaterally), by voluntarily refraining from sharing or exporting nuclear technology to others. Impressed by these facts the US agreed in 2005 and 2006 to cooperate with India in civil nuclear energy production and a few other high-tech programs.

India has already announced a policy of "no first use" and "no use against non-nuclear states" as a model for others to follow. It has already declared a moratorium on further nuclear tests too. Finally, India should develop a clear dividing line between its civil and military nuclear research and development programs. This was also a condition in the Indo-US agreement on civil nuclear energy production cooperation signed in 2006 and India has already complied with it. As one of the founder members of the IAEA, India can show its twin role of promoting peaceful nuclear technology utilization. Simultaneously it can help ensure that the nuclear know-how is not used by other countries for evil purposes. Therefore, it must organize a Global Conference in India for a Nuclear-Weapon-Free world and declare that it is willing to put its nuclear weapons on the negotiating table to force the P-5 and other nuclear nations to eliminate their arsenals in a phased manner, a stand it has been taking since 1954 (Chellany, 1993; Schmidt, 1999; Sondhi, 1998).

Prime Minister Vajpayee, in September 1998 at the UN stated that he was prepared to bring negotiations on India's joining the CTBT to a successful conclusion, so that the start of the CTBT is not delayed beyond September 1999. He added that New Delhi would participate in FMCT negotiations in good faith. However, on October 13, 1999 the US Senate turned down ratification of the CTBT, it had signed earlier. Therefore, apparently there is hardly any possibility for CTBT to start functioning as proposed earlier, unless the US decides to ratify the CTBT in future. The world is now worrying about what will happen if Pakistan's or the North Korean nuclear know-how gets released in Middle East to Islamic fundamentalists because the civil rule has been replaced in Pakistan by a military rule of General Musharraf, who was the main architect of the undeclared Kargil war and the nuclear arsenals remain under the control of the army in Pakistan, even during civil rule. Similarly due to its economic problems the North Korea, which has recently declared itself a nuclear power in 2006, may like to export nuclear technology to gain monetary benefits.

Some questions also arise whether the delivery aircraft

available in India, viz. F-16, Mirage III, Jaguar, MIG-23BN have been modified already to carry nuclear weaponry. After facing the US designs to hinder the question of nuclear capabilities and after aborted supply of super computers, cryogenic engines and associated technology for Indian space program etc. the belief is growing within India that there is no alternative to self reliance in scientific and technological endeavours. MTCR and other export controls retard Indian projects by 5 to 8 years. Unlike China and Russia, India has been seeking a way out of the logical Pokhran-II by indicating the willingness to sign the CTBT. It has also signalled a dilution in its robust nuclear doctrine, without any effective US or the European Union action to rein in Pakistan from its proxy war against India or open access to sensitive technologies. It is therefore clear that MEA is still desirous of entry into a US led- alliance rejecting the opportunity for joining the Russia-China Grand Alliance.

Nuclear Threats from Pakistan

Nawaz Sharif, at a public meeting at Neelbhatt town in GK/ POK on August 23, 1994, stated that the country possessed nuclear weapons and these would be used in the event of a conflict with India (Sharif, 1994). Earlier Mrs. Bhutto and General Aslam Beg had also declared production of nuclear arsenals and gave threats to India in December 1993. During Kargil war Pakistan again held out a nuclear threat to India. It seemed the new nuclear nations were going to start a nuclear war, although India had declared that it would fight to evict the invaders from Indian side of the LOC (Nanda, 1999). The US spy satellites were continuously providing information about Indo-Pak conflict. The US also knew that Pakistan had actually deployed its defence forces before it threatened India and had simultaneously positioned nuclear material and missiles.

Therefore, President Clinton warned Nawaz Sharif, over the phone to refrain from nuclear misadventure. Similarly, he called the Indian Prime Minister, who assured him that India had no intension to escalate the war. This was very well appreciated by the US and international community. However, Musharraf also later threatened with nuclear war (Times of India, January 20, 2002), which Vajpayee termed as nuclear black mail in the UN on September 15, 2002. In the absence of India's own spy satellite it had to share intelligence information with the US or Russia, as ISRO's CARTOSAT-1 does not measure up to being a spy satellite. Therefore, the sooner India has its own spy satellite the better it would be. India has to master remote monitoring to verify sensitive areas, identify troop movements of the enemy and to inform the army. Information from the spy satellite has to be augmented by AWACs or similar aircrafts. Pakistan has nuclear capable aircrafts and missiles like recently test fired Ghauri, Gaznavi and Abdali (Hatf).

Comprehensive network of air defence has to be created around the entire country, based on long-range radars and missiles. India's MIGs, Mirages, Jaguars and SU aircrafts must be made ready for a nuclear strike to make nuclear deterrence effective (Gupta, 2000 & Joshi, 2000). Fortunately Indian army has introduced jet trainer aircraft Hawk in 2008 to train its fighter pilots. The nuclear doctrine of August 1999 should have been formulated one year earlier, without going public. In 1998, India should have explained its rationale for nuclear program and deterrent nuclear capability to avoid threats from Pakistan because it would have known India's deployment of its nuclear capability if it had actually happened. Luckily, the US has now agreed to sell to India Phalcon radars and sensors to keep an eye on infiltrators. Russia has also offered to have joint projects with India on military requirements. Indigenous light combat aircraft was also tested successfully by India a few years back and with these Indian military is bound to become stronger.

Acquisition of nuclear capability in no way has reduced cross-border terrorism in Kashmir. India requires a very large well-equipped conventional force to retain its superiority over terrorism supporting neighbour. Unfortunately, despite nuclear threats Indian forces were neither reorganized nor were supplied with superior arms. Surprisingly, even the BJP alliance government had not heard the wake up call given by the Kargil episode and had been keeping quiet after Pokhran-II (Nanda, 1999). Is it because of the fact that the army has to fight the war and not the politicians or bureaucrats? Nuclear capability requires an absolutely reliable system of warning, well-equipped forces and a plan to meet every security threat. Further it also requires unified civil and military Command to overcome the threats. For Pakistan nuclear capability is the instrument for a war with India. Their leadership considers that the threat to use the nuclear weapons makes it clear that they want all of the Kashmir for themselves. Under such nuclear environment India cannot afford to remain content simply with the capability to counter Pakistani threat. According to Nanda (2001), under the nuclear capability umbrella, Pakistan chose to misadventure in Kargil for the following objectives:

1. Interdict NH 1 A to deny India winter stocking of the Leh-Kargil garrison.
2. To realign the LOC to dominate the highway to cut off Indian troops in Leh.
3. To hold on to occupied areas to nullify the Shimla Pact and internationalize Kashmir issue.
4. To Isolate the India troops in Siachin and capture the heights in Chusul valley etc.
5. To find a safe route for invasion by Mujahideens through Mashkoh and hold all heights in Dras –Kargil sector.

India has to be prepared for nuclear black mail by Pakistan, which has already threatened several times. Not only should India's minimum deterrence be in place but others should also know it. In the long run India needs to follow a policy like that of the US which led to the break down of the USSR and other Communist nations. It is unfortunate that every time an army General or a new Prime Minister takes over in Pakistan they have to follow the hate India policy to remain in power (Nanda, 2001). Accordingly with the history of about 60 years of locking in a spiral of action-reaction and terrorism, the state of J&K has become one of the causes of Indo-Pak hostility. More than ten thousand innocent people have lost their lives. Properties worth billions have been destroyed, besides tons of money wasted in arms and armaments lost in conflicts, despite abundance of poverty in both countries. Several decades of efforts for Indo-Pak reconciliations led to nowhere. The fate of Nehru-Liaquat agreement, Shimla Pact and Lahore Declarations show that even signed agreements are worth nothing. To secular India J&K is an integral part of the Indian Union. The only unfinished task is the vacation of GK/POK by Islamabad. To Islamic Pakistan religion is most important. Majority of people in Srinagar valley are Muslims and they should not be part of India, although in other two regions of the state they are in minority (Chibber, 1998) and should be a part of India.

On January 13, 2000 in Indo-US talks in London, the US desired that India must join the so called "international non proliferation norms". Indian analysts and politicians have serious reservations about the US commitment to NPT in view of its keeping quiet since 1993, on China's supply of missiles and nuclear plans to Pakistan, its silence on North Korean supply of missiles, the ring magnets sale of 1995-96 and China's role in Khusab reactor and reprocessing equipment. India's commitment to NPT is well known and the US has to reassure the world about its own commitment to NPT by ratifying CTBT first. Washington has to take clear stand on the question of its friend (China's) compliance with NPT. Without the US and China demonstrating their transparency, it will not be possible for India to generate a national consensus on signing the CTBT.

Another intriguing fact is the US reservations about the Indian nuclear doctrine. Due to increasing vulnerability of land based missile system to satellite spying, the US, Britain and

France have based most of their deterrence on submarines. Therefore, India too has planned a sea-based deterrent. It is a well known fact that after the NPT came in effect in 1970, none of the nuclear powers made any noteworthy effort to implement the item VI of the treaty, which requires them to work toward nuclear disarmament to abolish the weapons of mass destruction. The US did not agree to Soviet proposal of cutting the nuclear arsenals down. On the contrary, extension of NPT in 1995 allowed the P-5 to monopolize for forcing others to sign CTBT and bind them from conducting even peaceful nuclear energy researches for human welfare (Arundhati Ghosh, 1997; Chari, 1995; Subramnyam, 1986; Sondhi, 1998). Under these circumstances, Indian intellectuals and politicians were not in favour of signing discriminatory CTBT as shown in a limited survey conducted by the authors.

In April 2001, the Indian Prime Minister, speaking at a function of Jainism, offered to destroy its nuclear arms first if other nuclear countries are also prepared to do the same. However, under the present circumstances, there is hardly any possibility for it (Agencies, April 6, 2001). In 2009 President Obama said in Prague that the US is the sole country which has used nuclear arms therefore it is the moral duty of the US to end this dangerous inheritance of the cold war age. A similar action was proposed by Prime Minister Rajiv Gandhi in 1988. None of the other nuclear nations however has so far shown its willingness to do so. On the other hand the US had allotted funds for developing new arsenals and has maximum nuclear arsenals in several European countries despite end of the cold war long ago. North Korea on the other hand became another nuclear power despite pressure from others not to do the same. Iran too is on the way to become a nuclear power.

On Sunday the September 2, 2007 meetings North Korea agreed to account for and disable its nuclear program by the end of 2007. Kim Gye Gwan, head of the North Korean delegation stated his country was willing to cooperate in return for political and economic compensation. The US has decided to possibly remove North Korea from the list of terrorist-sponsoring nations and lift the sanctions. It is possible many other countries like Iran, Japan and South Korea may also declare themselves nuclear powers in the near future. There is lot of pressure on Iran to stop its nuclear programs, which it is not willing to do. Recently, Iran has test-fired dozens of missiles including the Shahab-3. Shahab-3 can carry a nuclear warhead and can reach Israel and is believed to be based on North Korea's Nodong missile. Iran is said to have funded Nodong missile development. Iran's President claimed on 2nd September, 2007 that his country is now running 3,000 centrifuges to enrich uranium for its nuclear program. Threats and economic sanctions shall not stop Iran's technological progress, President Mahmoud Ahmadinejad warned on 22nd September, before leaving for New York. At a large parade of missiles, jet fighters, torpedoes etc., showing off nation's weapon development program, Ahmadinejad cautioned the US and its European allies discussing a third round of UN sanctions (AP, September 22, 2007).

Indo-US Nuclear Deal

India's nuclear scientists and engineers had been working for years to test bombs to demonstrate nation's nuclear weapons capability, before US could interfere (Talbott, 2004). Reversing three decades of US policies, President Bush approved the long-stalled civil nuclear agreement with India, conceived in 2005. The House and the Senate had passed the measure earlier. The US, France, Russia and Britain have also begun to realize that India requires additional nuclear energy to meet its civil needs and is a responsible nuclear nation. These countries have therefore, signed agreement with India for cooperation in the matter (Subramanyam, 2005). President Bush is persuading world leaders and US politicians to support Indo-US nuclear energy agreement signed by him and Manmohan Singh in March, 2006.

The same was however not appreciated by the

proliferating nations like China and Pakistan and some critics in India. The joint pact included in the nuclear deal was the focus of controversy in both countries. Critics in the US argue that by allowing India's nuclear arsenal to keep growing and keeping some of its facilities off-limits, the pact establishes a double standard. The Left parties in India chipped away at efforts to improve relations with the US, Defence agreement of July 2005 and also with the nuclear deal. Sanjay Puri, Chairman of the US-India Political Action Committee, said some estimates had placed the potential economic value of the deal at US$ 30 billion in the US and India alone and that it could add 10,000 to 15,000 jobs in the US. It is therefore clear that the Bush government extracted a very heavy price from India for recognizing it as a nation with advanced nuclear technology.

On December 18, 2006 President approved the bill and the US companies are free to trade with India on civil nuclear energy programs. Bush hailed it as an important achievement for the world. Many analysts think this way India would cooperate with the NPT, which it had been denying to sign because of its discriminatory nature, although India is not willing for any legal binding on its nuclear testing, as informed by Prime Minister Singh in the Parliament. The deal allows India to trade civil nuclear fuel in return for its civil nuclear program under IAEA watch. The country's nuclear-weapon will not be subject to any added scrutiny. Nuclear experts are of the opinion that the deal was more than what India could have hoped for. Former Security Adviser Brajesh Mishra's view was that if India withdraws from Nuclear deal it would lose worlds confidence and would no longer be relied upon (Hindustan July 20, 2008).

However, India's left wing parties want it to be scrapped. They went to the extent of withdrawing their support to the alliance government with the result that the government had to seek vote of confidence, which the Congress alliance government won. The Left parties are still angry that the US pressured India into voting against Iran IAEA meeting in 2006. Prime Minister Manmohan Singh's reply was a firm 'NO'. Recently European External Relations Commissioner, Benita Ferrero-Walder, while discussing with Prime Minister Singh, however made it clear that India will have to take a 'few steps' like associating with NPT and CTBT before the 25 nation body can decide on cooperating with it in civil nuclear energy (PTI February 17, 2007). The External Affairs Minister Pranab Mukherji stated in the Parliament that Indo-US agreement is independent of the cooperation with Russia, which will help in building four more atomic plants in India.

This deal fortunately was approved in August by IAEA and in September by the 45 member NSG. US-India Business Corp. (USIBC) has started a joint move in Washington DC to persuade US Congressmen to approve the deal. In 2006 USIBC had started a move for making a change in the US ACT 1954 for doing business of nuclear materials with India. In addition Condoleezza Rice also pressed the Congress to approve the deal (AP September 7, 2008). US Officials said that selling peaceful nuclear technology to India would bring the country's atomic program under closer scrutiny and boost international non-proliferation efforts rather than undermining them. After approval of the nuke deal by the Congress and Senate, President Bush made it (HR7081) a law by signing the same on October 8. On October 11, US Secretary of State and Indian Foreign Minister put the final seal on 123 Accord in New Delhi to make it a legally-binding on both sides. It is also first step to India's cooperation with the world on civil nuclear energy.

The implications of the Indo-US nuclear pact are being continuously discussed by analysts and experts. As per views of Dr. A.N. Prasad, ex-Director of the Bhabha Atomic Research Institute, separation of civilian and military units under Indian conditions is next to impossible. Further, Indian army activities are not aimed at stockpiling nuclear arsenals. Indian objective is deterrence, which is based on the level of threat perception. However the US and the other P-5 nuclear nations desire stockpiling as they can afford to maintain military facilities for production and storage of nuclear weapons, although they are finding stockpiling as a costly affair. The main reason for high costs of stockpiling is the fact that weapons become old, their materials degrade and they have to be dismantled and replaced. He said, going down the route of stockpiling, which is the logic of the Indo-US joint statement, would be highly counterproductive and expensive (Koshi, 2006).

G. Parthasarthy, former Ambassador, and some others are however, happy with the deal. Signed by the President, the Act will allow Washington to restore civilian nuclear relations with New Delhi. Prime Minister Singh acknowledged in the Parliament that there were some areas of concern in the deal, which would be sought from Washington. Dismissing opposition charges that the deal would make India a client of the US, Singh asserted that nuclear 'swaraj' would be maintained and there was no reason for opposition leader Advani and others to worry about. According to the former Chairman of the Atomic Energy Commission (AEC), P.K. Iyengar, India should not sign 123 Agreement because part 2.1 is highly objectionable. According to many the US is trying to contain us quality wise and limit us size wise.

By May 2008 domestic opposition to the nuclear deal softened. Samajwadi party became willing to change its stance if the government puts the facts before it. Former Security Adviser to the NDA government, Brajesh Mishra, broke away with BJP orthodoxy by endorsing the deal. Former President APJ Abdul Kalam, doyen of the Indian missile and involved with the 1998 Pokhran nuclear tests, also endorsed the deal along with community of nuclear scientists. Therefore, it appeared that India could sign a safeguards agreement with IAEA after which the Nuclear Supplier Group (NSG) can move India specific amendment to its guidelines. With that the US Congress can discuss it for approval.

After approval by IAEA the US has assured India of all efforts to get the waver from NSG group. But what has added to India's concerns is a commentary in People's Daily, the official paper of Chinese Communist Party, calling the deal a 'major blow' to non-proliferation. Such an action was already suspected by some Indian political analysts (The Statesman 3 September, 2008). The US Congress completed final approval of the Indo-US nuke deal to end three-decade ban on nuclear trade with India. It is an historic deal under which India will get access to civilian nuclear technology, material and fuel. It would also give a boost to private firms, although National Power Corporation is presently the only corporation authorized for it. UK, France and Russia have been lobbying on behalf of their firms. Indian government's first concern is to produce more electricity as quickly as it can. The US House of Representatives passed the agreement. President Bush hailed the passage of civil nuclear deal and is expected to sign it in the 1st week of October. Indian National Security Adviser MK Narayanan said, "The world needs India as India needs the World." Pakistan which has been opposing the deal, demanded a civilian nuclear agreement with the US (AP October 3, 2008).

Fissile Material Control and Production Stoppage

Nuclear terrorism and proliferation have emerged as strong feasibility particularly after release of Dr. A.Q. Khan. About 1,670 tons of highly enriched uranium (HEU) has accumulated in the world. More than 95 percent of this is in the US and Russia and the rest spread all over the world. Total stock of weapon-usable plutonium is nearly 500 tons. Russia has about 180 to 190 tons, whereas the remaining 260 to 270 tons are spread around the globe. To begin with it may be a FMCT stopping further FM preparation. From the very beginning of the nuclear era the need for a treaty has been felt. As early as in 1946 the IAEA recommended prevention of production and stocking of FM. In 1967 a resolution was passed in General

Assembly for it but the cold war prevented it as formal negotiations have not yet been finalized. Several nations would like the treaty to cover existing stocks. Pakistan feels a FM production freeze would leave it with a permanent deficit vis-à-vis India. In 1993 India had supported a FM control regime by co-sponsoring UN resolution 48/75L.

Recently as part of Indo-US nuclear deal India agreed to cooperate with the US for conclusion of FMCT, although India itself is not ready to sign it. Agreeing to stop production depends on how big a nuclear arsenal the country requires. While negotiating the Indo-US nuclear deal India insisted that the fast breeders and six other power reactors be declared beyond safeguards. It would make FM produced from them available for weapon production. Pakistan too is producing FM in its Khushab and Kahuta facilities. The P-5, except China, declared a moratorium on FM production. China also seems to have stopped further production of FM. As P-5 have been producing FM for long time stoppage of FM production should not affect their strategic needs. FMCT would primarily affect India, Israel and Pakistan. It is likely that P-5 would agree on FMCT, if President Obama drops US objections of inspections. If that happens, India will be under pressure to sign it.

10

Indo-US-Pak Relations: Future Prospects

B.B. Nagaich

Sometimes an event in the history is so important that it can never be forgotten. This becomes apparent only after a passage of time, and to judge it in a short span of time is an indication of immaturity. At the golden jubilee of Indo-Pakistan independence, all the excitement revolved around separate celebrations of Pakistan and India. The freedom enjoyed by peoples of both countries was hard–fought and well deserved. There were reasons for separating the two countries in one land but it is sad to see that the two countries cannot live like two good neighbours and celebrate their freedoms together. Due to its faulty ideology one of these countries divided again into two separate nations. India or Bharat has been of the view that they will not get any help from the US in dealing with their neighbour, Pakistan (Talbott, 2004).

Today Pakistan's military, naval and nuclear development depends heavily on Chinese aid and advice. Hence India-Pakistan cooperation is tied to China-Pakistan relations. The growth of Indo-US strategic cooperation is intent to turn around Pakistan from its current role as hub of terrorism and nuclear proliferation to a position of nuclear transparency and anti-terrorism. These are the joint objectives of Indo-US diplomacy, which possibly had some positive results (Kapur, 2006). The infiltration of terrorists into J&K has declined slightly since 2002, although it has increased in other states of India. Pakistan's ISI continues its support to Taliban in Afghanistan and the Pakistan-Afghanistan border. In the nuclear field the facility and policy that encouraged the growth of Dr. A.Q. Khan's work is still obscure and continues with Chinese nuclear aid.

In population, natural resources, industrial infrastructure, technocrats & scientists, agricultural production, GNP, defence expenditure, defence production and military forces, India is one of the world's largest nations. With its stable democratic policy, the geography of India cannot be changed by organizing insurgencies or by supporting separatist movements morally, materially or politically. On the contrary, it can boomerang on Pakistan. The politically unstable environment in Pakistan also influences Indo-Pak relations. India or Hindustan after independence, dreamt of growing in a peaceful atmosphere of friendly relationship with Pakistan. The focus was on economic development, industrialization and improvement in quality of life. Defence had no priority. During 1950s, India visualized that a small defence program of less than 2-3 percent of GDP could meet its security requirements adequately.

India's Defence Expenditure

However, this estimate of Nehru was first jolted seriously by the Chinese attack of 1962 and later by Pakistan wars. Nehru's speech in Lok Sabha, on the No-Confidence Motion against his government on August 22, 1963, clearly reflected the psyche of the nation, leaders and citizens alike. He said, "We had been living in the world of unreality. This world is cruel. We had thought in terms of carrying the banner of peace everywhere and were betrayed. Pakistan betrayed us, China also betrayed us, World betrayed us. Our efforts to follow the path of peace have been knocked on the head. We are forced to prepare for a defensive war, much against our will" (Lok Sabha Debates, Series 5, 1963).

This is how India's defence expenditure began to increase in the sixties. Real defence expenditure more than doubled and the defence burden fluctuated between 4 and 4.5 percent of the

GDP (John Adams, 1966). For several years and even now India's defence spending has been pegged between 3.5 and 4 percent, but in 1982-83 it rose to about 5 percent of the GNP. Ever since Chinese attack in 1962, India has been compelled to keep up its defence expenditure at a particular optimum level. After the 1971 Indo-Pak conflict and subsequent massive military build up of Pakistan with the US support, India was left with no option but to increase its defence budget. It acquired French Mirage fighter planes at a cost of about $ 500 million and later British Sea Harrier fighter aircrafts were purchased for the Indian naval fleet. The existing mix of Soviet fighter planes, MIG-21, MIG-23 & MIG-27 was augmented by MIG-29s (Chopra, 1990). In 2006, India's spending on defence came down to only 2.6 percent of the GDP. Since its birth in 1947, Pakistan (a twin of India) for a variety of reasons has been striving to project itself as a countervailing power to India in South Asia. It continues to nurse this ambition till today.

The problem becomes serious when this self-image begins to impinge on India's security & integrity and retards normalization of Indo-Pak relations. Pakistan is much smaller than India—about eight times in population and five times smaller in area. In many indicators of socio-economic development, industrialization, export-import, literacy & education, science & technology, as well as agriculture, India has an edge over Pakistan (Ayoob, 1977). In per capita energy production, urbanization, health & medical care and per capita GNP Pakistan is ahead. Pakistan also spends more GNP per capita on defence namely between US$ 26-29, despite the US military help as compared to India which spends only US$ 9-10 and that too without any monetary help from other countries (Chopra, 1990).

In the eighties Pakistan's military budget increased significantly. Even during President Bhutto's time, the armed forces expanded by about 70 percent during 1972 to 1977, with equipment worth US$ 2 billion. Consequently, defence spending during Bhutto's period almost doubled. After general Zia's coup the defence budget kept going up continuously. It became double in 1983-84, and trebled by 1984-85, accounting for 30 per cent of Pakistan's total budget. This trend has been going up during the last decade also. In 1976, Saudi Arabia provided US$ 1.1 billion to Pakistan, of which US$ 550 millions went for modernization of armed forces, in addition to what was supplied by the US free of charges. This heavy expenditure on defence began to tell upon the fragile economy of Pakistan. Its growth rate fell down to 5.1 percent of GDP in 1988-89 as against 6.2 percent during the previous decade. The industrial growth of Pakistan also showed a downward trend. In one year it came down to 3.1 from 10 percent, partly also because of the ethnic conflicts within the country.

The large scale industry showed a miserable growth rate of 1.2 percent in 1988-89. It became only a dependent industrial sector in the sense that its manufacturing activity has remained confined to the production of cotton textiles, leather goods, surgical instruments, sugar, cement and fertilizers. The only heavy industry built in Pakistan is the Karachi Steel Mill, the gift of Soviet Russia (Chopra, 1990). The USAID study of Pakistan's economy noted in 1987 "Pakistan cannot continue on this path much longer without serious adverse consequences" (Chopra, 1990).

According to a leading economist of Pakistan, a "perverse relationship seems to be emerging between debts, development and defence; large defence expenditure is presumably made to preserve our national sovereignty. At the same time it looks up into a pattern of development that while increasing our dependence on fresh loans also generates fragile economic structure." It has to be admitted that Ms. Benazir Bhutto did make some attempts to save the economy of the country from collapse. The overall budget deficit was reduced to 1.7 percent of GDP from 8.4 to 6.7. Nawaz Sharif could not improve the economy people had expected from him. The latest available figure for 1998-99 is 23.95 percent.

The important point to note is that defence expenditure and debt servicing have been exceeding total revenue—422 billion against the expected revenue of 367 billion rupees in 1998-99. This makes it clear that it is in the interest of people of both Pakistan and India that confidence-building measures are taken up. Recently, there were several exchanges in the fields of culture, trade and sports. Taking lead, Prime Minister Vajpayee undertook a groundbreaking bus ride to normalize relations and a Declaration was signed between him and Nawaz Sharif at Lahore. However, in the summer of 1999 the Kargil conflict washed off all the goodwill that had emerged from the Lahore declarations (Nanda, 1999, 2001; Joshi, 2000; Mohan, 2000; Krishna & Chari, 2001).

However, even now if the two new governments can resolve conflicts and tension, defence expenditure can be reduced. It is not merely the comparative frame-work of Indo-Pak defence capability, including nuclear arsenals and missiles, which affect the security and stability environment of the region, it is the thinking of the people (which is generally not seen in Pakistan's governments). It is also a strange irony of the situation that each one of the army rulers in Pakistan had received the US sympathy and support. The single exception was the directly elected leader that Pakistan has had up to eighties, Z.A. Bhutto who in his last testimonial mentioned that he has warned by the US that he would be made a "horrible example" if he defied the US. Perhaps, he was, as he went to the gallows (Bhutto 1971, 1979).

During 1982 to 1984 there were frequent reports in the media that India, in partnership with Israel, had plans to strike Pakistan's principal nuclear complex in Kahuta. This was a great cause for Islamabad to worry about. India too was concerned because it had a large nuclear complex near Mumbai within easy, over-the-sea reach of Islamabad's newly acquired F-16 nuclear carriers. President Zia therefore, found a reason to visit New Delhi on December 17, 1985. During this visit six normalization measures, including an agreement not to attack each other's nuclear facilities, were accepted. Zia visited India several times.

Academies in the West have recorded the 54 years negation of the holistic identities of the countries (India, Pakistan and Bangladesh) by focusing on the history, economics, culture and politics of the post-1947 India, while giving Pakistan only a short drift. The fact is that despite the ascription of separate nationalities, the three countries share a long pre-partition history. Yet, these states have worked to alienate us from our roots. We have fought wars or *tamashas* (spectacles) for the world to witness. What is done is done – but it is not understood why, now that we have our separate houses, can we not live in them as a family? This is a big question even in the minds of most of the people in the world and gained further importance due to the 1999 Kargil conflict, just after signing the Lahore Declarations (Nanda, 2001; Behl, 2000; Krishna & Chari, 2001).

To be fair, some groups and local communities, like the Hyderabad based Confederation of Voluntary Association, have planned joint festivities. With the same objective, thousands of Indian enthusiasts flooded the moonlit Indian road leading to Pakistan Wagah border. Indian and Pakistani citizens were scheduled to meet at the Wagah post shortly before midnight on August 14, 1997. It was to be the first such post-partition meeting intended to melt away bitterness between cousins. However, the Pakistan citizens who wanted to take part denied permission to gather at the Wagah post. Thus, the Pakistani government prevented the handshaking between citizens of the two countries, which was to have been the high point of the "Indo-Pakistan Amity Vigil." This action is indicative of the mind of the Pakistani authorities.

Pakistan authorities did not stop with this. Indian and Pakistani forces exchanged heavy artillery fire at several border positions on the cease-fire line in Jammu and Kashmir, leaving about 10 Indians and at least 40 Pakistani soldiers dead. It was reported that Pakistan had launched the heavy fire because their powerful defence establishment wanted to scuttle peace talks between the two countries scheduled for September 1997. The artillery fire had another objective. It was to help Pakistani infiltrators who were entering India in an attempt to extricate Pakistanis who were trapped on the Indian side of the border following army ambushes. According to Indian army officials, "it is also a reaction to the frustration at not being able to stymie India's 50th anniversary celebrations, as happened in Pakistan—it is a periodic act of desperation." said the officer, who declined to be identified. "August is also the time when mountain passes open for about two months, and the maximum infiltration takes place.

This is the time to push in people and material—such firings serve to divert the attention of the Indian army and create gaps in security." A victim, Abdul Aziz and his family reached Srinagar on August 24th after fleeing Uri town, which witnessed heavy exchange of gunfire between Indian and Pakistani troops across the line of control. Many others like him left their houses in dozens of villages along the India-Pakistan border for safer areas in India. This has now become a ritual on the LOC due to frequent firing and shelling by the Pak army. Nearly all the border villages in Jammu and Kashmir often come under fire from across the border. The firing was reported to be the maximum in Kupwara and Uri sectors as well as on the Siachin Glacier (Joshi, 2000; Nanda, 2001).

In February 1999, while the Indian Prime Minister, Vajpayee was going to Lahore to sign an agreement with Pakistan, Nawaz Sharif had already consented to the sending of infiltrators in the Kargil sector to occupy the Indian territory and cut off the Leh-Srinagar highway leading to the Siachin glacier (Nanda, 1999, 2001; Joshi, 2000). Had he succeeded in his plans, the Siachin would have been his next target. During this period, the terrorists resorted to heavy firing on the office building of Srinagar Police Commissioner, where Vajpayee and Farookh Abdullah were supposed to visit. Fortunately, at the eleventh hour the plan was cancelled and none of the dignitaries go there and thus no harm could be done to them (Behl, 2000; Joshi 2000; Mohan 2000).

In the past few years, Karachi appears to have lapsed into a situation where murder and mayhem have become the daily routine for paramilitary rangers against Mohajir Quami Movement (MQM) activists. Mohajirs are the Urdu-speaking migrants from India's northern states who settled in Karachi and other cities in Sindh after partition and are alleged to have obvious sympathy for improving relations with India. Similarly, the Shia Muslims and the minorities have not only been ill treated but also converted to reduce their populations and contribute in making Pakistan a nation of purely Sunni Muslims. Similarly in Baluchistan residents are against Pak government. They blasted gas pipeline, because a lady doctor was molested and because Baluchistan does not get enough funds for development of the area.

Treatment of Hindus in Pakistan

The population of Hindus has been reduced to one-tenth of what it was at the time of partition in 1947. A Hindu judge, Rana Bhagwan Dass was first denied promotion in the High Court so that he would not be able to go to the Supreme Court in future. Later, on interference from some organizations he was promoted and now he is working as a judge in the Supreme Court. However, being a Hindu, despite his seniority he (Rana B. Dass) was not made the Chief Justice and instead his junior (a Muslim) had been promoted to the post of Chief Justice of Supreme Court by Musharraf's government in March, 2007. When he was being replaced by his junior as per order of the government there were agitations by the advocates and boycott by the bar council etc.

As a last resort the senior most judge of the Pakistani judiciary and the only Hindu judge, Rana B. Dass was sworn in as C.J. during the end of March and soon after he was asked to proceed on long leave. The case of suspended Chief Justice

Iftikhar Mohammad Chowdhuri was heard by the Supreme Court Judicial Council and Pakistan Government had to yield. Choudhuri was declared to be the rightful Chief Justice. A Pakistani newspaper 'News in Line' in its commentary during February 1991 and later others had mentioned that the minorities in Pakistan were and are being persecuted. There had been an attack on Christians during a prayer meeting at Bahawalpur in which 18 people died. It has mentioned several events in which Hindus, Christians and Ahmadis have been blackmailed or considered as Indian agents. The situation has become much worse after Ram Janam Bhumi temple in Ayodhya (earlier converted into Babri Mosque) was dismantled in India. Hindu temples were destroyed and Hindu families were attacked and given inhuman treatment.

Faced with this situation Chaman Lal born and brought up in Kotli (Sialkot) in Pakistan said good-bye to his birth country with a desire to settle in Indian permanently along his wife Shradho Devi in 1997 (Priti Jairath, Jalandhar, December 7, 2001). They moved to India for the sake of his religion, although they are sorry because several of their family members are still in Pakistan, being persecuted simply because they are Hindus. An unfortunate mother (Pushpa Devi) left Pakistan for good after her 2 daughters were molested and forcefully converted to Islam. She was accompanied by 2 daughters and a son. She narrated story at Atari Railway Station. She had to leave the country and property because of extremist Muslims (Amar Ujala, November 20, 2001).

Similarly, a minority leader and PPP's worker S.D. Chawla was murdered in Jakokabad on January 31, 2002 and Sindhi community organized a Bandh (closure of all activities) in the city on 1st February, 2002. On October 28th 2001 armed men attacked a Church in Bahawalpur, killed 18 people, including women and children. Four masked gunmen sprayed with bullets. Gyan Singh, a member of National Assembly, informed that a 14 year Hindu girl was forcefully confined in the house by Hazi Ramzan. She is being molested by Hazi and his son (Amar Ujala, October 24, 2004). The acts are apparently a reflection of hatred against minorities, as is apparent from the above mentioned and many other atrocities on Hindus. The hatred was further enhanced by the operation 'Enduring Freedom' and consequently there were several attacks later (Seattle Post Intelligencer, September 26, 2002). In Queta 4 Hindus were killed in a wine shop by tying hands first and then spraying with bullets (Amar Ujala, February 10, 2003).

In a few months later again in Quetta 3 Sunnis entered a Shiite mosque. Two of the suicide-squad 'Fidayeen' detonated their bombs to kill Namazis and the third sprayed them with bullets, which made 32 dead and several others injured (Agencies Islamabad July 5, 2003). On the other hand in India Pakistani children were given free treatment and open heart surgery in Delhi and Bangalore recently. Indian government too provided help in this matter (Amar Ujala, November 5, 2004). Despite mortar shelling by Pak forces, a 13 year old Aisha Shabas from Pakistan was operated, free of charge, in the Kerala Insititute of Medical Sciences. These and other free heart operations in the past are giving a good message to Pakistani junta (IANS, January 25, 2005).

The meetings of the Indian and Pakistani external affairs secretaries started again after Nawaz Sharif's government, helped by MQM, came into power in Pakistan. For several decades following the 1972 Shimla Summit, no official meeting was held between the two nations and consequently relations remained tense. A few short talks were held between the two governments and the voluntary societies. The June 1997 discussions were important, and much more important meetings were held in September 1997. But Pakistan, desirous of delaying solutions, did not respond to the severity of the problems. It argues that for about twelve years Indian security forces were not able to suppress terrorism in Kashmir. India argues that terrorists are brainwashed, trained, armed and even financed in occupied Kashmir and Pakistan.

Now that elections were held several times in J&K and popular governments were able to reduce terrorism and restore normalcy. Pakistan, on one hand, is still anxious to exploit religious fundamentalism to highlight the demand of self-rule despite several times elected government's resolutions stating J&K to be the integral part of India. On the other hand its ISI is discouraging public to take part in elections through its puppet Hurriat and terrorist organizations. However, Pakistan has neglected development of its occupied one-third Kashmir, for which demonstrations were held even in London years ago, in front of the Pakistan High Commission. In 2001 again residents of POK, Gilgit and Balistan demonstrated under the leadership of Shokat Ali Kashmiri in front of the UN Human Rights Commission in Geneva as also in Jammu because they were not allowed to vote for Assembly. Even children demonstrated on the streets of Jammu for liberation of GK/POK.

Two years before, thousands of GK people were killed or affected in riots and property worth billions was destroyed. Even the Police stations were put on fire and Police officers killed by the masses. In 2001 again nominations of all the candidates of Nationalist Kashmiri party were cancelled from State assembly elections because this party did not agree to merge the state with Pakistan. Sardar Sikandar Hayat, who was elected to the State Assembly as a leader of Muslim conference (which is in clear majority) has threatened to resign if the president of Muslim Conference party (Quayoom Khan) is prevented from becoming the President of the state. It may be stated that on several occasion Quayoom Khan had criticized the military regime.

Therefore, the military government is opposing Q. Khan. In 2002 GK public had again demonstrated for freedom from Pakistan on 'freedom day' under the leadership of Mahboob Ali Khan of Karakoram National Movement and Karakoram Students Organizations (INS, March 13, 2002). Indians are of the opinion that in 1947 Kashmir, ruled by Maharaja Hari

Singh merged into India (as per freedom agreement signed with Britain) and therefore, they (Indians) see no reason for it not being a part of India. When Pakistan forces and Mujahideens invaded Kashmir to occupy it, Indian forces were sent to throw out the invaders. In 1948 Nehru took the Kashmir issue to the UN. He was not merely complaining aggression but was rather seeking a solution to the problem (that is why he did not apply the invasion clause, VII) (Mahajan, 1963; Chopra, 1990).

In view of the above, as a part of the British Freedom Act agreement with India and Pakistan (Command paper 7136, 18.7.1947), the Indian Jammu and Kashmir is not at all 'disputed territory' as alleged by Islamabad and Washington. The disputed territory is the one-third Gulam Kashmir or POK illegally occupied by Pakistan, which it calls Azad Kashmir (Chopra, 1990). There has been no development in POK/GK and has not been vacated by Pakistan as part 2 of the UN resolution. The GK/POK Kashmiris have therefore, demonstrated even in London a few years back and later in Geneva against Pakistan for neglecting them and for settling more Sunnis to reduce Shia majority as well as for transferring terrorist training camps in the region. Therefore it is proper to hold a plebiscite in GK/POK to determine the wishes of people residing in that region. When Musharraf talked of Gujarat riots, Iranian President Sayeed Mohammad Khatmi reminded him of Shia-Sunni clashes in Pakistan and said such issues are common in the region. But for the development of the economy in the area India and Pakistan must solve bilateral problems (Amar Ujala, December 25, 2002).

Former Home Minister of India, Murli Manohar Jashi, speaking at the Centre for Strategic and International Studies (CSIS) in Washington in 1997, accused the US of fanning the fire of Kashmir conflict. He declared, "Kashmir solution will continue to defy so long as the United States of America goes on supporting Pakistan." Apparently referring to Frank Wisner, he wondered how India could believe that Washington wanted to eschew interference in Kashmir "when a particular ambassador (goes to the valley and) advises us to do like this, and do like that." Addressing the American officials directly, Joshi said that if Washington were sincere, it should not provide Pakistan with military aid and give Islamabad the impression that it can depend on the US support "on all counts".

Indo-US Fight against Terrorism

It is for the first time that India and the US have agreed to focus more intensely on combating terrorism, particularly the spill over from Afghanistan civil war. This was the result of two-day talks held in Washington in September 1999 and later in New Delhi as also in London in January 2000. The two countries agreed as to how terrorism is radiating out of Afghanistan and Pakistan, affecting almost the entire region. India allowed opening of an office of the FBI in New Delhi to help fighting the international terrorism. On September 11, 2001 terrorists hijacked four US planes. Two of them hit the twin towers of the World Trade Centre in New York; one plane hit Pentagon in Washington and the fourth crashed in a field in the state of Pennsylvania. The suicide squad's pilots had been living in the US and were getting flight training there itself. According to the President Bush of this act of "Attack on America" is once again Osama Bin Laden, residing in Taliban-ruled Afghanistan. Property worth billions was destroyed or damaged and thousands of people had died or were injured.

Consequently the US actively retaliated, in October 2001, to throw Taliban out of Afghanistan. Karzai was made the President of the new government, which has since then been trying to rebuild the nation. Where-about of Bin Laden and his host, Mulla Umar, are not known but evidence points out that they have taken shelter in Waziristan region. The US requested friendly nations to join its fight against terrorism. It has made requests to Pakistan to help arrest Bin Laden, who had harmed the US earlier also. Pakistan did conditionally agree to help the US provided it waved Pakistani debts worth billions and it would not allow the US to use its war equipment. The US poured dollars in Pakistan and supplied military hardware to this country. Before beginning international fight against terrorism the US gave Pakistan huge amount of sophisticated arms again along with a very big package of economic aid. But what to say of finishing terrorism in Afghanistan Hamid Karzai is able to control area around Kabul only.

During this period Taliban has been able to consolidate its position in the adjoining Pak areas and after getting shelter here Taliban has strengthened its extreme religious attitude. This has resulted in a great problem not only to NATO forces but also to Islamabad. Pakistani forces and ISI have been providing safe haven to extremists and in such a situation Islamabad has proven itself as a cunning partner in the international team to fight terrorism. It may be mentioned here that a few weeks earlier a group of Islamic terrorists was planning to attack the US embassy at New Delhi (in 2001) but due to timely action of the Indian Intelligence and the Police these terrorists were rounded up.

After 'Attack on America', India had given to the US whatever information it had on the terrorist-training camps operating in Pakistan-Afghanistan. It also offered to supply CIPRO worth $ I million to fight Anthrax and is also helping in rebuilding Afghanistan. Later, India supplied telephone equipment, school buses, minibuses, built roads, schools, hospitals and deputed Indian Doctors & health workers etc. India has also helped Iran in building Chabahar port in Sistan-Baluchistan. A road connecting Chabahar with Afghanistan has also been constructed by India to provide alternative and short route. It will facilitate import and exports to and from Central Asia and other nations. Over 2,000 Afghan citizens were trained in India in various fields. The harsh reality about Afghanistan however is that 5 years after the US invasion, the benefits are mostly confined to Kabul and nearby areas, with construction booms. Most of the remaining Afghanistan is apparently with little improvement.

The worst situation is that of the border with Pakistan, called by many as "Jehadistan". It is a region controlled by religious Pashtun radicals, who do not recognize Pakistan-Afghanistan frontier of 1893. The region extends beyond Pak border and the Jehadi militants have started calling themselves as "Pakistani Taliban". They have got further encouragement from the recent Pakistani agreement not to interfere in their affairs. They openly recruit young men to fight in Afghanistan and hold Islamic Kangaroo courts to stage public executions. On Sunday, Tuesday and Wednesday (December 13, 2006), President Hamid Karzai lashed out at Pakistan, continuously in a week, accusing Afghanistan's eastern neighbour. "Pakistan hopes to make slaves out of us, but we will not surrender," Karzai said at a school. "Pakistan wants you to be a gatekeeper at a hotel in Karachi", said he. Afghan and Western officials have blamed Pakistan for not doing enough to stop terrorism training on its soil and then crossing the border. The US and its Afghan ally say that Taliban have regrouped since their ouster, using safe havens in Pakistan and drug money.

Similar was the view of India for cross-border terrorism in that country. Reacting to a report that Pakistan had allowed CIA to operate in its border areas, Foreign Office spokesperson, Tasneem Aslam had said "We have no understanding with anyone in this connection, and such reports are speculative." "If there was any information about the pair (Laden and Zawahiri), it should be shared with Pakistan forces, who would take the necessary action. Whenever actionable intelligence had been provided Pakistan had taken appropriate action" (PTI March 8, 2007). As per BBC information, on June 10, 2008 the US had to launch an air attack in which at least 11 Pak soldiers (including a major) and 8 terrorists were killed. Entire Pak media (including TV) were discussing this attack loudly this chase of extremists who were as usual entering Pakistani areas to seek protection. Pak Prime

Minister Gilani branded this act as cowardice and interference in the freedom of the country. He also said that such incidence will not be allowed in their soil.

However, when the US showed the video of the attack the truth came out. Dawn has mentioned in its editorial that the new central government and the state government are giving different versions and it is difficult to decide with whom to talk to. Whatever the facts may be but relations between the two nations seem to have soured to some extent. Possibly both governments may be trying to whitewash the matter but such actions cannot control terrorism. In another incident Taliban attacked a jail in southern Afghanistan to release thousands of inmates in June 2008. About 15 dead bodies of security personals were found and it is expected more may be found. Despite all this the US Congress has decided to give ten more F16 fighter planes to Islamabad. Four reached Pakistan by the end June and the rest will reach in 4 months (Agencies, June 15, 2008). Pakistan's army Chief said, with regard to September 3 raid, that its forces have been ordered to open fire if US troops launched another attack across Afghan border.

This action of the main ally in the terror war raises stakes in a dispute over tackling militant safe havens in Pak tribal areas for attacks in Afghanistan. US Officers were of the view that Islamabad was doing very little to curb recruitment, training and supply to attack US forces in Afghanistan. In view of these Gary Ackerman Chairman of the Foreign Affairs sub-committee expressed concerns over Pak funding request to upgrade its aging fleet of F-16 fighter planes (AP, September 17, 2008). India had objected to the supply of F-16 to Pakistan in the 1st place, because the same was not required in counter-terrorism war. As per media reports Washington and Islamabad seem to have agreed on predator air strikes in tribal areas of Pakistan under which Pakistan would allow them and at the same would complain about them but the US will not acknowledge them (Times of India, November 17, 2008). The deal stopped ground assaults by the US Special Forces.

The US Coordinator on counter-terrorism A.F. Taylor went to New Delhi in January 2002 and stated in the Joint Working Group meetings that the US wanted to help India in border vigil. Later one MOU was signed for buying eight modern radars, un-manned sky aircraft, ground sensors and thermal imaging equipment by India from the US. According to the 'News Today', Nancy Powell, the US Ambassador in Islamabad said Pakistan should act on its promise to check cross-border terrorism and should not allow the country to become a centre of terrorism. US Secretary of Foreign Affairs, Colin Powell indicated to Pakistan that if it stops encouraging terrorism in J&K there will be a possibility for Indo-Pak dialogue. He further added that the US is interested in having good relations with both nations (Agencies Washington January 31, 2003). Pakistan Intelligence agency ISI has started encouraging the banned SIMI (Students' Islamic Movement of India) for bomb blasting in India. The ISI is training them on computer technology also for cyber-crimes. SIMI members are trained on 'net-surfing' so that they can carry out violence without being detected by the local police (Amar Ujala, February 1, 2003). To repeat 9/11 type of incidence in J&K or nearby states the ISI has given remote controlled planes to the banned organization, LET.

Despite Peace process started during Prime Minister Vajpayee's tenure, India and Pakistan did not agree completely on Kashmir issue. Pakistan still considers Kashmir imbroglio as the core issue and encourages J&K separatist leaders whereas India emphasizes overall good relations, increased trade and stoppage of cross-border terrorism. However both nations agreed on continuation cease-fire during Foreign Minister's meetings at New Delhi. They also agreed on starting additional bus service between Amritsar and Lahore as well as a train from Munabao to Kokrajhar followed by proposal for truck service. A source described the last round of Indo-Pakistan talks at secretary level on terrorism "We presented evidence, they trashed it." This statement clearly depicts the attitude of Pakistan when one presents the evidence on Pakistani role on terrorism. In May 2008 just before Foreign Secretaries meetings Pakistan carried out violation of peace on LOC three times. India lodged strong protests on such fires in which an Indian soldier died.

After the UK arrests, Pakistan is considered the real axis of evil. Anti terrorism squad (ATS) has found a close link between Dr. Tanvir Ansari, Faizal and Muzzamil Sheikh, who were arrested in July 2006. Besides these, Kamal A. Ansari, Khalid A. Sheikh, Mumtaz Choudhari and Zamir Sheikh are the other big fish. A poll survey conducted recently in U.K. shows one-third of young British Muslims justify the 7/7 bombings as a response to U.K.'S role in international terror war.

George Pickart, a senior State Department official had stated that the US had no intension of changing its position that Kashmir is a "disputed territory" and therefore not an integral part of India. He also refused to promise that the US would veto any resolution, which came up in the UN to internationalize the Kashmir issue. Previously, India had resented it strongly when one of the US magazines had shown Indian Kashmir as disputed territory, because India considers only GK/POK as disputed area (Mahajan, 1963; Chopra, 1990; Dixit, 1998; Ganguly, 1991). Similarly, actions like lifting of embargo on US military training funds to Pakistan because of concerted lobbying by a coalition of pro-Pakistani group and by support from US administration, were received in India as anti-Indian leanings in the US. One ship carrying some nuclear energy material for use in Pakistan, alleged to have originated in the US was intercepted in Britain. The Omega Engineering Co., the supplier of the equipment accepted its fault and has been fined US$ 3 lakh and 13 thousands. Senator Frank Pallone and others have gone to the extent of asking the US to declare Pakistan a terrorist country, which is supporting mass killings in J&K.

On resumption of economic and military aid to Pakistan,

Senator Pallone criticized military aid to Pakistan. Later he and Senator Crowley suggested that out of 176 million dollar military aid US$ 7.5 million dollars should be reduced, which was not accepted by the Senate (Agencies, April 3, 2003). He also asked the US government to allow the sale of missile defence technology to India. Despite a plethora of intelligence reports on China's clandestine transfer of nuclear weapons and ballistic missiles (M-11 and Hatf) equipment and technology to Pakistan, the Clinton administration had informed Congress that there was no hard evidence to justify penalizing Beijing or its close ally Pakistan. However, it was deeply concerned and deeply disturbed because the CIA said that the alleged transfer had indeed taken place. This occurred despite the fact that in 1994 China had indicated to the US that this would not occur.

Republican Eliot L. Engel called the US to strengthen its bonds with India and advance constructive dialogue to reduce tension in South Asia in the interest of encouraging non-proliferation. The same administration (Clinton's) blacklisted several nuclear centres in India without proper investigation, giving the message to India that it cannot hope to acquire the US dual-use technology items as long as it maintains a nuclear option or develops ballistic missiles. Not only this, it also asked Russia and Israel not to help India in military matters. In ignoring the fact that joining of hands between Pakistan and China and arming Myanmar military dictators by China create security problems for India, the US is favouring those countries. Due to such stands, Indians do not perceive the US as being friendly to their country. Even Henry Kissinger, former US Secretary, also expressed similar opinions by criticizing China in his article in Newsweek.

On November 21, 2000 the US Department of State admitted to what has been known to the intelligence community and the members of Congress for years, when it imposed sanctions against Pakistan and Iran for receiving Chinese technology transfers. But because China again assured the US that it will not provide such equipment to third countries, Washington waved sanctions against China. Thus despite considerable economic partnership, which exists between India and the US, Indians still consider the US to be pro-Pakistan (Dixit, 1995; Ganguly, 1991; Joshi, 1991), pro-China, and an unfriendly superpower (Harrison & Subramaniyam, 1989; Venkataramani & Arya, 1996).

This perception was reinforced when former US Assistant Secretary of State, Robin Raphel, made anti-Indian statements, and when his successor told Congress that the US administration would prevail on Russia to eschew selling nuclear reactors to India. There exists a strong lobby in influential politicians for whom the US support of China and Pakistan and pressure on India to join the US-led initiatives of the CTBT and the Fissile Material Cut-Off treaty (FMCT) are calculated steps to make India a satellite nation dependent on the US for trade, money and security (Chari, 1997). As a art of its 'threat reduction programs' the US has desired that India , Pakistan and Israel should sign CTBT, although it has not signed the CTBT itself besides China, Egypt, Indonesia, Iran and North Korea (PT Washington, June 9, 2009).

The former Indian Defence Minister, Mulayam Singh Yadav, declared that India would not shelve its medium range Agni missile program. The timing of this statement was significant because it came on the eve of his (Yadav's) visit to Moscow and days after Karl Inderfurth said that Washington would pressure Moscow not to aid India's nuclear program. Since then, both Agni and Prithvi missiles have been test fired in India and Pakistan has deployed Ghauri and Shahin missiles. India has been able to produce a light aircraft capable of carrying 14 passengers or 1200 kg payload.

It is unfortunate that without a valid reason, the US had threatened India with economic controls for agreeing to establish a pesticide factory in Iran. Similarly, uncalled for were the comments on India's 1997 declaration to the Chemical Weapons Convention admitting to having chemical weapons and protection facilities. The US directed that it be determined whether India had revealed the full scope of its chemical program. India became the 62nd nation to sign the agreement in 1997 and international inspection of its facilities began. In fact, that should be a model for other nations to follow despite the risks and hazards. India is the first country to allow inspection of its weapon stores and production sites. The production site in Maharashtra was inspected, and prior to that an Organization for Prohibition of Chemical Weapons (OPCW) team visited the Defence Research and Development Organization (DRDO) factory.

Many nations in Asia, Africa and Europe have not signed the agreement, and some others who signed are delaying confirming. Russia, Pakistan and Bangladesh have yet to confirm the agreement. If Pakistan and Myanmar do not sign and confirm the agreement it will be dangerous for India and under that circumstance, with hostile neighbours on three sides India will continue to keep its options open. This question of security has assumed more importance to India, as Pervez Musharraf, the general who staged Pakistan's military coup on October 12, 1999, is a battle hardened soldier. He was the Chief architect of intrusion in Kargil and was at the ranks at the time of independence when Hindus were massacred in Pakistan. He several times declared continuity of support to organizations responsible for terrorism in Kashmir.

In light of the foregoing, it can be concluded that US policy on South Asia is not yet clear and realistic (Brown, 1999; Chellany, 1993; Cohen, 1998; Dhar, 2000). Sometimes the US favours Pakistan, and on other occasions it supports Indian actions, but it desires peace in South Asia (Dennis Kux, 1993; Gould & Ganguly, 1992; Gupta, 1977). President Clinton's confirmation that the Indian subcontinent is hardly a priority on the agenda of his administration was well known for a long time to South Asia watchers. If India and Pakistan were economic powerhouses like Southeast Asian "Tigers" the US would have perhaps paid more attention, Therefore, this is the proper time for both India and Pakistan to live like cousins in their separate houses, and pay more attention to their trade and economics, and to the long history of their civilization. What happened to our age-old freedom struggle fought by our fathers (Hindus and Muslims) together against colonial rule? Only if we become Asian "Tigers" we will get world attention and respect. By cooperating with each other and, therefore, being able to reduce the spending on defence and security, both nations can alleviate poverty through population regulation, increase their gross national product, control environmental pollution, and develop drug control programs. Recently, Indian and Pakistani senior port officials discussed opening of sea trade between Mumbai and Karachi. Presently many items have to be rerouted through Middle-East (Hindustan Times, May 29, 2004).

A sound realistic United States policy must devote proportionate to America's diverse interests in South Asia. A leading think-tank of the CATO Military Institute, Ted G. Carpenter suggested to President Bush that it is proper time for the US to have some defence agreement with India. Russia and China and others are keen to have defence alliance with India because of its growing power in the region. The policy must be realistic i.e. it must be achievable with the minimum available resources. The Indian subcontinent does not need elaborate aid programs in the post cold war era. Costly military commitments or the diversion of huge American resources are not required. Personal indulgence of the senior policy makers and Congress is useful. In other words, such a policy would be low in cost and resources. So far there is no coherent policy worth the name, at times different versions of the US interests in South Asia were presented by the Ambassadors, State Department Officials, and Senior Intelligence Officials testifying before Congress.

According to Professor Stephen P. Cohen (1987 and 1998), the new policy should be based on the confluence of the five different clusters. The first cluster is the continuation of economic liberalization, which has provided a new opportunity for Indian and Pakistani relations with the US. Market reforms, tariff reduction, elimination of subsidies, and promotion of free trade zones are in America's interests as much as in India's or in Pakistan's. According to Professor Cohen, India and Pakistan are sensitive to distortions and inequalities generated by uneven economic growth. Growth without social justice will be unacceptable in multiparty democracies. Apart from intrinsic values of democracy, democratic countries are less likely go to war than monarchies or dictatorships. Mature democracies develop interests in calculating gains or losses in the use of force. Second, the US has an important ideological interest in India: a democratic India and continued democratization of Pakistan are not only more compatible with the further movement toward market reforms, but will be sensitive to the abuses that market systems may develop. Elections are powerful tools for economic growth and for insuring that gains are equitable in terms of class, creed and religion. Democracy also insures prevention of human rights violations. The third and fourth goals for the US policy in South Asia are closely linked.

It is difficult for the weak or unstable democracies to accommodate the views of the hostile nations. The US has tried for the forty years to arrange a deal on Kashmir but has failed. Therefore, the US should not press for a quick solution of the Kashmir problem but rather help create the conditions under which satisfactory solutions can emerge. In fact, the United States should assist the Indian and Pakistani nuclear weapon programs in the opinion of Professor Cohen. Nuclear weapons provide Pakistan the confidence to deal with India. For India they are an additional incentive for its security as well as to normalize its ties with Pakistan and China. They act as deterrents to both countries to deploy them. It is unlikely that India or Pakistan will give up their nuclear programs in the near future (Cohen, 1991).

Hence, a realistic goal for the US should be to create situation in which neither visualizes gains in moving their nuclear weapon programmes further. In fact in 1998 both countries detonated their nuclear arsenals and missile programs. Pakistan received aid from China and North Korea etc. whereas India developed its programs indigenously. Both nations are now working for medium- and long-range missiles (Cohen, 2001). Professor Cohen is of the opinion that the United States has let the best become the enemy of the good. According to him the fifth policy goal should be to develop a dialogue about short-term and long-term strategic cooperation with India and Pakistan. India has already given the most favoured nation status to Pakistan but the latter has not reciprocated the same to India so far. In short run, India and Pakistan may be able to expand their peacekeeping roles (Cohen, 1998). In the long run, China's emergence as an aggressive power could raise profound issues for all three nations. In such a context, Pakistan would have to decide whether its quasi-alliance with China might not drag it into conflicts for which it would be ill equipped. India also must decide whether it is easier to wean a totalitarian, powerful China away from Pakistan, or whether it is easier to wean a newly democratic Pakistan away from China.

In the past, American policy towards India and Pakistan was formulated from the top down. Today, there is less interest at the top but more in the grass roots. Investments from the United States have increased many folds in India during the past few years. There are now active and affluent lobbies of Americans, of Indians and Pakistani origins in every congressional district eager to influence votes that affect countries of their origin. William Delly, while addressing a conference at Calcutta (now Kolkata) in 1997, said President Clinton desires to improve business ties, political, cultural and war agreements with India but these involve long processes and difficult work. He said that by removing controls and by liberalization the opportunities for better trade with the US are increasing and can lead to higher living standards of Indians (Cohen, 2001).

Kashmir Fatigue in Pakistan and India

Professor Cohen returned, in 2003, from a 3-week trip of Pakistan, where he had gone for researching a book, 'Pakistan: Search for a Future.' In an interview to Aziz Haniffa, he said (a) Kashmir is not a major problem to a lot of Pakistanis; (b) Pakistan is an ally in short run but it should be a problem in the long run; (c) Pakistan is, in some ways, the most anti-US country in the world (India Abroad, September 5, 2003). Almost similar was the opinion of 50 Indians, comprising members of Parliament, journalists and experts on South Asia, who had visited Islamabad from August 9 to 13 to attend the South Asians Free Media Association Seminar. The event turned into a peace delegation to support Prime Minister Vajpayee's efforts to usher peace. They met President Musharraf, Prime Minister Jamali and Foreign Minister Kasuri and were accompanied by local journalists wherever they went. Their views can be summed up in the statement, "There is a Kashmir fatigue visible in Pakistan" (India Abroad, August 22, 2003).

Similarly, Peoples Forum delegates too felt the warmth of Pak hospitality, who visited that country a little later. The new cease-fire between India and Pakistan brought an atmosphere of happiness and enjoyment right from the border areas to interior of the country, after 14 years. Bus journey from Lahore to Delhi started again after remaining closed for about 18 months. The process of rehabilitation of Kashmiri Pandits began. Rousing reception was given to about 250 delegates at Karachi railway station (Times News network, December 13, 2003). A four-member delegation from Pakistan reached India to work out running of Samjhauta Express railway. After 2 years Pakistan International Airlines flight reached New Delhi in 2004 and was received warmly. The Secretary general of the UN termed normalization of relations as a happy news and so did the US, Britain, France, Germany, Australia and Japan etc. On Indian side Kashmiris were also jubilant and the elections were held peacefully in J&K, despite threats from a few outlawed, who would like to internationalize the Kashmir issue (Amar Ujala, April 21, 2004).

The Council of Indian Muslims in London stated that if the good relations are to be continued Lashkar-e-Toiba has to be controlled (Agency, June 17, 2004). The welcome that the Indian cricket team received in Pakistan in 2004 showed the hearts of people of both nations. India has always been on the side of permanent cease-fire and for no cross-border terrorism. Indian President Abul Kalam appealed to both India and Pakistan to fight the common enemies, i.e. poverty and diseases and not over Kashmir. As one of the CBMs, India and Pakistan exchanged the list of nuclear facilities on 1st January, 2007 and agreed to continue exchanging such lists each year to prevent accidental or deliberate destruction of nuclear facilities of both neighbours. The peace moves went on and as a part of the same Wagah border was opened for truck transport between the two nations in July 2008.

President Asif Ali Zardari, in an interview to Wall Street Journal said, "India has never been a threat to Pakistan, and that militants in Indian-administered Kashmir are terrorists." He also stated that his government has given consent to US-air strikes in Pakistan. These U-turns unorthodox views are in contrast to those held by the powerful military, which views India as a persistent threat to give militants a covert backing against India and it is also adamant that the US and its coalition forces do not have permission for cross-border raids (BBC News, October 5, 2008). According to the decision taken last month, trading across the LOC in Kashmir started in six decades, raising hopes of further reducing tension in the disputed region as well as reducing illegal trade between India and Pakistan.

It is a well-known fact that the US administration is neglecting India as compared to China. Even the then US President during his participation in the G-8 meetings in London accepted that India has been neglected for a long time and now it should be taken more seriously. After nuclear detonations in the subcontinent this has become more important to give due recognition to India for its democratic institutions and economic achievements plus international peace keeping roles. Professor Sumit Ganguly (now holding Tagore Endowment Chair) discussed the new challenges to Indian policy makers in the post cold war era. According to him there are three alternatives for the Indian policy makers. One is the renewed focus on 'rich-poor' state issues and mobilization of international coalitions to resist economic pressures from the developed world. Another is developing India to be a nuclear, great power state, which would be seen as an equal by other major powers. This may risk intensification of tensions and be inconsistent with Indian rapid economic growth and development. This would envisage India's continuing its policy and is the best option to lead to the strengthening of New Delhi's international stature. This can partially be met when South Asian association for Regional Cooperation (SAARC) becomes stronger and effective (Ganguly, 1999).

The second alternative, i.e. India becoming nuclear power has already been achieved by the minimum deterrent nuclear explosions carried out in May 1998 by India, following Ghauri missile tests by Pakistan. The Indian tests were followed by Pakistani Chagai nuclear tests and the tension in the subcontinent did increase as was expected when Pakistan purposely started firings on the J&K border. However, to ease tension India voluntarily announced unilateral NO First Use (NFU) of its nuclear power against Pakistan or any other non-nuclear states. The US and Japan as also some other countries imposed economic sanctions on India and Pakistan both, not understanding the necessity of these tests. Later, President G. W. Bush waved off the sanctions imposed on both countries, after working out the US plan for uprooting Bin Laden and his terrorist network, Al-Qaida. Japan also followed the suit by lifting the economic sanctions. However President's waving off sanctions imposed on Pakistan despite military coup was considered by many as a bribe to Pakistan to help the US in Security Council on Iraq issue (Agencies Washington 16th March, 2003). After lifting the sanctions on India, President Bush said that he would like to improve mutual ties with India as he considered its role in South Asia as very important (IANS, May 16, 2003).

President Clinton had intended to pressurize India and Pakistan to resurrect the Lahore Declaration and resolve mutual differences bilaterally when he visited New Delhi and Islamabad. He wrote to Representative Gary Ackerman, a member of the International Relations Committee and the Co-Chairman of the Caucus on India & Indian Americans, "Encouraging the resumption of Indo-Pakistani bilateral discussions has my personal attention, and I intend to pursue this when I visit the region within the next year," In his letter he further mentioned that he was "very pleased to see an easing of the fighting in Kashmir, but I remain extremely concerned about the continued confrontations between India and Pakistan. These clashes remind us of how important it is for India and Pakistan to resolve their bilateral problems and end over 50 years of enmity." He agreed with Ackerman, saying he shared the latter's "views on the importance of strengthening our economic relations with India and (have) long believed that our two countries should enjoy broader and more productive relations." Clinton acknowledged that, "the potential gains for both the United States and India are enormous. My trip to South Asian region will seek to promote a deepening of our ties with India, Pakistan and Bangladesh." He also said, "we can pursue such a goal as we seek India's and Pakistan's cooperation in the non-proliferation realm."

In reality, the US considered China as the natural Asian leader and not India and that the US and China could form a bilateral bargain to stabilize Asia on the basis of partnership between the two. In this respect India was assigned the position defined by the US, China and Pakistan as that of a difficult regional bully, who had to be contained by the development of Indo-Pak balance. This is why the US never worked seriously to prevent China from supplying nuclear technology and material to Pakistan for long-time. According to many analysts, this is where Pakistan is to China as Israel is to the US. Consequently the US did not object to Chinese nuclear and missile help to Pakistan, despite its agreement with China not to encourage proliferation. All the three nations decided that containing India is more important than curbing Pakistani nuclear proliferation.

The US Congress during 1st week of October 1999 gave the President an authority to wave off all sanctions against India and Pakistan, including the Pressler Amendment. Two years later, after the president was given power, Bush lifted the sanctions on Pakistan and later on India too. In 1998 the US, which had never before agreed on the need for third world association, for the first time expressed an interest in participating in Non-Aligned Movement (NAM), in Durban, to which it was invited along with Britain, Japan and South Korea. While attending these meetings as a guest it offered (113-member movement) to make common cause in fighting global terrorism and to deny the terrorists financial resources and other support. James Foley of the State Department said that the US desired to engage constructively with NAM and similar organizations on major global issues.

It is worth mentioning that during and after the cold war era the US did not agree with any movement as non-aligned. In the cold war era, the US used to think that any nation not aligned with it was against it. Therefore, developing and implementing a coherent policy in South Asia and addressing challenges and opportunities for the US interests will indicate the strategic maturity of the policy of the US in the next millennium. With the new government in New Delhi; with the view of the President in Washington (in the new millennium) and a likelihood of the new government in Islamabad there is an opportunity for friendlier relations between the three nations. There are however, many important obstacles, like an old mind-set in Delhi, locked in 1950s and lack of US sensitivity on Kashmir in the past and unnecessary statements that often appear in the press are good examples. Prickliness in India's bureaucracy while dealing with the US, the question of universal non-proliferation and the way debate was publicized and defeated, lack of interest on Indian subcontinent among senior US policy makers/ administrators, strong hostility for India in Pakistan, based on religion, all are important hurdles to be crossed for better US-Indo-Pak relations, in the new century (Dixit, 2000; Subramanyam, 2005).

Representative Frank Pallone, the founder and former Co-chairman of the Congressional Caucus on India and Indian Americans, had assailed the provisions adopted by the House-Senate Congress Committee on Defence appropriations saying that these would inevitably result in renewal of the US arms transfers to Pakistan. Pallone termed the action a "grave mistake", and said "He was concerned that administration would move to renew the US-Pakistan military relationship." The opinion that Pakistan must not be helped militarily has now materialized in the US and consequently the US has refused to give 81 million dollars, which Pakistan had requested in February, 2008 (Los Angeles Times). The reasons is because whatever financial help the US had given to Islamabad, it had been misused to buy such equipment which can be used against India and not against terrorists and the purpose of that help was to crush the terrorists. Because Pakistan was an important ally against terrorism, the US had been giving financial help since 2001 as 'coalition support fund' to crush Taliban and Al-Qaida on Afghanistan border (Press Trust, May 10, 2008).

Expert's Advice to Musharraf

Michael Krepon, President of Henry Stimson Centre, which has an exclusive Confidence Building Measures (CBMs) programme on South Asia, has advised Musharraf to give more time to the "myriad of domestic problems" than

Kashmir or Afghanistan. "Pakistan's will must be won in Pakistan and not elsewhere", said Krepon. He stated Indian Prime Minister's reluctance to resume dialogue with Pakistan unless it stops help to terrorists in Kashmir was "a reasonable position", but added that India should adopt an Israel type approach of supplementing counter-insurgency with political reconciliation and conflict resolution. Not realizing this, Indian government relies heavily on one-track policy of counter insurgency operations. It places heavy burden on Indian forces. Krepon also said few believe that assertions made by government in Islamabad that its support to militancy is limited to moral and diplomatic initiatives. He told the Senate panel that, "Pakistan's military and politicians have been deeply involved in helping militancy in Kashmir and Afghanistan."

He further said militant groups educate and train new cadres in Pakistan and openly hold conferences. He also stated that Pakistan, like India, has a one-track strategy on Kashmir. Its strategy revolves round inducement and support for insurgency, while India's strategy revolves round counter-insurgency. "Diplomatic efforts by both countries are designed to place the other in a negative light, not to resolve basic issues," he concluded (POT, November 24, 1999). White House officials discussed the alleged threat to the Indian Prime Minister by LET with the Pakistani government and showed their displeasure. Since this information was published in several Pak newspapers they raised this issue with Islamabad and expressed their serious concern.

Army Takeover Censured in the US

On Sharif government's overthrow on October 12, 1999 the US Secretary M. Albright was blunt and said the coup created a new level of uncertainty and made it difficult to continue business. The House of Representative Committee passed a resolution, censuring Pakistan for October military coup, urging the administration not to renew aid "until democracy is restored" (The News 12/11). The resolution showed growing criticism of military change in Pakistan. "We do not support the waving of sanctions against Pakistan or the resumption of military sales and assistance or military education and training programs in Pakistan," it said. Moved by Congressman Sam Gejdenson, the resolution was co-sponsored by Sherrod Brown. "I urge my colleagues to send a clear message that USA stands in support of democracy and human rights and against military coups," he added. Brown said if General Musharraf was unhappy with his Prime Minister, he should have resigned his Commission and entered the political arena. "That is how the democracy works. It works for us, it works for Taiwan, and it works for India," he commented. Brown added, "I believe the House must send a strong and unequivocal message that the USA is not in the business of supporting military dictatorship. We do not do it in Burma, we don't do it in North Korea and we shouldn't do it in Pakistan," he said (POT, November 24, 1999).

President Clinton's Visit to South Asia

Pakistan's special envoy Yaqub Khan was told that presidential visit was conditional on a timetable to restore democracy. After Khan's visit a change in official statements was visible. They (US) started saying that unless the movement on time table for democracy was seen early in 2000 the visit to Pakistan may not materialize. Khan warned the US leaders of anti-American and anti-Indian reactions in Pakistan if Clinton visited India only (POT, November 24, 1999). President reconsidered Islamabad's desire and obliged with a visit, under a very heavy security to Pakistan for a few hours only, even though democracy was not restored till then, after he visited Bangladesh. The Indian American Forum for Political Education held a special meeting in Washington, DC to discuss India-USA relations before President Clinton visited India in March, 2000.

A Call for Dialogue and Cooperation

Karan Singh (son of the last ruler of Kashmir, a former minister in the Union government and a former ambassador to the US) now a member of Rajya Sabha, said in his address on August 29, 2000 that a plurality of paths to the divine is one of the most striking features of human history and no one formulation has ever been able to establish its superiority over all others. More people have been killed, tortured and persecuted in the name of religion than in any other name. India's first major commitment, therefore, is to move toward a culture of peace and conflict-resolution. "But for that to begin, it is important that constant support to cross-border terrorism must be stopped." He did not subscribe to the theory that India cannot talk to the military leader. We have, in the past, negotiated with other military rulers around the world. Same way, a leading think-tank in the US considers that although in the past efforts for peace in Kashmir have failed, they have generated strings of hopes and creativity. It was the first time a Kashmiri group have put itself in the driver's seat. He urged all sides to try again to open a dialogue with Kashmiri groups and warned New Delhi that its efforts to handle Kashmir simply as a law & order problem will only feed insurgency.

Fatima Bhutto a social worker and the niece of Late Benazir Bhutto, has written in her article for Al Jazira that India does not believe Pakistan because of its week legal system. Particularly after 29/11 Mumbai terrorist attacks New Delhi lost confidence in Islamabad completely. She and Ginva Bhutto wrote that Prime Minister Gilani had promised that they are trying to find out the culprits of 29/11 terrorists and had also promised that if India's allegations are found correct the culprits will be tried under Pakistani laws. But watching the law and order situation in Pakistan, India was not sure of Pakistani trials. Agreeing with India's view, they also wrote that Mumbai attacks were very serious, entire world wants to see that terrorists/ organizations responsible for the same must be punished severely. Islamabad should improve its trustworthiness.

Kashmir Issue

After realizing that independence is nearing the British government sent Lord Mountbatten as the last Viceroy of India with hidden mission of divide and quit policy as a foothold to be used later as pawn against USSR. Thus it was in British interest to create Pakistan, shortly after it was conceived to divide India (Azad, 1960; Hodson, 1969; Gandhi, 1981; Menon, 1985). Having carved out Pakistan it was natural for them to support it on Kashmir issue for making it a friend in need. On September 13, 1947 Maharaja Hari Singh, the last ruler, approached Delhi for deputing Lt. Colonel K.S. Katoch to replace Major General Scott. He also requested for telegraph, telephone and wireless communications to be established with India, as also improvement of Pathankot-Jammu road including a boat bridge over Ravi. On October 1 the State Government sent its indent for ammunition and military equipment as well as concentration of Indian troops around Madhopur for early induction, as and when needed, as he was considering joining India very strongly.

Unfortunately no action was taken on any of these points by Indian authorities. Because of British civil and military officers holding senior and top positions in government of India no advance preparations were to be done to meet any future emergency in Kashmir as the Viceroy desired Kashmir not to remain with India after the independence. Even Lieutinent Colonel Katoch was not allowed to replace Major General Scott. And none of the proposals of Maharaja were agreed upon purposely. This formed the basis of their post-independence diplomacy in Kashmir. The determination of India to send its troops to Kashmir seemed to have ended the game-plan. If the government of India had not made merger of the state subject to the wishes of the people Pakistan had no claim on it. Thus it is this commitment, conceived and nourished by Mountbatten, which formed the crux of the

Kashmir imbroglio (Mahajan, 1963 & Chopra, 1990). It is unbelievable that Indian historians and politicians did not visualize Mountbatten's diplomacy. The independence act gave a right to the Maharaja to accede or to remain independent. Maharaja was thinking of the welfare of his subject. He knew while Muslims would be safe in secular India, there would be no place for the minorities in theocratic Pakistan. Later it proved to be true from the treatment minorities receiving in sovereign Islamic Pakistan where their population has been reduced from 12.5 percent to 2.5 percent.

Therefore, Maharaja's delayed decision was in reality his rejection of Mountbatten's pressure as also of Jinnah's request to merge Kashmir with Pakistan. Even after relinquishing his post of the Head of government of India, Mountbatten continued to send his views to Nehru, in the name of his "continued responsibility". India made mistake by not claiming GK/POK every time the Kashmir issue was raised. Both countries may not admit openly today but the fact remains none of them is in a position to change by force the cease-fire agreement reached by them. Kashmir has already been divided between India, Pakistan and later China too with the courtesy of Pakistan (Chopra, 1990 & Chibber, 1998). Pakistan made several futile attempts in 1965, 1971 and in 1998 to capture J&K. The proxy war, although cheaper, which Pakistan has been waging against India will end the same way as did the open wars (Barnds, 1972; Dixit, 1995; Prasad; 1979; Singh, 1998).

Thus it is best for Pakistan particularly and India too to agree to the 2001 advice of Kofi Annan, Secretary General of the UN, and work for mutual agreements based on Shimla and Lahore pacts. According to Kofi Annan there is no possibility of further involvement of the UN in Kashmir issue. Many other Hindu and Muslim Politicians and diplomats have said the same thing that LOC (with necessary modifications) should be accepted as the international boundary between the two neighbours. After Kargil battle the whole world has accepted the present LOC as de-facto border between the two nations. The desire to create problems (directly or indirectly) to Indians and Kashmiris to force them to agree to Pakistani view should be given up. For India it is best to forget POK and to accumulate enough economic and military power to make waging proxy or open wars a highly risky as well as losing adventure. This will however require strong will and hard work.

The US once again pressed Pakistan to hand over 20 wanted culprits to India or to sue them in courts. George Bush, Colin Powell and senior officials have several times asked culprits to be handed over to New Delhi but Musharraf did not pay any attention to this suggestion. Thus it appears that the US demand regarding Indian affairs has no value to Islamabad. During his visit to New Delhi, Islamabad and Beijing, Richard Armitage stated that no doubt cross-border terrorism is going on but they are not sponsored by Pakistan. This statement was made in Islamabad after talking to Musharraf, Inamul Haq and Moinuddin Haider. As a reply to Musharraf's comment of not promising to stop cross-border terrorism, the US embassy's spokesman at New Delhi, while commenting on Musharraf's interview published in Newsweek said President had promised Richard Armitage that terrorist-infiltration in J&K shall be stopped for good. Similarly, British Foreign Minister Jack Straw talked to Indian Foreign Minister Jaswant Singh and explained that promises made by Islamabad will be fully implemented (Agencies New Delhi, June 24, 2002).

However, Pakistan on the contrary released, some culprits demanded by India, earlier put in jail. As far as underworld don Dawood Ibraheim is concerned, Pakistan is in debt to an extent of more than 10 million dollars and therefore, Musharraf is not at all willing to send any outlawed person to India (Amar Ujala, January 19, 2002). Under pressure from Interpol, Dawood has shifted his last base recently from his posh bungalow in Karachi to a more secure home in Rawalpindi and also in Dubai (as per information of Altaf

Ansari, the prime culprit of attack on American Centre at Kolkata). Most of the leading experts, including senior defence officials, are of the opinion that if Pakistan does not agree to a reasonable solution as happened in 2001 Agra Summit, India should take a proactive role and offer Islamabad negative incentives like pushing the LOC towards it. According to them India is well within its right to undertake necessary air-strikes on training camps, ammunition stores, supply depos and communication centres to discourage Islamabad from indulging in cross-border terrorism. There are plenty of precedence of such actions in strikes carried out by the US, Russia, Turkey and Israel etc. Some experts however are not in favour of 'hot pursuits' (Nanda, 2001).

The international community has observed India's restraints as a responsible nation. Musharraf once said, "Pakistan is willing to solve the Kashmir issue through peaceful means if India shows sincerity for resolution of the issue." Yet at another forum he stated, "Pakistan is Kashmir and Kashmir is Pakistan." "I want to reiterate that there is a change in the policy towards India. Earlier we used to say that we will negotiate all issues, including Kashmir. But now we will discuss the Kashmir issue first. There are no negotiations, no talks." These statements show inconsistency. India can only hope that the need for Musharraf to make such vehement statements for domestic consumption is over and he can face the issue more squarely (Nanda, 2001). USA may be changing opinion about Indian perception yet India has to accept that Pakistan has been USA's dependable ally for more than 50 years. The US may dislike some its wrong policies but it will continue to remain Pakistan's well wisher and shall not declare it a state sponsoring terrorism in spite of reams of information. The US is against North Korea and also against Iran for their misdeeds but not their partner Pakistan. Does this fact not make the US-policy clear?

While addressing the Asia Society in New York on September 7, 2000 Vajpayee said, "We reject and we call upon the international community to reject attempts to cloak cross-border terrorism as Jehad." "India has consistently sought to build good relations in South Asian region. In pursuit of this approach we have displayed a generosity of spirit that few countries can match" (AP, September 8, 2000). Obama administration's advice to remove Indian soldiers from the Pak border is unreasonable. The US and the world community know that India has been suffering from cross-border terrorist attacks mainly from this border. Therefore asking removal of soldiers from this border indicates that the US is interested only in that terrorism which affects its interests. Positioning extra Pakistani troops by Islamabad on this border is full of trick because no terrorist from India has ever crossed this border and American administration should not have asked for such a silly thing or does it mean that only the US has right to end terrorism and every body else should continue to suffer from the same. The US Security Adviser James Jones, while addressing foreign press reporters in Washington, said that Kashmir is a separate issue and the US does not want to meddle in the same but Washington does want to help in increasing the mutual Indo-Pak understanding. India appreciated the statement and anticipates a positive change in the US policy.

Commonwealth Expels Pakistan

After the coup by Musharraf in October 1999, leaders of Commonwealth nations, at their Dublin summit, agreed on November 12 to expel Pakistan from the group and a formal announcement was made on November 15, 1999, reports the newspaper Dawn (3/1). A decision was also taken that unless democracy is restored Pakistan will remain outside Commonwealth. Islamabad's efforts to get its suspension revoked did not succeed, as democracy has not been restored fully (PTI, December 6, 2003). Pakistan's membership, which was restored in 2004, is again under threat as UK warned Musharraf that unless democracy is restored Islamabad would again lose its Commonwealth membership. On the recommendation of Commonwealth Ministerial Action Group, Secretary General Don McKinnon said Pakistan was again being suspended on November 23 "pending restoration of democracy and the rule of law".

Human Rights Violations in Pakistan

In January 1999, Foreign Rights Groups found that 50,000 enslaved industrial labourers in Pakistan were chained to their cots at night so that they may not be able to escape (Margolin, 2000). Pakistan faced strong criticism in UN Human Rights Commission meetings in Geneva in April 2002. The GK/POK leader, namely Sardar Sowkat Ali and others of European Union Public Relations said banned terrorist organizations are active in GK/POK, particularly in Takir and Domal areas of Balistan. These terrorists have carried out outrageous activities, tortures and murders. For this Pakistan is to be blamed because it wants to deprive GK people from self-determination, which it is demanding. ISI should stop terrorization of innocent people, said he. Mumtaz Khan, a representative of the same organization stated that Pakistan as per its plan is advertising so that it can divert world attention from inhuman treatment meted out to its occupied Kashmir. The public in this area is struggling for its basic rights of justice, education, freedom of expression, free voting etc. (Press Delhi, April 7, 2002).

According to the Human Rights Watch, nearly half a million women in tribal areas were de-franchised from October 2002 elections by a Jirga (self-appointed Court of Law) of tribal leaders, passing a rule to destroy houses of those, who let their women exercise the voting right (India Abroad October 18, 2002). Pakistani police arrested four persons for attacking a Church near Lahore on the occasion Christmas. In the grenade-attack 3 persons died and 15 were injured. In the arrested persons one is a Mulla (Muslim priest), who has been advocating killings of Christians (Amar Ujala December 27,

2003). Similarly, 4 Hindus were killed in Quetta city in Baluchistan, after tying their hands and spraying them with bullets. Later in Quetta again, 3 Sunnis entered a Shiite mosque. Two suicide squad men detonated their bombs to kill them and also several other persons during Friday Namaz and the third fired shots. Thus 32 persons were killed on the spot and several others were injured (Agencies Islamabad, July 5, 2003).

Therefore, in a US report on Human Rights, it has been pointed out that rights of minorities, Ahmadias and ladies are being frequently violated. Crimes against them are increasing and they are being treated as 2nd grade citizens in comparison to Sunnis, even in politics (Agencies Washington March 5, 2003). Three international organizations, working for freedom of Press, have criticized President Musharraf for not giving the basic rights to press in Pakistan. (Agencies May 13, 2003). Similarly Asma Jahangir, a lawyer and human rights activist, had complained that in a firing on peacefully demonstrating farmers in Okara, one farmer Amir Ali died because of excessive use of force to prevent human rights on May 11 (Agencies N.Y. May 17, 2003). She demanded that the case may be investigated. In 2006 she pleaded for stoppage of army action against farmers in Baluchistan and she herself was mistreated during these demonstrations.

Human Rights Agency in Pakistan has stated that situation of law and order is deteriorating fast in the country (Amar Ujala, April 10, 2007). Pointing out that devolution of power to woman was easy in India due to democratic way of life Asma Jehangir said. However in Pakistan the system appeared to be "smug" and needed to overcome prejudices, she said. Even economic condition of people is so bad that they commit suicide. In comparison to 2006, suicide cases in 2007 have increased at a fast rate in the beginning of the year itself. In a report prepared by Parliamentarian B.E. Nicholson for External Relations Committee of the European Union and Amnesty International have shown their concern for J&K

refugees in POK, Gilgit and Balistan. Without telling any reason the refugees are arrested, terrorized and even killed. Their religious freedom is always at stake. In a factory in Karachi a Hindu worker was killed by his Muslim colleagues. Jagdish Kumar was beaten till his death in his house in Mirpurkhas on April 8, 2008. After a survey in several countries on Human Rights in 2007 the report pointed out that Hindus suffered religious persecution in several countries like Pakistan, Bangladesh and in the Indian State of J&K besides some other nations like Malaysia.

Pakistani newspaper 'Daily Times' claimed that Karachi has become the headquarters for Harkat-ul-Mujahideen, Hizbul Mujahideen, Jaise Mohammad and Al Badar etc. They have opened their new offices and are openly advertising from this port city. After lot of pressure from different quarters in the country President Musharraf resigned from the post of President and decided to stay in Pakistan. Immediately after his resignation Fidayeen attacks occurred and some analysts predict that extremists and Taliban are likely to gain with Musharraf's resignation. Already a serious blast was carried out in the heart of the capital involving destruction of Marriott hotel in which more than 50 people died in September. Signs of involvement of Al-Qaida and Taliban were seen in this blast carried out by using a truck. In May 2009 there were demonstrations in Jammu against crimes on Pakistani Hindus and Sikhs by Taliban. In these crimes a large number of families were displaced and the government practically did nothing.

In the report issued by the Bush Administration's Foreign Ministry for the year 2007 the human right situation of the nationals in Pakistan and China has not been found satisfactory. For this purpose 42-day emergency imposed by President Musharraf has been cited as the main example along with suspension of the constitution, dismissal of the judges of the High Court and Supreme Court. According to the report all these actions were directly responsible for human rights violation. In China the government put riders on media, restrictions on internet, reduction of rights of the Buddhists in Tibet and of Muslims in Zinjiyang province in China.

Amnesty International has criticized Pakistan because of its failure in protecting rights of women in the country. In its report 'Insecurity of Women' it has been mentioned that the country has become a market for sale of South Asian women (Agencies London April 18, 2002). Ms. Bhutto, former Prime Minister, in an interview to CNN criticized President by stating that Musharraf has two faces, one was before September 11, when he was pleading for the rights of terrorists and Taliban, the other is the one after 9/11, when he has agreed to fight against terrorism. In 2002 Musharraf ordered arrest of 2,000 militants, who were trained in Pak camps. Weeks later, he released nearly all of them. Likewise after 9/11 Musharraf promised to rein in about 25,000 Islamic schools, incubator of terrorists but never took any step to do so. After attack in the Indian Parliament in 2001, Islamabad had assured Western nations to control the activities of LET.

However even in 26/11 Mumbai attacks and Lahore shootings, LET has been found to be mainly responsible for all these terrorism activities. Therefore Pakistan is in a difficult situation. According to the US intelligence sources Pak religious institutions not only provide money to the terrorist organizations but also carries out propaganda for them. Taliban destroyed 11 houses of minority Sikhs in the tribal area of Orakzai and imposed Zajia tax on non-muslim minorities. This started a movement of Sikhs from tribal areas (Agencies May 6, 2009).

According to many Iraq and Iran are dangerous places, but Pakistan is the most precarious nation on the globe. It has nuclear weapons. Its top nuclear scientist sold nuclear technology to many rogue nations. This country harbours extremist Islamic movements. Bin Laden is supposed to be resting and working here in hiding. Its President imposed 'emergency' on 4th November, 2007 for desperately clinging to power, suspended the constitution, sent troops into the cities to arrest more than 3,500 opposing leaders, lawyers, media persons and democracy advocates, despite worldwide opposition. Despite several demands from the US Pakistan did not bring their elite units in tribal areas against Pashtun radical elements. Till recently Pakistani authorities favoured radical Muslims at the cost of moderates and democracy. For instance President Musharraf imprisoned lawyers because they protested for the rule of law and democracy but appeased extremists and Taliban on the pretext of Pashtun code of conduct enforced in tribal area. The Al-Qaida leaders and Mujahideens are handing over leadership to young Taliban. Baitullah Mehsud is the typical example. He wanted to set the agenda rather than follow orders. Despite pressure from ISI and religious leaders to push him to fight infidel troops in Afghanistan, Mehsud insisted to take the battle to Islamabad and not Kabul.

Surveys on Indo-US-Pak Relations

A poll conducted by A.C. Nielson in the urban areas of Srinagar and Anantnag in Muslim dominated districts of J & K and in the cities of Jammu and Udhampur in the Hindu dominated districts of Jammu region showed strong liking for remaining in democracy. As per average of all the surveyed cities, a larger share of respondents (over 49 percent) said that Kashmir valley should remain with India (Prawin Swami, 2000 "The Game of Numbers," Frontline, Vol. 17 No. 21: 14-17) {Fair, 2004}. Two years later in a limited survey, by B. B. N., in a few cities in Kashmir, Delhi and U.P. states towards the end of year 2002 revealed that that about 52 per cent of people in Northern India think that the US has a soft attitude for Pakistan as compared to India and the US prefers to remain silent on Pak-supported terrorism in India, despite its (US) statements against global terrorism. If it had paid enough attention to militancy about a decade ago the problem would not have been so bad. Considering the crusade against global terrorism, jointly spearheaded, the US took more than two days to condemn the hijacking of IAC flight from Kathmandu to New Delhi.

Approximately 15 percent people feel that the US is neither pro-Pakistan nor is indifferent to Indian perspectives. It views each issue in the best interest its own benefits. Nearly 17 per cent of the Junta is of the opinion the US is not impartial in the international issues and mostly acts in the larger interests of welfare of its allies. The rest of the Junta is confused. To the US is a powerful and rich country and they are not aware of the US policies. Another opinion poll, conducted on the solution of the Kashmir imbroglio, disclosed that nearly 48 per cent Junta in the northern states of India expressed that the present LOC should be modified (wherever essential) to make it an international boundary between the two cousin-nations (as agreed in Shimla Accord). Forty one per cent stated that all of Kashmir, including GK is an integral part of India and no compromise should be made with Pakistan by handing over any area to it. Islamabad has already gifted some area to China illegally and they are sore about it. The remaining people are indifferent. They do show interest in saving money from wars imposed by Pakistan on us and instead would like this to be spent on development. Interference in the internal matters in the name of religion is also not liked by them.

On January 27-28, 2002 the Herald carried out a poll to gauge where urban Pakistanis stand on the issues confronting to the country. As expected the interesting finding was that for a majority of Pakistanis economic issues are the most important and not Kashmir. The two most pressing concerns, along with the threat of wars with India, are the unemployment and inflation. Men are more worried about unemployment than women, who are more concerned about inflation. To answer extremism increase in last 5 years, 63 percent said yes. As expected, 51 per cent respondents have said the army should not inject itself in politics (Times of India, February 17, 2002).

A Maverick academic based in Europe has advertised as

book 'Divide Pakistan To Eliminate Terrorism' written by Syed Jamaluddin, a chartered accountant with a degree in conflict management. The book gives an in depth analysis of the role of Pakistan's ISI and Tablighi Jamaat, which are involved in producing future terrorists. The book also claims to provide information about actual tactics and their strategy to disrupt international peace in the name of Islamisation of the world through holy wars and martyrdom (TNN March 11, 2007).

LOC as Permanent Boundary

According to Altaf Hussein, the Chief of MQM, the LOC should be converted into a permanent boundary line to solve the 54-year Kashmir imbroglio (INS London, January 15, 2002). In 2004, he repeated the same suggestion in an exclusive interview to Hindustan Times in November. A similar view was also expressed by Senator Joseph Biden, the Chairman of the US Foreign Relations Committee. Senator was speaking at a FICCI meeting organized at Washington (INS 19th June 2002). The conversion of the LOC into border and autonomy within India are the two most likely concepts for attaining peace in Kashmir. For Pakistan it will be difficult to sell the idea of autonomy within India because the same will be viewed as a partial failure of its strategy Islamabad followed for about six decades. It can however sell it by claiming that India has stopped suppression of Kashmiri Muslims because in recent years it had been emphasizing suppression more than the right of self-determination. Stopping institutional hostility is as much a problem in Pakistan as it is in India but in dealing with religion based philosophies, Pakistan's problem is much greater (Verghese, 2004).

Rigged Elections in Pakistan

To have a government of his choice, Musharraf adopted all measures to achieve his objectives. Ms. Bhutto, earlier Prime

Minister of Pakistan, while giving interview to Gulf News stated candidates of her party were being terrorized, her nomination was cancelled and information was broadcasted one hour before Election Officer announced it. On the other hand nomination of a terrorist leader Molana Azam Tarik, who is in jail, was accepted (Agencies August 3, 2002). Incidentally, Nawaz Sharif's nomination was also cancelled. According to Imran Khan, another political leader, all top political leaders were being deprived from being elected. "In the three years since coup, Pakistan has witnessed a consolidation of military power rather than a transition to democracy," said Brad Adams, Executive Director of Asia Division, of Human Rights Watch. In a prognosis that calls the October 2002 election for provincial and national assemblies of Pakistan a farce, the Centre for Strategic and International Studies says the elections would be at best 'a transition to civilian rule under Musharraf's control rather than a transition to fully functioning democracy'(India Abroad October 19 2002). Already police and government offices were shaken by a series of parcel bombs that exploded in Karachi, injuring nine people. One package had 'from MMA' written on it. MMA is a partner in United Action Front, a coalition of anti-American religious parties that won in the October election. Zafarullah Khan Jamali was elected as Premier to lead Pakistan government and was replaced later by Showkat Aziz.

US Should not Support Pakistan any Longer

North Korean and Iran's secret enrichment of uranium for weapons with the help of Pakistan shows the danger of having faith in a liar nation (s). Supply of nuclear technology and uranium to N. Korea should shatter the US faith in Pakistan as a reliable member of coalition to fight global terrorism. Monetary aids are not enough to contain Pakistan unless a provision is also made for punishment if not utilized properly. It is a centre from where nuclear technology, fundamentalism and drugs radiate. Minorities are treated as 3rd rate citizens and killed at will. Musharraf is pretending to lead the country toward democracy but in reality is only a move for military guided civil rule. Huge amounts of US aids are being poured in, without proper monitoring on spending. Just after 9/11 an emergency aid package of more than US$ 1 billion was given. The aid also included funds to off-set one-third of debt. Islamabad received more than 1 billion in various forms in 2002.

It subsequently received economic and military aid of about US$ 495 million and US$ 385 million in 2003 and 2004, in addition to reimbursements from the US for military operations. In the second half of 2003, the US Congress first authorized as much as US$ 581 million for logistic support. After addressing Islamabad's immediate needs the US negotiated a new comprehensive economic and military assistance program. The proposed program provides for US$ 3 billion. The new relationship developed between, the US and Pakistan after the successful visit of Musharraf to the US in February 2002. Washington is neither telling the truth about Musharraf's lies nor is holding him accountable. The US is appeasing with huge sums, needed by Islamabad. In Pakistan even the US diplomats cannot stay for long. Their dependents do not accompany them. Flawed election, after constitution modifications, must not be lauded nor treated as a step for functional democracy. Not allowing political parties or their leaders in election led to orthodox Islamic coalition, which favours Islamic Sheriat. Joint US-Pak military exercise was held after lifting military cooperation sanctions.

Earlier Clinton administration also suspected a foul nuclear deal but did nothing. Recently D.E. Sanger of the New York Times exposed that Pyongyang sent missiles and its technology in exchange for Islamabad's nuclear technology and uranium. These nations have helped Iran also in nuclear and missile technologies. Secretary Colin Powell knows about the deals but prefers to keep silent to continue helping Islamabad. Pakistan also desires that the US should not take any action against Iran on nuclear issue because Islamabad is also involved in this proliferation. The world community is likely to press for punishment to Dr. A.Q. Khan, whose pernicious activities were within the reach of Pak military establishment. Pakistani air force C-130 carrier could not leave for Pyongyang from Islamabad and return with a cargo of ballistic missile components without connivance of military.

Under these circumstances Musharraf will have to face stiff opposition within the country. But Pakistan and China keep criticizing Indo-US agreement on civil nuclear energy. Musharraf pledged to stop cross-border terrorism but later denied even discussing it with President Bush in their New York meeting. Before coming to the US, he alleged India's nuclear test, which turned out to be wrong. Therefore, Musharraf's saying that he is not helping North Korea cannot be relied upon. He knows, he is continuously rewarded and protected by the US despite lies. Thus, why should he care? Jim Hoagland, columnist of Washington Post, in his article has stated that Musharraf succeeded in getting huge amounts of economic and military aids from the US in Camp David discussions.

However, the Indo-US relations are likely to be affected by the same and he turns out to be right (Agencies May 30, 2003). Despite all this, additional help is being poured into Pakistan, not withstanding the fact that Pakistan is probably the "most anti-American country", as viewed by the Congressional Research Service. Taliban and Al-Qaida terrorists, supported by Pakistani extremists, used Pakistan as a safe haven for hit and run attacks inside Afghanistan. Consequently tensions between Islamabad and Kabul rose alarmingly. Even the Pakistanis residing in the US have started agitation against President Musharraf. They are demanding that General Musharraf should resign from the post of General and hold a fair and free election in Pakistan. Even Sharif and Ms Bhutto have joined hands against Musharraf. Bhutto has written in her autobiography 'Daughter of the East' that

Musharraf wanted permission to attack Kashmir in 1996, which she had refused seeing the fate of Kargil war. She had also refused to give him the post of her Military Secretary because of his nature. She had till recently agreed to cooperate with him for mutual benefit. However because of imposition of emergency the relations have soured again.

Despite US desire, Pakistani officials made it increasingly clear that they were not interested in stopping cross-border attacks by terrorists into Afghanistan, promoting frustration among Americans, who did not like infiltration in Afghanistan. Cross-border attacks doubled in 2008 and presented an increasingly lethal challenge to the US and NATO efforts to wind up the war and deny the Taliban a sanctuary. The Deputy Secretary of the Foreign Ministry of the US said that their government believes that the new Pak government is likely to have agreement with terrorists, which would amount to a great danger not only for Afghanistan, America but also to other nations of the globe. According to him Osama bin Laden and Taliban leaders are hiding in northern and southern Waziristan (Agencies). The news which is likely to invite more anger in Pakistan is the missile strike in August, 2008.

In this American-led blast that killed at least four people in North Waziristan, part of tribal area where Laden and his deputy are considered hiding, embarrassed the government and is supposed to have eroded support for pro-American presidential candidate a few days before election (AP August 6, 2008). With reference to September 18 US strikes in Waziristan both Prime Minister and Army Chief said that no incursions would be allowed in Pakistan. On 23rd September, 2008 Pakistani Shiite Muslims burnt the US and Israeli flags to condemn the alleged US strikes in tribal areas along Afghanistan border but Washington denied the allegations and said that the helicopters returned to Afghanistan after the tribesmen opened the fire. Pakistani religious fanatics and Taliban are furious about October 2008 US missile strikes in N.W. tribal Pakistan, in which civilians also got killed along with militants. The US has intensified cross-border strikes to target Al-Qaida and Taliban hideouts in Pak tribal areas bordering Afghanistan.

Pakistani politicians and religious people are against the attacks as they are considered violations of sovereignty. The fact that senior leaders of Taliban like Mulla Omar are hiding for long in Baluchistan province near Queta and there is no drone attack in these areas is baffling. It is known that these leaders are being helped not only by ISI but possibly also CIA. The US possibly thinks that they may ultimately have some sort of agreement with them. Unfortunately Obama administration presented Al-Qaida and Taliban separately and later Taliban was divided into Afghani and Pakistani Taliban. The US army was asked to attack Taliban led by Bettullah Mehsud and not Taliban led by Mulla Omar. It is therefore necessary for the US to change its attitude of limiting the terrorism to a particular area to the attitude of defeating the terrorism completely.

President A.A. Zardari continues to deny that 26/11/08 Mumbai blasts terrorists came from Pakistan, despite tons of information coming from Pakistan. However international community demands are beginning to tell Islamabad to crack down on exporting terror. High profile visitors from US, U.K. and Europe visited India. Close on the heels Of Condoleezza Rice and Mike Mullen, British Prime Minister Gordon Brown and John Kerry came calling couple of weeks after 26/11. It appears the world paying the attention it should have long ago on export of terror from across Indian border. Both Indian government and FBI of USA have submitted strong information about involvement of Pak citizens in planning and execution of 26/11 Mumbai attacks and world is waiting to see what action Islamabad is taking on the same.

According to a report in Wall Street Journal Zarar Shah (LET commander arrested from POK) and another terrorist commander Zabir H. Lakhvi were involved in Mumbai attacks. But to protect Lashkar, Islamabad government has denied on

1st January 2009 that Shah has given any statement, as per news in 'Dawn', 'The News', 'Frontier Post', 'The Nation' and 'Daily Times' etc. Five weeks after the attacks and solid Indian government evidence, Pak officials for the first time agreed that Kasab is their citizen. Senior security officials told Dawn News that the terrorists themselves had planned the attacks and to protect Lashkar they further told that no organization was involved. The Chief of ISI, General Pasha expressed his desire to go to India to cooperate in Mumbai attacks investigations (Hindustan, January 8, 2009). In court trials, Kasab accepted all the charges and disclosed information about training in Pakistan and also about trainers.

After flinging around disinformation for the past 79 days and tossing names from Austria to UK, the US and Bangladesh, Zardari's government had to tread straight. It is considered that the pressure from US & West had its effect. A threat by the US to cut off aid had its own effect. This was also supplemented by Washington's desire to undercut its dependence on Islamabad for the War on Terror. Islamabad also demanded answers to thirty questions posed to New Delhi. After gathering information India supplied the answers to all the thirty questions and is waiting for proper action to be taken by Pak government on culprits of 29/11 attacks. Hardly 2 days after Zardari declared that "Taliban was trying to take over Pakistan", his government pleased the same Taliban by signing an agreement to make Sharia as law (Agencies & TNN February 17, 2009) and within a few months the government had to withdraw the Swat valley peace agreement after Taliban started capturing areas like Buner, which are nearer to Islamabad.

Highlighting the dilemma Lee Hamilton, the Vice Chairman of the 9/11 Commission, stated while the US has problems with Pakistani President Musharraf on terrorism, nuclear issues and lack of democracy, it needs his support in anti-terror war (PTI, August 25, 2004). Twenty Senators under the leadership of Gary Ackerman, appealed to President Bush to with draw the status 'non NATO' member given to Pakistan, because of its irresponsible role in nuclear proliferation (Agencies, April 7, 2004). Senator Frank Pallone wrote a letter to President Bush stating that Pakistan must be prevented from supporting Taliban and encouraging cross-border terrorism in J&K. The US gave US$ 100 million to Pakistan each month for war against terrorism. Pakistan on the other hand objected to crossing the border by US helicopter for the same purpose (Agencies, March 23, 2004). Musharraf declared that all the necessary measures will be taken to improve the nuclear program (Amar Ujala, August 7, 2004).

Nevertheless, India continued its strong support for the US-led global war on terrorism mainly for 2 reasons. 1. Anti-terrorism war served to highlight India's view of itself being a long-time victim of (Pak-sponsored) terrorism. 2. India was happy to have the US drive out Taliban (Pak- associates) from power in Afghanistan to replace with a regime that is friendly towards India. To sum up, it can be stated that Indians like the US and its citizens but not its international policies and the same appears to be true for majority of the nations that I have personally visited. With the presence of NATO in Afghanistan and the US presence in Pakistan, a long-term anti-terror war is going to be an important challenge for India.

If Russia does not join NATO will India like to join Russia-China-India group? Will the US like it? India understanding the US and the US understanding Indian security needs, which can at times differ from those of the US, will be the major diplomatic challenge in Indo-US relations for many decades. CPI (Centre for Public Integrity) and CSF (Coalition Support Funds) studies said, "CSF money has constituted to flow despite growing US concerns over Pakistan's assistance in the global war on terror." Congressional Research Service estimates Pakistan's total take of CSF through August 2006 at 4.75 billion. CSF money is independent of bilateral aid to Pakistan. A recent study by Centre for Strategic and International Studies estimated the total value of all American aid to Pakistan since 9/11 at more than US$ 10 billion. According to the New York website the US administration has spent about US$ 100 million to secretly guard the Pakistani nuclear weapons for the past six years.

Recently Rand Corporation has published a report in which Pakistan has been blamed for helping Taliban. It was alleged that ISI has associations with Taliban and has been giving even monetary support to Afghan Taliban. Not only monetary support but they have been arranging' rendering medical help to the injured extremists. Pakistani resources were giving information secretly to Taliban about NATO operations. This adversely affected several US/NATO operations. But Pakistan has always been denying the same or declaring these allegations as baseless.

Indo-US Strategic Relationship

Growth of Indo-US strategic relationship became fast after the fall of USSR. USA's role in Kargil war was a significant step in strengthening Indo-US strategic relations. Later Bush administration enabled the Indo-US ties achieve its full potential. During the second term of Bush USA made conscientious decision in March 2005 to help India become a major world power. The first step was the new frame work for Indo-US defence relationship, including fight against terror and religious extremism, preventing spread of WMD, encouraging free flow of commerce, joint exercises as well as two-way defence trade. Bilateral trade from the US in 2002 was US$ 5 billion and crossed US$ 25 billion in 2006. This was followed by civil nuclear energy cooperation. The inability of Pakistan to have a similar pact symbolized advancement of Indo-US strategic ties. Islamabad said China will build two more nuclear power plants, besides Chinese nuclear plant at Chashma and another nuclear plant already being built to rival Indo-US nuclear pact. The nuclear pact among a dozen accords signed during Zardari's visit to China after becoming President in 2008.

Today US needs India much more than at any time earlier because of the impact of terrorists in Pakistan. According to a report of Asia Society in the years to come India will be important in the foreign policy of the US. It is quite clear that if the US maintains close friendly relations with India it (the US) will find a reliable partner like Britain, Japan, Israel.

The Indo-US relations became very friendly during Bush's second term. The US desired India to achieve major world power status and agreed with the need for an energy deal. This was followed by the recent framework for the Indo-US defence agreement signed in June 2005, a step in strategic partnership. India and the United States remained engaged in negotiations for a civilian nuclear deal, even during President's stop over in Kabul. After President Bush landed in March, 2006 in New Delhi, Prime Minister Singh and President Bush were involved in lengthy discussions on common values, commitment to democracy, institution of freedom, free press, independent judiciary, freedom of religion, war on terror, trade issues, Doha round of talks and agriculture besides shortage of energy in India. Discussions also included Indian plan for enhancement of ability to provide secure clean energy to its people. During this trip, which was the fifth visit of a President of USA in India, an historical deal on civil nuclear energy was signed. President Bush's visit also included his visiting an agricultural institute and business school funded by USA in Hyderabad.

For the past nearly half a century, India has been telling the US about misdeeds of Pakistan and misuse of funds given by the US to it. Unfortunately US was not paying due attention to these facts. Now not only India but also Afghanistan and the American CIA have confirmed what India has been telling all along that Pakistan and its ISI have been encouraging violence in India and Afghanistan. Deputy Chief of the CIA informed Pakistan government and presented evidence showing that ISI officers and terrorist organizations are in league with each other and are spreading violence in tribal areas in Pakistan and in Afghanistan. For the first the US has taken a serious view of the same to warn Islamabad with consequences. According to Sunday Times, President Bush had warned Prime Minister Yusuf Raza Gilani about attack on Indian embassy in Kabul in July 2008 and said CIA has got enough proof of involvement of the ISI in the same and cautioned that tribal areas have become a safe haven for terrorists. According to a US Official ISI helped Serajuddin Haqqani, a Taliban commander, who arranged bombing of Indian embassy in Kabul. CIA again stated that they have evidence showing good relations of ISI with terrorists in tribal areas. This was told by a senior officer of CIA to New York Times after a long tour of Pakistan. Accordingly two senators wrote to the Bush administration to stop US$ 226.5 million aid to Pakistan. A few days later similar statement has been made by the Foreign Secretary Condoleezza Rice (Agency, August 8, 2008).

During his second term, Prime Minister Singh asked Pakistan (in a speech in Parliament) to punish Mumbai Taj Hotel attack planners before they expect India to begin talks with Pakistan. Just after that William Burns came to New Delhi and had talks with Prime Minster and other Ministers for restarting talks with Islamabad. However all the authorities told him firmly that talks cannot begin with Pakistan unless culprits are properly punished and not released as has already been done. Following this Islamabad is again pressing for talks to show the world that it is India which is not keen for talks. The US on the other hand is interested in talks to favour Pakistan for attacks on Taliban in Waziristan. They desire that before the visit of Foreign Secretary in July the talks should begin. Prime Minister Singh asked President Zardari in Russia to first punish Mumbai culprits, rather than releasing them, to resume Indo-Pak peace talks.

During the visit of Richard Holbrook to New Delhi, he mentioned that the US fight against terrorism in Af-Pak region depends on the success of Washington movement and India has to play an important role in the same. The Indian diplomats, Shiv Kumar Mennon and Narayanan however made it clear that the US should not expect India to cut its troop on LOC and New Delhi can begin the talks with Islamabad when Pakistan dismantles its terrorist structures and arrange to punish Mumbai attack culprits (PT April 9, 2009).

There is a famous saying, 'you reap what you sow.' Pakistan had planned and financed terrorism against India for a very long time. Now it is harvesting the fruits of terrorism in its own soil. Lately terrorists had been creating problems in Pakistan too and the list is given below:

1. October 19, 2007: Fidayeen attack on former Prime Minister Bhutto killing 139.
2. December 21, 2007: Fidayeen attack in a mosque in NWFP killing 41 people.
3. December 27, 2007: Attack on Benazir Bhutto killing her and 16 others.
4. February 29, 2008: Fidayeen attack in Swat valley killing 40 persons.
5. March 2, 2008: Human bomb attack in tribal area killing 40 persons.
6. March 11, 2008: Attack on Pak Security Force H.Q. causing death of 24.
7. August 19, 2008: Attack on a hospital in Dera Ismael killing 23 persons.
8. August 21, 2008: Fidayeen attack in front of army cantonment killing 50.
9. September 20, 2008: Attacking Mariott Hotel and killing 55 persons.
10. December 5, 2008: Car bomb blast in Peshawar killing 20 persons.
11. December 28, 2008: Attack in election booth in NWFP killing 30 people.
12. February 5, 2009: Fidayeen killing of 27 in a Shia mosque in Dera Gazi.
13. February 20, 2009: Death of 27 Shia in Dera Ismael in a Fidayeen attack.

14. March 3, 2009: Lahore attack on Sri Lanka cricket team.
15. Mach 27, 2009: Human bomb attack in a mosque in Khyber killing 37.
16. April 5, 2009: Fidayeen attack on a Shia Imambara killing 35 people.
17. April 6, 2009: Terrorist attack on police academy in which 13 persons were killed.
18. May 29, 2009: Militants blasted in front of ISI office in Lahore in which 35 died.
19. June 5, 2009: Fidayeen attack in NWFP mosque resulted in the death of 40 people.
20. June 9, 2009: Bomb blast in 5-star hotel in Peshawar resulting in the death of 15.
21. June 12, 2009: Blast in a mosque in Noshera killing 15 persons.

Because of fight between Taliban and the army in NWFP more than 28 lakh people were displaced and more than 200 schools particularly those of girls were destroyed by Taliban and about 400 students were abducted. All these show great insecurity in Pakistan. But to the US India seems to be unsafe and not Pakistan. Therefore an advisory has been issued to public refraining them for visiting India. Thus Obama administration seems to be using the same old spectacles which earlier governments were using and constantly giving lavish aid to Pakistan. Many analysts view this as a self-centred interest of the US because it has to show to Islamic nations that it is friendly to them and this is why President Obama was on a visit to Middle East Muslim countries. The US has to act in this manner because Pakistan is one of the countries which encouraged Muslim Jehad to oust Russia from Afghanistan.

This ultimately developed into global terrorism. Thanks to CIA of the US and ISI of Pakistan for fattening Jehad. If the US is really seriously after terrorism why it is not taking strong steps against terrorism inciting nations? The same US had vowed in 2001 to arrest Bin Laden (dead or alive) and it is known he is taking shelter in Pakistan. Despite this fact the very same US is generously raining dollars on Pakistan continuously (on the pretext of fight against terror war) at the cost of welfare of its own citizens and bulk of this aid is going to be spent either on making nuclear weapons or on defence spending for which it has already declared an increase of 15.5 percent over previous budget.

According to a report of Pentagon large quantities of arms were supplied to Islamabad. Surprisingly, these arms had nothing to do with terror war. For example eight P-3 C Orion Sea watch planes were purchased by Pakistan and the same were not for terror war. Similarly more than 5,000 toe missiles were ordered and 2007 were already supplied. Even F-16 fighter plane-kits were also purchased which had nothing to do with terror war. All these facts were known to President Bush and Defence Secretary yet the new government has arranged to triple the aid at a time when its own people are facing hardship (PT, Washington). Foreign Relations Committee of the Senate has approved under the act "Pakistan Enduring Assistance and Cooperation Act 2009" that for the next five years Islamabad shall be getting three times more aid than what it was getting earlier. According to the Analysts attacks on Taliban in Southern Waziristan is more to please America to extract money than to carry out real anti-terror war (PT, Washington 18th June, 2009). According to them this will result only in some deaths and destruction of property and nothing else. The majority of Pakistani army is still posted on eastern border ready for fighting with India (Islamabad, Agency June 19, 2009).

In 1949, Maulana Abul Kalam Azad, a freedom fighter (who became a very senior cabinet minister several times in the government of India) delivered a convocation address at the Aligarh Muslim University, the institution which can claim that it has done as much as Jinnah to create Pakistan. There, Azad stated, "I am not aware what the state of your minds is today, nor in what colours the future appears to you. Does it bring to you the message of closing doors or of the opening gates that introduce you to new vistas of experience? I do not know your visions but I will tell you what visions I see. I see the doors that were closed have now opened." As per Persian poet- translated in English:

"What you and I hear are different;
You hear the sound of closing doors,
But I of the doors that open."

11

Strategies and Relations among *Star Nations*

B.B. Nagaich and Rajiv Nagaich

For more than sixty years, relations between India and the US have had several ups and downs, always with Pakistan affecting the same (Gary, 1992; Gold & Ganguly, 1992; Harrison & Geoffray, 1993). They were occasionally friendly, sometimes indifferent and a few times estranged (Dennis Kux, 1993; Dixit, 1998; Cohen, 1998). Under their different historical, social and economic conditions both countries were bound to adopt different policies on various issues. Why have the two old democratic nations found themselves at loggerheads with each other? The root cause lies in national security matters of importance to them. For India, the stumbling block has been the US-Pakistan ties. For US, the problem has been India's ties with the USSR and the non-alignment (Gupta, 1996; Harrison & Subramanyam, 1998; Limaye, 1993). As stated earlier, Indo-US mutual relations are guided by their relations with other countries, mainly five or six (called star nations hereafter).

Star Nations

Therefore, it would be interesting to discuss the strategy and relations between these, i.e. Bangladesh, China, India, Pakistan the US, and USSR from the beginning of India's freedom and birth of Pakistan. It is said that the tribal invasion (supported by Pakistan) of Kashmir in 1947 was planned by the former ruler, Great Britain and implemented by the newly created Pakistan in their own interests. By the very fact that Kashmiris bravely fought the plundering invaders, proves that the raiders were not Kashmiris and had no sympathy with Kashmir. The defeat of invaders by the people of Kashmir, supported and guided by Indian forces is one of the most glowing chapters in the history of struggle for the multi-religion democratic unity of the Indian or Hindustani dominion (Azad, 1960; Bhattacharya, 1994; Chopra, 1990).

After his visit to Lahore, Mountbatten (noted by Campbell Johnson, 1951) started exploring the Indian Cabinet for the acceptance of his new line, cease-fire and plebiscite under the auspices of the UN. Now that the Kashmir Maharaja has signed accession papers, Mountbatten could not object to the use of Indian troops in Kashmir. His new argument (again noted by Campbell Johnson) was that if the Indian army advanced beyond Uri town, near the border, for throwing out infiltrators remained in occupation of their illegally occupied part of Kashmir, it will start an open war. This is a mysterious question to Indians, which has never been answered satisfactorily up till now.

However it is interesting to note that there were plenty of British Officers in high positions in the Indian army at that time. One cannot condone the fact that Mountbatten and Commander-in-Chief, General Lockhart, who should have been loyal to India, also did what was in the interest of Pakistan. Evidently Mountbatten's actions showed his pro-Pakistan policy with regards to Kashmir. First it was on his insistence on the "wishes of people" before accession though there is no provision for it in the India Freedom Act. Second was, creating 2-day delay in sending Indian troops to Kashmir even though the invaders were nearing Srinagar. Third was making the accession provisional. Fourth was, committing the country to a plebiscite while complaining to the UN, under a wrong clause. Fifth, making the military operations slow by frightening the country with possibility of a war. Sixth, a premature cease-fire to enable Pakistan to retain a big chunk of Indian territory.

Although later (in 1951) a Constituent Assembly was

actually elected on the basis of adult-franchise and this assembly also confirmed the accession of Kashmir to India, which was in 1947 signed by the Maharaja on the support of the National Conference party. Therefore, a plebiscite under the U.N. would question the independence and sovereignty by permitting an internal matter being decided under a foreign organization. The Government of India finally referred the Kashmir issue to the Security Council on December 31, 1947 (Mahajan, 1963; Lamb, 1967 and other). Pakistan's representative, Zafrullah Khan did not question the legal validity of accession of Kashmir, as Jinnah, the Pakistani President was himself a legal expert.

It may be recalled that the invaders were not only trained and equipped by Pakistan but even regular units of army were sent along with them. Pakistan admitted these facts in 1948, when the UNCIP members visited Kashmir areas. Who then stampeded in the Security Council in brushing away the simple question of aggression and its vacation as well as substituting it by the question of free plebiscite? It is very interesting to note what Warren Austin, the US representative said in the UN after India and Pakistan had stated their case. He said, "How are you going to ask the tribesmen to retire? Only when they are satisfied that there would be a fair plebiscite, assured through an interim government, you can give a peaceful settlement."

On the heels was the Noel Baker, British representative. He said, "The main thing is the plebiscite itself. The plebiscite is a vital part of the whole settlement. This plebiscite must inspire confidence in everybody, including those fighting. I, therefore, arrive at the conclusion, as other members, that impartial interim administrative arrangements must be made." With this mandate the US-British allies in the Security Council naturally chimed in the same tune with a purpose (Chopra, 1990). Why Mountbatten counselled India to send its case in the UN under the chapter VI dealing with disputes and not under the Chapter VII dealing with aggression, speaks for a pre-meditated plan. This view finds strength in Mountbatten's earlier decision of cease-fire instead of driving invaders across the border and in his pressing for a plebiscite under the U.N. India wanted the prince's to decide on accession on the basis of the views of people. Jinnah argues that it was not the people who should decide but it was the prince's who should decide in their sovereign discretion. The British agreed to it. No plebiscite was suggested for Hyderabad princely state. In fact they would have created similar problems there but for a swift action by the Indian army.

All these facts point out to a premeditated British plan for creating problems in the region, after giving freedom to the subcontinent , to retain their influence even after they leave, as they had done in the Arab countries. On April 21st, the US-British team succeeded to increase the membership of the commission to include Belgium and Colombia, both dependent on the US. They also kept a provision for inclusion of the US in the Commission, although, both India and Pakistan objected to this resolution. After inclusion of the US in UNCIP, it asked the UN to send a high-ranking military survey. The UNCIP carried out several political and economic surveys, but no effort was made for rapprochement between India and Pakistan. It rather gave conflicting statements to the two governments to create further difficulties. This has even been published in the newspapers in England. On January 1, 1949, Indian and Pakistani governments decided to formalize the military stalemate, with a cease-fire. By February 36 military observers were sent; of these, majority was from the US. Thus the US and its allies were firmly entrenched in Kashmir. The UNCIP then suggested a Plebiscite Administrator, with wide governing powers. Nehru suggested General Walter Bedell Smith but the UN replaced him with Chester Nimitz.

The UNCIP (although originally for meditation) was always averse to brining the two countries to the same table. It cancelled a joint meeting and instead, at the stance of the US, proposed arbitration by Admiral Nimitz. President Truman and

Nimitz both pressed India and Pakistan to accept arbitration. India refused. Pakistan increased its forces to 32 fully armed battalions, despite the supervision of the Commission, which did not object to it. The US was now anxious to send Nimitz as supreme arbitrator and administrator. India objected. The US, Cuba, Norway and Britain obtained Security Council's approval to appoint a mediator. They agreed on Sir Owen Dixon, who had been an Australian Minister to Washington. The UN promptly appointed American army officers as advisor to Dixon. A few months later, Dixon formally proposed partition of Kashmir and a plebiscite only in Srinagar valley. In 1951 the US-British allies again obtained Council's approval for another mediator first in General Dwight Eisenhower but later decided on Frank Graham, who, after about a year, desired that Admiral Nimitz should also be brought on the scene.

Thus it may be seen that during 1947-52, the US played a leading role and by virtue of the US-British control over the Security Council they were in reality working for a division of Kashmir. Hence there was an emphasis on a plebiscite and opposition to a Constituent Assembly to decide between independence and accession. Sheikh Abdullah , the undisputed leader of the National Conference, who was later elected as the Chief Minister of Kashmir declared in 1948, "Most of the members (of the Security Council) saw Kashmir only as a neighbour of Russia and therefore an essential base in the encirclement of Russia for future aggression." In 1950 Nehru said that Kashmir was not being considered on its merits. He declared that Anglo-American powers looked at Kashmir as a strategic area from their own point of view. In 1951, Indian News Chronicle said in an editorial on January 18th, that the Anglo-Americans "have considered Kashmir less from the point of view of interests of Kashmiris and more as a potential strategic base against Russia and China in a world war."

The decisions of the Security Council, which made aggressor and the aggrieved as equal, were attacked by the

Indian Press. Throughout the functioning of the Commission, only Czechoslovakia worked for a genuine solution of the Indo-Pak conflict. The rest were toeing the line put across by the US member. A formula was at last agreed and put in the form of UNCIP resolution of August 13, 1948, which was agreed by both India and Pakistan. India at that stage had agreed clearly on the condition of Pakistan's withdrawal of its forces and tribal invaders from Kashmir. But when it was not implemented, in early fifties, both in Parliament and outside, there was a persistent demand in India that the issue should be withdrawn from the U.N. Nehru himself began to re-examine this question.

In 1951 in his speech in Parliament, he said: "I am not quite sure", if the "issue can be withdrawn from the Security Council." Two developments were simultaneously going on in fifties. On one side Pakistan was being promoted for all round military build up, including in the areas of the POK and on the other side India was being dragged into discussions for phased evacuation of Indian and Pakistani forces from Kashmir. Simultaneously, India was being pressed to hand over administration to Admiral Nimitz of the US navy. Both, British Prime Minister Atlee and President Truman pressed India to accept Nimitz's arbitration. Even in the Commonwealth Conference, a proposal to send a Commonwealth Peace force was suggested for Kashmir. A known favourite of the US, the Australian Jurist, Sir Owen Dixon was sent as a representative, who suggested for a tri-partition of Kashmir.

Tri-partition has also been lately suggested by the Rashtriya Swayam Sevak Sangh (RSS). Dr. frank Graham, another representative, proposed increasing number of UN observers to several thousands and equipping them with military weapons to demilitarize Kashmir. Both Czechoslovakia and the USSR were against intriguing in Kashmir. The real issue of aggression by Pakistan receded into background and created a false impression in some countries that substantial issue was one of plebiscite and not the aggression in Kashmir (Chopra, 1990; Chibber, 1998; Ganguly, 1999).

Pakistan has therefore, time and again raised demands for plebiscite in Kashmir but it neither held elections in GK/POK, like those held in J&K nor made proper developments in that region. The infiltration by Sunnis is creating a suspicion in the minds of Shias, who are in majority in GK that their proportion is being deliberately reduced by influx of Sunnis. Therefore GK/ POK public has often been asking for their basic rights, fair elections, development and the most important freedom from Pakistan, if developments are not carried out (INS Delhi March 13, 2002). They are also unhappy with Al-Qaida and other terrorist organizations, being given a safe haven in the region because the militants have created problems not only in J&K but also locally (Times News Network, New Delhi, 2002).

The UN resolution had proposed "As the presence of troops in the territory of Jammu and Kashmir constitutes a material change in the situation since it was represented before the Security Council, the Government of Pakistan agrees to with draw its troops from the State." The admission by the Security Council of a "material change" by presence of Pak troops has been forgotten by Pakistan as well as by its mentor countries, including the US. They ask India for a plebiscite but never Pakistan to vacate aggression first. Additional changes which took place are massive military aids to Pakistan, including building of air bases, more importantly flushing out Kashmiri Pandits as well as nationalist Muslims and finally the four wars that have been fought, all have changed the situation. Prime Minister Indira Gandhi had explicitly mentioned in 1960 at New York that after Pakistan fought wars over Kashmir, the situation changed substantially and it is too late to talk of plebiscite (Gandhi, 1981).

Pakistan, with US help, built airfields in Gilgit, Muzzafrabad and in other occupied areas, even transferred land to China, in complete violation of the cease-fire arrangements and UN resolutions. What action did the UN take? On Kashmir, the UN Secretary General Kofi Annan during his visit to Pakistan in March 2001 stated that UN resolutions cannot be applied. He also suggested that Lahore Declarations should form the basis for solution of Kashmir Issue (Agencies March 11, 2001).

The growing crisis in Sino-Indian relations had expected impact on Indo-Pak equation. At the Conference of Commonwealth Prime Ministers in 1961, General Ayub Khan said that Kashmir was the burden on the armies of both countries and, if that were settled, the relations would become cordial. He proposed that Kashmir be made a separate unit like Switzerland. This is how the concept of independent Kashmir was being put across through the back door. They had been quietly planning that Kashmir should not be a part of India; it should either be a part of Pakistan or else independent. Following this, Galbraith, the US Ambassador at New Delhi, suggested that India should convert the cease-fire line into a 'soft boundary' to Pakistan for easier entry or share of trade and commerce.

However, he neither talked of vacation of aggression nor making GK/POK with 'soft boundaries' for India. This vague proposal was naturally rejected by India on the ground that such concessions could only follow, if Pakistan accepted the entire Kashmir as integral part of India. Such arrangements existed between India and Tibet, before Chinese occupation of Tibet. Another proposal that came from the US was the proposal from President Kennedy. He offered the services of Eugene Black, the World Bank President, as mediator to assist in reaching accommodation or compromise. Eugene Black was earlier successful in the conclusion of Indus Waters Treaty between India and Pakistan. This shows that in Sixties Washington also realized that the demand for plebiscite had lost its significance.

The fact that the US became once again active in

suggesting mediation either by Russians, Americans or later Chinese shows that possibly Islamabad is again playing the old game of attempted internationalization of Kashmir issue, the moral right to which it lost after Shimla Pact in 1972. To keep the issue alive in the UN, Pakistan created a conflict in Kargil sector in 1999 summer knowing fully well it cannot grab Kashmir by insurgency or through political pressures (Nanda, 1999; Krishna & Chari, 2001). It appears to some experts that behind all these sweet talks by some western nations, cajoling mediations, negotiations there is something more than what meets the eyes. In the context of turmoil in this region (Afghanistan, Pakistan, Bangladesh and southern parts of Russia), the geopolitical importance of Kashmir has increased manifolds (Ganguly, 1999; Gupta, 1996; Raza, 1996).

To understand this, we have to go back to late 1940s, when several major events took place in quick succession. One was India becoming independent from Britain and Pakistan was born simultaneously. Second was the explosion of atomic bombs by the Soviet Union in 1949 and 1953. Henry Kissinger (then a scholar) and General Vandenburg warned more or less in similar words: we face an enemy who has more modern jet fighters than we have and enough long-range bombers to attack the US in a quick all out atomic effort. Third was the establishment of a Communist Government by the Chinese Communists on the mainland, forcing Chiang Kai-Sheik to go to Formosa. The loss of China brought to the consciousness of the US policy makers the importance of friendly relations in the Indian subcontinent, whose total population and resources could match those of China.

Therefore, President Truman first invited the Indian Prime Minister Nehru to the US in 1949. He was possibly confident of involving Nehru into the American scheme of alliances for regional security. However, Nehru desired to remain what he called non-aligned (in spite of getting a warm welcome) and insisted to include the same in his foreign policy program for the country. Therefore, Washington was disappointed and began to look towards Pakistan. Prime Minister Liaquat Ali was then invited in 1950. His country was in need of a prosperous and powerful ally, to help in economic development and for protecting its strategic interests in relation to India. He assured the US that Pakistan would be a dependable ally (Dennis Kux, 1993 & Cohen, 1990). Therefore, according to Francis Fukuyama, a former member of the US Policy Planning Council, Pakistan should serve as extremely important entrepot for Rapid Deployment Force for moving into Middle East from Diego Garcia or the Philippines. In the event of a war with communist powers, Soviet Russia and China, airfields in Pakistan or northern Kashmir (GK/ POK) would be ideal (Nanda, 2001 & Krishna and Chari, 2001).

Korean War

On June 25, 1950 the North Korean troops crossed the 38th parallel and attacked South Korea. On the US initiative, the UN adopted a resolution condemning North Korea's aggression and decided to take enforcement action against North Korea immediately (unlike that in Kashmir). The UN appointed General Douglas Mac Arthur to command military operations of the UN at the very outset of crisis. India condemned the aggression. Nehru stated in Parliament...it is perfectly clear that North Korea indulged in a full scale and well laid out invasion and this can only be described as aggression in any sense of term...That is wrong; that has to be condemned; that has to be resisted. New Delhi supported the Security Council resolution calling for the withdrawal of North Korean forces (Nehru, 1950), but it did not support the second resolution on the assistance to put an end to fighting and instead asked to settle dispute by mediation (same way as in Kashmir). Security Council, without working for mediation, passed a third resolution quickly for setting up a joint UN Command force. India abstained from voting, again emphasizing mediation efforts.

Thus it did not agree to send combat forces (because of desire for mediation). India wrote letters to Dean Acheson and Joseph Stalin stating, "...the USSR, the US, and China, with an assistance and cooperation of other peaceable States, can find a basis for the final solution of the Korean problem. Acheson did not appreciate Nehru's stand and the correspondence continued, although India played an important role in cease-fire and the management of the prisoners of war in South Korea, which were highly appreciated (Alan, 1969; Cohen, 1987; Ganguly, 1993). Regarding the entry of Communist China in the UN, Dean Acheson was most critical (to which the US had to agree later). In our opinion, the decision between competent claimant governments for China's seat in the United Nations is one which must be reached by the UN on its merits. The US newspapers were also critical of Nehru's stand. Pakistan's full support in voting with the US in the Korean issue and subsequently in signing of Peace Treaty with Japan strengthened the American thinking that Pakistan was likely to be a better promoter of their interests in Asia. Therefore, the US began siding with Pakistan on Kashmir issue in the UN along with Britain. Later, the US also came forward with military and economic aids and security partnership programs with Pakistan (Cohen, 1992 & Venkataramani and Arya, 1966).

Therefore, apart from modernizing Karachi port, ports and airfields began to be developed at Jawani, Gwadar, Ormara and Pasni. Sophisticated equipment was also supplied for army modernization despite complaints from India, as a part of the US strategy in the region. Besides US$ 38 million worth gifts of naval weapon systems, Harpoon missiles were also sold to Pakistan, in the name of Afghan situation and due to vital sea-lanes and approaches to Gulf. This was indicative of the US designs in the post-Khomeini Iran. The famous US columnist Jack Anderson revealed the 4-point US Program for military partnership with Pakistan.

Indo-Pakistan War

While General Ayoob was making friendship with communist countries, he was also preparing for a battle with India, as he had plenty of sophisticated arms and armaments. In 1965 Pakistan's army, started a war on the western borders of India. Prime Minister Shastri accepted the challenge. The Pakistani army could hardly match the Indian forces. The cease-fire was declared on September 23, after 3 weeks of fighting. Again the US equated aggressor and the aggrieved equally and suspended military aid to both (Jha, 1983 and Ganguly, 1999). In this war, India had gained vital Pakistani territory but returned it as per Tashkent Agreement. Pakistan became unhappy with the US for stopping military supplies (Dixit, 1995 and Gary Hess, 1992). Luckily for Pakistan, Nixon (a strong supporter of that country) became the President in 1968 (Immerson, 1999 & Thornton, 1992). Washington and Islamabad concluded an agreement, as follows. 1. Pakistan "to allow US planes to use Pak airfields should the Soviet bombers threaten..." 2. In return for the abovementioned facility, in addition to the US$ 3.2 billion aid, the US will share intelligence information with Pakistan. 3. General Zia agreed to let US weapons be sent to Afghanistan rebels through his special force, and 4. The US agreed to train the Pak presidential bodyguards.

Despite protests from India for building an arms race, for resulting in the cold war rivalry in South Asia, the military relationship between Pakistan and the US became an all time high in the eighties as a treaty (Dennis Kux, 1993). The US weapons continued to pour in (some of which were later used against the US by ISI trained Talibans), now in the name of Afghan rebels through Pakistan. The continued supply of military hard ware to Pakistan evoked sharp criticism and denunciation from different quarters in the US itself (Harrison & Subramanyam, 1989; Harrison & Geoffrey, 1993). The frontline personalities were Senators Kennedy, Fulbright and Saxbe. Kennedy stated, "Unfortunately, the fate of America today in South Asia is not much different from its image over the past years in South East Asia." Senator Saxbe, in a speech on the Senate floor condemned the US actions (Kennedy, 1971).

The mediation by Pakistan in Sino-US relations cost the US a lot of goodwill in the international community and the intellectuals in the country (Kissinger, 1994). Some of these dignitaries were the Columnist, C.L. Sulberger of New York Times and Professor Stephen P. Cohen of the University of Illinois (now at the Brookings Institution). Continued US support to Pakistan and Chinese hostility towards India were significant factors that led to the birth of Indo-Soviet Union Treaty of 1971 (Gandhi, 1981). This treaty of peace, friendship and cooperation was an event that the US could not overlook and thought of re-fashioning its future course of action towards Indian subcontinent. However, even the visit of Prime Minister in 1971 could not bring about significant improvement and the US government continued its earlier policies in the region. Consequently, Indo-Soviet ties became steadily more cordial as compared to Indo-US relations, barring a few moments. Towards the end of the millennium, US-Pak military, Sino-Pak military and Sino-US friendly relations are continuing to make India suspicious about the US and Chinese moves, particularly in the post nuclear-explosion era (Harrison & Subramanyam, 1989; Hoffman, 1990; Dixit, 1998; Gupta, 1997). Each of the Star nations, i.e. Bangladesh, China, India, Pakistan, Russia, and USA is viewing strategy and regional securities from its own angle, as discussed earlier and hereafter.

Regional Security System

As mentioned earlier, the US has long time back evolved an arrangement of 'Regional Security System' to be able to respond quickly to any crisis in the globe. Under this arrangement, it has involved several regional strategic allies to share responsibility to overcome the crisis. Due to its excellent economic condition it can bear the expenditures incurred in overcoming the crisis. The pursuit of commercial interests is underpinned by geopolitical interests. The US is primarily interested in preventing emergence of a major power in the region. Undertaking the task of safeguarding access to oil resources is another important US goal. The US thus desires to ensure free flow of energy source to itself and its allies (Haider, 2004). In 1950s and early 1960s the US followed a "balance of power" approach in South Asia, first balancing Pakistan against India and then balancing India against China. In the process the US earned estranged relationship with India (Cohen, 1987; Dennis Kux, 1993; Dixit, 1995). In the 1970s, after liberation of Bangladesh, the US accepted, half-heartedly, India's importance in Asia and international community (Kennedy, 1971; Kissinger, 1994).

In 1973, President Nixon, while addressing the Congress, said that the US was "prepared to treat India in accordance with its new status and responsibility on the basis of reciprocity." Henry Kissinger, the Secretary of State, during his visit to New Delhi in 1974 specifically said, "the size and position of India gave it a special role of leadership in South Asia and world affairs" (Kissinger, 1994). The 1976 Democratic Party spokesman stated, "India has now achieved a considerable hegemony over the subcontinent...and future American policy should accept this fact." This was recognition of the reality and an attempt to wean India away from Soviet Union. Sino-US-Pak relations, India's nuclear explosions in 1974 and 1998, the Diego Garcia base issue held back the progress of improvement in Indo-US ties. Reagan administration strengthened Pakistan economically and militarily to balance the forces in the subcontinent.

This increased India's security concerns. At the same time, the US admitted that India was not a 'proxy' of the USSR and that the Indo-Soviet treaty was not a military alliance. The US began to realize that it should not take sides in the bilateral problems of India and Pakistan. During the eighties, particularly after the Soviet help to a particular government in

Afghanistan, Pakistan again became a major conduit for supply of arms to Mujahideens (Vinod, 1991; Yousaf & Adkins, 1993; Wolpert, 1982), but the main thrust of military build up assumed distinctly an anti-Indian character. The US is now considering China as a major power of Asia, with the break up of the USSR. China has therefore been engaged as a regional partner, in the US scheme of regional security for the South East and South Asia. Clinton administration had accorded China the 'most favoured nation' status for increasing trade relations, considering it as a booming market (Cohen, 2001; Nanda, 2001; Dixit, 2001).

It is much easier to deal with dictators or monarchs and difficult to deal with democracies, although the latter maintain long- lasting relations. The so called 'human rights' slogans are assigned back seats for the sake of strategic partnership. Republican leadership has been seething over the administration's apathy in this matter. They are unhappy over the State Department's attitude to recent revelations about China by the Intelligence Community. According to some experts, the US condemnation of India's 1998 nuclear tests and imposition of economic sanctions have been even handed with a hidden tilt toward China and Pakistan. Since Pakistan has been an old blind follower, it is seen as a continuous strategic partner. Pakistan provides access to oil rich areas in Middle East. It also allows its airfields to be used against Russia, Iran and Afghanistan. Therefore, the US has always been supporting Pakistan's views in the UN. Because of its own strategy and affinity with Pakistan, Kashmir has been high on US agenda (Cohen, 1998). In 1998, the US has openly suggested 'third party' intervention on Kashmir issue by China, much to the annoyance of India.

President Clinton on other occasions mentioned that the US cannot inject itself into the dispute unless both India and Pakistan desire it. The same has been echoed again during Indian Prime Minister's visit to the US in September 2000 and later proposed in 2009 by Hillary Clinton to Obama, by appointing Richard Holbrook as special Ambassador because he is known for his ability to bring peace in Bosnia (Agency January 9, 2009). Pakistan is ready but India points out to agreements to resolve bilateral issues mutually, through discussions. According to many experts, the US, Pakistan and China seem to have reached some sort of working compromise, which allows China to quietly help Pakistan's nuclear programs.

On May 1, 2001 US spy satellites detected consignment as it arrived by truck at Chinese Pakistani border. It was at least 12 missile-component transfers sent by China. The most recent shipment sent by China's National machinery & Equipment Import and Export Corporation supplied components for Pakistan's Shahin-1 and Shahin-2 missile programs, able to carry nuclear warheads (India Abroad, September 14, 2001). One senior intelligence officer said G.W. Bush called China a 'strategic competitor' and scoffed at Clinton administration. He however anticipated nothing will change. China will simply continue transfers. "No American administration can afford to be hostile to China for more than a week or two," agreed Professor Cohen of the Brookings Institution in Washington, D.C. Despite protests from Senators, the administration is not taking any action against China because the business lobby is very strong and powerful. The K-Marts and Wall-Marts are totally dependent on cheap Chinese goods (India Abroad August 17, 2001).

Finally, irrefutable evidence provided by CIA ultimately forced the State Department to slap sanctions on a private Chinese Corporation 'China Metallurgical Equipment Corporation'(CMEC)-working closely with government. The company had been transferring missile technology to Pakistan intended for Shahin-1 and Shahin-2 missile programs. These clandestine transfers are in clear violation of the MTCR and other international agreements. The US had earlier demanded from China to stop such exports and China had always told lies & denied such transfers.

According to Intelligence sources, this time Deputy/ Assistant Secretary of State (Vann Van Diepen) led a delegation to Beijing to discuss the matter. He pressed Washington to impose sanctions on CMEC and the National Development Complex of Pakistan that received the missile technology. The officials pointed out that transfer of category 1 refers to whole missiles for which CIA reported its satellites had captured China delivering whole M-11 missiles to Pakistan. Category 2 technology transfer to Islamabad clearly violated international non-proliferation guidelines. This time foolproof evidence as well as pressure from Senators Joe Biden (now Vice-President) and Arlen Specter made slapping of sanctions possible. Similarly it was disclosed recently that North Korea supplied missiles & its technology in exchange for nuclear know-how and Uranium from Pakistan. This year Pyongyong announced its nuclear missile tests, which created serious concerns in South Korea, Japan and USA. Intelligence officials described these nuclear tests as slaps at Washington and its allies, who were pressing North Korea not to detonate nuclear bombs. It may also be mentioned that the Pakistani plane used in secret payload, a few years back, was the US-built C-130, part of the army force that Musharraf had promised President Bush to be devoted to hunting down Al-Qaida terrorists and this was the hunt Musharraf had planned in his mind (New York Times November 24, 2002).

The pity is that Bush administration was hailing Pakistan's cooperation in the counter-terrorism war and had been pouring money and military supplies, without any monitoring. Both Pakistan and North Korea equipped Iran with nuclear and missile technologies. President Clinton's administration also knew about the clandestine deals and later Bush administration too was very well aware of it but instead of taking any action it was continuously helping Pakistan with money and military supplies. According to the New York Times website Bush administration has spent about 100 million dollars in secretly guarding the Pakistani nuclear arsenals for the past six years.

Every body knows that very soon Iran will follow the same path North Korea has taken.

It is pertinent to recall that Pakistan vies with Turkey for the third place among aid recipients, after Israel & Egypt and knows the US will not take any adverse action against it and China. During its fight against terrorism, the US made Pakistan as one key player by lifting economic sanctions, rescheduling payments of debts and carried out not only dollar rains but also military aids, despite protests from its own lawmakers. In this process Islamabad has gone higher than Turkey in receiving American aid. The same Pakistan has been supporting Al-Qaida and Taliban, whenever possible, by giving money, medical aid, information or shelter etc. With the result American forces were requesting their top commanders to permit them to crush extremists after entering Pakistani boundaries. Recently RAND Corporation alleged that Pak ISI had been cooperating with Taliban secretly by giving information about US or NATO operations with the result that several times these operations were adversely affected. According to New York Times reports the US forces had requested Pakistan to crush guerrilla activities in their territory but Pakistan did not take proper action.

The recent findings of Iran's aspirations to become a nuclear power nation with the help of Pakistan the known proliferating nation are disturbing for South Asian nations' peace. Iran has recently refused to stop uranium enrichment program, as proposed by the United Nation resolution of 2004. On the top of it, the work has been hastened and missiles test-fired. Its trucks line up daily on Iraq border carrying food articles, appliances and other materials for boosting trade. Washington has been accusing Iran of sending arms and even militants to help Shiite Muslim militias in Iraq to target US troops like a "proxy war". According to the US intelligence sources Iran is supplying the Afghani Taliban surface-to-air missiles capable of destroying a helicopter. Taliban want to use the SA-14 Gremlins missiles to launch an attack against coalition forces in Helmund (TOI March 2, 2009).

Recently, the US arms manufacturer, Raytheon supplied Indian army 12 Weapon Locating radars at a cost US$ 200 million. Another deal is the acquisition of the amphibious transport vessel called USS Trenton by Indian army at a cost about US$ 87.25 million. Trenton vessel was supplied along with six UH-3H helicopters to operate from it. The US Defence Security Cooperation Agency (DSCA), which supervises foreign sales, notified the US Congress about request of India for delivery of the military equipment in 2006.

After September 11, 2001 Bush administration had been giving huge sums from time to time to Pakistan for the fight against terrorism but chairman of the Foreign Relation Committee said that Pakistan must tell what happened to the money given to them as nothing has been told to the GAO office by Pakistan regarding this amount. It is suspected that Islamabad had used this money for developing border roads and army issued false receipts to appropriate the funds (PT). According to the GAO office Pak air force had taken money from the US for purchasing radars but neither Al-Qaida nor any other terrorist organization has any thing like air force. The GAO report thus concludes that Islamabad had used all these funds to increase its defence needs but did nothing to prevent or fight terrorism for which the money was given. In some cases the Pakistan navy had used money given in 2007-08 for repairing the cars used by navy officers. The same has been questioned by the US (PT).

Newsweek magazine had claimed that ISI had developed friendly relations with Betullah Mehsud and keeps on giving secret information to him so that he can escape any action against him taken by police or army. Further Pakistani government and the US administration both have information of the same but they do not want to comment on ISI and Mehsud relations or ISI Taliban and Al-Qaida relations (PT, New York). According to an American Think Tank Pakistan has not allowed American Diplomats (Holbrook and Mike

Mullen) to meet ISI Chief.

World Opinion Organization arranged to carry out a survey in 20 countries between 10th January to 6th May 2008 from a total of 1 lakh nine thousand seven hundred fifty one persons. In the survey it was found that among the leaders Musharraf was rated the least reliable person. Only in China he was rated by 30 percent people as reliable. Next to Musharraf President Bush was rated as unreliable. On an average 67 percent persons rated him as unreliable. Ahmadinejad, the President of Iran was rated as not reliable by persons of 13 countries. About 52 percent people were against him (Agency).

President Obama apparently is not able to judge Pakistan (which has become a fort of terrorism) properly because on one hand he is stating that the country is reluctant to play its part properly in the fight against terror and on the other hand he is tripling monetary help. He does not believe that Islamabad will sincerely fight the terrorism. This is natural because several sources are indicating that its ISI is helping not only Taliban and terrorist groups but also Al-Qaida (PT, N.Y.). All major terrorist groups have a safe haven in Pakistan to operate from creating a big "problem" to the terror war defence Secretary Robert Gates has said. I think it is safe haven on Pakistan side of the border not just for Al-Qaida bur for the Taliban for the Haqqani network, for Gulbuddin Hekmatyar and other affiliated groups that are still working together (PTI). Facing similar problem Switzerland has refused to sell important war materials to Pakistan. Specialist on Af-Pakistan affairs, Richard Holebrook reprimanded Pakistan for blaming India helping terrorists in Afghanistan. In fact he appreciated India's developmental activities and asked Pakistan to give maximum concentration on the problem of controlling terrorism prevalent in Pakistan.

Russian Stand on Kashmir

Geopolitical importance of Kashmir has to be seen in the

context of the fact that Kashmir occupies a strategic position, which is close to the international boundaries of China, Soviet Russia, Tibet, Afghanistan and Pakistan. With this background in view, the star nations had an eye on the Kashmir issue, solution or otherwise, most favourable to them. The Soviet Russia considered US-British attempts to make Kashmir a Pakistani territory or independent, as a neighbour of Russia on the southern side. This would have enabled them to use Kashmir as an essential base in the encirclement of Russian territory for future aggression. Some thought Anglo-American powers looked at Kashmir as the most suitable region for strategic bases from their own point of view and not from the point of view of the inhabitants of Kashmir. This is how the local dispute over Kashmir developed into an important international issue (Chibber, 1998; Chopra, 1990; Ganguly, 1991; Grover, 1995; Lamb, 1967; Mohan, 2000).

Therefore, Soviet Union opposed Security Council's first resolution, which equated aggressor and the victim of aggression, politically and morally. In the UN, the Soviet Union representative, Y. Malik, reiterating that the Soviet Union considered the entire Princely state of Jammu and Kashmir as integral area of India, sternly warned the Anglo-American powers against intriguing in Kashmir. He stated: "These plans, as regards Kashmir, aim to achieve the bringing of American-British troops into the territory of Kashmir and to convert it into an American-British colony and a military-strategic strong point." Russia had then announced that rather than using its stockpile only when its very existence was threatened, Moscow would employ atomic weapons in case other means for settling a crisis "have been exhausted/ prove ineffective."

This sharply lowers the "use" threshold for such weapons, and is in line with similar shifts in China's nuclear doctrine. This was near explicit signal from USSR that any bid to help provinces such as Chechnya to breakaway may lead to nuclear war. China, Russia and four other central Asian nations have signed an agreement called Shanghai Cooperation Organization (SCO) mainly to deal with Islamic terrorism. They wanted to include India in the organization but not Pakistan (INS June 15, 2001). The SCO opposed the US National Missile Defence Program but agreed to cooperate with the US to curb terrorist activities internationally and bring Bin Laden to justice. Russia disagreed to supply the engines for Super-7 fighter planes to Pakistan, for which it had earlier shown inclination. Using these engines, Islamabad wanted to build fighter planes. Later China agreed to supply these engines to Islamabad.

Prime Minister Vajpayee and President Vladimir Putin discussed the world affairs and agreed to fight international terrorism (Agencies November 23, 2003). About a month later Russia agreed to supply 12 Sukhoi fighters to India. After prolong discussions sale of airplane carrier 'Admiral Gorshkov' was finalized between the two countries (Amar Ujala January 21, 2004). With this deal mutual cooperation is likely to improve further. Moscow is unhappy with India's new defence relations with the US as indicated by recent acquisition of military supplies. Therefore in an arm twisting tactic, Russia asked for more money from India for the sale of airplane carrier 'Admiral Gorshkov' and Su-30 fighter aircraft on the plea of recent weakening of the US dollar. Even as they work towards resolving the escalated cost issue of airplane carrier, India signed a US$ 1.2 billion deal with Russia to buy 80 Mi-17 V-5 helicopters. For this India brushed aside criticism on outdated technology and high life-cycle costs. It was stated that the choppers will be able to land at a height of 18,000 feet in Siachin and Ladakh areas. Russia became the third country to sign a civil nuclear cooperation pact with India (TNN, December 6, 2008).

Spokesperson of the Chemical Weapons Destruction Organization stated that Russia has started working to destroy its chemical weapons and it is expected that by 2012 chemical weapons will be completely eliminated from Russia. The instrument which is being used for this purpose is the sixth instrument of the project intended to destroy all the chemical weapons. To boost relations with Russia a nuclear deal was signed in May by the US and Russia and is now before the Congress. This deal would give the US access to modern Russian nuclear technology and simultaneously clear the way for Russia to establish a lucrative centre for import and storage of spent nuclear fuel from US supplied reactors around the world. But now it is suspected that the US is planning to punish Moscow for invading Georgia, a former Soviet republic, by cancelling the nuclear deal with Russia. The time is not right for the agreement cancellation, Secretary of State said during her visit to North Africa (AP September 7, 2008).

Soviet invasion of Georgia in riposte to Georgia's attack on South Ossetia is suspected to be the beginning of another cold war between Russia and the US or the US-led alliance. This is however predicted to be low intensity as compared to the previous one. The suspicion between the two sides however is expected to take a long time to heal. Fortunately, Adm. Michael Mullen and Russian Gen. Nikolai Makarov discussed a wide range of issues, including the future of NATO, missile defence in Europe, Georgia episode and Afghanistan on October 21, 2008 in Finland. It was a highest-level military meeting between the two nations, signalling thawing relations between the two powers.

Russia will respond to the US missile shield plans in Central Europe said President Medvedev on 8th October, 2008. Further, Russia will not resort to hysterics over the issue and would be prepared to talk with the US on nuclear weapons.

China's Strategy

Main Land China had its own strategy on Kashmir, which till recently supported Pakistan's stand on Kashmir. India and China developed an understanding when A. B. Vajpayee, External Affairs Minister visited China. Afterwards there was a shift in China's position, when it began to advocate the Indo-

Pak conflict on Kashmir should be resolved bilaterally on the basis of Shimla Pact of 1972. Gilgit, Hunza, Nagar, Yasin, Ponil, Chitral and Skardu all occupy a strategic position and came into focus due to Pakistan's annexation to merge them with the northern parts of Pakistan. As mentioned before, these areas are close to the boundaries of several countries. With this background, the question of building strategic highways like Karakorum all-weather road, passing through GK/POK is worth examining. By constructing this road, China has clearly shown its interest in the area, as it has spent about Rs. 1000 million on construction of roads in this area. It is also in agreement with Pakistan for building another road linking Skardu with Yarkand and for starting an air service between Skardu and Sinkiang. It may be mentioned that there is an important military base and a terrorist training camp near Skardu, wherefrom infiltrators were sent to start the Kargil conflict in the summer of 1999 (Nanda, 1999; Krishna & Chari, 2001).

Keeping in mind the internal economic problems of China these constructions, up to 19,000 feet height is revealing. However, with the construction of these roads China has an access not only to GK/POK but also to the North-West India. The Karakorum highway starts north of Islamabad and goes through Khunjerab pass (about 16,000 ft. high). Beyond this pass the highway is connected with western Tibet road network, linking Sinkiang province, where China's military base is located. Through the Karakorum highway China has found a new access to Arabian Sea. Chinese security persons have been permanently positioned all along the road. There are many other roads and other strategic passes on the Indian border with China, currently under illegal possession of Pakistan, some of which are very important to China.

In the opinion of G.S. Butt of Pakistani army, all kinds of communications between Pakistan and China have become easier. China also tried Nepal in the same manner but did not get much success. In addition, there are considerable deposits of minerals, including radioactive elements, gold and costly stones in GK/POK. In 1963, about 3,400 sq. kilometres of the territory of Kashmir has been gifted by Pakistan to China has its own strategic interests in Kashmir (Chopra, 1990). China has its own strategic interests in Kashmir (Chopra, 1990). To pay back as a good partner, China has not only been supporting Pakistan on the Kashmir issue in international forums but has also been giving massive military aids to Islamabad. After the visit of Prime Minister Rajiv Gandhi both nations agreed to set up a joint working group. In 1996 Chinese President Jiang Zemin came to India both sides signed an accord on CBMs.

China shamelessly prepared nuclear plans, supplied its test data to Pakistan, which reached Libya before it abandoned its nuclear program in 2004. China also gave heavy water, magnetic rings etc, and provided training on nuclear technology as well as supplied missiles, although it was under agreement with US not to do so. Therefore, many specialists consider it was done with prior consent of the US. Since in spite of Intelligence reports US administration preferred to keep quiet, many take it as a confirmation of the story of prior consent to the deal. Beijing has also moved away from NFU stance to that of "active nuclear defence" using all available means. It has indicated the employment of nuclear weapons against Taiwan or Tibet should these territories proclaim their freedom or any bid to help break away may lead to nuclear deployment.

As a signatory of the NPT China had an obligation not to export nuclear technology and materials to other countries but it did precisely that since the 1980s. Although China talks of peace and cooperation with India, exchanges high level visits, started direct air service to Delhi, trade promises and promises of a strategic partnership, the real aim is to divert India away from a policy of cooperation with the US. At the same time it has strengthened its military ties with Pakistan. China has transferred Super-7 fighter planes to Pakistan, which are to be fitted with Italian radars. It has also agreed to supply these planes without taking any advance money to help Islamabad, promised to build nuclear plants, naval frigates and a submarine port at Gwador. It has already helped Pakistan to develop A1 Khalid tank as the main battle tank of Pak army. These are supposed to be better than T-90 tank of Russia. In March-April, 2008 large quantities of Chinese made hand grenades and mortars were found in the Rajauri district of Jammu to promote terror. Garwal Rifles has therefore been deployed to make an intensive search in the region. China is also planning to divert Brahmaputra water to its Yellow river for a hydroelectricity project. This will affect North East India adversely by stopping the water flow or flooding as it had done in 2006-07 in Arunachal.

China has proposed an increase of about 17.7 per cent in its defence budget. China has been continuously increasing its defence expenditure since 1998. It has nuclear capability, nuclear submarines and ICBMs. Its navy is the biggest in the East Asia. It has established several large military centres in Tibet and has been building its bases in far off places like Coco islands and Myanmar near India. On December 22, 2001 China has again shown its continuous interest in ICBM program by successfully testing its missile DF-31 covering a range of 5,000 Kms. The first test of DF-31 was carried out about a month earlier.

According to the 'The News' of Pakistan on January 8, 2002, China had increased military supplies to Pakistan. As a result F-17 MG fighter planes etc. with extra spare parts have already reached Karachi. China is also trying to develop military ties with Bangladesh, Myanmar and Nepal to surround India. Pakistan is its gateway on west; Bangladesh on its east; Myanmar is the gateway to the Bay of Bengal, also on east. China is building railroads and highways in Tibet to develop Nepal as a gate way on the north of India. In South it has agreed with Sri Lanka to build a harbour at Hanbantota, which will get completed in about three years. This is the second big

Chinese project which has surrounded India completely.

These developments reveal emergence of the two competing alignments with divergent interests. In view of these developments it is in the interest of India to develop close ties with the US, Japan, Taiwan, and Australia (Kapur, 2006). The fear of encirclement by China has driven India's plans to build up its long-range military capability. The Indian Air force is now planning to send its Su-30s to Andaman Islands so as to give the military a strike capability that can reach Southeast Asia. Obviously, the mission intents stopping a possible hostile Chinese incursion into the Indian Ocean. Indian nuclear submarines, armed with the 300 kilometre Klub missile or the BrahMos PJ-10 supersonic missile, can give the Indian navy deterrence against China (Gupta, 2005). China has the third largest nuclear- missile-arsenal in the world and it has been deploying more accurate mobile ballistic missiles. For the year 2008, the country has increased its defence budget by 17.6 percent. Improvements appear to be directed toward increase in yield-to-weight ratio of warheads, improving multiple re-entry vehicles and accurate survivable delivery systems. This has great implications for China's neighbours since most of the China's arsenals have rationale only for them.

About 2 weeks after the fighter plane supply to Pakistan, Chinese Premier Zu Rongji visited India in January 2002 accompanied by 25 businessmen and signed pacts on space, agriculture, science & technology etc. He also told Indian Prime Minister that Beijing would not be a party to the Indo-Pak dispute. Two years later, Indian Defence Minister and also the Prime Minister visited China to herald a new era. For the first time China has shown Sikkim as part of India in its "World Affairs Yearbook". China has also stated that Indian Defence Minister visited China and after the visit of Chinese Defence Minister to India our relations would improve further. A senior Indian government officer looking after security of the International border informed in Kolkata that recent moves by Chinese army along the Sikkim-Bhutan-Tibet tri-junction, culminating in a demand for removal of two Indian border bunkers near Batang La indicated that Beijing is pushing southward. Batang La is located about 50 km southeast of Nathu La, the main border post in Sikkim. Tibetan spiritual leader Dalai Lama said for the first time that Tawang in Arunachal is part of India and is being wrongly claimed by China (TNN, June 5, 2008).

On November 11, China took a strong stand on India's view that Arunachal is an integral part. The Chinese Foreign Ministry challenged a statement made by the Indian External Minister saying that Arunachal was a part of the country. China does not want to recognize McMahon agreement made in Simla (Shimla) with Great Britain. Foreign Secretary (Shiv Shankar Menon) said the issue of Tawang, leave aside the Arunachal Pradesh, is out of range of border negotiations (Times of India November 12, 2008). At the same time Beijing and Delhi have agreed to discuss issues on trans-border rivers. One of them which bothers India the most is the dam on Brahmaputra river at its Great Bend in China. The project is for generating 40,000 MW electricity and subsequent diversion of waters northwards. This will be disastrous to India and Bangladesh both. During his return flight from Beijing in October, 2008 Prime Minister Singh informed journalists that his conversations with Chinese President Hu Jintao focused a lot on the future of trans-border rivers.

In January 2008, Indian Prime Minister Singh had visited China and discussed many issues and agreed on many aspects of interest to both nations. On March 12, 2008 Tibetan Youth Congress women demonstrated in front of Chinese Embassy in New Delhi, Nepal and later in Sydney. Demonstrations were organized in different countries in Asia, Europe and America. South Korea and Nepal presented a much stronger protest. After agitations at many places, including Lhasa, Tibetans entered the Chinese embassy in Delhi, and shouted slogans in front of UN Office against suppression of Tibet citizens,

Olympics in China as well as for Tibet's cultural freedom. After the demonstrations Delhi Police and Police in other cities arrested the intruders and later released them. More than 100 people have died in Lhasa and in China in similar demonstrations to save Tibetan culture and internal freedom. Some of the EU countries were thinking of boycotting Beijing Olympics.

United Nations however decided not to interfere in the matter. China is blaming Dalai Lama for the demonstrations, whereas Dalai Lama is blaming Chinese policies and atrocities for continued demonstrations. He has been pleading Tibetans for peaceful demonstrations. Although Dalai Lama was trying to solve the problem peacefully, China was imposing conditions for talks. During talks with representatives of Dalai Lama China imposed condition that Dalai Lama should prevent Tibetan youths from violence and from creating problems in Olympic. Only then the atmosphere for talks would be appropriate. Spokesperson of the Foreign Ministry Liu Jivanchao said it had not been decided where and when the talks with Dalai representatives would be held. Since French President said that only after watching the progress of talks between China and Dalai representatives it would be decided whether he would go to China during Olympics or not. In retaliation Chinese in several cities demonstrated and appealed for boycott of French products because China considered talks with Dalai representatives as purely internal matter of China (PT). After a long wait for final talks on autonomy for Tibet within China, Dalai Lama said he has given up. Now it is up to Tibetans to deal with the matter as they like.

Because of China's close involvement with Pakistan in key strategic areas like telecoms and seaports, New Delhi has not let Chinese firms come close in the field of security business. China has been helping Pakistan in construction of at least two nuclear reactors. Therefore, India will not be very happy in involving Chinese firms in building nuclear reactors in the country. However China would like its firms to get involved because the stakes can be more than US$ 100 billion because of the Indo-US civil nuclear energy deal. Chinese President Hu Jintao visited India in 2006 and had discussions with Prime Minister Singh. President Hu declared that "India's growth is an opportunity, not threat", indicating Beijing's new thinking. Beijing seems to have been driven by business possibility, demonstrated by its U-turn over the Indo-US nuclear deal, which has the prospects of business contracts amounting to about dollar 100 billion. China has positioned five nuclear powered submarines near Indian Sea. Chief of the Indian navy, Admiral Suresh Mehta informed the reporters that this step very dangerous for Indian security. Satellite photos have shown that China has converted a big area into submarine port (Agencies May 6, 2008).

Latest satellite pictures have pinpointed a large area in central China which has 58 launch pads for nuclear powered ballistic missiles. According to the US scientist, Hans Christensen's report it has become clear that in the central area of China nuclear powered DF 21 ICBMs have been positioned, which can attack north India and southern Russia but not Japan and Taiwan. Similarly last year it had developed secret port near Andaman Nicobar. China and Pakistan have joined hands with each other to hack the Indian Web sites or e-mails. Indian security forces are busy to keep a watch where cyber space is affected or where the main computer is disturbed. According to the experts recently in May, 2008 Chinese 'IP Address' carried out maximum attacks. A senior official of the information technology ministry has confirmed 10 hacking cases of Indian government websites by Chinese hackers. After Godhra incidence Pak hacking group 'G Force' is very active. Recently in a European country a Chinese hacker hacked the e-mail of Indian Ambassador, Nirupama Rao.

On one hand China keeps a tight rein on Chinese Muslims on the other it has been encouraging Pakistan to become an arch rival of India in military matters and nuclear-energy plant-construction. The fasting in the sacred month of

Ramadan and the hajj pilgrimage are carefully controlled. Students and government servants are compelled to eat during Ramadan. Similarly passports of Uighurs are confiscated across Xinjiang to force them to join government-run hajj pilgrimage rather to let them visit on their own (Seattle Times October 19, 2008). To patronize Islamabad China has clearly spoken against Indo-US civil nuclear energy pact in international forums. A major investor and arms supplier China shares Pakistan's constant regional rivalry with India and had already helped building a nuclear plant at Chashma along with another nuclear power plant construction of which in progress. During the recent visit of President Zardari to China about a dozen agreements were signed between the two nations. To help ease Islamabad's resentment on Indo-US deal China will help construction of two more nuclear power plants. Pakistan's nuclear program gives the US a constant worry because of its past record of proliferation.

Information Warfare Monitor's (IWM) internet research group headed by Greg Walton has informed that a 'Ghostnet' hacker group of China is involved for the past two years in cyber crime of 103 countries, including Indian Embassies. It has been able to gather secret information available in the computers of various countries particularly embassies and NGOs in Washington.

Pakistan's Desire for Equality with India

Since its creation Pakistan has considered itself as an equal rival of India and tried to equate with India in all the spheres (Azad, 1960; Barnds, 1972; Dixit, 1995). Since the origin of Pakistan is based on religion and hatred to Hinduism, it had strong desire to merge Muslim majority Kashmir too in Pakistan (Sharma & Sharma,1997; Singh,1998). If that was not to be, it preferred Kashmir to remain independent but never with India. First, Maharaja Hari Singh desired to merge with Pakistan but when he took time to decide, Liaquat Ali started an invasion (planned by British?). That is why Mountbatten (who had earlier pressured Maharaja to merge into Pakistan) persuaded Prime Minister Nehru to take the issue to the UN (against the wishes of other leaders as well as military), under the clause of dispute and not aggression. In addition, he managed the halt of Indian troops and started advocating plebiscite even before the UN resolution.

All these facts indicate manipulation according to some prior plan from top. The US was probably later involved in the UN scene by the British to cooperate and use its influence. The natural beauty and the cool climate of Srinagar valley had attracted English people as a summer resort to escape from the searing heat of Indian summer in the plains. Pakistani aristocrat leaders also found a heaven in Kashmir. They considered Kashmir a great attraction for the tourism to earn additional revenue for the empty treasuries of Pakistan. Its attempts to take advantage of ethnic pluralism have been worse. The dictatorial leaders of Pakistan ignored and suppressed East Bengali nationalism, thus undermining its own claim on Kashmir because it is a Muslim majority state. East Bengal (East Pakistan) crisis and subsequent war showed the fragility of Pakistani view. The nation, which could not hold on one of its components, had little basis for claiming a part of a neighbouring country (Prajapati, 1998 & Ganguly, 1993). The GK/POK was, on purpose, not developed and consequently its residents have been extremely unhappy.

As a result they consider that they have been given a choice to either remained undeveloped or may separate. The minority populations are further dwindling and are treated as second/ third rate citizens. Pakistan took advantage of the geographic importance of this region and made agreement with China to build an all weather Karakorum highway and other roads in the strategic areas, touching boundaries of several nations including northern border of India. As a gratitude for the support of their case in the UN and also to make their friendship permanent, they gifted a part of illegally occupied Indian territory to China, despite protests from India (see

Indian map). Similarly they allocated lands for building airfields and army bases as well as they let their existing airports be used by the US for spying purposes. Certain Arabian countries are also helping Pakistan with financial assistance for modernizing army. China and North Korea too are supplying nuclear arsenals and missiles and technology for their own benefits (Dennis Kux, 1993; Cohen, 1998; Nanda, 1998). Just as the US wanted to encircle Communist China with its regional security allies, China has encircled India through its allies in Pakistan, Tibet (now occupied by China), Myanmar and Coco islands etc. This is a clear indication of their new strategy for establishing its military striking ability outside their own country.

Pakistan is buying airborne warning and control system (AWACS) to boost its air defences. China started producing AWACS in 2004 and a US$ 278 million agreement had been made in 2008 to supply this system to Pakistan. China is not happy with India because this is the only country in the region which can challenge it and also because of India's refusal to toe the Chinese policy in Tibet. In addition India has border dispute with China (Hoffman, 1990). Therefore, China normally supports Pakistan. As a result Pakistan is in a very comfortable position as long as China, US and Islamic nations are sympathizing with it and helping it monetarily from time to time. Recognizing the inferiority of its conventional warfare in 1971 and onwards, Pakistan embarked on a program of nuclear armaments and it received impetus after the Indian nuclear explosion in 1974. The usual trend in Pakistan is to raise a slogan of cooperation with neighbours during elections and once elected raise slogans on Kashmir problem to keep the conflict alive in the UN and simultaneously divert public opinion from domestic problems or the economic failures. Iranian diplomats and Afghan leaders too encouraged Kashmiris to take training in Pakistan (Ganguly, 1999; Grover, 1995; Gupta, 1996).

Tehran organized support against India at the Organization

of Islamic Conference (OIC). M.I. Sheker informed Iran had exerted pressure. Tehran also cancelled Indian Prime Minister Gujral's visit to show its solidarity with Pakistan on Kashmir. Iraq was one of the countries supporting India. Therefore, India took a mild attitude towards Saddam Hussein's annexation of Kuwait and also did not send its forces to invade Iraq without UN sanction. Some analysts suspect that Pakistani nuclear technology or some of its arsenals may already have reached in the hands of some Islamic fundamentalists or nations or organizations to create further problems. The fact that for long time Pakistan had become a safe haven for terrorist organizations and their mentors attacking India has been reconfirmed by the US strikes in Afghanistan when 'martyrs' of Harkat-ul-Mujahideen (HUM) were brought back to be buried in Pakistan. According to Pakistan's newspaper "The Friday Times" parents of Pak nationals, who went to Afghanistan for Jehad, are buying them back by paying high charges to Tahrik-e-Insaf-e-Mohammadai (TNM).

The leader of extremist TNM Molana Sufi Mohammad met Mulla Omar and sent Jehadis (Agencies January 5, 2002). After Prime Minister Vajpayee's 2003 peace feelers there had been exchanges of several visits by social workers, students, artists, Parliamentarians, journalists and traders all advocating friendly relations, resumption of buses- and trains- journeys between the two nations. Despite all this Pakistan has yet to give MFN status to India, although India has already given this status to Pakistan long back and trade is also improving. The sea routs between Mumbai and Karachi has yet to be opened. The peace process continued during Prime Minister Manmohan Singh's period too and several CBMs have been taken. Guns on the border are silent most of the time but the cross-border terrorism has not stopped. In fact the peace-process measures like increasing Indo-Pak travel were misused to increase terrorism.

After May 13 serial blasts in Jaipur, police arrested six Pakistanis from Karachi-Jodhpur Thar Express after they were found with tempered visa-papers. With these arrests, the number of illegal Pakistanis caught in the past one year sneaking into India with invalid papers increased to 92, proving the suspicion that the militants will misuse these facilities for their nefarious purposes. Instead of working for economic development seriously Zardari administration has decided to build two more new atomic plants with the help of China for production of nuclear weapons. Each of the plant is supposed to be of 340 megawatt capacity. The equipment will come from China and Pakistan government will pay in foreign exchange as it is already getting lot of help from the US, Japan Europe, Iran and Saudi Arabia. The US help to the tune of US$ 5.2 billion is supposed to be for containing terrorism. The new US administration is also committing the same mistakes which its old administration was making by donating huge sums without proper controls and the money was being diverted for other purposes. Although Obama has been the President for quite a few months, his steps still are not firm and he has been using the same terms 'hope', 'chase', and 'we can', as he was using during his election campaign.

'You Help We Destroy' Policy of Pakistan

You be helpful and peaceful but we will be destructive has been the policy of Pakistan government and ISI-sponsored terrorism. Because of this policy India has lost more than 50,000 lives from 1990 to 2,000s. However in October, 2005 POK suffered one of the worst tremors and lost over 85,000 lives. Therefore, India, USA and many other countries provided help to Pakistan. India sent plane-load of relief material. It also offered to provide helicopters. Islamabad however declined to accept pilots. Therefore, India did not send helicopters. Where fences are OK, people from Pakistan can cross LOC for getting relief and medical treatment as well as also to talk to relatives on phones, provided by India, without any payment. Despite all the relief measures terrorist organizations have vowed to continue destruction in India.

Therefore, security forces have no option but to encounter terrorists and shoot them down, if necessary.

As a result Indian government had become in a fix whether to continue sending earth quake relief material or stop it because the material was either handled by Pak army or the terrorist organizations like Jamait-ul-Dawa a branch of LET. Indian intelligence agencies were continuously reminding that the money and material were reaching the hands of terrorists to be used against India only. According to many analysts whenever India acted seriously on any move for peace or help Pakistan's Jehadi personals or supporting army/ ISI created bloodshed (preferably of minorities) right from the period of Nehru to Vajpayee and Manmohan Singh. After long denial of existence terrorist training camps in Pakistan, former President Musharraf came forward with statement, during his trip to the US, that Pakistan does have areas which provide safe havens to militants (ANI January 25, 2009).

The problems created in Delhi during Diwali holidays (October 2005), Varanasi (March 2006), Kashmir (May 2006), Mumbai (July 2006, 2008) and Hyderabad (2007) are the typical examples of the ISI thinking. After 26/11/08 Mumbai terror attacks Indo-Pak relations soured again and Islamabad has put additional forces on Indian border and even threatened to use nuclear weapons in the event of Indo-Pak war. No one with right mind would ever think of handing over the culprits by Zardari despite world opinion to do so because the military will never allow it (Hindustan Times December 11, 2008). Even though Condoleezza Rice is refusing to accept possibility of war between the nuclear powers, Islamabad is ready for the same. Pakistani army chief General Ashfaq Kayani has assured the President Zardari that his army is ready to attack India within minutes.

As per information of the Wall Street Journal, Pakistan had to agree involvement of LET in 26/11 attacks because its commander Zarar Shah, when arrested with Zaki-ur-Rehman in POK, accepted training 26/11 terrorists. In 1994 Pakistan had decided to create a monster called Taliban without bothering for its future impact on its own soil. ISI'S policies for bleeding the Indian army in Kashmir and making Afghanistan virtually a Pakistani state had blinded them to the future consequences. Eventually Pakistan has become a big loser in both places because the same fanatics threatened the creator- Pakistan. Along with the ISI the late Benazir Bhutto is also to blame because the movement was created during her tenure as Prime minister and she had to pay for it with her own life. Another example is the kidnapping of Pak Ambassador Tariq Azizuddin in Kabul for which Taliban demanded payment of US$ 500 million and release of 10 Taliban supporters from Pakistan for releasing the Ambassador as well as carrying out fidayeen and frequent terror attacks in one part of the country or the other.

Faced with unrelenting global pressure and solid evidence by India and the US, Islamabad agreed that 26/11 strikes were partly planned in Pakistan and Kasab is Pakistani. Terrorists were launched by LET from Karachi. Three rubber dinghies and one engine were supplied to them. Nine persons were named in FIR and six were already arrested. VoIP phones for culprits were bought in Spain, paid for in Italy and internet domains were traced to Houston, Texas (TNN & Agencies February 13, 2009). VoIP calls made by terrorists to their handlers were traced to a colonel and a major general Sahab, whose name cropped up repeatedly in the talks of the terrorists. New Delhi may be making a mistake by overemphasizing Mumbai strikes, forgetting that it was one of the hundreds of terrorist strikes during the past decades. Islamabad emphasizes arrest of six culprits to show it has changed. Even if these six men are hanged what about the 20 culprits India has been demanding for long and what happens to the main issue of terrorist groups operating from Pakistan and what about involvement of ISI and army in cross-border terrorism or what about the debt of Rs. 300 crore that Pakistan owes to India since 1948-49 along with its 3 percent interest.

Therefore India should ask nothing less than declaration of Pakistan a terrorism sponsoring nation or must ask for acceptance of Indian hot pursuits in cases of cross-border terrorism in its territory.

India's Security Concerns

Even before its independence from the colonial rule in 1947, India got involved in the internal problem of religious hatred resulting in communal riots, population migration and ultimately invasion, by its twin, in the north-western state called Kashmir (Azad, 1960; Bhattacharya, 1994; Singh, 1998). Due to inapt handling of the situation by the then government, the country is still suffering and trying to recover. After the Kashmir issue was taken to the Security Council in 1947, several interested nations worked for confusing the issue to suit their needs rather than solving the matter for the benefit of the inhabitants. In contrast to the Korean war, the aggressor and the aggrieved both were treated as equals, in Kashmir imbroglio and were asked to hand over the territory to the UN so that the Anglo-US team could arrange to settle the issue as per their desire (Chibber, 1998; Chopra, 1990; Dixit, 1995).

Not succeeding in the same, they kept on delaying settlement by introducing new plans, as discussed in detail earlier. To sum up, various Anglo-US plans did not succeed in dragging India into a plebiscite net. But admittedly, the real issue of vacation of Pakistani aggression receded into background. This created a false impression in many countries that the plebiscite was the real issue and not the aggression by Pakistan (Chopra, 1990). After independence India arranged to propose in the UN a resolution on peaceful uses of atomic energy for human welfare. Nehru wrote to the Secretary General of the UN, which became the basis for partial test ban and later for the CTBT.

Unfortunately, none of the super powers took lessons from the Indian example and kept expanding their nuclear stockpiles. They also did not give India any assurance for security against a nuclear attack (Noorani, 1967). Therefore, after Chinese efforts to arm Pakistan with nuclear arms and missiles, India declared itself a nuclear weapon state in 1998, although it could have done so decades earlier with more advantages (Chari, 1995 & 1997; Dhar, 2000; Gupta, 2000). Presently India needs a system as well as government which enable the country to become very powerful militarily and allows it to use its forces without hesitation for safeguarding its own security, because it is surrounded on all sides by failed/quasi-failed countries like Nepal, Pakistan, Bangladesh, Myanmar and Sri Lanka. On the top of it China is bent upon to follow the policy of expansion of its borders.

On the invitation of President Truman, Nehru went to the US and received a warm welcome in 1949. However he refused to align with any super power and preferred to stay rather non-aligned. This disappointed the US, who thought India needed funds and technology for development and would surely become its ally for regional security against communists. Next year, the US invited Pakistan. Pakistan obliged the US by promising to become its strategic ally against communists. Pleased with this action the US began to supply arms and monetary funds to the little brother of India. Thus the arms race started in the region. Having sufficient sophisticated arms, Pakistan thought of annexing Kashmir by force and invaded India several times but was humiliated on each occasion, culminating in peace agreements. These agreements had in reality no meaning to Pakistan and after it got back its lost territory and prisoners of war, the agreement ended. It is therefore apparent that India had to fight five wars (4 times with Pakistan and 1 time with China) in the sixty years of its independence. Therefore, it is crystal clear that security and integrity of India is high on its priority, particularly in view of its size and hostile neighbours.

The Indian Ocean stretching over 75 million kilometres of water is about one fifth of the total area under oceans and about 15 percent of earth surface. It takes within its sweep several states accounting for almost one third of the total membership of the UN. There is a marked variation in socio-economic situations and political systems. Amongst these, India is the biggest country, with a coastline covering about 5,000 kilometres, almost equal to India's land frontier. Its western side is an integral part of the defence environment of the South, South West, West Asia, covering Gulf and East African belt. Its eastern side has a chain of states in South and South East Asia. No state is geo-politically so situated as India is, to become affected as a consequence of any military or defence system in the entire region. It is therefore relevant for the security purposes to have 'strategic consensus' covering the states from West Asia to South Asia and South East Asia, coupled with establishment of Rapid Deployment Force. India has unfortunately hostile neighbours, had to fight several wars and now terrorism.

Therefore, it is very much concerned for its internal and external security, with no military alliance and has decided to introduce modern technology on 7,400 km borders with Bangladesh and Pakistan. Thus, it has to have modern equipment for army with minimum nuclear deterrence, missiles, naval units to guard its long coastline and an air force with modern jet fighters and radars etc. If we compare the 1998 budget of 15 biggest military powers in the world, which spend more than US$ 10 billion per year on the armed forces, India ranks 10th. In the same manner, if we compare defence spending per capita, India ranks 12th and not 6th or 7th, where it should have been seeing its size, population and its problems with neighbours. Going by the man-power, India has the 4th largest army in the world, the commencement of a blue water navy and nuclear capability contrasted with a slow growing economy (far slower than many other Asian nations) and inefficient as also corrupt public sector enterprises. Outburst of the anti-US feelings from time to time led US to remain unfriendly or indifferent to India, trying to keep it down and unwilling to treat India as pre-eminent power in South Asia or as a leader of the world's poor nations.

During recent meeting of Secretary Rice with Manmohan Singh at New Delhi in 2005 she said the goal of the US is to help India become a major world power in 21st century. The new policy was not the case of statement only. Washington was willing to work for co-production in the defence sector. It was willing to sell India F-16 or F-18 fighter planes. It was also willing to discuss the early warning systems for missile defence etc. There was also the promise of cooperation in the civil nuclear energy sector. But it is strange because till now the US was considering Kashmir as one of the most dangerous places in the world and the same nation feels it is worth cooperating with India. At the same time it feels it is promoting security by supplying nuclear capable strike F-16 aircrafts to Islamabad to fight terrorism.

Therefore, instead of jumping at the offer India decided to wait and play cool for further discussions between the Prime Minister and President in early 2006 and for finalization of the civil nuclear energy agreement in both Houses. Simultaneously it was also watching the US role for the permanent seat in the Security Council of the UN (The Hindu July 17, 2005). In this connection it may be stated that on November 2, 2006 meeting the Chairman, US Senate Foreign Relations Committee said, "India is an important emerging power....It enjoys a vibrant democracy, a rapidly growing economy, and increasing influence in world affairs...It is clearly in the interests of the United States to develop a strong strategic relationship with India," and the bill was passed. Same way it was also passed later by the House. On December 18, 2006, the President finally signed by the bill to make US Companies free to deal with India on civil nuclear energy projects.

Despite Indian Prime Minister's assurances in the Parliament many Indian leaders were sceptical of the Indo-US nuclear pact. A clear sign that Indo-US relations have changed came in March when George Bush and Manmohan Singh signed historical agreement in New Delhi. For allowing IAEA inspection of its nuclear reactors, India was promised an assured supply of enriched uranium and technology for civil nuclear energy projects. At long last USA is recognizing the potential of India in Asian security affairs. New Delhi and Washington think alike in the post September 11, 2001 world. Both nations are concerned about Pakistani nuclear proliferation as well as South Asian Islamic extremism as shown by Taliban and Al-Qaida. American administration has a school of thought which recognizes India as a bulwark against abovementioned security concerns.

As far as India is concerned Indian government, after horrific 26/11 Mumbai blasts (2008), had to create federal agency called national investigation agency (NIA) and tough laws unlawful activities prevention act (UAPA) to fight terrorism, although anti-terror laws like TADA and POTA were rolled back earlier. The fact that Jehadi terrorism originating from Pakistan is a major part of global problem became well known by brutal 26/11 blasts, using Indians, Americans, British and Israelis as cannon fodder. According to a Washington Post report Indian and US investigators collected the names of the handlers of brutal attacks and also have proof of close associations between LET and ISI. They have identified Yusuf Muzammil, a Lashkar leader, as the mastermind behind the attacks. Former Secretary Rice asked Pakistan to turn in Muzammil and other suspects. India invited ISI Chief to come to join investigations, similar to the police inviting culprit leader to join the probe. Entire world community knows that Kabul embassy and 26/11 attacks were creations of ISI.

After the dangerous moves from China on eastern side of India, particularly in Arunachal Pradesh, where China constructed 14 air bases. China border is only 170 km from here and Myanmar border is about 80 km. Although the latter is friendly to India but it is close to China also. At present the situation was not critical according to the Commanding Officer, M.S. Venkateshwar, who was talking to the Press but it could be anytime later. Therefore, India began to modernize seven air bases in the region and move is there to place modern fighter plains in these bases to counteract the future dangerous moves from China, if any. After building of Lhasa railways India had decided to increase vigil on China border also and soon one squadron of Sukhoi-30 MKI will be deputed. In the year 2008 China had crossed the border 270 times and in 2009 60 such incursions have come to the notice of Home Ministry of India. With active help from China and North Korea, Islamabad has surged well ahead of New Delhi in the missile development field (TNN February 2, 2009). Only Prithvi is fully operational but improved version of Agni series is still in trial phase. Agni V can strike up to 5,000- km range.

Indo-US relations need no longer be hostage to US-Pakistan-China and Indo-Soviet relations. Whether the 'Star nations' will take advantage of the altered international environment of the end of cold war is still to be seen, although the beginning of the Indo-US-Russia relations in the millennium year and afterwards have been encouraging, particularly after operation 'Enduring Freedom'. The trend of negotiations held elsewhere to resolve mutual issues, is not being witnessed in South Asian region. It may therefore, be worthwhile for the above mentioned 'star nations' to have their meetings with open mind and discussions to solve out the problems plaguing their mutual ties and also to set in motion a new climate in this region. The example of Germany is worth mentioning in this connection. India and the US are now working on economic and trade issues, but also on military cooperation and civil nuclear energy.

The revered Sathya Sai Baba of India, who is operating to promote human values, wrote that,

"There is only one nation, the nation of humanity;
There is only one religion, the religion of love;
There is only one language, the language of heart;
There is only one God, and he is omnipresent."

Annexures

Annexure 1

Tashkent Declaration January 10, 1966

The Prime Minister of India and the President of Pakistan met at Tashkent and having discussed the existing relations, hereby declare their firm-resolve to restore normal and peaceful relations between their countries and to promote understanding and friendly relations between their peoples. They consider the attainment of these objectives of vital importance for the welfare of the 600 million people of India and Pakistan.

I. The Prime Minister of India and the President of Pakistan agree that both sides will exert to create good neighbourly relations in accordance with United Nations Charter. They reaffirm their obligation not to have recourse to force and to settle their disputes through peaceful means. They considered that the interests of peace in their region and particularly in the subcontinent and indeed, the interests of the peoples of India and Pakistan were not served by the continuance of tension between the two countries. It was against this background that Jammu and Kashmir was discussed and each side set forth its respective position.

II. The Prime Minister of India and the President of Pakistan have agreed that all armed personnel of the two countries shall be withdrawn not later than 25 February, 1966 to the positions they held prior to 5 August, 1965, and both sides shall observe the cease-fire terms on the cease-fire line.

III. The Prime Minister and the President have agreed that relations between India and Pakistan shall be based on the principles of non-interference in the internal affairs of each other.

IV. The Prime Minister and the President have agreed that both sides will discourage any propaganda directed against the other country, and encourage propaganda which promotes the development of friendly relations between the two countries.

V. The High Commissioner of India to Pakistan and the High Commissioner of Pakistan to India will return to their posts to restore normal functioning. Both Governments shall observe the Vienna Convention of 1961 on Diplomatic Intercourse.

VI. Both Governments have agreed to consider measures for restoration of economic and trade relations, communications, cultural exchanges and to make measures to implement the existing agreements between India and Pakistan.

VII. The Governments have agreed to give instructions to carry out repatriation of prisoners of war.

VIII. Both Governments agreed to continue discussion of questions of problems of refugees/illegal immigrants. They further agreed to discuss the return of the property and assets taken over by either side during the conflict.

IX. The Prime Minister of India and the President of Pakistan have agreed that the sides will continue meetings on matters of direct concern to both countries. Both sides have recognized the need to set up joint Indian-Pakistani bodies, which will report to their Governments in order to decide what further steps should be taken.

Both Prime Minister and President record their feelings of deep appreciation and gratitude to the leaders of the Soviet Union, the Government and personally to the Chairman of the Council of Ministers of the USSR for their constructive, friendly and noble part in bringing about present meeting which has resulted in mutually satisfactory results. They also express to the Government and friendly people of Uzbekistan their sincere thankfulness for their overwhelming reception and generous hospitality.

They invite the Chairman of the Council of Ministers of the USSR to witness this Declaration.

Annexure 2

Bilateral Agreement between India and Pakistan (Shimla Pact, July 1972)

The Government of India and the Government of Pakistan are resolved that the two countries put an end to the conflict and confrontation that have hitherto marred their relations and work for a promotion of a friendly and harmonious relationship and the establishment of durable peace in the subcontinent. Both countries may henceforth devote their resources and energies to the pressing task of advancing the welfare of their people.

In order to achieve this objective, the Government of India and the Government of Pakistan have agreed as follows:

(i) That the principles and purposes of the charter of the United Nations shall govern the relations between the two countries.

(ii) That the two countries are resolved to settle their differences by peaceful means through bilateral negotiations or by any other peaceful means mutually agreed upon. Pending the final settlement of any of the problems, neither side shall unilaterally alter the situation and both shall prevent the organization, assistance or encouragement of any acts detrimental to the maintenance of peaceful and harmonious relations.

(iii) That the prerequisite for reconciliation, good neighbourliness and durable peace between them is a commitment by both the countries to peaceful co-existence, respect for each other's territorial integrity and sovereignty and non-interference in each others internal affairs, on the basis of equality and mutual benefit.

(iv) That the basic issues and causes of conflict which have bedevilled the relations between the two countries for the last 25 years shall be resolved by peaceful means.

(v) That they shall always respect each other's national unity, integrity, political-independence and sovereign equality.

(vi) That they will refrain from threat or use of force against each other.

(vii) Both Governments will prevent hostile propaganda directed against each other. Both countries will encourage dissemination of information to promote friendly relations:

(viii) In order progressively to normalize relations, it was agreed that: (i) Steps shall be taken to resume communications, postal, telegraphic, sea, land including border posts, and air links including over flights. (ii) Appropriate steps shall be taken to promote travel facilities for nationals of the other country. (iii) Trade and co-operation in economic and other agreed fields will be resumed. (iv) Exchange in the fields of science and culture will be promoted.

The delegations from both countries will meet periodically for working out necessary details.

(ix) In order to initiate the process of establishment of durable peace, both Governments agreed that: (i) Indian and Pakistani forces shall be withdrawn to their side of the border. (ii) In J&K, the line of control resulting from the cease-fire of December 17, 1971 shall be respected by both sides. Neither side shall seek to alter it unilaterally, irrespective of any interpretation. (iii) The withdrawals shall commence upon entry into force of this agreement and shall be completed within a period of 30 days thereof.

This agreement will be subject to ratification by both countries in accordance with their respective constitutional procedures, and will come into force with effect from the date on which the instruments of ratification are exchanged.

Both Governments agree that their respective heads will meet again at a mutually convenient time in the future and that, in the meanwhile the representatives of the two sides will meet to discuss further the modalities and arrangements for the establishment of durable peace and normalization of relations, including the question of repatriation of prisoners of war and civilian internees, a final settlement of Jammu and Kashmir and the resumption of diplomatic relations.

Annexure 3

Text of the Documents Signed at Lahore at the Conclusion of the Indian Prime Minister's Visit on February 21, 1999

The Prime ministers of the Republic of India and the Islamic Republic of Pakistan:-

1. Sharing a vision of peace and stability between their countries, and of progress and prosperity;
2. Convinced that durable peace and development of harmonious relations and friendly cooperation will serve the vital interests of the peoples of the two countries, enabling them to devote their energies for a better future;
3. Recognizing that the nuclear dimension of the security environment of the two countries adds to their responsibility for avoidance of conflict between the two countries. "
4. Committed to the principle and purposes of the charter of the United Nations, 'and the universally accepted principles of peaceful coexistence;'
5. Reiterating the determination of both countries to implementing the Shimla Agreement in letter and spirit'
6. Committed to the objectives of universal nuclear' disarmament and non-proliferation;
7. Convinced of the importance of mutually agreed confidence building measures for improving the security environment.
8. Recalling their agreement of 23rd September 1998, that an environment of peace and security is in the supreme national interest of both sides and that the resolution of all outstanding issues, including Jammu and Kashmir, is essential for this purpose.

Have agreed that their respective governments: -

- Shall intensify their efforts to resolve all issues, including the issue of Jammu and Kashmir.
- Shall refrain from intervention and interference in each other's internal affairs.
- Shall intensity their composite and integrated dialogue process for an early and positive outcome of the agreed bilateral agenda.
- Shall take immediate steps for reducing the risk of accidental or unauthorized use of nuclear weapons and discuss concepts and doctrines with a view to elaborating measures for confidence building in the nuclear and conventional fields, aimed at prevention of conflict.
- Reaffirm their commitments to the goals and objectives of SAARC and to prevent their efforts towards the realization of SAARC vision for the year 2000 and beyond with a view to promoting the welfare of the people of South Asia and to improve their quality of life through accelerated economic growth, social progress and cultural development.
- Reaffirm their condemnation of terrorism in all its forms and manifestations and, their determination to combat this menace.
- Shall promote and promote and protect all human rights and fundamental freedoms.

AtaI Bihari Vajpayee
Prime Minister of the Republic of India

Muhammad Nawaz Sharif
Prime Minister of the Islamic Republic of Pakistan

Annexure 4

Lahore Declaration, February 21, 1999

Before Vajpayee's 27 hour visit to Lahore concluded he and his Pakistani counterpart Nawaz Sharif signed a 23 para Lahore Declaration setting out 8 points within which they will attempt to resolve outstanding bilateral issues. The declaration commits the two countries to refrain from intervention in each other's internal affairs, intensify and upgrade their ongoing composite dialogue process and step up efforts to resolve all bilateral issues including J & K.

In an eight point MOU signed by Foreign Secretaries K. Raghvan and Shamshool Ahmad, the two countries agreed to reduce the risk of accidental or unauthorized use of nuclear weapons under their respective control.

The most substantial gains of Prime Minister A.B. Vajpayee's visit to Lahore seems to have been in the area of augmenting confidence building measures (CBMs) between the two countries to prevent a possible nuclear war, Vajpayee and Pakistan Prime Minister Nawaz Sharif had two rounds of one to one talks within a duration of 24 hours.

Although the hope of a no-war declaration that many had hoped would emerge from these current negotiations was belied, in a memorandum of Understanding signed between the foreign secretaries of India and Pakistan, both nations agreed to provide each other with advance notification in respect of ballistic missile flight tests. Besides this, both nations will undertake national measures to reduce the risks of accidental or unauthorized use of nuclear weapons within their respective control.

In the event of an accidental or unauthorized incident that could create the risk of fallout with adverse consequences for both sides, and an outbreak of a nuclear war between the two countries) the two sides undertook to notify each other about the development.

The two sides will not identify/establish the appropriate communication mechanisms for this purpose. While they agreed to abide by their respective unilateral moratorium on conducting further nuclear test explosions, there was qualifying clause: "Unless either side, in exercise of its national sovereignty decides that extraordinary events have jeopardized its supreme interests".

These CBMs will be periodically reviewed and, where necessary, appropriate consultative mechanisms to monitor and ensure their effective implementation would be put in place. The two sides will also review existing communication links and to provide for fail-safe and secure communications.

In reply to a question whether the two sides had discussed the issue of signing of the CTBT, Prime Minister Vajpayee replied in the affirmative but added that no decision has been taken on it.

The Memorandum of Understanding was one of the three documents that emerged at the end of the talks, the others being the Lahore Declaration and a Joint Statement

In the Lahore Declaration, signed by both Prime Ministers in front of an assembly of media persons in the majestic wood-panelled Durbar Hall of the Governor's House, both governments agreed to "intensify their efforts to resolve all issues, including the issue of Jammu and Kashmir.

They also undertook to refrain from intervening and interfering in each other's internal affairs, and shall "intensify their composite and integrated dialogue process".

Interestingly, this clause came in particularly handy for both Prime Ministers when confronted with sticky questions from the media, like progress on the Kashmir issue for instance. They just reiterated that the dialogue process was going on.

Under the Joint Statement, the two leaders agreed to meet periodically to discuss all issues of mutual concern, including nuclear-related issues. Consultations on WTO and those related to information technology particularly in tackling the problems of Y2K will take place. It also identified Prime Minister Vajpayee's invitation to Prime Minister Nawaz Sharif to visit India at mutually convenient date.

According to Sharif the biggest gain was that the ice was broken. "Both sides have agreed to consult each other" said Sharif and added that both nations must now desist from blaming each other constantly for whatever happens in their mutual countries. Earlier that evening, speaking to a large gathering of Lahore's elite, at a civic reception on the well-manicured lawns of Governor's House, Vajpayee had already touched upon the theme. "I believe that the distance between Delhi and Lahore has shrunk" he said. Seeking to explain why he a poet and a man who had written about the horrors of Hiroshima, had presided as Prime Minister over the Pokharan explosion last May he said that it was not intended to attack but to defend, an attempt to use shakti for shami. He recognized that being nuclear states imposed new responsibilities on both nations. "It is vital that Pakistan and India come together. There is no alternative to dialogue" he said, "because we can change history but not geography." "Enough of enmity, give friendship a chance was the message".

Glossary

Glossary

Abdullah, Sheikh Mohammad. He was a Muslim freedom fighter and President of the National Conference Party. He became the first Chief Minister of Jammu & Kashmir state after merger of Kashmir with India.

Abdullah, Farookh Ahmad. He is the son of Sheikh Abdullah. He also became the President of the National Conference after death of his father. Later he was elected Chief Minister of J&K several times.

Acheson, Dean. He was the Secretary of State at the time of President Truman. He could not build a good rapport with Nehru and did not agree to Nehru's suggestion to include main-land China a seat in the Security Council.

Ackerman, Gary is a member of the International Relations Committee and the Co-chairman of the caucus on India and Indian Americans.

Adams, John has been a Professor of the Department of Economics at the North-Eastern University at Boston, N.Y. He is an expert on Indian Economy.

Advani, Lal Krishna. He is the top leader of the Bhartiya Janata Party and the two-time Home Minister. He was also the Deputy prime minister in a BJP alliance government.

Afghanistan. An Islamic nation North-West of Pakistan. Till recently, majority of its area was under the control of Taliban, a fundamentalist Islamic group, supported by ISI. Now Hamid Karzai is its President. Bin Laden has taken a refuge in this country for long time.

Agni, Prithvi, Akash, Nag and Trishul are different Indian missiles, which were test-fired and improved upon recently.

Ahinsa (Ahimsa). A form of non-violence movement started by Mahatma Gandhi, first in South Africa and later in India against British Raj.

Alan Greenspan was the Chairman of the Federal Reserves of the USA.

Ali, Liaquat. A top leader of the Muslim League, who wanted a separate Islamic nation-Pakistan. After partition, he became the first Prime Minister of Pakistan and was later killed. He had encouraged invasion of Kashmir in 1947.

Ambedkar, Baba. He was a nationalist Harijan (schedule caste) leader. He worked for improvement of Harijans and was the main architect of the Indian constitution. After freedom, he became the first Law Minister in Nehru's cabinet.

Asgar Khan. Former Air Marshall and an important political leader of Pakistan, known for his frankness.

Ashok. He was the most famous emperor of ancient India in the third century BC. He extended his rule to cover entire India and established Srinagar in a beautiful valley of Kashmir, inhabited by Hindus. As a symbol of unity, his Chakkra or wheel has been put on the Indian national flag.

Asian 'Tigers' are the Southeast Asian countries, i.e. Indonesia and Malaysia, whose economies jumped very high in the last decade or so.

Austin, Warren and Noel Baker were respectively the US and U.K. representatives in the UN who pressed for plebiscite in Kashmir and pushed the main issue of aggression to back burner.

Azad, Abul Kalam was a top nationalist Muslim leader of the Indian National Congress Party or the Congress party. He rose to an important position of a Cabinet Minister of the government of India.

Azad, Chandra Shekhar was a great freedom fighter and the top leader of Indian revolutionaries. In 1931, he died in a freedom fight in Allahabad. When surrounded by British soldiers, he shot them and turned the last bullet on himself.

Bhagat Singh was another great revolutionary and, a colleague of C.S. Azad, who was hanged in 1930, by the British, for his role in second freedom struggle of India.

Bangladesh was earlier East Pakistan, having more Muslim population then in West Pakistan. Both parts [separated by India] had struggle in the East for separation, in which India helped the East and the US supported the West.

Bhabha, Homi Dr. He was the pioneering nuclear scientist of India. He established the first atomic reactor at Tarapore. Unfortunately, he was killed prematurely in Kanishka airplane crash, when he was returning to India.

Bhagwan, Dass is a learned Hindu judge in Pakistan. Timely promotion was denied to him because he is a Hindu. If he had got timely promotion as a judge in the High Court, he would have become a judge in Supreme Court earlier.

Bhagwat Gita or Gita is originally a Sanskrit book. It basically comprises of the preaching or the philosophy of Lord Krishna, which advocates Karma or work/ duty, without desire for benefits in return. It has now been translated in many languages.

Bhartiya Janata Party. BJP is a rightist Hindu political party, earlier called Jana Sangh. It emphasizes Indian culture. RSS, Bajrang Dal, Vishwa Hindu Parishad and Durga Vahini are its cultural associates. During BJP's rule Indian economy had improved significantly.

Bhutto, Benazir was the daughter of late Pakistani Prime Minister, Z.A. Bhutto, who was hanged. She accompanied her father to sign Shimla Pact in 1972. Later, she became Prime Minister. Afterwards she moved to live in England and returned to Pakistan and was shot dead during elections.

Bio-diversity and genetic diversity are the natural variations in plant materials. They allow development of new varieties through manipulations of genetic make-ups.

Blackwill, Robert was the Ambassador of the US at New Delhi.

Blue Star Operation was organized during Indira Gandhi's time to flush out Bhinderanwale Sikh terrorists from the Golden temple in Amritsar (Punjab).

Boeing Company is the famous airplane manufacturing company based around Seattle.

Bokaro Plant. A large Steel Plant in eastern India, which the US had originally promised to help but did not. Russia came forward to help build the steel plant and got lot of credit.

Bose, Subhash Chandra. Netaji as he was called was a very popular leader of the Congress. He was well known for his leftist views and left India. He organized the Indian National Army in Burma, during 2nd world war. He supposedly died in a plane crash in Japan.

Brown, Sherrod is a Senator and an International relations Committee member, who had cautioned the US about the dangers of the US-China nuclear agreement.

Buddhists are the followers of Gautam Buddha. He was originally a Hindu Prince and started Buddhism when Hinduism needed cleansing. Buddhists are a majority in Ladakh region of Kashmir. There are many Buddhist shrines in India and neighbouring nations.

Burkha. A veil put on by the Muslim ladies on their dress to cover the entire body, head to feet, excepting eyes. Generally it is black in colour.

Bush, George. He is a former US President of Republican party during whose period the US-Indian relations improved slightly.

Bush, G.W. is the immediate past US President. He defeated Vice President Al Gore to become the first President of the millennium. Earlier, he was the Governor of Texas. Father and son both are Republicans. During his period Indo-US relations improved to a great extent. He signed civil nuclear agreement with Prime Minister Manmohan Singh.

CARE. The Cooperative for Assistance and Relief Everywhere, working internationally on different projects to benefit human society. They normally support child care.

Celeste, Richard. He was the former Ambassador of the US at New Delhi.

CENTO. A US led military treaty of which Pakistan and some other nations in the Gulf are or were the members.

China. Communist China or mainland China is in East Asia, having maximum population in the world. It is one of the P-5 nations, supporting Pakistan. After preparing for mountain war it had attacked India as it has border dispute with it.

China Metallurgical Equipment Corporation. A corporation, which has been cunningly passing on missile and nuclear technologies to Pakistan, despite China's commitment to the US not to do so. Later, sanctions were imposed on it.

Christina Rocca. Defence Security Adviser of the US.

CIA. The Central Intelligence Agency of the US working internationally to collect secret information and appoint agents for the same.

CID. The Criminal Investigation Department of the Indian police, which collects information on secret matters.

Clinton, Bill J.A. Former Democrat President of the US for two terms. He visited India and received a warm welcome.

Clinton, Hillary. Present Defence Secretary of the US. She is the wife of former President. She too visited India to induce good relations.

Coco-Islands. The Indian Ocean islands where China has built its bases to establish military striking ability outside its own territory.

Cold War. It refers to rivalry between USA led western nations and the USSR led communist nations of Eastern Europe and China. This ended after the split of the USSR.

Cohen, Stephen P. is a former a Professor and expert on South Asia at the University of Illinois. Presently he is a senior scholar at the Brookings Institutions in Washington DC.

Condoleezza Rice. She is the immediate past Foreign Secretary of the US.

Cummins, Ralph W. Dr. Former Director of the Rockefeller Foundation's Field program.

CTBT. Comprehensive Test Ban Treaty of the UN, which prevents any state other than the P-5 nations, to become nuclear-power State by manufacturing or by acquiring nuclear weapons.

Dalai Lama. He is the highest religious authority of Tibet, who administered Tibet but was thrown out by China. He has his government in exile at Dharamshala (H.P.) India. But he is not getting serious help from world community for autonomy of his country.

Deendar Anjuman. An Islamic group based in Pakistan, having cultural centres in India. After its nefarious activities in South India, it was banned.

Desai Morarji was the first Janata Party Prime Minister of India. Earlier he was Finance Minister in the Congress Party government.

Diego Garcia. Is the island where the US established its base in the Indian Ocean after displacing the native population. The islanders won a court case to go back to occupy their land. India did not appreciate establishment of a base here.

Dixit, J.N. He was formerly a Secretary and later Security Adviser in the Ministry of Foreign Affairs of the government of India. He has authored many books and articles on Indian Foreign policy.

Dixon, Owen Sir. He was an Australian Jurist who served as the minister to the US. Being a US favourite, he worked as Head of the UN Commission on India and Pakistan.

Dong Pederson is a leading think-tank of Conway Pederson Economics of the US.

Dulles, John Foster. A Former US Secretary of State, who had said "Those who are not with the US are against it". He was not happy with India and favoured Pakistan.

DUMA. The Parliament of the Soviet Russia is called DUMA.

Durand Line. It is the old international boundary between India (Later Pakistan) and Afghanistan.

Ecosystem. It refers to the ecological variations, in a region/ nation, which influence productivity.

Einstein, Albert & Louis Fischer. The famous scientists of the US and Nobel Laureates.

Eisenhower, Dwight D. He successfully led the allied forces in the 2nd World War and later became the US President. He and Nehru liked each other. During his visit to New Delhi he was given a warm welcome.

Eliot, R.S., Mellville Herman, Satyanand George Stokes and Whitman Walt. The US luminaries of their period, who were all well informed about India in their respective fields.

Emerson, Ralph Waldo was a famous US author.

Enron. Is a famous energy corporation of the US, which was working on an energy project in India. It is now reportedly involved in money scandals.

Enterprise. is a US nuclear powered warship carrier of the 7th fleet, which was sent to India in 1971.

Fernandes, George. He has been India's 2-time Minister of Defence in BJP government and a leader of Samta party.

FMCT. It is the Fissile Material Cut-off Treaty of the UN dealing with elimination of material used for preparation of nuclear arsenals.

Ford Foundation. A philanthropic organization working internationally to help further development.

Galbraith, John K. and Bowles, Chester. Former US Ambassadors to India, who were much appreciated by the Indians.

Gandhi, Mahatma or Mohandas K. Gandhi fought against colour bar in South Africa and later for freedom of India from Britain. His philosophy was non-violence (Ahinsa). He is referred to as 'father of the nation'. Unfortunately for his help to Muslims and Pakistan he was assassinated.

Gandhi, Indira and Rajiv. Rajiv Gandhi was the elder son of Prime Minister Indira Gandhi, the only daughter of Nehru. Both Rajiv and Indira Gandhi were killed when they were Prime Ministers.

Ganges, Bramhaputra, Sindhu (Indus), Yamuna, Satluj, Ravi and Vyas are the important rivers of North India, nourishing the crops in North and in the Indo-Gangetic belt called Doab. Narmada, Godavri and Mahanadi are the rivers in other parts of the country.

Gates, Bill. The richest person in the world, who is the Chairman of Seattle based Microsoft. Melinda Gates is her wife, who has a charity organization in her name.

Gates, Robert. Defence Secretary of the US.

GATT is the old General Agreement on Tariffs and Trade, which was signed by 23 countries in 1947 to liberalize trade after World War II. Later, many more countries signed it. In 1994, it was amended to create the World Trade Organization (WTO).

GDP. Gross Domestic Product is a value measure of flow of domestic goods and services produced by an economy over a period of time, say- a year.

Ghadar Movement. The first freedom movement of India in 1850, which failed. After that the British Government assumed the administration of India from the East India Company.

Ghauri, Gaznavi and Shahin. Pakistani missiles modified from their North Korean and Chinese versions. They were named after Muslims who had invaded India.

GNP. Gross National Product comprises of GDP plus net income or loss stemming from transactions with foreign countries. It is a broad measurement of the output of goods and services by an economy.

Gokhale and Tilak. Top leaders of the Indian National Congress before Mahatma Gandhi. Gandhi and the Indians have high regards for their contributions in the freedom struggle.

Golden Temple is the most revered religious temple of Sikhs managed by a committee (SGPC). For some time Bhinderanwale occupied it and he had to be flushed out.

Green Revolution. It refers to very high production of grains, potatoes and sugarcane to meet the increased demands of food to eliminate food shortage in India.

Gujral, Inder Kumar. He was the second Prime minister of the Joint Front government and proposed the Gujral Doctrine but did not last long as Prime Minister.

Gulf War. A war between Iran and Iraq, which lasted for nearly a decade.

Harappans, Hunes, Shaks, Aryans and Greeks were the invaders, who came to India in olden days from North and settled in India. In due course of time they were absorbed into the Sanatni (everlasting)/ Vedic culture, which is referred to as Hinduism.

Hardayal, Lala. A famous Indian Freedom-Fighter, who came to the US and founded a Freedom (Ghadar) Movement. It received support in California and other parts of the US.

Harriman, Averell. He was the US Ambassador to India.

Harkat-ul-Ansar. A terrorist group based in Pakistan, funded by some Islamic nations and Pakistan, creating insurgency in India. After being banned by the US it has changed its name to Harkat-ul-Mujahideen.

Helmes, Jesse and Faircloth, Lauch are the Senators, who urged the President Clinton to work closely with the Congress to improve Indo-US economic ties.

Hinduism. An old civilization of Indian subcontinent called Vedic or Sanatni culture. In fact, more than a religion, it is a way of life more than four thousand years old. It is against taking life. Its followers are called Hindus. Majority of Indians are Hindus and most of them speak Hindi language. Some of them speak regional languages too.

Hizbul Mujahideen. It is a pro-Pakistani organization of fundamentalist and fanatic Muslims.

Humphrey, Hubert and Rusk, Dean. The US dignitaries, who were sympathetic to India.

ICBM. Inter-Continental Ballistic Missiles being developed by many countries.

Ichogil Canal. A large water channel with swampy areas on both sides near Lahore.

Indian National Army. INA or Azad Hind Fauz was founded by Subhash C. Bose, who escaped from prison and contacted leaders in Europe & Japan to mobilize support for Indian freedom. He founded INA in Burma to fight the British Army.

ISI. The secret intelligence service of Pakistan called Inter-Services Intelligence, organizing terrorism, counterfeit currency and drug trade for nefarious activities in India.

Jammu. A city and southern region of Kashmir with primarily a Hindu population.

Jehad or Jihad. An Islamic holy war in which torturing/killing of non-Muslims is pious.

Jha, A.N. He was the Chief Secretary of U.P. when an Agricultural university was established in Pantnagar, with the collaboration of the University of Illinois.

Jinnah, Mohammad Ali. He was the leader of Muslim League, which wanted a separate Islamic Pakistan, by dividing India due to hatred for Hindus. He became its 1st President.

Joe Biden and Arlen Specter. US Congressmen, who made slapping of sanctions on Chinese and Pak Corporations possible for the clandestine deals on nuclear technology. Joe Biden is now Vice-President of US.

Johnson, Lyndon. He was the US President during Indo-Pak was of 1965. He asked A.N. Kossyginof the USSR to mediate and bring about an agreement.

J.K.L.F. A group of staunch Muslims linked with Pakistan, named Jammu and Kashmir Liberation Front, creating militancy in India.

Joshi, Murli Manohar. He is the 2-time Minister of Human Resource Development. Formerly, he was Home Minister of BJP government. Earlier he was a Professor at Allahabad

University.

Karakorum Highway. An all weather road, built & guarded by the Chinese in GK/POK to get an access to Gulf countries and North India, where India has relatively higher hills.

Kargil is a hill town near J&K border, where Pakistani invaders occupied strategic hills in 1998 and early 1999, resulting in an undeclared Indo-Pak war in summer.

Karzai, Hamid. The present President of Afghanistan government founded after overthrow of ISI trained Taliban regime. He was attacked but he is working hard to improve Afghanistan.

Kashmir, Arunachal, Uttar Pradesh (U.P.), Himachal Paradesh (H.P.), Bengal, Bihar, Rajasthan, M.P., Orissa, Haryana, Karnataka, Sikkim and Punjab are a few Indian States. Kashmir (Princely state) merged with India as per Freedom Act and only a part later occupied by Pakistan as a disputed territory. The US considers Kashmir as disputed.

Kennedy, John F. President of the US, who was very friendly to India and helped it against China at a time when India required help urgently but Russia did not come forward. He was unfortunately assassinated during his tenure.

Khan, Ayub was a General of Pakistani army, who became a President of Pakistan through a military coup and remained President for long-time.

Khan, Zafrullah. He was the representative of Pakistan to the UN and did not question the legal validity of accession of Kashmir into India in the UN but the US does question it.

Khorana, H.G. and S. Chandrashekhar. The US scientists of Indian origin, who won Nobel Prize because of their excellent work and became famous in their respective fields.

Laden, Osama Bin. He is a Us-trained Saudi Arabian

billionaire terrorist, who was living in Talibani Afghanistan. He supported bombings on US embassies, World Trade Centre and Pentagon. After 'Enduring Freedom' operation he is hiding in Pak-Afghan border.

Lahore is a city in Pakistan near Indian border. Before freedom it had a very large Hindu population.

Lahore Declaration is the bilateral Indo-Pak agreement signed in 1999. Prime Minister Vajpayee took a bus ride to sign this agreement with Nawaz Shariff to solve bilateral problems after mutual discussions.

Lajpat Rai and Sarojni Naidu. Famous freedom fighters of India. Lajpat Rai died before freedom. Sarojni Naidu was a poet and became the governor of U.P.

Lalitaditya and Awanit Varman. They were the Hindu rulers of Kashmir after Kanishkan Empire. They ruled to develop Kashmir into a most famous valley of South Asia.

Lashkar-e-Toiba and Jamat-e-Islami are other rabid and fanatic organizations, which receive money from Pakistan and Islamic nations for creating militancy and to convert non-Muslims to Islam or kill them if they do not become Muslims.

Leh and Ladakh are the towns in J&K in difficult hilly and snow covered region in west Kashmir. This region is the second non-Muslim majority area of the State of J&K.

Liang, Ting Wen. The Ambassador of Malaysia, who succeeded in CBD recognizing the sovereignty of nations over their biological resources.

License Raj. The legal requirement for industrial firms to obtain permission for setting up production units or to add more equipment or to produce different products. It takes long time to complete all the formalities.

Madarsa/Madrasa is a Muslim school for Quran and religious studies. Extremists in Pakistan and Afghanistan are using them as centres for terrorism teaching against infidels or Kafirs, i.e. non-Muslims.

M-11 and Hatf Missiles are the medium range missiles, supplied by China to Pakistan.

Magnetic Rings are required in nuclear energy programs and missile production. China supplied such rings to Pakistan.

Maharaja of Kashmir. Hari Singh was the last Kashmiri Maharaja. He was not popular. After freedom, he took time to decide whether to stay free or merge into India. Pakistan invaded to annex it and then only he merged his state with India.

Mc. Dermott, Joseph. A Democratic Senator from Seattle known for his anti-war attitude.

Mc Mahon Line. 1914 decided international boundary between India and Tibet, with free trade all along the border. China did not accept it and called it as 'imperialist-forced line'.

Menon, Krishna V.K. was High Commissioner of India at London and later, the Defence Minister in the Indian Government, who participated in J&K debates in the UN. His frankness and outbursts were not liked by the Western nations.

MIGs are the Jet fighters manufactured in Russia and were later purchased by India.

Mishra, Brajesh. India's former National Security Adviser and Principal Secretary in Prime Minister's Office. He was earlier Foreign Affairs Secretary to Indian government.

MTCR. Missile Technology Control Regime agreed in March 1992 to stop missile-proliferation.

Mohajir Quami Movement is an organization of discriminated Urdu speaking Indian Muslims, who settled near Karachi or in other cities in Sind and desire better relations with India. The MQM leader Altaf Husain is living in exile at London for long time.

Most favoured Nation. An economic status given to a country for having good trade and commerce dealings. US gave this status to China. India gave it unilaterally to Pakistan.

Mountbatten, L.F. Lord was the last Viceroy of Colonial India and the 1st Governor General of free India. Nehru was very friendly to him. Many regard Kashmir problem as Mountbatten's gift, by stopping the Indian troops at Uri and not to drive invaders across as well as asking Nehru to approach UN.

Moynihan, D. He was the US Ambassador at New Delhi, who made untiring efforts to make Indian- USA relations cordial. Later he became a Senator.

Mujahideens are the so-called holy war fighters. They think it holy to create problems to non-Muslims. They are paid from funds to support fundamentalism and they go blindly to fight wherever they are sent for the sake of religious fights.

Mukti Bahini was a force of liberators of Bangladesh (Earlier East Pakistan) from West Pakistan. East Pakistan-Bengalis, though Muslims, were not given due rights in Pakistan.

Mukherji, Pranab is the present Finance Minister of India.

Musharraf, Pervez was a General in Pak army. He planned a coup to become Chief Executive by overthrowing Sharif. Later he modified constitution to become President with power to dismiss elected government. He continues to be President and Army Chief, now retired from both.

NAM/Non-Alignment Movement was started by Nehru, Nasser and Tito, in which more than 145 countries are now the members. Its last meeting was held in Cuba in 2006.

Namaz is the prayer of Muslims. They are supposed to pray five times a day.

NATO camp refers to Western powers- the US, UK, France and Germany etc. WARSAW camp was of the East European Communist countries led by Soviet Russia.

Natwar Singh was External Affairs Minister of India. Earlier he was Foreign Secretary.

Nayyar, Shushila Dr. was a disciple of Mahatma Gandhi, who managed several refugee camps in India, after freedom. She was also a leader of the Indian National Congress.

Nehru, Jawaharlal Pandit was a Kashmiri, settled in Allahabad, educated in U.K. He became a disciple of Gandhi Ji and a leader of the Congress party. He was the 1st Prime Minister of India and founder of NAM. He had socialistic leanings and friendly to China.

Nixon, Richard M. was former President of the US, who had strong pro-Pakistani views and therefore was disliked by Indians.

Nuclear Powers are the P-5 nations with stockpiles of nuclear arsenals. They are the US, Russia, UK, France and China. Later India and Pakistan declared themselves as nuclear powers. Israel is undeclared Nuclear power. In 2006, North Korea declared itself a nuclear power. It is expected that Iran, Japan and South Korea may also join the club.

NPT is the Nuclear non-Proliferation Treaty of the U N, which has not proved effective.

NWFP. North-West Frontier Province, which had a nationalistic Muslim leader Khan Abdul Gaffar as the Chief Minister. With advice from Mahatma Gandhi Khan's party did not take part in referendum for Pakistan. Therefore, NWFP was included in Pakistan and Khan (also called Frontier Gandhi) was sent to jail.

Obama, B.H. The current Democratic President of the US. He is the first African American to occupy this post.

Onco-mouse or Harward-mouse. The cancer prone animals are susceptible due to their genetic make up, which can be manipulated through genetic engineering.

Pal, B.P. Dr. was a plant breeder from Burma (earlier a part of India) and a Director of the Indian Agricultural Research Institute for long time. Later, he became the first Director General of the reorganized Indian Council of Agriculture Research.

Pallone, Frank is a Democrat Representative from New Jersey and is a founder and Co-Chairman of Caucus on India and Indian Americans. He had introduced legislation to prevent the administration from waiving the Pressler Amendment.

Panchayats are the elected village bodies of, at least, five persons in India. These bodies look after planning, development and to some extent also legal and social matters since ancient times.

Panchsheel is a theory of five principles of co-existence in peace propounded by Nehru.

Pant, G.B. was a Congress party leader, who was the Chief Minister of U.P. and later became Home Minister in Central government cabinet, during the period of Nehru.

Pant, K.C. is the son of G.B. Pant. He has been a minister in Indira Gandhi's government. He is also a former Deputy Chairman of the Planning Commission of India.

Parmanand, Pandit is also called Parmanand of Jhansi or Dadaji. He was a revolutionary, who was first imprisoned at the age of eight years. He escaped from jail and travelled to Japan, Europe and America for seeking support for freedom struggle. The title of Pandit was given by Mahatma Gandhi for his knowledge.

Parker, F.W. Dr. was the Chief of the USAID at New Delhi in the 1950s.

Patel, Ballabh Bhai Sardar. He is commonly called Sardar Patel. He was the Iron man of the Congress party, who became the first Home Minister of India. He was known for his ability to merge Goa, the princely states in India, particularly Junagarh and Hyderabad.

Pearl Harbour is a Hawaiian port, which was bombarded by Japan, initiating World War II.

Phipps, Henry. He was an American philanthropist, who donated liberally to help establish an Agriculture Research Institute and College in Pusa (Bihar), in eastern India.

PL-480 is a US public law, which allows food aid to the needy nations worldwide.

Poonch, Rajauri and Doda are the remote areas on J&K border, full of forests where militants take refuge after massacres or mass murders and run away.

Powell Colin. The former Foreign Affairs Secretary of the US, who visited India and Pak.

Privy Purses is the allowance agreed to be given to the ex-rulers of the princely states, on their merger with India.

Proxy War. It is an undeclared war, which goes on through insurgency supported by some organization or country to create trouble and destruction in another country.

PVOs or the private voluntary organizations, which carry out constructive work. NGOs are also similar cooperatives, which help in social activities locally or on regional basis.

Quasim, Syed Mir was the Congress party liberal Chief Minister of J&K. In the interest of the state he did not mind stepping down from the post of Chief Minister.

Radcliffe, Cyril Sir was the Chairman, Boundary Commission, who was assigned the job to demarcate India and Pakistan in Punjab, a few months before independence.

Radhkrishnan, Sarvepalli Dr. A famous Indian Educationist and philosopher, who became the President of India. Earlier, he was the Ambassador and before that the Vice-Chancellor.

Randhawa, M.S. Dr. was the Chief Commissioner of Delhi at the time of freedom. Due to his Botany background, he was made Vice President of the old ICAR in Agriculture Ministry.

Rashtriya Swayam Sevak Sangh (RSS) is an Hindu organization intent to support nationalism. Vishwa Hindu Parishad and Bajrand Dal have more or less similar views.

Rao, Narsimha was a minister in the Congress government at the centre. Later, he became Prime Minister and started liberalization in India, crafted by Manmohan Singh.

Reagan Ronald was a US President, who was able to improve Indo-US relations slightly.

Reliance Corporation is an upcoming Indian industry involved in several projects in the nation. Oil sector is a new addition. Recently it has been split into two corporations.

Rockefeller Foundation is a philanthropic organization founded by the Rockefeller, the US billionaire. This foundation is helping in several countries including India.

Rotaviral Vaccines are the vaccines for controlling special group of viral diseases and rotaviral infections prevalent in humans in India and the US, both.

Rumsfeld, Donald was the former Secretary of Defence, who visited South Asian nations.

Rupee. It is the currency of India and Pakistan. Presently about 46 Indian rupees and about forty nine Pak rupees are equivalent to one US dollar.

SAARC is an organization for mutual cooperation between seven South Asian nations i.e. Bangladesh, Bhutan, India, Maldiv, Nepal, Pakistan, Sri Lanka and now Afghanistan also. SALT is a treaty on the limitation of strategic offensive arms but it has little contribution.

Samuel E. Stokes was an American settled in H.P., India to improve apple cultivation. He changed his name to Lal Chand Stokes and married an Indian lady.

Sandhu, H.S. was a retired army Major, who settled in Tarai of U.P. He was keen to see that an agricultural university be established in Tarai region and worked towards that end.

Sanskrit is an old language of India in which most of the Hindu religious books have been written.

Saund, D. Singh is an Indian farmer, who migrated to California and became a Senator.

Savarkar, Vir was a learned Hindu revolutionary from Maharashtra, who survived to see freedom for India.

SEATO is a US-led military treaty covering South Asia and South East Asia, of which Pakistan also became a member. Later, it withdrew from the membership of the SEATO.

Sahrif, Nawaz was the former Prime Minister of Pakistan, who signed Lahore Declaration in 1999 and also invasion of Kargil. After Kargil cease-fire, Sharif was overthrown by Musharraf (promoted by him) in a coup and he had to leave the country. Later, he came back to Pakistan

Shastri, Lal Bahadur. The Indian Prime Minister, who took over after Nehru's death. Earlier he was a Minister in U.P. Afterwards, he had become a minister in Nehru-cabinet.

Sheikh, Hasina Begum. Former Prime Minister of Bangladesh in whose period Indo-Bangladesh relations improved considerably and Farakka dam-water accord was signed.

Shias are the minority Muslim sect of Islam in Indian subcontinent. They are in majority in POK but are unhappy because of influx of Sunnis in the area to reduce their majority.

Shimla was earlier called Simla, the capital of H.P., where McMahon line pact was signed between British and China and another pact between India and Pakistan. Under the latter pact territory captured by India and about 94,000 Pak military POWs were returned.

Shaukat Aziz is the immediate past Prime Minister of Pakistan, who replaced Jamali.

Siachin is a glacier in J&K on the border between India and Pakistan. Because of its strategic importance Pakistan has its eyes on the glacier often claims it to be in Pakistan.

Sikhs are originally a Hindu Marshall race created to fight invasion from North-west. One member from each family used to be a Sikh in Punjab. They grow beard, keep a sword & comb, use iron-ring and turban. Often by mistake, they are considered Muslims. Now Sikhism is considered separate religion.

Singh, Jaswant was the Foreign Affairs Minister in BJP government and met with the US Officials and Secretaries to sort out differences in Indo-US relations and nuclear issues.

Singh, J.J. was an Indian, who had settled in California and worked for India's freedom.

Singh, Maharaja Gulab was a Dogra ruler, who purchased Kashmir and ushered a Dogra rule in the region, which lasted up to 1947, when Hari Singh merged the state with India.

Singh, Maharaja Ranjit was a Sikh ruler of Punjab, who took over Kashmir from Muslims and ruled it till 1886.

Singh, Manmohan is the present Prime Minister of India, who had crafted liberalization policy as a Finance Minister. He signed civil nuclear energy bill with President Bush.

Singh, Mulayam is the past Chief Minister of U.P., who was earlier the Defence Minister at the Centre. He is also the President of 'Samajwadi' party.

Singh, Sardar Swaran was External Affairs Minister in the Congress government at the Centre and participated in several Indo-Pak discussions.

Singh, Karan Dr. is the son of Maharaja Hari Singh. Dr. Singh is the founder of 'Vishwa Hindi Parishad' and several Hindu trusts to maintain historical shrines in Kashmir. He became Health Minister in the government of India. He was also the Ambassador to the US. Presently he is an M.P.

Singh, Tara Master was a leader of Akali Dal. He was extremely unhappy with massacres of minorities in areas which were to become Pakistan or in the trains going to India. He desired retaliations to end the massacres of Sikhs, Hindus and other minorities.

Singh, V.P. was former Prime Minister of India. After breaking away from Indian national congress, he formed the Janta party government at the Centre.

Sinha, Yashwant was the Minister of Foreign Affairs in BJP government. Prior to this he was Finance Minister in the same government and visited the US.

START is the Strategic Arms Reduction Treaty meant for verification and other aspects.

Stinger Missiles were supplied by the US to Pakistan for the use in Afghan war. Pakistan however used them against India in Kargil war. Taliban used them against the US troops during the operation 'enduring freedom'.

Sunnis are the majority Muslim sect in Indian subcontinent, who often fight with Shias.

Srinagar is the summer capital of J&K situated on a beautiful Dal Lake in a cool valley. It was established by the emperor

Ashok in the third century.

Tagore, Rabindranath was a great Bengali poet, who won Nobel Prize. He visited the US several times. His poem collection called Gitanjali was translated in many languages.

Talbott, Strobe is the former Deputy Secretary of the State Department of the US, who dealt with South Asia. He had several meetings with Jaswant Singh on Indo-US relations.

Taliban is the group of staunch Islamic extremists and wanted to take control of entire Afghanistan. Earlier US helped them through Pakistan to fight Russians. Later, US attacked the Taliban as part of its 'enduring freedom' operation.

Tamils are the residents of Tamil Nadu state in southern India. They speak Tamil Language. Lots of Tamils have settled in northern part of Sri Lanka and desire autonomy.

Tashkent is an important city in erstwhile USSR. An Indo-Pakistan agreement was signed there with the mediation of USSR in 1966. L.B. Shastri died there after signing the pact.

Taslima, Nasrin is a famous writer of Bangladesh, who was living in exile in Sweden and now in Kolkata. In her novels she wrote how Hindus and women continue to suffer in that nation. For this she was exiled. She is now desirous of living permanently in Kolkata.

Terminator Technology makes the seeds lose germination capacity. Therefore, the farmers cannot use their own produce or the home-grown seeds, as is the practice in developing countries in Africa, Asia and South America etc. Thus, seed producing MNCs gain a lot by using this technology.

Thoreau, Henry David was an old time US literary giant with great appreciation for India.

Tiger Hill is a strategic snow-covered peak on the Indo-Pakistan border in Kargil sector.

TRIPS are Trade Related Aspects of Intellectual Property Rights including patents on agriculture and allied fields.
Tricolour is India's National Flag, having white, orange and green colour horizontal stripes, with Ashok's wheel in the centre depicting unity in diversity.

Tritium is a gas required for nuclear-bomb preparation, which China gave to Pakistan.

Truman, Harry was the US President at the time of Indian freedom. He pressed India to accept a plebiscite and also arbitration as well as administration of Kashmir by Admiral Nimitz of the US navy to which India did not agree.

Union Jack is the British Empire Flag.

UNCIP. A UN Commission on India and Pakistan, to establish the line of control and watch it in relation to the UN resolutions on Kashmir imbroglio.

UPOV is the International Convention for Union for Protection of New Plant Varieties held in Geneva in 1961, for recognition of rights of plant breeders on global basis.

Vajpayee, Atal Bihari is the former 3-time Prime Minister of India. He is Ex-President of the rightist party, BJP. He is a poet and was Foreign Minister in Morarji Desai's cabinet. During his period, India developed economically

VAP. Under this Indo-US collaborative project researches are carried out on Vaccine Action program on rabies, HIV/ AIDS, Leishmanias (Kala Azar) etc.

VDC is a Village Defence Committee, armed and trained with the help from the government in areas prone to terrorism in J&K.

Verma, Inder is a leading US Geneticist of Indian origin, who works on Stem Cell Research.

Veto Power. The power enjoyed by the P-5 nations in the

Security Council to block any proposal.

'Vijay' is the operation to throw out Pak infiltrators from Kargil sector, which was started in May 1999. After more than 2 months fierce fight the Indian territory was recovered.

Vijaylakshmi Pandit was Ex Indian ambassador to the US & Indian representative to UN.

Vishnu Purana is one of several Puranas, which are the religious Hindu books written in Sanskrit and translated in several other languages, including foreign.

Vivekanand, Swami is a disciple of Swami Ramtirth. Vivekanand was a very learned Swami and participated in World Religion Parliament at Chicago. After the meetings, he travelled to many places and founded the Society of Vedanta in the US.

Wattumal, Govindram was a prosperous resident of Honolulu with philanthropic attitude. He founded the Wattumal Foundation, which awards fellowships to further the Indo-US understanding.

Yatra is a religious travel to some holy places like the Amarnath cave or Vaishnav Devi temple in Kashmir or Rameshwaram temple etc. in South.

World Bank is informal name used to designate a group of four affiliated international institutions: the IBRD, IDA, IFC and MIGA with a purpose of providing loans for raising living standards in developing nations established from 1945 onwards.

Zia-ul-Haq, General was the President of Pakistan, who came to power through a coup to throw out an elected government. He ruled for long time and was close to the US.

Zia, Khalida Begum is the past Prime Minister of Bangladesh.

Bibliography

Bibliography

Abul Kalam, A.P.J. 2003. Ignited minds- Unleashing the Power within India. Penguin Books, New Delhi.

Adams, John. 1966. Reforming India's Economy in An Era of Global Change. Current History. April, pp. 151-157.

Ahmad Imtiaz. 1993. State and Foreign Policy. India's Role in South Asia. Vikas Publishing House, New Delhi.

Aijauddin, F.S. 2006. When Bush Comes to Shove. Sange-e-Meel Publications, Lahore.

Akbar, M.J. 1985. India: The Siege Within - Challenges to Nation's unity. UBS Publishers, New Delhi.

Alan James. 1969. Select Bibliography. The Politics of Peacekeeping. Chatto & Windum, London.

Anonymous. 2004. People, Progress, Partnership: The Transformation of US-India Relations. Embassy of U.S.A., New Delhi.

Arundhati Ghosh. 1997. The CTBT and Nuclear Disarmament- The Indian View. Journal of International Affairs. 51 (Summer), p. 252.

Ayoob, Mohammad. 1977. Thirty years of India's Freedom. Indraprastha Press, New Delhi.

Azad, Maulana A.K. 1960. India Wins Freedom. Longman, Green & Co., New York.

Babu, Ramesh B. 1994. Domestic Dynamics and Indo-US Relations since 1965. In Four Decades of Indo-US Relations by A.P. Rana. Har Anand Publications, New Delhi.

Barnds, William J. 1972. India, Pakistan and the Great Powers. Praeger, New York.

Behl, Y. (Maj. Gen.). 2000. Kargil Blunder; Pakistan's Plight India's Victory. Manas Publications, New Delhi.

Bhatt, S. and V.S. Mani (Eds.). 1999. India on the threshold of the 21st Century. Lancer books, New Delhi.

Bhattachrya, Ajit.1994. Kashmir- The Wounded Valley. UBS

Publishers Distributors, New Delhi.

Bhutto, Z.A. 1971. The Great Tragedy. Vision Publications, Karachi.

Bhutto, Z.A. 1979. If I am Assassinated. Vikas Publishing, New Delhi.

Bose, T.C. 1994. Indo-US Security Relations. 1965-1990. In Four Decades of Indo-US Relations by A.P. Rana. Har Anand Publications, New Delhi.

Brown Sherrod. 1999. Congress from Inside: Observations from the Majority and the Minority. The Kent University Press.

Campbell-Johnson Alan. 1951. Mission with Mountbatten. Robert Hale, London.

Chau Chee Khoon. 1999. Whose Body Is It? Far Eastern Economic Review, October 15, 1999.

Chari, P.R. 1995. Indo-Pak Nuclear Stand Off- Role of the United States. Manohar Publications, New Delhi.

Chari, P.R., Parvaiz Iqbal Cheema and Iftekhauz Zaman. 1996. Nuclear non-proliferation in India and Pakistan. Manohar Publications, New Delhi.

Chari, P.R. 1997. FMCT: Issues in contention. The Hindu March 4, 1997, page 12.

Chibber, M.L. 1998. Pakistan's Criminal Folly in Kashmir. Manas Publications, New Delhi.

Chellani, Bramha. 1993. Nuclear non-Proliferation-The US Indian Conflict. Orient Longman, New Delhi.

Chopra, V.D. 1990. Genesis of Indo-Pakistan Conflict in Kashmir. Patriot Publishers, New Delhi.

Cohen Stephen P. 1985. Pakistan: Army Society and Security. Asian Affairs (New York) Vol. 10 No.2 (Summer).

Cohen Stephen P. 1987, Balancing Interests: The US and the Subcontinent. National Interest (Fall), pp.80.

Cohen Stephen P. 1991. Nuclear Proliferation in South Asia: Prospects for Arms Control. Lancer International, New Delhi.

Cohen Stephen P. 1992. The Pakistan Army. Oxford

University Press, Karachi.
Cohen Stephen P. 1998. The United States and India: Recovering the Lost Ground. Sais Review, XVIII, No. 1:93-107.
Cohen Stephen P. 1998. South Asian Features- A Strategic Assessment. ACDIS report of the University of Illinois, Urbana-Champaign. October, 1998.
Cohen Stephen P. 2001. India: Emerging Power. Brookings Institution Press, Washington D.C.
Daruwalla, K.N. 2000. Pakistan: State, Policy and ISI. USI Jour. CXXX, Jan.-March: 61-88.
Dettman, Paul R. 2001. India Changes Course: Golden Jubilee to Millennium. Praeger Publishers, Westport, CT.
Dhar, P.N. 2000. Indira Gandhi, the Emergency and Indian Democracy. Oxford University Press, New Delhi.
Debroy, Bibek. 1998. Intellectual Property Rights. B.R. Publishing Corporation, New Delhi.
Dennis Kux. 1993. Estranged Democracies: India and the United States (1949-1991). Sage Publications, New Delhi and Thousand Oaks.
Dinshaw Mistry. 1998. Domestic-International Linkages: India and the CTBT. The Non-proliferation Review, Fall, 1998.
Dixit, J.N. 1995. Anatomy of a Flawed Inheritance: Indo-Pak Relations, 1970-1994. Konark Publishers, New Delhi
Dixit, J.N. 1996. My South Block Years. UBS Publishers, New Delhi.
Dixit, J.N. 1998. Across Borders: Fifty Years of India's Foreign Policy. Picus Books, New Delhi.
Dixit, J.N. 2001. India's Foreign Policy And Its Neighbours. Gyan Publishing House, New Delhi.
Dixit, J.N. 2002. A big change in war strategy in Asia (in Hindi). Amar Ujala, April 15, Kanpur.
Dudley, Williams (Ed.). 2003. India and Pakistan. Greenhaven Press, Farmington Hills.
Dutt, V.P. 1990. India And the World. Sanchar Publishing House, New Delhi.

Fair, Christine C. 2004. The Counter-terror Coalitions. Cooperation with Pakistan and India. Rand, Santa Monica.

Friedman Thomas L. 2002. Globalization alive in post 9/11 world. Seattle Post Intelligencer, September, 24.

Gandhi, Indira. 1981. My Truth. Vision Publications, New Delhi.

Gandhi, Rajiv. 1988. A World Free of Nuclear Weapons: An Action Plan. Address to Third Special Session on Disarmament. UN General Assembly, June 9, New York.

Ganguly, Sumit. 1986. The Origins of War in South Asia. Indo-Pakistani Conflicts since 1947. Westview Press Boulder and London.

Ganguly, Sumit. 1991. Avoiding War in Kashmir. Foreign AFFAIRS, (Winter) 1990-91.Vol.89, No.5.

Ganguly, Sumit. 1993. Ethno-religious Conflicts in South Asia. Survival (Summer) Vol. 35, No. 2.

Ganguly, Sumit. 1999. The Origins of War in South Asia: Indo-Pakistani Conflicts since 1947. Vision Books, New Delhi.

Ganguly Sumit, Brian Shoup and Scobell Andrew. 2006. US-Indian Strategic Cooperation into 21st Century. Routledge, London & New York.

Gary R. Hess. 1971. America Encounters India. The John Hopkins University Press, Baltimore, Md.

Gary R, Hess. 1992. American Perspective on India, 1947-90. In Four Decades of Indo-US Relations. Har Anand Publications, New Delhi.

Gehlot, N.S. 2002. New Challenges to Indian Politics. Deep & Deep Publications, New Delhi.

Gould A. Harold and Sumit Ganguly (Ed). 1992. The Hope And the Reality (US-Indian Relations from Roosevelt to Reagan). West view Press Inc., Colorado.

Greenspan, Alan. 2007. The Age of Turbulence: Adventures in a New World. The Penguin Press, New York.

Grover, Verinder. 1995. The Story of Kashmir: Yesterday and Today. Vol.III. Deep & Deep Publications, New Delhi.

Gupta, Amit. 2005. The US-India Relationship: Strategic partnership or Complimentary interests? At http:// www. Carlisle. Army. Mil./ SSI.

Gupta, K.R. 2000. Selected Documentary on Nuclear Disarmament. Vols. I & II. Atlantic Publishers and Distributors, New Delhi.

Gupta, R.C. 1977. US Policy towards India and Pakistan. B.R. Publishing Corporation, New Delhi.

Gupta, Sisir.1966. Kashmir: A Study in India-Pakistan Relations. Asia Publishing House, New Delhi.

Guruswami, Mohan. 2006. India's World- Essays on Foreign Policy and Security Issues. Hope India, Gurgaon.

Haider, Salman. 2004. The Afghan War and its Geopolitical Implications for India. Manohar Publishers and Distributors, New Delhi.

Harrison, Selig S. and Kemp, Geoffrey. 1993. India and America after the Cold War - A Report of the Carnegie Endowment Study Group on US-India relations in a changing International Environment. Carnegie Endowment for International Peace, Washington, D.C.

Hodson, H.V. 1969. The Great Divide: Britain-India-Pakistan. Hutchinson and Company, London.

Hoffman, Steven A. 1990. India and China crisis. University of California Press, Berkeley.

Immerson Richard H. 1999. John Foster Dulles: Piety, Pragmatism and Powers in US Foreign Policy. Scholarly Resources Inc., Willington, USA.

Jackson, Richard L. 1983. The non-Aligned, the UN and the Super-Powers. Praeger, New York.

Jacques Chirac. 1999. Personal Views. Times of India, 22nd December 1999, New Delhi.

Jain, B.M. 1987. India and the United States: 1961-1963. Radiant Publishers, New Delhi.

Jha, C.S. 1983. From Bandung to Tashkent: Glimpses of India's Foreign Policy. Radiant Publishers, New Delhi.

Joshi, Manoj. 1991. India, the United States and the World: An

Indian View. In Nicolas X. Rizopoulos (Ed) Sea Changes: American Foreign Policy in a World transformed. Council on Foreign Relations, New York, 1990.

Joshi, Arun. 2004. Eyewitness Kashmir: Teethering on Nuclear War.Marshall Cavendish Academic, Singapore.

Joshi, Ashok. (Lt. Gen.). 2000. Restructuring National Security. Manas Publications, New Delhi.

Kapur, Ashok. 1971. India's Nuclear Option: Atomic Diplomacy and Decision Making. Praeger Publications, New York.

Kapur, Ashok. 2006. India from Regional to World Power. Routledge, New York.

Kathleen C. Bailey (Ed). 1994. Weapons of Mass Destruction: Costs versus Benefits. Manohar Publications, New Delhi.

Kennedy Edward M. 1971. A report to the subcommittee to investigate problems connected with refugees and scope of the Committee on the Judiciary, 1 November.

Kennedy, Paul. 1988. The Rise and Fall of the Great Powers. Foutanna Press, Hammersmith, London.

Khan, Akbar. 1970. Raiders in Kashmir- Story of Kashmir War 1947-48. Pakistan Publishers, Karachi.

Khan, Humayun and G. Parthasarthy. 2004. Diplomatic Divide. Lotus Collection, New Delhi.

Kissinger, Henry. 1994. Diplomacy-A Touchstone. Simon and Schuster, New York.

Koshi, Ninan. 2006. Under the Empire India's New Foreign Policy. LeftWord Books, New Delhi.

Krishna, Ashok and P.R. Chari. 2001. Kargil: The Tables Turned. Manohar Publications, New Delhi.

Krishnan, G.V. 1994. PSLV Launch Puts India in Select group. Sunday Times, October16, New Delhi.

Lakhera, M.M. 2000. Plebiscite a Dead Issue in Jammu and Kashmir. USI Jour. CXXX, Jan. –March: 56-60.

Lamb, Alistair. 1967. The Kashmir Problem. Praeger, New York.

Limaye, Satu P. 1993. US-Indian Relations: The Pursuit of

Accommodation. West view Press, Colorado.

Mahajan, Mehar Chand. 1963. Looking back: An Autobiography. Asia Publishing House, New Delhi.

Malik, Yogendra K. and Ashok Kapur. 1998. India- Fifty Years of Democracy and Development. APH Publishing Corporation, New Delhi.

Malthus, Thomas R. 1978. Essays on the Principles of Population. Penguin Books Hammondsworth, 1982.

Margolin, Eric S. 2000. War at the Top of the World. The struggle for Afghanistan, Kashmir and Tibet. Routledge, New York.

Matin Zuberi. 1999. The proposed Indian Nuclear Doctrine. USI Jour. CXXIX, July-September: 314-23.

Menon, V.P. 1985. The story of the Integration of the Indian States. Orient Longman, New Delhi.

Mohan, Sulakshan Maj. 2000. Kashmir: Is there a solution? Indian Publisher & Distributor, New Delhi.

Mishra, J.P. 1999. Biotechnology and Intellectual property Rights. Yojna, May 1999: 15-20.

Mishra, J.P. 1999. Plant Variety Protection including UPOV Convention and Biodiversity: An Indian Perspective. Proceedings International Seminar, New Delhi: 1-24.

Mohite, Dilip H. 1995. Indo-US Relations: Issues in Conflict and Cooperation. South Asian Publishers, New Delhi.

Mohite, Dilip H. and Amit Dholakia. 2001. India and the Emerging World Order: Foreign Policy and Security Perspectives. Kalinga Publications, Delhi.

Moynihan, Daniel P. 1978. A Dangerous Place. Little Brown and Co. Boston.

Maroof Raza. 1996. The Kashmir Issue: Rhetoric and Reality. USI Journal CXXVI, July-September: 370-373.

Morgenthau, Hans J. 1967. To Intervene or Not to Intervene. Foreign Affairs, 45 (3):425-436.

Nagaich, B.B. 1981. Potentialities of Potato Production and Export from India. Jour. Indian Potato Association, 8(3), Shimla.

Nagaich, B.B. 2003. Indo-US Relationship: A Perspective. The Front Page Vol.II, No.320, New Delhi.

Nagaich, B.B. 2004. A Quest for Development of India. Hindustan Times, November 4, Lucknow.

Nanda, Ravi. 1999. Kargil: A Wake up Call. Lancers Books, New Delhi.

Nanda, Ravi. 2001. Kashmir and Indo-Pak Relations. Lancer Books, New Delhi.

Nayak, Polly. 2007. Prospects for US-India Counterterrorism cooperation. National Academic Press Washington, DC.

Nayyar, Kuldip.1992. India House. Penguin Books, New Delhi.

Nayar, V.K. 1998. Low Intensity Conflict: Jammu and Kashmir. USI Jour. CXXVIII, July-September: 405-424.

Nehru, Jawaharlal. 1946. Discovery of India. Asia Publishers, Bombay (Mumbai).

Nehru, Jawaharlal. 1946. Interviews with George Jones of the New York Times, 30th August: 46.

Nehru Jawaharlal. 1948. India's Foreign Policy. Publications Division, New Delhi, 1960.

Nehru, Jawaharlal. 1950. Parliamentary Debates, Vol. 3rd, August 1950.

Noorani, A.G. 1967. India's quest for Nuclear Guarantee. Asian Survey, Vol. VIII, No.7 (July).

Ohajunwa Emeka.1992. India-US Security Relations (1947-1990). Chanakya Publications, New Delhi.

Palmer Norman D. 1984. The United States and India, Dimensions of Influence. Praeger, New York.

Prasad, Bimal. (Ed) 1979. India's Foreign Policy: Studies in Continuity and Change. Vikas Publications, New Delhi.

Prajapati, Vishnu. 1998. South Asia- Power and Politics. Vols. 1, 2 & 3. Commonwealth Publishers, New Delhi.

Rai, Vinai 2005. Rethinking India. RF Publications, New Delhi.

Ram A.N. 2000. Historical Perspectives, in Seminar 'Looking East', March 2000, New Delhi.

Rana, A.P. (Ed). 1994. Four Decades of Indo-US Relations. Har Anand Publications, New Delhi.

Randhawa, M.S. 1986. A History of Agriculture in India. Vol. IV. Indian Council of Agricultural Research, New Delhi.

Rose, Leo E and Eric Gonsalves (Ed). 1992. Towards a New World Order: Adjusting India-US Relations. Institute of East Asian Studies. University of California Press, Berkeley.

Salman, Khurshid. 1994. Beyond Terrorism: New Hope for Kashmir. UPSPD, New Delhi.

Sandy Gordon. 1995. South Asia after the Cold War: Winners and Losers. Asian Survey, Col. 35 No.10 (October): 879-895.

Sathasivam, Kanishkan. 2005. Uneasy Neighbors: India, Pakistan and US Foreign Policy. Ashgate Publishing, Burlington.

Schmidt, Karl J. 1999. Atlas and Survey of South Asian History. Vision Books, New Delhi.

Sethna, N.H. 1977. Address at the General Conference of the IAEA. Nuclear India, September 16.

Sharif, Nawaz. 1994. "Bombshell". India Today, September 4, page 47.

Sharma, Shri Ram. 1999. Indo-US Relations (1947-71). Discovery Publishing House, New Delhi.

Sharma, Sita Ram and S.R. Bakshi. 1992. Bill Clinton's Victory- A New Era in World Politics. West Vill Publishing House, New Delhi.

Sharma, Urmila and S.K. Sharma.1997. International Relations: Theory and History. Atlantic Publishers & Distributors, New Delhi.

Sidhu, Waheguru Pal Singh. 1998. Enhancing Indo-US Strategic Cooperation. Oxford University Press, New Delhi.

Singh, A.K. 1973. Impact of America on Indian Economy. Vora & Company, Bombay (Mumbai).

Singh K. Bramha. 1998. British Diplomacy in Kashmir.

Reliance Publishing House, New Delhi.

Singh, Karan Dr. 1982. Heir Apparent: An Autobiography. O U P, New Delhi.

Sinha, Aditya. 1996. Farookh Abdullah: Kashmir's Prodigal Son- A Biography. UBS Publishers, New Delhi.

Sinha, Ajoy. 1994. Indo-US Relations. Janaki Prakashan, Patna.

Sinha, S.P. 1998. Insurgency in Northeast: The External Dimensions.USI Journal CXXVIII, July-September: 438-446.

Sondhi, M.L.1998.Nuclear Scrutiny: A Challenge for Indian Diplomacy. Times of India, April 12.

Specter, Leonard S. 1988. The Undeclared Bomb. Bellinger Publishing Co., Cambridge, Massachusetts.

Srinivasan, M. 1995. The Eagle and the Peacock: US Foreign Policy towards India since Independence.

Srivastava, B.K. 1994. Issues in Indo-American Economic Relations in the Eighties. In Four Decades of Indo-US Relations by A.P. Rana. Har Anand Publications, New Delhi.

Srivastava, Siddharth. 2007. Americanization of the Indian military. Asia Times WWW.atimes.com

Subramanyam, K. 1986. India and the Nuclear Challenge. Lancer International, New Delhi.

Subramanyam, K. 1998. India Interactive: Talking Terms with the US. Times of India, July 20, 1998.

Subramanyam, K. 2005. Indo-US Relations in the Coming Decades. USI Jour. CXXXV No.561 (July-September).

Sunderji, K. General. 1993. Blind-men of Hindustan. Indo-Pak Nuclear War. UBS Publishers & Distributors Ltd., New Delhi.

Talbott, Strobe. 2004. Engaging India- Diplomacy, Democracy And the Bomb. Brookings Institution Press, Washington DC; Donnelly, Harrisonburg, VA, 2nd Ed.

Thakkar, Usha and Mangesh Kulkarni (Eds). 1999. India in the World Affairs: Towards 21st Century. Himalaya

Publishing House, New Delhi.

Thakur, Ramesh. 2000. Role of the United Nations in the Changing World Order. USI Journal CXXX. January-March: 153-162.

Tharur, Shashi. 2007. India from the midnight to millennium and beyond. Penguin Books, New Delhi.

Thornton, Thomas P. 1990. India, the United States and the World: An American View. In Nicholas X Rizopoulos. Sea Changes: American Policy in a World Transformed. Council on Foreign Relations, NewYork.

Thornton, Thomas P. 1992. US policy in Nixon-Ford Years in fold. In the Hope and Reality (EDs. Harold & Ganguly). West View Press, Colorado.

Vas, Eric A. (Lt. Gen.) 2000. The Muslim World and Globalization. USI Jour. CXXX No.540: 315-328.

Venkataraman, R. 1998. Nuclear Explosion and its aftermath. USI Jour. CXXVIII, July-September: 303-328.

Venkataramani, M.S. and H.C. Arya. 1966. America's Military Alliance with Pakistan: The Evolution and Course of an Uneasy Partnership. International Studies Vol.8 No. 1-2:76.

Vinod, M.J. 1991. United States Foreign Policy towards India: A Diagnosis of the American Approach. Published by S. Kumar. Lancer Books, New Delhi.

Vohra, A.M. 2000. Pakistan's Kashmir Fixation. USI Jour. CXXX, April-June: 340-344.

Wallace, James. 1985. Why Another US Treaty Is Going Down the Drain? US News and World Report, December 23, 1985.

Waslekar, Sundeep. 2005. The Final Settlement: Restructuring India-Pakistan Relations. Strategic Foresight Group, Mumbai.

Weisman Stem and Herbert Khosney. 1981. The Islamic Bomb. Times Books, New York/ Vision Books, New Delhi.

Wolpert, Stanley. 1982. Roots of Confrontation in South Asia.

Oxford University Press, New York.
Woodman, Dorothy. 1969. Himalayan Frontiers. The Cresset Press, London.
Yousaf, Brigadier Mohammad and Adkins, Major Mark. 1993. The Bear Trap: Afghanistan's Untold Story. Jang Publishers, Lahore.
Zachariah, Benjamin. 2005. Developing India: An Intellectual and Social History. Oxford University Press, New Delhi.

Government Publications and Institutional Reports

British Government- Indian independence Act Command Paper 7136, July 18, 1947.
Department of Public Information, United Nations, New York.
Indian Government- Indian Foreign Office Records, August 1963. Loke Sabha Debates, Series 5.
Military technology. 1988. No.1/88, World Defense Almanac, Wehr &Wissen, Netherlands.
Report of the Carnegie Study Group on US-Relations (Carnegie Endowment for International Peace, 1993).
Report of the Nuclear Debate in the US House of Representatives, Washington, DC, November 16, 2005.
Report of the Nuclear Debate in the US Senate, Department of State, Washington, DC, November 2, 2005.
SAARC Survey of Development and Cooperation Research and Information System for the non-Aligned and other Developing Countries, New Delhi, 1995.
The World Today, published by Royal Institute of International Affairs, London.

Personal Interviews

C.P. Upadhyay, Additional Secretary to M.M. Joshi, former Minister for Human Resource Development, earlier Minister of Home Affairs and prior to this a Professor at Allahabad University.
Pandit Parmanand of Jhansi, a great revolutionary of India, who had survived to live in independent India but did not

accept any position in the government.

Shankar Dayal Sharma, Former President and a Freedom Fighter.

T.N. Kaul, Former Ambassador to the US and USSR, earlier a Foreign Secretary to the Government of India.

Index